Natural Hierarchies

Natural Hierarchies

The Historical Sociology of
Race and Caste

Chris Smaje

Copyright © Chris Smaje 2000

The right of Chris Smaje to be identified as author of this work has been asserted in accordance with the Copyright, Designs and Patents Act 1988.

First published 2000

2 4 6 8 10 9 7 5 3 1

Blackwell Publishers Inc.
350 Main Street
Malden, Massachusetts 02148
USA

Blackwell Publishers Ltd
108 Cowley Road
Oxford OX4 1JF
UK

Library of Congress Cataloging-in-Publication Data has been applied for.

ISBN 0-631-20948-4 (hardback); 0-631-20949-2 (paperback)

British Library Cataloguing in Publication Data

A CIP catalogue record for this book is available from the British Library.

Typeset in 10 on 12 pt Galliard
by Ace Filmsetting Ltd, Frome, Somerset
Printed in Great Britain by MPG Books, Bodmin, Cornwall

This book is printed on acid-free paper.

Contents

Preface

In this book I develop a sociological theory of culture which, I argue, can illuminate the way that race and other status hierarchies that are grounded in ideas of natural difference have been sustained and transformed. The argument is illustrated empirically through an analysis of race and caste systems which is focused mainly upon the Caribbean region (but also refers to North America) and the Indian subcontinent. My principal aim is to provide an overview of what a sociological approach to these "natural hierarchies" can (and cannot) achieve through a comparative historical perspective which addresses itself to existing writings on the topic in a slightly unusual but, I hope, illuminating way. The book is intended to be read as an integrated whole, but each chapter engages with rather different scholarly literatures, and some readers may prefer to focus on specific parts of the argument. In particular, those who are interested in the way sociological theory can address the question of race or caste might focus upon chapters 1, 2, and 7, while those who are interested in the structuring of historical societies in relation to natural hierarchies might focus upon chapters 3–6, although distinctions of this kind are something that I try to transcend in the following pages. Chapter 1 introduces the major theoretical issues and empirical material which are pursued in the book, while chapter 2 – drawing critically upon existing writings – develops a theoretical approach to the topic which is put to work in the following chapters. In chapter 3 I show how the logic of exchange relationships and state formation which emerged in the medieval and early modern period were to produce different configurations of natural hierarchy in the Indian subcontinent and the extended polities of the European colonial powers in the Americas; this point is developed in chapter 4, which examines the nexus of race, slavery, and colonialism in the Americas during the early modern period. In chapter 5, the way that particular cultural constructions of the person invest forms of natural hierarchy is examined, while chapter 6 considers the way that state formation and constructions of the person have combined to create particular problems in forging postcolonial "nations" in race and caste-ordered societies. Finally, the implications of the preceding analysis for political questions about the transformation of race and caste identities in contemporary societies are addressed in chapter 7.

It is my perception that the English language literature on race in sociology has tended to focus upon a critique of the essentialist categories through which ideas of race are sustained in the contemporary or near-contemporary USA and Western Europe, somewhat to the exclusion of attempts to place this into a broader ethnological and historical framework which might inform greater reflection upon sociological theory itself as a particular, historically grounded phenomenon. For this reason, I have chosen to adopt a comparative approach which destabilizes not only much criticized but still routinely invoked distinctions like modern/premodern or Western/non-Western, but also positions which merely negate them. In doing so, I have synthesized a good deal of scholarship in anthropology, history, sociology, and the humanities. Whether or not the reader judges my efforts a success, I hope that I have provided a convincing case for the merits of adopting such an approach, and avoided inordinate oversimplifications in some of the more specialist topics covered here in which I am far from expert.

In writing this book I have incurred debts to several people to whom I owe some words of thanks. Above all, my wife Cordelia Rowlatt and my children Jake, Oliver, and Dan Smaje have sustained me through the many vicissitudes of the writing process; I cannot repay what they have given me, or what I have learned from them. Sara Arber first suggested that I write the book, and has wholeheartedly supported me throughout the writing. John Solomos advised me wisely at various points in the project, and also kindly read an earlier draft of the manuscript. Martin Bulmer encouraged me in practical and intellectual ways to pursue my interest in the topic at several crucial stages. The Department of Sociology at the University of Surrey awarded me a grant to cover some of my expenses in writing the book, and also a sabbatical leave for a semester which enabled me to complete much of the writing. I spent the leave in Seattle, where Pierre van den Berghe and his colleagues in the Department of Sociology at the University of Washington extended a warm welcome to me. Rick and Nanette Goss went far beyond the call of friendship to make the stay in Seattle a happy and productive one at a time in their lives when they had more pressing things to do. Back home, several people commented on an earlier draft of the manuscript. I'm particularly indebted to Declan Quigley for providing a detailed, incisive, and patient reading beyond what I could have asked from him. Geoff Cooper, Keith Macdonald, Mike Hornsby-Smith, and an anonymous reader also gave me much useful advice, as, at an earlier stage, did several readers of the original proposal for the book. All of these people share some of the responsibility for the fact that the book is better than it might have been, and none of the responsibility for the fact that it's not as good as it could have been. Finally, I'm grateful to Jill Landeryou of Blackwell Publishers who received my initial idea for the project with such enthusiasm, and to Susan Rabinowitz and Ken Provencher who steered it through to its conclusion.

Chris Smaje

1 | Race, Caste, and Hierarchy

In the beginning there was but one concept – the concept of I
Then Arose Apaleon the Devil, claiming that it's you and I
And from that day on, there is trouble in the world and the
world's gone astray
Bunny Wailer, 'Amagideon' From *Blackheart Man* (Island
Records)

When they divided Purusha, into how many parts did they
apportion him?
What do they call his mouth, his two arms and thighs and feet?
His mouth became the brahman; his arms were made into the
rajanya, his thighs the vaishyas, and from his feet the shudra were
born

Rig Veda

Race and Caste as Natural Hierarchies

The two passages cited above could be read as summaries of the prevailing
approaches to race and caste in sociological theory until quite recently.
Race, in accordance with the passage from Bunny Wailer's song, involves
an act of differentiation in which a "you" or an "other" is separated from
an "I" or a "self." This constitutes a degeneration from a prior unity, a
historical wrong turn which is the source of much contemporary trouble
and which needs to be transcended. Caste also stems from an originary
differentiation in the division of Purusha, the original "cosmic man," whose
sacrifice is described in the hymn from the *Rig Veda*. In this case, however,
the division is a necessary foundational act, creating a stable and
hierarchalized social order of the castes. Both passages draw attention to
the differentiation and hierarchalization of a primal human "substance"
but, to the extent that they are representative of sociological approaches,
they do so in ways with quite different analytical and normative implications. Thus, Oliver Cromwell Cox – whose work in the 1940s was perhaps

the last programmatic attempt to analyze jointly systems of race and caste relations – felt able to describe caste as "ancient, nonconflictive, nonpathological and static" (Cox, 1987: 37), as against the putatively modern, conflictive, pathological, and dynamic character of racial systems. Cox's efforts to sunder the study of the two phenomena were successful, and subsequent analysis was to conform to a particular theoretical and disciplinary division of labor within the social sciences. Race largely became the object of a materialist sociology, which attempted to explain its appearance as an epiphenomenon of a modern and specifically Western or Euro-American process of capitalist development. Caste, on the other hand, largely became the object of an idealist anthropology, which sought to lay bare the cultural grounds upon which manifestations of caste hierarchy rested.

In recent years, some of the main bulwarks of these divergent traditions have been eroded, and my aim in the present book is to reconsider the way that sociological theory can address questions of race and caste hierarchy in the light of newer approaches in sociology, anthropology, and history. In doing so, I will reject Cox's view. Race, I will argue, is not to be so lightly dismissed as a "pathological" consequence of capitalist development, but evinces a much deeper relationship with some of the most fundamental aspects of "Western" societies. And caste, in turn, is not quite as stable, normative, or consensual – that is, not quite as "nonpathological" – as Cox supposed. But against the tendency in much contemporary writing to dismiss the ideas of both race and caste as fictions in the political, economic, and intellectual discourse of Western modernity, I will suggest that the social phenomena to which they refer are continuously recreated in relation to distinctive cultural repertoires within which the analytical categories of sociological theory can themselves be located. Moreover, a revised analysis can point to similarities between ideologies of race and caste. Each can be regarded as different kinds of "natural hierarchy," by which I mean they involve the idea that people can be divided into ordered collectivities on the basis of some transcendent or extra-human principle which seemingly establishes these groups as *sui generis*. However, my intention is not to suggest that race and caste are really the same thing. They differ from one another because the ordering principles involved are not the same, although it is possible to examine a range of affinities and differences between them across distinct cultural dimensions. To anticipate my general argument, I shall suggest that race and caste can be analyzed comparatively by considering their relation to three factors: the separation or identity between persons and things; conceptions of cosmic order and its relation to worldly diversity, particularly with respect to political boundaries; and the character of the person and the "substance" that they embody. The particular, albeit overlapping, resolutions effected in the Indian and Euro-

American contexts to the complexities thrown up by these conceptions involve certain tensions or "aporia," establishing social processes and conflicts which continue to invest contemporary life. To make this argument, we shall have to take up various positions in contemporary sociological theory. However, sociological theory cannot be regarded as a neutral or transcendent means for analyzing natural hierarchies, as if its generative force lies in some quite different order of reality. One only sees aporia from particular standpoints, and I will argue that both sociological theory and racial ideologies too are precipitates of a particular European (and, more specifically, Christian) intellectual trajectory.

A comparative context can be instructive here. Sociological theory and cognate political ideologies such as Marxism tend to oppose the everyday sense that race is some tangible or essential property of the person which people "have," counterposing to this "essentialist" idea the "relational" view that race denotes a particular kind of social relationship *between* people which is established historically. This involves an implicitly egalitarian view that there is no inherent essence or substance which makes some kinds of people superior to others. However, when we turn to Indian conceptions of caste we find that ideas concerning the inherent superiority and inferiority of particular kinds of people have often attained their highest justification precisely in the relational view that these kinds are parts of a broader whole, to which one "egalitarian" response has been to counterpose a naturalizing essentialism, viz. that there should be no such relational hierarchy because each individual person is born equal in nature. This egalitarian essentialist critique of caste hierarchy does not just emerge from the viewpoint of Western "outsiders," but also underpins indigenous understandings. Consider, for example, the earthy essentialism in the following poem by Kabir, an Indian *bhakti* poet of the sixteenth century:

> It's all one skin and bone
> one piss and shit
> one blood, one meat.
> From one drop, a universe.
> Who's Brahman? Who's Shudra?
> (Hess, 1983: 19)

These observations suggest that the idea of essences is not a mere projection from some real, objective ground of social relations, which the clear-sightedness of sociological analysis can reveal once and for all. Relations and essences are better seen as mutually entailed moments in ideologies of a particular kind – ideologies of natural hierarchy – and it is worth appreciating that the sociological penchant for turning substances into relations, immensely revealing though it is, has its own specific cultural grounding. This unremarked continuity between the categories of sociological analysis and the hierarchical ideologies it takes as its object therefore requires a deeper kind of intellectual mediation to make explicit its undergirding assumptions.

This establishes one rationale for the present book. It is, I contend, no longer necessary for sociology to offer a critique of naive racial essentialism through postulating naive concepts of relationality, because naive essentialism no longer has any serious intellectual credibility. It continues to have credibility outside the critical discourse of the social sciences, but this is unlikely to be undermined through the proselytization of the sociological critique, because it is predicated structurally upon different logics of transformation with respect to those European modes of thinking wherein lie the common roots of (essentialist) racial and (relational) sociological thought. Moreover, too single-minded a focus upon mere deconstruction of essentialist identifications like race can obscure the complexity of the worlds that people create through such identifications in everyday life, worlds that grow out of but also transform their aporia and possibilities. Later in the book we shall consider several concrete examples of such transformations. But let us first turn to consider some of our key terms in a little more detail.

Race

One way in which race is often differentiated from other kinds of identification is the suggestion that it refers to circumstances where human variation in physical or somatic traits – skin color, hair type, facial appearance, etc. – are deployed to establish distinctions between people of different kinds, particularly where these distinctions are socially consequential (I take as granted that no systematic biological schema can be identified which corresponds to the social significations associated with these traits). However, when we look at cases where social distinctions are elaborated on the basis of somatic criteria we often find that these distinctions are *not* simply established on the basis of physical appearance. For example, in chapter 5 we will encounter the example from nineteenth-century Cuba of a woman who cancelled her wedding engagement upon learning that her intended groom was not white but a "mixed race" *pardo*. This "fact" was clearly not evident from his physical appearance, and was only discovered through inspection of parish records. A rather different example comes from Charles Kingsley, an English scholar of the nineteenth century who, while traveling in Ireland, professed to be

haunted by the human chimpanzees I saw along that hundred miles of hor-
rible country . . . to see white chimpanzees is dreadful; if they were black, one
would not feel it so much, but their skins, except where tanned by exposure,
are as white as ours. (Cited in Curtis, 1968: 84)

So, in Kingsley's worldview, it is not simply that on the grounds of their
physical appearance the Irish are white, full stop. Rather, their whiteness is
a problem, because there is a dissonance between what Kingsley wishes it
to connote – that is, civilized or nonbestial behavior – and the bestiality he
believes he has witnessed in the Irish people he has encountered, the model
for which he immediately draws from another, "non-white" race.

Both of these examples involve white people who are not "really" white,
suggesting that somatic characteristics are acting as referents for some other
kind of identification, which is social in character. We might perhaps suggest that, in general, "racial" identification has to do with the idea of an
inherent and nonmodifiable social rank, for which the heritability and vis-
ibility of somatic traits stands as an imperfect referent. This somatic referent emerged from a specific history of European colonial expansion which
was already some 400 years old when Kingsley was on his travels, but to
understand how this process came to invest somatic characteristics with
such weight requires, among other things, an appreciation of the way that
much older concerns in Europe with issues of political order and of the
relationship between persons and political communities had, by the late
medieval and early modern period, concretized around particular forms of
national identification which shaped the course of European colonial expansion. In this book I do not therefore understand "race" principally in
terms of somatic traits, but in terms of a specific engagement between
political ideology and the colonial expansion of Europe. Other aspects of
the relation between social identification and political ideologies, specifically those associated with those modern forms of nationalism which arguably first emerged in Europe from the eighteenth century onwards, are
often rendered through the concept of "ethnicity." However, my focus in
this book is upon race as defined above in relation to the colonial and
postcolonial history of America (which, throughout the book, I take to
refer not just to the USA but to the whole North, South and Central American mainland, as well as to the Caribbean region, upon which we shall
particularly concentrate) and then to consider the problems of transformation that have arisen in forging "ethnic" nationalisms within racially stratified American societies.

As I suggested earlier, race can be regarded as one of a broader class of
social phenomena we might term *essentialist identifications*. A fundamental point of departure for a specifically sociological approach to race and to

other similar identities is to oppose the idea that some actual, substantive quality or qualities exist which unambiguously and unfailingly differentiate some kinds of people from other kinds. In other words, it opposes the idea that race involves "natural" properties which define groups of people. Rather than inhering in persons, race is instead seen to inhere in relations of a particular kind *between* persons, relations which are symbolized or denoted by the concept of "race." This is equivalent to a distinction between *categories* and *groups*; whereas in everyday life we might think of a number of distinct groups, each comprised of actual people who possess an identical "race," the sociological approach suggests instead that "race" denotes categories or devices through which particular ideas of groupness are constituted. It is as if these categories are generic collective nouns, empty but always with the potential to be filled in some way or other. Against the idea of race as a given, "natural" property, the sociological approach therefore substitutes the idea of a relation which is created in specific historical or social contexts, usually involving exclusion or discrimination of some kind. For this reason, many analysts prefer to discuss "racism" rather than "race," in order to capture the sense in which the latter is actively constructed. Moreover, since this construction occurs in contextually varied ways, it has more recently become common to talk of "racisms" rather than just "racism." Indeed, it is sometimes suggested that this plurality of racisms vitiates any attempt to construct a general theory of race or racism. For example, Paul Gilroy (1993a: 22) has argued that "the plurality of forms in which racism has developed . . . underlines the idea that there is no racism in general and consequently that there can be no general theory of race relations or race and politics."

There is much to commend this argument. It is easy to apply terms like racism or race relations to aspects of social life in nineteenth-century Cuba or Britain, or to many other times and places, but equally easy to see that there are enormous differences between these cases which demand their own specific forms of explanation or analysis. Nevertheless, the term "racisms" necessarily implies similarity as well as difference; racisms must be sufficiently different from one another in order to warrant the plural form of the noun, but sufficiently similar to be regarded as specific examples of the same social domain – they are racisms, and not some other kind of thing. Robert Miles (1993: 85) has aptly criticized those writers who invoke the idea of "racisms" without specifying grounds for this putative similarity, but the merits of attempting to find an unambiguous *a priori* definition as the basis for empirical comparison are doubtful. It is worth referring to Wittgenstein's concept of "family resemblances" in support of this point. In a famous passage, Wittgenstein (1953: 31ff.) argued that no single trait can be found which uniquely distinguishes "games" from other

classes of phenomena; games can only be defined by their "family resemblances" to other games with reference to a set of non-exclusive criteria
(like "amusement," "competition," "skill," and so on), none of which are
necessary conditions for any particular game. But this does not mean that
the concept of "game" is hopelessly ambiguous. People are usually fairly
sure about what is and is not a game. Analogously, we might suggest that
"race" can be defined in relation to a set of non-exclusive criteria (natural
difference, inherent collectivity, somatic distinctions and their fetishization
as a moral project, rankings of blood, body, mind, or culture, and so on).
The point can help us to avoid arid and reductive typological exercises
which define empirical examples of racial sentiment only in relation to some
particular phenomenon which is given *a priori* theoretical privilege, but I
do not wish to go wholly in the contextualist direction arguably implied by
Wittgenstein's philosophy of language. Instead, I wish to suggest – against
both the idea of merely coincidental or contingent racisms and the idea of
a unitary racism – the persistence of certain historical structures to which
different and changing manifestations of racial sentiment are, as it were,
organically related. I attempt to defend this rather old fashioned position
in chapter 2, but its relevance can be seen in relation to the view set out
above that race is a category through which particular social relations are
constituted. Kenan Malik expresses this idea as well as anyone in arguing
that

> The concept of race . . . is not an expression of a single phenomenon or
> relationship. Rather it is a medium through which the changing relationship
> between humanity, society and nature has been understood in a variety of
> ways. (Malik, 1996: 71)

The point is well taken, but it raises several problems. One of them is the
question of identity which was posed in the preceding discussion of racisms.
How can we reconcile the *changing* character of the relationship between
the three entities mentioned by Malik with the concept of race which, in
his schema, is worked into a singularity as their apparently *unchanging*
medium or context, even though it is itself regarded as a set of different
representations? If race is a medium which codes changing social relations,
what confers its unchanging capacity to act as their context?

In this book, I offer a variety of theoretical answers to these questions.
But theoretical analysis alone has no force in the absence of empirical reference to actual societies where racial ideologies are, as it were, put to work.
So while I have argued that it is untenable simply to reject on principle the
idea of a general theory of race, any theory must be grounded in specific
empirical contexts which will affect the kind of theory deployed. This is

reflected in the structure of the book, which moves from an apparently contextless theoretical exposition to detailed discussion of particular societies.

We began this section with a particular definition of race which was based upon a certain amount of analytical abstraction. Another possible approach is to allow oneself to be guided by considering those cases where the idea of race is an explicit feature of public discourse and debate. Intellectual histories of the race concept generally converge on the eighteenth century as the period when it began to rise to prominence as a matter for intellectual debate in Europe (e.g. Poliakov, 1971; Mosse, 1979; Hannaford, 1996). But much of the context for these debates had emerged over the preceding two to three hundred years, in processes of European colonial expansion which historians often call the "first imperial age" (Scammell, 1989). Beginning with the Portuguese explorations of the West African coast in the first half of the fifteenth century, and proceeding through the Spanish conquest of America to the later colonial adventures of the English, French, and Dutch in the Americas and South Asia, the first imperial age was the period when many of the political and economic institutions familiar to us today began to take on their contemporary form. It was, above all, the period when diverse peoples from around the world were incorporated into an increasingly global political economy, sometimes as willing participants, often forcibly. But in a sense its initial movement reflected the dynamic of medieval societies whose political assumptions were predicated upon notions of a divine hierarchy. As we shall see in chapters 2 and 3, this provided a complex prior context for notions of human similarity and difference. The eighteenth-century emergence of race as an explicit feature of intellectual discourse coincides with the denouement of a long crisis in this medieval worldview which was manifested intellectually in the putatively rational, secular, and egalitarian philosophy of the Enlightenment.

This new egalitarian rationality was, however, accompanied by yet more ramifying forms of colonial enterprise. It also rested upon metropolitan projects of nation-building which were increasingly incorporative in character. Thus, insofar as we might speak of the racial context of these two colonial moments, we confront a change in its character from the hierarchical to the liberal or egalitarian, although this represents just one way of segmenting a longer-term trajectory of historical transformation. Indeed, the "liberal hour" of the second imperial age in the early nineteenth century – especially evident in British policy in the Caribbean and India – was to be replaced later in the century by an imperialist discourse of racial inferiority as violent and inflexible as anything preceding it (Bayly, 1989; Holt, 1992; Pagden, 1995). Perhaps it is these vicissitudes which allow analysts to identify the emergence of racial ideology at any number of wildly different periods. So, Kenan Malik (1996) argues that racism emerged in the nineteenth century as a rationale for inequality in an age which espoused egalitarianism, while Barbara Fields (1990) argues that it emerged in the seventeenth century as a rationale for enslavement in an age which espoused free labor. Only one of them, it would seem, can possibly be correct. This need only be true, however, if the meaning of "racism" is regarded as stable and constant. If, alternatively, we suggest that different kinds of racisms have manifested themselves at different times, then the two positions may not be so incompatible. But we have already encountered the problem of imputing an unchanging "racial" context to the changing social relations through which a sense of race is fixed. Ann Stoler has referred to this problem in her book about the idea of racism in the thought of Michel Foucault. Stoler draws attention to a "fundamental paradox of racial discourse":

> Namely, that such discourse invariably draws on a cultural density of prior representations that are recast in new form; that racism appears at once as a return to the past as it harnesses itself to progressive projects; that scholars can never decide among themselves whether they are witness to a legacy of the past or the emergence of a new phenomenon all together. Foucault's analysis suggests that these scholarly discrepancies are irresolvable precisely because they mirror what is intrinsic to the paradoxical power of racist discourse itself; namely, that it is, as George Mosse once noted, a "scavenger" discourse or as Barbara Fields writes, a "promiscuous critter," but not in unpatterned ways. (Stoler, 1995: 90)

Compelling though this argument is, there remains a certain awkwardness of expression in describing a dispersal of meaning which is nevertheless referred back to "racial discourse" as a seemingly unitary thing, a "promiscuous critter" which cunningly hides its singular purposes behind a variety of masks. This reflects the same problem of identity and differentiation which we encountered earlier in the idea of "racisms" or in Malik's view of race as the medium for changing social relations. To preserve the identity of racism as a distinguishable phenomenon, Stoler concedes that the ramification of racist discourse proceeds in *patterned* ways. A satisfactory theory of race must attend to the character of this patterning, and this cannot be done either by simply pointing to its relational nature or by arbitrarily according a unique theoretical privilege to some particular factor as a necessary and implicitly prior causal phenomenon. For Foucault – at least in one of his moods – and in this book also, such a theory involves describing processes of historical transformation which subsume both the "hierarchical" racism of medieval Europe and its forms of colonial domination together with the "egalitarian" racism of bourgeois capitalism and the second imperial age. Existing sociological writings on race have, in my view, devoted adequate attention to the latter but have given curiously short shrift to the former, while also somewhat neglecting to address the question of race in studies of the nineteenth- and twentieth-century transformations between colonial dependency and postcolonial nationalism. That this book grounds its historical analysis of race upon discussion of premodern and early modern Europe and the colonial and postcolonial Caribbean will hopefully seem less empirically quixotic in this context.

But let us nevertheless consider briefly some approaches to modern egalitarianism as a context for examining racial ideology. Several authors have noted that the emergence of explicitly racist ideologies which emphasized the natural inferiority of particular peoples coincided in Europe with the parallel emergence of the idea of natural equality, whereby the aristocratic order of the *ancien régime* was rejected in favor of the idea that people enjoyed a formal, natal equality in nature. Among the least persuasive of explanations for this phenomenon is Louis Dumont's argument that

> racism fulfils an old function under a new form. It is as if it were representing in an egalitarian society a resurgence of what was differently and more naturally expressed in a hierarchical society. Make distinction illegitimate, and you get discrimination; suppress the former modes of distinction and you have a racist ideology. (Dumont, 1980: 262)

Dumont, whose writings on caste and individualism are of incomparable influence and importance, here reveals one of the major defects of his approach in postulating a process of simple change or "modernization" from hierarchy (of which he considers Indian caste society to be one example) to a modern egalitarianism which cannot, however, complete itself. This reflects a belief in an inherent human tendency towards discriminations of status, so that if hierarchy is flattened in some particular domain it necessarily pops up again somewhere else. A more convincing approach is provided by Gunnar Myrdal – from whom Dumont derives much of his argument – in suggesting that racism mediates the contradiction of a *specific* political ideology (in this case, US egalitarian individualism) in a society that was manifestly not equal. In Myrdal's words,

> The dogma of racial inequality may . . . be regarded as a strange fruit of the Enlightenment. The fateful word *race* itself is actually not yet two hundred years old. The biological ideology had to be utilized as an intellectual explanation of, and a moral apology for, slavery in a society which went out emphatically to invoke as its highest principles the ideals of the inalienable rights of all men to freedom and equality of opportunity. . . . *The need for race prejudice is . . . a need for defense on the part of the Americans against their own national Creed, against their own most cherished ideals. And race preju-*

dice is, in this sense, a function of equalitarianism. The former is the perversion of the latter. (Myrdal, 1944: 89. Original emphasis, as in all subsequent quotations.)

In this passage, Myrdal captures the sense in which racial hierarchy and individualist egalitarianism represent two poles of a single sociocultural system articulated in relation to the increasingly instrumental order of economic relationships associated with capitalist production. Understanding the apparently paradoxical way in which particularist categories of social being are objectified within the putatively universalizing instrumental logic of capital constitutes a central analytical and normative question for any approach to the question of race. Not illogically, Myrdal singles out the Enlightenment as the generative moment of racism because this movement gave clearest expression to an ideal of a secular political order and a world rationally comprehensible in terms of a system of differences. This was the precondition for the later state penetration of the social order in which other writers have traced racial imperatives, as, for example, in Foucault's (1981) discussion of the nineteenth-century articulation of "biopower" by states newly creating and disciplining a national "population," though unlike Myrdal, here Foucault emphasizes the *transformation* of a prior discourse.

Myrdal's view of racism as a perversion of Enlightenment egalitarianism therefore seems apposite in many respects. However, to use the word "perversion" in this context commits us to the historicist belief that Enlightenment thought contained within itself some necessary historical trajectory which was upset by the emergence of racism. This is also a problem with Kenan Malik's (1996) attempt to locate race as a nineteenth-century degradation of eighteenth-century universalism. Taking the biological racism of the later nineteenth century as the essence of the race concept writ large, Malik finds such a differentialist reading of natural hierarchy lacking in earlier periods. Although he is broadly correct to suggest that "race" in the eighteenth century did not generally carry the connotations of biological evolution that it did in the succeeding century, there are other ways of approaching the concept. If, for example, we adopt Michael Oakeshott's useful view of race as an antonym to politics (Hannaford, 1996: 13), we might suggest that Malik not only neglects the increasingly precise definitions worked out in theory and practice from medieval times onwards regarding who was and was not to be included in the political communities of Europe and their later colonial extensions – definitions accompanied by a pervasive language concerning the constitutional inferiority of those that were excluded – he also overlooks the striking coincidences between Enlightenment thought and what I shall argue was the racialized disciplining of the body in the slave systems of the eighteenth-century Americas, a colonial context with which Enlightenment thinkers were deeply engaged in complex ways by no means reducible to simple opposition. He thereby detaches only the most "progressive" elements of Enlightenment thought as representative of its time. This raises an important theoretical issue which can be discerned in the following point of tension in Malik's text as he articulates the historical disjunction through which race emerged:

> That in the nineteenth century science, reason and universalism came to be harnessed to a discourse of race is a development that has to be explained through historical analysis; it is not logically given by the nature of scientific or rational thought. (Malik, 1996: 41)

The "historical analysis" offered here is implicitly functionalist; the harnessing of universalism to a discourse of race is read as the outcome of human action which took it in that direction because it suited practical purposes to do so. But those practical purposes are built upon a particular, prior ordering of assumptions. The difficulty with Malik's argument, then, is that "historical analysis" is abstracted from its specific historical grounding, so that the context for the critique of racial ideology is detached from the context of racial ideology itself, allowing the analyst to arrogate the role of a contextless arbiter – what Craig Calhoun (1995) has called social theory from the "umpire's chair" – without appreciating the sense in which he or she is participating in a racial discourse which provides its own context for critique. My argument is that sociological analysis needs to make explicit such contexts and the range of reversals they permit, and thus needs to find a different ground or perspective from which to do so. This is the aim of chapter 2.

Caste

Caste relations are archetypically associated with the area of Indic cultural influence (see below, and chapter 2, for a discussion of the "culture area" idea) which corresponds roughly with what are now the modern countries of India, Pakistan, Bangladesh, and Sri Lanka, though extending somewhat into Southeast Asia. Since the idea of caste is probably less familiar than that of race to Euro-American readers, we will devote a little more definitional space to it.

As with race, definitions of caste threaten to fix and reify that which should be seen as fluid. This is a particular danger in cross-cultural or comparative sociology where essentialized views of a phenomenon like caste are made to bear the onus of explanation for an entire culture-history, a point much to the fore in contemporary critical writings. Instead of a reductionism which invokes the singular phenomenon of caste to portray India as a society of separate, ranked, and religiously validated corporate groups, contemporary scholars have emphasized a plethora of alternative bases of social identification, including kinship, kingship, locality, gender, sectarian religious affiliation, and locality-based politico-economic institutional complexes. A pertinent question, then, which could be anticipated from our preceding discussion of race is the extent to which these phenomena constitute, independently or conjointly, an alternative way of conceiving Indian social realities or whether they are only refractory to the realities denoted in the concept of caste. Some contemporary scholars now reject the idea that caste has been a distinctive and fundamental organizing principle in India, pointing instead to the complex interplay between other factors of the sort mentioned above as constitutive of what has been understood as "Indian society" (Appadurai, 1986; Inden, 1990). Other writers preserve the idea of caste as a distinctive phenomenon, but one that is explicable mainly in relation to universal social-structural processes so that caste is stripped of its cultural or geopolitical specificity, being identifiable in principle or in practice elsewhere in the world, and being absent in India where those processes do not obtain (Quigley, 1993; Milner, 1994). Although there is much to commend these views, I think they involve their own forms of reductionism in neglecting the culturally specific – if not necessarily entirely unique – grounds upon which the manifold complexities and contradictions of social life are systematized, a point which applies not only in this case to the categories of Indian social life, but also to the sociological theory which purports to provide an account of it. In this context, to pursue the treacherous path of relating caste relations to a broader "civilizational" culture-history is, I argue, a valuable complement to other approaches.

We will return to this question later on, but let us now turn to a more straightforward appraisal of the way that caste has traditionally been understood in Euro-American scholarship. The word "caste" itself is Portuguese in origin, and it is usually regarded as conflating two different indigenous terms, *jati* and *varna*. *Jati*, etymologically associated with ideas of "type," "kind," and "origin," has generally been taken to refer to particular and more or less localized groups of people who marry and procreate among themselves and pass on their particular *jati* identification to their offspring, so that the *jati* can be regarded as a closed, ascriptive social group. These groups are parts of a hierarchy, so that people from different *jatis* would usually be regarded as being of different social status. *Jatis* are also traditionally associated with particular occupational specializations, though the extent to which such associations have ever been anything but fictive is debatable (Béteille, 1967; cf. Quigley, 1993).

In practice, however, things are rather more complicated than their portrayal in this rather idealized sketch. Although in some circumstances group boundaries are very clearly demarcated, this is not always the case. For one thing, two people who apply the same *jati* identification to themselves might nonetheless regard themselves as belonging to different and incommensurate groups. In such circumstances, it is tempting to break *jati* identification down to posit "subcastes," but the same kind of objection holds. A general finding of much ethnographic research has been that there is no basic unit of caste which unambiguously identifies a definite group of people. Thus, even though *jati* identification, not unlike racial identification, often involves a very clearly delimited sense of corporate group membership, *jatis* can nevertheless be thought of as *categories* and not *groups* in the sense defined earlier. Similar ambiguities attend the hierarchalization of *jati* identity; while people might readily agree that different *jatis* are unequal in status, there may be very little agreement on where those *jatis* stand in the status order. This is not just because of inevitable local dispute about the "true" status order, but because – as we shall see – the principles of hierarchy are contextual and intrinsically antithetical to any singular accounting of what the "true" status order might be (Dumont, 1980; Quigley, 1993).

The foregoing description of *jati* identification was fixed rather ahistorically in the ethnographic present. A more historical argument might suggest – though not uncontroversially – that the ramification of *jatis* emerged in medieval Indian history when larger imperial formations gave way to regional polities, was given further impetus under Muslim and particularly British colonial rule, and is today breaking down in the face of class stratification and ethnic nationalism. We will examine these points in more detail in later chapters, where I will argue that a more consistent logic can nevertheless be discerned. But let us now turn to the *varna* categories, which are of greater antiquity. While there is a vast proliferation of locally specific *jati* identifications, *varna* categories are pan-Indian in scope. They are mentioned in works associated with Brahmanism, the Vedic religion of ancient India and one of the precursors of modern Hinduism, most notably in the famous hymn from the *Rig Veda* cited at the start of the chapter. That hymn neatly enumerates the fourfold *varna* taxonomy of *brahman* (priest), *kshatriya* or *rajanya* (warrior or ruler), *vaishya* (farmer or "people'), and *shudra* (servant). The hierarchy of the *varnas* emerges clearly in the hymn from their reference points to the body of "the Man," Purusha, whose sacrifice was the primal act which generated the world; the *brahmans* (the mouth) occupying the most exalted position, followed by the *kshatriyas* and the *vaishyas* (these three constituting the "twice-born" castes), with the *shudras* at the lowest point of the hierarchy. Although these identifications clearly refer to actual social divisions which parallel to a limited extent those in other agrarian societies such as medieval Europe (see below and chapter 3), they are manifested in the Vedic literature largely as ritual functions in the sacrificial order of Brahmanism. However, there are some further complexities involved here. For one thing, positioning within the *varna* hierarchy is contested not only in terms of historical actualities like the putative superiority of farmers over kings or warriors in South India, but even within the very logic of Brahmanic thought where, as I shall argue, *kshatriyas* and *brahmans* act as a kind of double apex, each professing to encompass the other (Malamoud, 1981; Heesterman, 1985; Shulman, 1985; Burghart, 1996).

The *varna* identifications do to some extent reflect actual occupations; *brahmans* are associated with priestly functions, *kshatriyas* with political rule, *vaishyas* with mercantile activities, and so on. But, as with *jati* identification, the match is imperfect. For example, most brahmans are not actually priests. In fact, *varna* identification might be better thought of as a set of different idealized lifestyles or functions; Brahmanic mores are ascetic, contemplative, vegetarian, while the *kshatriya* lifestyle is a martial one, less discriminating and not so concerned with the niceties of Brahmanic ritual observation. To a degree, these lifestyles are appropriable as caste identifications. For example, local rulers sometimes have suspiciously obscure origins – perhaps they were *shudras* or something even more unseemly – and yet by behaving like kings they are assimilable to the *kshatriya* category, just as certain groups attempt to improve their caste status by adopting Brahmanic mores, a process which Srinivas (1956) has termed "Sanskritization." In other words, the *varna* scheme can once again be thought of as providing a set of potential categories which actual groups seek to realize in attempting to achieve status closure within them.

This touches upon the question that was raised earlier concerning the extent to which caste relations can be understood in universalist terms of status contest, or evince a more culturally specific grounding. The first of these positions is exemplified in Murray Milner's elegant discussion of the *varna* scheme through a neo-Weberian analysis of its status implications. Milner (1994: 63–79) argues that there is a recurrent status order in many societies based upon a fourfold division into three types of elite classes and one non-elite class, each of these four classes itself being further divisible by two. In brief, his argument posits an initial distinction between a class of economic producers and a class of warriors or rulers who are charged with protecting the producers from arbitrary or extraneous violence, in return for an economic claim upon them. It is in the producers' interests to minimize this claim and the rulers' interests to maximize it, but this tension is mediated by a third elite class whose status claim rests upon neither economic nor military–political force, but upon access to knowledge, typically of a religious kind, and is therefore able to act as a legitimacy-conferring third party. The fourth class is the non-elite mass, which nevertheless enjoys a humble respectability and can make certain claims on the services or protection of the elite classes. Each of these classes is in turn bifurcated by an inherent tension. Thus, where the rulers' militarily enforced economic claim upon the producers becomes overbearing, the distinction between rulers and the forces of predatory violence against which they were supposed to protect becomes blurred, so that the category of the ruler/warrior is complemented by that of the bandit. Among the class of producers, particularly in agrarian societies, the bifurcation is between controllers of extensive resources like productive land and intensive resources like commerce or finance, leading to a tension between landed gentries and merchants or bankers. Among the religious elite, the tension is manifested between those who are institutionally tied to one of the other elites, such as a church or priesthood established under the umbrella of the rulers, and those, such as mendicant religious ascetics, who adopt a more autonomous path in pursuit of transcendent religious goals and who are therefore able to mount a critique of the compromise entailed in the institutionalized religious order. And among the non-elite, there is a tension between the respectable citizenry, and an excluded class of the destitute, enslaved, or outcaste.

As Milner shows, it is fairly straightforward to apply each of these four categories along with their "alter egos" to the Indian *varna* scheme. Thus, the alter ego of the *kshatriya* is the would-be warrior-king of obscure origins, archetypically from the class of bandits, whose martial prowess threatens those traversing the wilderness between stable political domains. In fact, the *kshatriya* category rather conflates this distinction between the bandit or wandering warrior, and the king (*raja*) of a particular domain, a point to which we shall return in chapter 3. The alter ego of the *brahman* is the renouncer. Although the Brahmanic lifestyle is ascetic, contemplative, and religious, the *brahman* – whether a priest or nonpriestly householder – is very much tied to this-worldly social and political relationships. The archetypical renouncer, on the other hand, gives up all connections with such worldly concerns, other than the most basic requirements of sustenance and shelter, in order to pursue a wandering, individualist path of transcendence which is not hidebound by ideas of caste hierarchy. In this respect, the renouncer radicalizes the Brahmanic ideal of asceticism (even though he – and renouncers usually are male – may not actually be of Brahmanic origins). But it should also be pointed out that less extreme forms of renunciation exist, combining ascetic wandering with monastic or temple-based religious forms. These perforce have a greater involvement with worldly affairs, and are usually associated with sectarian religious affiliations which we shall examine shortly.

The renouncer constitutes a Brahmanic alter ego because it is he who pursues most uncompromisingly the path to release from the soul's wandering which is the Brahmanic goal. But in another sense, the *brahman's* alter ego can be regarded as the untouchable. Some words of clarification on this somewhat problematic term are necessary. In general, untouchability refers to "outcaste" groups who constitute the lowest of the low in the order of caste. However, the term is to some degree an invention of tidy-minded British colonial census-takers, who organized a rather disparate set of local groupings under pan-Indian terms like "outcaste" or "untouchable." For this reason, even though untouchability has subsequently been the focus for considerable political organization there remains no consensus on the meaning or validity of the term; here, I follow Mendelsohn and Vicziany (1998) who argue that untouchability does refer to an identifiable class of person, even if it is subject to characteristically blurred boundaries. The range of groups connoted by untouchable or "outcaste" status is nevertheless wide, and can include "tribal" groups who seem to be more or less outside caste society (though see below), groups who are literally "untouchable" in the sense that physical contact with them is thought to be especially polluting – often on the basis of "polluting" occupations such as leatherworking or sweeping (removing faeces) – and other groups of low status who shade into the *shudra* category and whose lifestyle often contains elements which offend higher caste mores, such as beef consumption. But insofar as untouchables act as removers of impurity there are affinities with *brahmans* in the latter's priestly function, since the *brahman* priest is also considered a vessel for the removal of the patron's impurity or "sin" (Parry, 1980; Raheja, 1988). In theory, brahmans have access to restitutive, purifying forces which render safe the impurity they take on (Shulman, 1984), therefore differentiating them from untouchables, but in the light of this association with impurity the idea of Brahmanic status preeminence is questionable at best.

Finally, the alter ego of the *shudra* is also the untouchable, since the latter represents the depths to which the *shudra* could easily sink in the absence of rigorous attempts to preserve appropriate differentiations of status. Indeed, untouchable strategies of status improvement typically involve the ramification of *jati* distinctions among their ranks for this reason (Mosse, 1994), and status improvement in India more generally has often followed the model of Sanskritization.

Milner's model, though to some degree adaptable to local circumstances, is essentially predicated upon a universal claim about the character of the status order in human societies which tends to blur the distinction I have made between categories and groups, so that its tensions always figure as fundamentally political contests between actual groups. Shulman (1985), on the other hand, offers a rather different model which is at once more specific to India (particularly, but not exclusively, to medieval South India) and more alive to the *varna* scheme as categories. He postulates a series of complementarities between king, bandit, brahman, renouncer, untouchable, and also clown which are incompatible with Milner's general model, and which he derives from a specific inner mentality, "a certain dynamism and tension, an urge to transformation; an open-endedness in principle" (ibid.: 7) that is reflected in the politics of everyday life. We will not consider this argument in detail here, because we will return to its theoretical and substantive implications in later chapters, but it is worth quoting Shulman's characterization of the associated differences between medieval India and medieval Europe, where

> a stable, neatly bounded cosmology – the earthly realm clearly separated from heaven and from God – allows for a far more stable vision of social order and of the state; control of power and resources is a legitimate goal for both king and Church, and there is, therefore, a long historical struggle between these two powers to seize control, to demarcate their respective jurisdictions, to resolve the contradiction in their rival claims to authority, and ultimately to stabilize their relations. . . . The South Indian king, in contrast, never even approaches enduring stability, since his authority, such as it is, proceeds out of a creative imbalance, an impulsive emotionalism, a playing with power and identity, a recognition of his limitations in the light of transcendent forces that eat away at the polity. (Shulman, 1985: 371–2)

We will return to consider this distinction between Indian and European kingship in some detail. For the present, I wish to suggest that in Europe the stress has fallen mainly on three of Milner's eight categories, namely the king, the priest, and the citizen, and that this is an "ideological" or "civilizational" difference between the two regions. In this respect, I shall argue that Indian kingship is "weak" *vis-à-vis* European kingship, not in the sense that it has failed empirically to prevail in political or military terms, but because the very idea of kingship is constitutionally mired in a sense of its precarious and ambiguous character in ways that are unparalleled in Europe. This difference is certainly not the only relevant factor in contrasting the political forms of Europe and India, and their transformation in ideologies of race and caste, but it is, I will suggest, an important one.

The discussion so far has made various references to ideas of status hierarchy, purity, and pollution. For some scholars, these are the central principles of caste. Purity is what defines caste hierarchy, so that those who are more free from pollution occupy a higher position on the status hierarchy. This hints at an issue upon which we shall later place some emphasis, namely a difference in the way that the boundaries between persons and things are conceived in the thinking that underlies race and caste ideologies, boundaries which are typically less secure in the latter case (see also chapter 3). In fact, the term *jati* does not just refer to different kinds of person but also to different classes of object, which are also hierarchalizable. Thus, the objects and substances with which people deal impart themselves into the person while, concomitantly, people impart themselves in these objects and substances. The significance of this goes beyond contact with especially polluting substances such as faeces and leather; traditionally, local caste relations are based upon often exceedingly complex interactional orders, particularly concerning food (who can cook – or accept – food, of what kind, from whom, under what circumstances) and gifts of other kinds (Marriott, 1968). More broadly, all action in the world is thought to create disorder, pollution, or "sin," manifested in objectified forms which require ritual restitution. At issue here is a quite fundamental sense of order; according to one view, the hierarchical order of the *varnas* is largely to do with this idea of preserving order by ensuring the purity of the highest caste, though quite which caste this is remains a disputed matter both in indigenous ideologies and among scholars.

In his *Homo Hierarchicus*, first published in 1966, Louis Dumont set out his influential theory of caste which addressed these points. Here, I will only provide the most summary description of his position; Quigley (1993) provides an especially lucid overview and critique. As we have already seen, Dumont is essentially a theorist of modernity, a point which becomes more evident in later works devoted to European ideology (e.g. Dumont, 1977; 1986). Modernity for Dumont is characterized by an ideology of egalitarian individualism, whereas traditional societies are characterized by hierarchical and holistic ideologies. From the perspective of modern, egalitarian individualism hierarchy implies inequality, whereas from the perspective of traditional society it merely implies ordering or ranking in relation to a whole. India is an example of a traditional society in which purity constitutes the ranking principle. Thus, for Dumont, superiority of status in India is identical with superior purity. Since the brahmans are preeminent in terms of purity, they stand at the top of the hierarchy. This leads to the curious situation whereby political or economic elites are, in theory, inferior in status to powerless Brahmanic ritualists; in India, as Dumont formulates it, "power" or temporal political authority is subordinated to "status" or the priesthood (Dumont, 1980: 71–2). The approach is structuralist in the sense that emphasis is placed not upon the substantial reality of particular units of the system – such as a specific caste group – but upon the predication of these units from broader systemic principles, so that caste society emerges as a system of (contextually variable) differences, driven by an underlying ideology of purity expressed in terms of a relation to the whole.

Dominant in anthropology during the 1960s and 1970s, Dumont's approach has more recently been subjected to intensive criticism and is now widely regarded as presenting an idealized Brahmanical ideology rather than a convincing contemporary sociological portrait of caste on the ground. It has given way to a more historical approach which emphasizes political relationships previously neglected because of the leveling effects of British colonialism on indigenous political processes. One way of broaching this alternative approach is by considering caste at the level of local (or "village") relations.

Perhaps the best-known formulation here is the concept of the "dominant caste" first developed by Srinivas in the 1950s (Srinivas, 1987). At the local level, much political and economic action is organized in relation to the dominant caste of local land controllers, which does not necessarily occupy an especially high position in the *varna* scheme. From this perspective, caste is understood in terms of relationships between a central, dominant group and a set of groups arrayed around it in relationships of patronage and clientship. For economies based upon agrarian production – of which India has been an example for most of its history, and very substantially still is – control over the productivity of the land is the *sine qua non* of political control, and the dominant caste of the Indian village is usually the one with preponderant ownership or control over land.

The dominant caste model has the merit of relating caste to economic control as well as transcendent ideologies, though it also suffers from several limitations in this respect (Mendelsohn, 1993). For our purposes, its principal insight lies in the way it substitutes a view of caste relations as a clustering around or radiation from particular points rather than the simple rank ordering associated with the traditional view of the *varna* hierarchy. But whereas Srinivas emphasized economic processes of domination, more recent approaches have restored a ritual or ideological element to them in emphasizing the way that *every* identifiable caste unit acts as a nodal point in local economic, social, and political relationships, yielding a model of caste as a complex set of overlapping center–periphery relations at the local and supra-local level (see especially Raheja, 1988: 243). The principles of connection or articulation between the units in this "radial" model are by no means straightforward, and have been the subject of scholarly disputes which we shall examine in later pages. One issue which is worth anticipating at this point, however, is the nature of political rule. From the viewpoint of those "Western" discourses on political sovereignty (which, I have argued, underpin racial ideology) it is hard to conceive of political orders in which sovereignty is invested in more than one entity or at more than one level within the social order. This, however, is one possible implication of the "radial" model; local suzerainty falls to dominant castes or "little kings," who possess an autonomous legitimacy even though, at higher levels of political encompassment, they might be beholden to greater magnates and thence up to the great dynastic kings who have at various times held sway over a greater or lesser proportion of the Indian subcontinent. In this sense, the radial model can serve at a number of levels, applying to relations of patronage and clientship between castes at the village level, but also to relations between local rulers and those of a higher order. In this model, then, "power" does not submit to "status," or at least not in the way that Dumont conceives it; caste can always be conceived in terms of political relations in different contexts.

Some of the strongest criticisms of Dumont have come from those who feel his "Brahmanic" account of caste society effaces its exploitative character. Berreman, for example, has argued that

> The human meaning of caste for those who live it is power and vulnerability, privilege and oppression, honour and denigration, plenty and want, reward and deprivation, security and anxiety. As an anthropological document, a description of caste which fails to convey this is a travesty. (Berreman, 1979: 159)

The violence and oppression at the heart of caste society is indeed underemphasized in many scholarly writings, but it does not follow that it is of the same character as that which characterizes class and race conflicts in the West. On this point, Dumont (1980: 253) opposes those who draw parallels between race and caste on the basis of particular features like the exercise of violence by arguing along Durkheimian lines that such features must be considered in their relation to systemic wholes and, when examined thus, two putatively identical features of different systems cannot necessarily be considered the same. The argument is compelling from a sociological standpoint; it is perhaps less compelling from the standpoint of the people bearing the brunt of oppression, though it may nevertheless be wise not to assume that oppression is everywhere experienced and responded to in the same way, so that the specific forms of inequality in other societies are read reductively as mere variants of those recognized in Western contexts, like the oppression of women by men or the poor by the rich. Indeed, where Dumont offers a rather universalizing contrast between the traditional and the modern (and between caste and race as specific manifestations of them), I will argue that there are more culturally specific features of India and Europe – each following its own trajectory of "modernity," until they collided under the aegis of British colonial expansion – which underlie caste and race ideologies.

Part of my argument will involve an appraisal of the relationship between caste and Hinduism. Some brief introductory comments on the latter are therefore in order. First, we should note the argument that Hinduism does not really constitute a religion in the same sense as, say, Christianity or Islam, with an organized church exerting control over religious doctrine and acting as a political institution with or against the organs of secular rule. It is instead a rather looser composite of cultural traditions. One of those traditions is the ancient sacrificial Vedic religion mentioned earlier, which was associated with the Aryan-speaking peoples who migrated into India during the second millennium BC. This was to inform a new Brahmanic synthesis which took shape during roughly the first half-millennium AD and whose soteriology emphasized the ultimate aim of release (*moksha*) from the cycle of reincarnations, where the soul escapes the individual to rejoin cosmic unity (*brahman*). Later religious forms in India were more theistic, particularly with the emergence of Vaishnavism and Shaivism, which emphasized worship of the gods Vishnu and Shiva respectively as the supreme god, Vishnu generally being viewed as a rather majestic "royal" figure, Shiva as a more austere and ascetic one. These forms intersect with the *bhakti* movement, which took shape initially in South India during roughly the second half of the first millennium AD and is today largely constitutive of popular temple-based Hinduism. *Bhakti* emphasizes devotional worship from a crowded pantheon of deities rather than the austere ritualism of Brahmanism. Buddhism and Jainism constituted earlier responses to Brahmanism which, on the contrary, redoubled the emphasis on the ascetic pursuit of release, but contained a critique of Brahmanic hierarchy. These and other non-Brahmanic traditions constituted a vital religious force which rivalled Brahmanism until they were finally marginalized by the end of the first millennium AD. Some of their elements found their way into the *bhakti* movement, although the movement itself represented a critique of anti-Brahmanic heterodoxy and became intertwined with Brahmanism (Shulman, 1984; Thapar, 1992). Indeed, the contrast between Brahmanism and more theistic forms is not easy to draw. From one perspective, they share a root conception of an "encompassing" divinity. In other words, lesser gods appear as manifestations of particular aspects of greater gods, and even the phenomenal form of greater gods is but an aspect of a larger cosmic reality, of which humans and animals also partake. Strong domain distinctions are not entertained between the divine, human, and natural worlds and between the objects (like individual humans) comprising them. This encompassing aspect is perhaps particularly true of *Vaishnavism*, with its doctrine of the avatar, whereby gods like Rama and Krishna appear as specific manifestations of Vishnu. Thus, there is much scope for fluidity of religious belief and organization. There are nevertheless certain tensions between local folk deities and Hindu cosmology which cannot always be assimilated away and sometimes have significant implications for sociopolitical organization (Schnepel, 1995).

In relation to caste, we might say that Brahmanism, with its *varna* ideology of Brahmanic preeminence and ritual purity, is closest to the principles of caste hierarchy. Theistic traditions are less hidebound by considerations of hierarchy, but are nevertheless amenable to the broad logic of Brahmanic encompassment. This raises the question mentioned earlier concerning the extent to which caste, if it is given any credence at all, should be regarded as a social-structural feature of limited compass in Indian history or whether it conforms to a more general cultural context. The point can be addressed to debates concerning the extent to which particular kinds of people or ideology should be regarded as "outside" the caste order, such as untouchables (Moffatt, 1979; Deliège, 1991), "tribals" (Sinha, 1997; Skaria, 1997), or even the discourse of contemporary Hindu nationalism (Fox, 1996; Hansen, 1996a). In his ethnographic study of untouchables in contemporary Lucknow, Khare (1984) makes an important distinction between what he calls "Hindu" and "Indic" values. The cosmology of Khare's untouchable informants shared aspects of the Hindu traditions examined above, but they represented these as part of broader "Indic" civilizational values of which they regarded Brahmanic Hinduism as but one, not very legitimate, derivation. Perhaps this suggests that to participate in a singular cultural tradition does not necessarily preclude the possibility that social conflicts and political struggles might be articulated through its "shared" values or cultural assumptions. Indeed, later I will argue that caste does relate to broader "Indic" values, just as race draws from Euro-American values which might otherwise seem to have little to do with it, while attempting to avoid any commitment to the view of unitary, ossified "cultural tradition." But in order to establish the terms of this argument, let us now examine the notion of "hierarchy" in a little more detail.

Hierarchy

In everyday usage hierarchy is typically thought of as an ordering of discrete units which ranks them from superior to inferior. This appears to be the sense of hierarchy employed by Gerald Berreman, who regards both race and caste as amenable to description as "a hierarchy of endogamous divisions in which membership is hereditary and permanent" (Berreman, 1979: 2). There are indeed understressed parallels between caste and race systems on the basis of endogamy (i.e. marriage and procreation within the group) and inherited rank; these are discussed in chapter 5, which nevertheless shows some of the limitations to the analogy. But in this section I will suggest that race and caste conform to two different kinds of hierarchy, a point which has significant implications not only for their sociological analysis, but also for an appreciation of the character *of* sociological analysis.

The starting point for this argument is Dumont's important discussion of hierarchy (Dumont, 1980: 239–45), from which figure 1.1 has been derived, with modifications. Dumont identifies one situation, shown pictographically in figure 1.1 (a), where a universe of discourse is completely divided into two (or, conceivably, more) non-overlapping classes. In this schema one must either belong to class A or class B; it is not possible to belong either to both or to neither. The schema permits a transitive hierarchalization; one or other of the classes may be defined as superior (or, where there are more than two, they can be placed in a consistent rank order). This kind of scheme broadly characterizes Euro-American ideologies of racial hierarchy, as well as common conceptions of gender and class inequality. A different situation obtains in figure 1.1 (b). Here, class A is coextensive with the universe of discourse, but class B is set within – encompassed by – A. Thus, we encounter unity at the level of A (A encompasses B) and diversity at the level of B (B is different from A). Dumont reserves the term "hierarchy" for the second case, and considers Indian caste relations to be a paradigmatic example. In his words, "In hierarchy thus defined, complementariness or contradiction is contained in a unity of superior order" (Dumont, 1980: 242). In order to posit hierarchy in this sense, then, it is necessary to define the particular level at which it is situated. This is the more true because hierarchy is two-dimensional, so that a class which at one level is superior to another can, from a different level, be inferior. Superiority "cannot be true from one end of experience to the other (only artificial hierarchies make this claim), for this would be to deny the hierarchical dimension itself, which . . . offers the possibility of reversal" (ibid.: 244).

I do not find it useful to call one kind of hierarchy "artificial" in comparison to another, so I shall henceforth refer to figure 1.1a-type hierarchies as "ranking hierarchies" and figure 1.1b-type hierarchies as "encompassing hierarchies." The schema has some obvious parallels with Lévi-Strauss's discussion of dual organizations, in which ranking and encompassing hierarchy roughly correspond with what Lévi-Strauss calls "diametric" and "concentric" organizational structures (Lévi-Strauss, 1963:

(a)   (b)

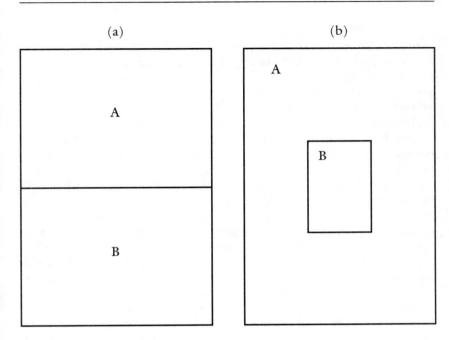

Figure 1.1   Forms of hierarchy
(Derived from L. Dumont, *Homo Hierarchicus*, Chicago: University of Chicago
Press, 1980: 242)

132–63). For Lévi-Strauss, diametric structures may evince equality insofar
as their two elements are viewed as complementary, but are often unequal
after the fashion of the ranking hierarchy model discussed above. Concentric structures, on the other hand, are *always* unequal because they are
arranged around, or emanate from, a supreme central point. On the face of
it, this contrasts both with Dumont's model of encompassing hierarchy,
which permits reversals or eversions vitiating any consistent orientation to
a center, and with the "radial" model of caste relations examined earlier,
which denies that there is any single, central point of hierarchical
preeminence. But there is another aspect to Lévi-Strauss's argument. Concentric structures, he suggests, are mediators between diametric structures
and a triadism in which the distinction between a hierarchically preeminent
or "sacred" center and its subordinate or "profane" periphery or satellites
requires a third element, an external frame of reference which encompasses
it (ibid.: 151–2). Analogously, I would argue that the "radial" model of
caste as a multiple set of context-specific center–periphery relations, associated with writers like Raheja (1988), can be further encompassed within a

more singularly hierarchical model along these lines in ways to which Dumont's theory is in principle more alive, that this has manifested itself in a basically unitary political conception underlying the multiple sovereignties of the caste order, and that the critique of Dumont which emerges from the radial model is therefore not as damaging to his general approach as is often supposed (see also chapter 3).

Dumont's argument, as a theorist of modernity, is that figure 1.1b describes the hierarchy of traditional society which gave way to conceptions of ranking hierarchy in modern society; thus, with a hierarchical conception as in figure 1.1a, "moderns" can only think of difference as inequality (if A and B are not equal, they succumb to a rank ordering), whereas in traditional society difference is thought of in relation to a whole. Furthermore, Dumont sees figure 1.1b as a model not only for caste but also for conceptions of social order in other premodern societies, including Europe (Dumont, 1986). On this point, my own argument diverges from his. While accepting that such transformations are logically possible, I shall argue that although the idea of encompassing hierarchy captures some, but not all, aspects of caste, the political thought of European Christendom has been consistently oriented to conceptions of ranking hierarchy which, in the long term, underpinned the emergence of racial thinking. It is true that there were elements of encompassing hierarchy in early Christian thought, such as in the philosophy of Origen, which were increasingly subordinated to ranking hierarchy as the Christian church transcended its roots as a sectarian reform movement to incorporate itself with first the structure and then the legacy of the Roman empire (Caspary, 1979; Dumont, 1986). However, this transformation was not just politically contingent, but reflected a dominant developmental possibility of Christian cosmology.

The difference can be made explicit with reference to Dumont's (1986) discussion of the "Great Chain of Being," a way of conceiving the natural world which emerged in classical philosophy, and later on in Neoplatonic thought, remaining influential in Europe up until the eighteenth century. The Great Chain of Being mediates the idea of the wholeness or unity of nature with its diversity; there is a continuous gradation of beings from the lowest to the highest, the difference between each successive form being vanishingly small so that the gradations represent the continuity of Being as a whole. In this sense, it has been common to think of the Great Chain of Being as an infinitesimally divided ranking hierarchy. Dumont wishes to refute this view, citing the sixth-century Neoplatonic Christian writer Pseudo-Dionysius Areopagitus, who first coined the term "hierarchy" and who argued for a disjunction between inferior and superior (divine) forms which required mediation. Thus, Dumont infers, "the Great Chain of Being appears as a form for acknowledging differences while at the same time subordinating them to and encompassing them in unity" (Dumont, 1986: 256), thereby assimilating it to the encompassing hierarchy of traditional society. What this neglects is the fact that the unity of Being constituted a deep problem for Christian thinkers working in the Neoplatonic tradition, because Judeo-Christian thought posited an absolute disjunction between God and the world. God precisely did *not* encompass differences; in Peter Berger's words, God "stands *outside* the cosmos, which is his creation but which he confronts and does not permeate" (Berger, 1967: 115), and a major axis of Pseudo-Dionysius's text is an attempt to reconcile the monism of the Neoplatonic tradition in which all things emanate from the first principle of Being (rather as in Lévi-Strauss's concentric structures) and the dualist, anti-emanationist Judeo-Christian conception in which the world of objects, God's Creation, is divested of God's own numinous presence (Gersh, 1978). In contrast to an absolute monotheism, however, Christianity posits the liminal man–god figure of Christ who mediates between a secular Creation and the divine. This is better represented through the ranking hierarchy depicted in figure 1.1a, where the everyday world of objects stands beneath and is absolutely distinguished from a superordinate divine order, except that now, through Christ's mediation, the subordinate world of objects possesses a kind of direction or intendedness which would reconstitute it into the divine order. Absolutely distinct from God, but uniquely forged in God's image, human beings are differentiated from and stand above the object world (persons are separated from things). In Christianity, these objectifications became further entrenched when the early church rejected the millenarian belief that Christ would return to establish a kingdom on earth with the eschatology of an afterlife as the domain of salvation. The separation of the human from the numinous established a tension between them which promised transcendence if the mundane human world could be reconstituted after the fashion of the divine, fueling a general Christian tendency to construct economic and political action as secular domains which required some kind of reconnection with transcendent goals.

This Christian sense of ranking hierarchy has also underlain the peculiarly monadic idea of political sovereignty in Europe, concerning which worldly person can, as it were, appropriate Christ's singular mantle as mediator with the divine order. The battles in medieval Europe between the secular authority of kings or emperors and the clerical authority of priests or popes can be understood in this context, representing as they do different fragments of the same moral entity (see chapter 3). Thus, Dumont (1986: 68) is simply wrong to imply that emphasis upon the conflict between them is an anachronistic affectation of observers in the modern period, where the distinction between secular and divine authority has been firmly drawn, who thereby fail to perceive that in medieval Europe, just as in India, secular authority was encompassed by clerical authority. On the contrary, I would argue that this conflict is immanent in the fundamental Christian logic of the mediated ranking hierarchy in ways barely paralleled by the more monadic political categories of pre-British India. For example, the *Brhadaranyaka Upanishad* (1.4) posits an originary, cosmic substance (*brahman*), which differentiates in accordance with the principles of encompassing hierarchy outlined by Dumont, so that the *varna* categories emanate from the original unity of *brahman*, and evince different kinds of superiorities with respect to one another. Similar emanationist thinking exists in contemporary India (Daniel, 1984; Fuller, 1992). Neoplatonism shared something of this emanationist approach whereas, as we have seen, the matter was much more problematic in the Judeo-Christian tradition. Berger (1967) argues that Judaism constituted a kind of "reform" of the emanationist doctrines among the ancient civilizations of the Middle East, one that, in positing a God absolutely outside Creation and preceded by nothing, established a logic of secularization which proceeded through various reversals to the "death of god" in the disenchanted modernity of the post-Reformation period (cf. Dumont, 1986; Wagner, 1986).

Transformations of the same logic, I will argue, partly underlie the political ideologies associated with European colonial expansion in the "first imperial age" through which modern ideologies of race took shape. But we should be attuned to continuity as well as difference across the premodern–modern divide. Habermas (1987) has argued that Hegel (1770–1831) was the first philosopher to come fully to grips with the problem of modernity, settling in his *Phenomenology of Spirit* upon a conception of unitary substance or spirit with an immanent intendedness towards differentiation, reconstituted as wholeness through an intellectual reason which traversed all its forms. The identities between this and the Christian idea of a reconstitutive mediation of the secular into the sacred are obvious. In "turning Hegel on his head," Karl Marx substituted human practice for Hegel's intellectual abstraction as the vehicle for mediation, but did not upset the Christian parameters of the model whereby mediation was directed at some wholeness or redemption beyond the extant order, a point which I would argue holds true for much contemporary thinking on race and inequality. Chapters 2 and 7 involve a more detailed appraisal of this theoretical implication that racial identifications together with their critique in sociological analysis and in a good deal of political activism are actually predicated on much the same underlying presuppositions. But in the final section of this chapter I want to lay the groundwork for this in addressing some of the more immediate issues which emerge from the contention that race and caste can be understood in relation to specific culture-histories.

History and Ambivalence: A Place in the Sociological Debate

There is a problem with analysing race or caste identifications in relation to specific culture–historical grounds because it can plausibly be argued that a historical sociology which purports to demonstrate the "development" of these identifications over linear time is not the means for their analysis so much as itself representing a particular modality of them, grounded as they are in notions of deep historical origins and rootedness. This point is addressed in the following chapter, which develops a theoretical approach to structural transformation in arguing that changing social representations are nevertheless entailed in the dynamics of more uniform social logics. Subsequent chapters will illustrate the point by showing how race and caste relations have been shaped in accordance with such logics over the *longue durée*, logics which now articulate somewhat awkwardly in the contemporary condition of a putatively global modernity. In developing this argument, I am influenced – but not wholly swayed – by two rather antithetical bodies of writing. On the one hand, I draw from the traditions of comparative historical sociology, originally formulated by the pioneers of the discipline like Marx and Weber and developed more recently by writers like Immanuel Wallerstein (1974), John Hall (1985), Michael Mann (1986), Jean Baechler (1988), and Charles Tilly (1990). On the other hand, I draw from contemporary postcolonial theory which, under the disparate theoretical influences of Antonio Gramsci, Frantz Fanon, and Michel Foucault, has developed out of the writings of Edward Said (1978) and has been especially influential on Indian historiography through the later Subaltern Studies school and the work of writers like Gayatri Spivak (1996). Let us briefly consider the main issues that these writings raise.

The fundamental question posed by comparative historical sociology is why Western Europe, and some of its derivatives like the USA, has been so globally dominant politically and economically over the past several centuries. Imbibing from a tradition which dates to the very beginnings of secular political thought in Europe, the answer proposed by recent writers like Mann and Baechler just as much as their forebears is that the economic and political structures of Europe have engendered a radical, modernizing dynamic which has been missing in other places. This literature is of interest to us because it places emphasis on tracking the specific structural transformations wherein the particularity of European social forms can be located, although we shall be less interested in the spectacle of its "economic miracle" and more interested in the especially uncompromising forms of racism and colonialism that accompanied it. Indeed, whereas the contemporary orthodoxy in comparative historical sociology has it that Europe differed from the rest of the world in the autonomy of its economic order, and that its politico-religious ideologies were a largely irrelevant superstructural gloss on this fundamental fact, I shall argue on the contrary that there was relatively little to distinguish Europe's economic order until the eighteenth and nineteenth centuries, but that its politico-religious traditions had an immense influence upon emerging forms of colonial domination and racism. Thus, while Michael Mann's view that scholarly conceptions of societies as totalities should be replaced with the idea that they are "constituted of multiple overlapping and intersecting sociospatial networks of power" (Mann, 1986: 1) is persuasive, his approach to power and politics belies a sociological reductionism which is a common feature of writings in comparative historical sociology. In chapter 2 I attempt to develop a similar conception to Mann's, but one more alive to the constitutive effects of political ideology. And I therefore reject the view inherited in this literature from Weber and Marx that the non-European world was a static one in comparison to the "rational restlessness" of Europe, first by showing the relative stasis and continuity in Europe's own politico-religious thought, and second by showing the relative dynamism outside Europe. Moreover, whereas orthodox comparative historical sociology tends to regard "modernity" – that secular sense of alienation whereby the legitimacy of social institutions has to be self-consciously created (Habermas, 1987) – as tied ineluctably to processes of "modernization" which are regarded as the singular achievement of the "European dynamic," I argue that there is nothing especially recent or culturally specific about this sense of modernity as alienation (cf. Simmel, 1968; Miller, 1994: 58–81). It can be found for example in medieval India, with its literature on the contradictions of kingship, and Brahmanic conceptions of the *Kaliyuga*, the last and most chaotic age in a cycle of epochs. By the same token, the sacralization of rationality itself as the transcendentally empirical and normative basis of the social order in modern Euro-American thought can be regarded as no more than a transformation of the premodern concern to reconstitute the mundane world into the transcendent order via the mediation of an embodied divinity (cf. Inden, 1995). Thus, I suggest, there are specific forms of "rationality" and "restlessness" which contribute to particular logics of stasis and change.

A word on the ideas of "Europe" and "India" may be in order at this point. Although there was much diversity among them, the European countries which engineered colonial expansion in the "first imperial" age substantially shared the political, religious, and cultural traditions through which racial ideologies were shaped in colonial encounters (Pagden and Canny, 1987). More important, perhaps, was a *self-conception* of an essential European singularity and distinctiveness which began to develop in the medieval period in relation to a sense of political community under unitary, sovereign rule and grounded in notions of territorial identity of varying scales. This, I will argue, has been crucial to the later emergence of racial ideology. Thus, it is quite possible to accept that what we now tend to think of as "European" culture has drawn much of its inspiration from the people of the African and Asian – and, indeed, American – continents (Bernal, 1987), without abandoning the view that "Europe" has played a significant historical role as a constitutive idea. At the same time, whereas standard imperialist and anti-imperialist histories share a common tendency to privilege Europe as the agent of world-historical integration, so that the story of the modern world can be described as that of "Europe and the people without history" (Wolf, 1982), it is equally possible to counterpose a "history of peoples without Europe" (Asad, 1987). By adopting race as a major key to the historical narrative in this book, I risk fixing colonial history to European history, thereby understating the indigenous grounding of colonial histories (a point we shall discuss further in chapter 6). My aim, however, is not first and foremost to tell the history of particular places in their specificity, but to provide a historically grounded account of racial ideologies which, I suggest, did largely originate in the way European encounters with non-Europeans were refracted through its antecedent political categories. I recognize that this slants my historical account in a "Eurocentric" direction. Still, by focusing on the emergence of race rather than "modernity" as Europe's contribution to the universe of cultural representations, perhaps a more sober appreciation of this contribution is possible.

Precolonial India, on the other hand, was not on the whole characterized by a sovereign sense of a unitary political community (though see chapter 3). Instead, as Dipesh Chakrabarty (1995) has argued on the basis of Sudipta Kaviraj's work, people in precolonial India might have described themselves in given contexts according to any number of religious, regional, caste, locality, or other identities. Although people could place themselves and others precisely within these identities, Kaviraj argues, they did not generalize them so that it would have occurred to them to quantify themselves as "populations" within these identities or to think of them as an exclusive basis for collective political action. This contextual aspect to identity is hardly unique to India and it therefore reveals the very specific cultural framing of the view which permits leftist thought to dream of global proletarian majorities (Rigby, 1996), even as the globalization of a homogenizing and exploitative capitalism makes such identifications possible (though see Miller, 1994). Nevertheless, I do want to suggest that there are some more specific "Indian" aspects to this idea of plural identities, enabling us to posit an Indian culture area which, paradoxically, is unified by its very lack of unity. This plurality, in other words, is not just actual but reflects a unified ideology which is able to countenance plurality of certain, delimited kinds. Here, we might draw upon Sheldon Pollock's (1998) analysis of the astonishingly rapid spread of Sanskrit as a court language throughout much of the vast area of Southern and Southeastern Asia from around AD 150, a spread which – unlike the spectacular progress of other cultural or politico-religious ideologies such as the Christianization of Northern Europe or the Islamicization of the Mediterranean and beyond – involved no political center, military conquest, or population movement. In Pollock's words it was "periphery without centre, community without unity" (ibid.: 13). But it involved more than just the adoption of a language, since the language implied a determinate moral, social, and political order which was self-consciously conceived within specific geopolitical boundaries (ibid.: 14–16). A millennium after its rise to hegemony, Sanskrit gave way to regional vernaculars, a change which seems to be associated with the transformation in political aspiration from universal overlordship to more limited regional suzerainty. However, to paraphrase his argument, Pollock warns that these events should not be understood (as, for example, writers like Mann are inclined to do) with reference to the "cultural" legitimation of "political" power, a reductionism which emerges from contemporary Euro-American intellectual discourses formulated in relation to the logic of capitalism, and making it extraordinarily difficult to reconstruct what might have been a potentially radically different cultural logic in a part of the "nonmodern non-West" (ibid.: 32).

The obstacles to any such reconstruction, epistemological as well as empirical, may well be insuperable, but what seems especially valuable in Pollock's analysis is his empirical demonstration of a cultural context not tied deterministically to a specific social process which can be reduced to some putatively universal and constraining dynamic like Mann's "networks of power." The point leads directly to one of the major contributions of postcolonial theory in its various forms which, rather than focusing analytically upon a singular conception of a power which yields coercive domination in colonial contexts, have emphasized instead the way that colonial situations involve a poetics or a performance of different kinds of power, a performance which is always multilayered and ambivalent. For example, Edward Kamau Brathwaite (1977) shows brilliantly how Samuel Sharpe – the enslaved Baptist preacher who led the 1831 slave uprising in Jamaica – was later fashioned into the embodiment of several quite different versions of political action by ideologues of the different political discourses in Jamaica which were associated with its social disjunctions between an elite white plantocracy, a missionary movement which offered a critique of plantation slavery from within a colonial ideology, an aspirant middle class comprising "mixed race" free people of color, and the mass of black slaves who sought an autonomous cultural tradition which entirely avoided the colonial plantation order (see also chapter 6). Brathwaite shows how Sharpe's uprising can be portrayed as a power strategy of the aspirant middle class, but equally as an expression of the sensibilities of the enslaved masses who turned away from that model. This is a specific example of a broader move in postcolonial theory to posit ambivalence as a general feature of colonial society, so that the basis of political action as the performance of some particular group's collective interest can always be destabilized by showing its multilayered and ambiguous provenance. Such insights have permitted some exemplary empirical studies of colonial political struggles, but in the theoretical discourse of postcolonial theory they have also led to the kneejerk postulation of ambivalence itself as the ontological condition of colonial societies (e.g. Prakash, 1990; 1992). The question here is whether simply to approbate ambivalence within academic writing, or whether to incorporate its manifestation within a specific sociological account. There is, I think, a complacency in postcolonial writing which adopts the former strategy – often, indeed, as a critique of more orthodox sociological metanarrative. The simple substitution of ambivalence for structure – indeed, the whole irony of regarding ambivalence unambivalently as *better* analytically or politically than its antecedents – betrays a common root in progressivist Western intellectual traditions steeped in Christian ideas which promise a single key to redemption or a critique which supersedes its antecedents. This involves a failure to recognize that unitary ideas of structure or culture which recourse to the notion of ambivalence sought to overcome are merely recuperated through "ambivalence" as a unitary theoretical abstraction encompassing the possible ("cultural") configurations of contest and resolution. My claim in this book is that by attending historically to the ways in which power is performed and contested it is possible to provide a systemic account of the way ideologies of natural hierarchy are reproduced and transformed according to distinctive cultural logics. Nevertheless, I acknowledge that this claim has its own specific cultural grounding. Scholarly discourse in the social sciences reaches out beyond itself to incorporate those phenomena it takes as its object (a point which is as true of postcolonial theory as the "modernist" theories it opposes), but in doing so mounts a transcendent epistemological claim which can never wholly be sustained. This is essentially Habermas's point about the self-consciousness of modernity which was described earlier. For this reason, strongly materialist or naturalistic epistemologies which might wish to subject sociological models to the rigors of empirical testing cannot really be entertained. In the words of Talal Asad,

> the important thing always is to try and identify that combination of elements . . . in the past of a given population that will serve to explain a particular outcome – in the narrative (or weak) sense of "explain," not in the

natural science (or strong) sense, because the past of human societies cannot be tested, it can only be made more or less plausible as part of the same story as the present. (Asad, 1987: 602)

This incitation to make history plausible as part of the story of the present comes from the contested intellectual juncture of the present, even if this in turn depends upon the ones preceding it. Postcolonial theory has been particularly attentive to the epistemological implications of this point in directing critical scrutiny towards the world-constituting assumptions underlying social science. So, for example, Said (1978) and others, in their critique of "Orientalism," have focused upon the tissue of prior assumptions necessary to codify social relations into an objectively knowable system. These assumptions, it is argued, are systematically associated with European colonial domination in its attempt to characterize and control the non-European, by working the irreducibly manifold world of meanings, actions and intentions into a singularity which, through devices such as the concept of culture, constitutes the non-European as "other." The critique of Orientalism has been influential in drawing much closer scholarly attention to social science itself as a particular kind of cultural practice, which uses characteristic devices to inscribe a knowledge of the world. By the same token, it has contributed to the dissolution of an older anthropological culture theory insofar as it questions the essentialism involved in counterposing, for example, an Indian "world of caste" with a Euro-American "world of race." In this, however, it creates something of a paradox, in that it recuperates a notion of *cultural difference* (India cannot be understood through Euro-American concepts) at the same time as it tries to undercut the representation of difference as an artifice of particular (Euro-American) modes of thought. This "forked stick" threatens to disable any kind of sociological representation, but it involves rather totalizing claims of its own. One problem is that it is not just colonial discourse which works multiplicity into singularity; all representations of the social world do so, including the critique of Orientalism, and this objection is as true for those postcolonial writings which celebrate the ambivalent, the fragmentary, or the unique as it is for the "metanarratives" they reject. In this book, I knowingly construct two metanarratives of Euro-American and Indian culture-history of very great generality, although in later chapters I do attempt to ground them in much specific detail. In doing so, I acknowledge that to talk of cultural specificity or "otherness" necessarily means implicitly to invoke a "self," but there is no reason to suppose that it means *only* to invoke a self, and the "Orient" that I construct in these pages is emphatically not just a mirror image or distortion of my Occident. This, I hope, will become clear in subsequent chapters.

2 | Theoretical Constructions

Introduction

In the previous chapter it was argued that there are some problems with
the way that ideologies of natural hierarchy are commonly approached in
the sociological literature through a critique of essentialism which opposes
relations to essences, because the mutual entailment of these qualities within
a broader cultural context of European thought is thereby elided. The
present chapter develops this argument in greater detail in order to lay the
basis for an alternative theoretical approach which will inform the substantive analysis undertaken in later chapters. Thus, it will not be concerned
with particular theories of race or caste so much as with the intellectual
underpinnings of the kinds of sociological theories through which these
phenomena have been understood. In classical or "modernist" social theory,
these have characteristically involved an understanding of the social world
predicated on the idea of *value* created in the tension between distinctive
orders of social reality. Two influential thinkers whose work we shall examine shortly – Marx and Lévi-Strauss – conceive these distinctive orders in
relation to the separation of the natural and the human worlds. In this,
they broach the classic philosophical antinomy of idealism and materialism
whose transcendence is a necessary but difficult goal for any moderately
sophisticated sociological theory. But they also pinpoint the generative
moment for ideologies of natural hierarchy in ways that are richly suggestive for their sociological analysis, even if this was never very explicitly their
intention. Although the universalist or "scientific" aspirations of their thinking have more recently succumbed to critical scrutiny, their genius lies in
their ability to articulate intellectually the "Western" traditions which form
the premise of sociological thought and also of one type of natural hierarchy, namely race. In this respect, the grounding of this "modernist" or

"structuralist" literature is, I suggest, more germane as a point of departure for a sociology of natural hierarchies than "postmodernist" or "poststructuralist" writing, although the argument developed here is framed through the tension between modernist social theory and its later critique. In this chapter, we will address both the antinomy of idealism and materialism, and the cultural specificity of Euro-American conceptions of "nature" which provide the context for sociological theory as well as racial ideology. But first let us prepare for this by appraising the duality of relations and essences mentioned above a little more deeply.

Essentialism and Anti-essentialism

To say that a cultural representation such as the idea of race is "relational" does not in itself specify the issue fully. It is necessary to define that with which it stands in a relation. Here, anti-essentialist critiques adopt one of two strategies: either race is an (imagined, constructed) figure projected from some (real) ground, or it is defined as a relation by its difference from other representations. The former strategy requires a convincing argument to establish the "reality" of the ground it supposes, while the second needs to supply an encompassing context which provides the axis for the relational character of the representations it posits in order to establish their systematic and enduring character. It is not easy to do this without laying oneself open to the charge of simply deferring essentialism onto the higher-order ground or context. Often, therefore, anti-essentialist critique provides a deconstruction of the *sui generis* character of race or other hierarchical ideologies, but leaves the context through which it is able to do so implicit or exogenous, perhaps lest the essential grounds or contextual assumptions for its own critique are undermined. We will encounter this objectivism or "problem of exogeneity" several times in the following chapters.

The point can be pursued further by discussing the idea of "naturalization." Natural hierarchies, it is often argued, are not founded upon fixed qualities of the person, but constitute markers for changing social relations. So, for example, the ideological strategy of racial thought, it is suggested, is to make those relations appear fixed and *sui generis*. Racial sentiment in fact constitutes a *naturalization* of social relations, generally in circumstances of unequal power. The argument is one that I wish thoroughly to endorse as the point of departure for a sociology of race. Yet it is no more than a point of departure. Often, it or something like it is proffered as the closing gambit in a sociological onslaught against the race concept which brooks no further argument. But what do we really mean by "naturalization," and why does it seem so effective?

Sociologists commonly proceed by showing that things which have a taken-for-granted or "natural" character in everyday life have actually been the product of specific human actions. From this perspective – and beyond rather banal generalizations about human beings as social or moral creatures – no particular complex of social arrangements can be deemed inherent or preferred or, in other words, "natural." Each comes to be seen as natural through legitimizing processes which are bound in the structure of the social arrangements themselves. "Naturalization" then becomes a piece of sociological jargon to describe generically the way that people conceal from themselves by cloaking their institutions with the aura of unquestioned truth their own creativity – the human capacity for culture – which produces conceptions of human relationships whose variation is ultimately arbitrary. In this respect, "naturalization" could apply to the basis of any human interaction, which is competently executed without the need for conscious speculation among participants as to its origins or conditions of possibility. All routinized or institutionalized human action is "natural." But the idea of "naturalization" has a peculiar resonance in relation to natural hierarchies, because they can be understood as a particular legitimating form for social relationships predicated upon an explicit conception of "nature" itself as a warrant for human hierarchy. The sociological question then becomes how and to what extent this legitimating form succeeds in the conceptual closure demanded of "naturalization" in its generic, sociological sense; how is it that an explicit concept of "nature" becomes the "natural" recourse for arguments about inherent difference?

At issue here is the way in which the concept of nature stands for a sense of a hard, unyielding "reality" in contrast to the uncertainty and subjectivity of human feelings and behaviors. Thus, those who stop at the idea that cultural representations like race "naturalize" social relations participate in the hold of this particular construction of "the real." Indeed, sociological analysis of racial ideology has been overly dominated by arguments against the "reality" of the race concept. This idea stems from the sociological insight, which was sketched above, that social relations are ultimately arbitrary configurations which are given the appearance of necessity by particular forms of legitimation. But the idea that race, or the social relations warranted by the concept, is not "real" only has analytical force if it is also established that some kinds of social relation are non-arbitrary, or "real." Otherwise, one could establish that all social relations are "real" in just the same measure that they are "unreal"; the notion of their reality would thus be entirely redundant. In fact, this sense of the unreality of race *is* usually accompanied with the contention that some kinds of social relations have a real, *sui generis* character. As we shall see shortly, the most influential theory of this kind stems from Marx's materialist argument that the practical activity of human beings in transforming the objective conditions of their existence constitutes the foundation of the social, whence the idea of class struggle as the "real" basis of social relations derives. The general thesis of this book, however, is that such an argument concedes too much to the force of the legitimating ideologies which sociological analysis professes to unmask. To find the reality of race wanting against the reality of class is to measure one legitimating ideology against another, whereas the more radical implication of the sociological critique is to illuminate the structure of legitimating ideology in general. For example, the "unreality" of the race concept is often theorized through the idea that race is a kind of phantasm of *racism*, the latter understood as a particular legitimating ideology which rationalizes a political order of hierarchical social relations. The implicit suggestion is that racism distorts the "natural" basis of social relations which is predicated upon the absolute equality of all human beings. Yet it is not too difficult to see that this idea of "natural equality" itself constitutes a form of legitimation for particular kinds of social relations which are as fully ideological or "constructed" as the idea of "natural hierarchy." Analysis of the race concept, I suggest, does not need to abandon the principal insight of sociological thought by suggesting that some kinds of social order are more natural than others, and that there is, as it were, some gravitational pull towards particular kinds of social order which is only offset through the distorting energy of ideologies like racism.

This, then, is the problem with anti-essentialist critiques on the figure–ground model. Later in the chapter, we shall attempt a more historicized argument about the provenance of natural hierarchies by recourse to Roy Wagner's (1986) concept of figure–ground reversal which can include within its purview the emergence of social science. But let us now consider the problem with the other, "contextual" strategy. We have already encountered Kenan Malik's (1996) argument that the race concept acts as context for the relationship between humanity, society, and nature. Here, the unitary character of race is dissolved by locating it in the play between these three other phenomena. Yet one could equally well question the stability of *these* categories, or of any others against which race might be contrasted as a determined outcome, thereby leading quickly to a situation of infinite regress in which the substantive character of any category melts away in an ever-proliferating series of refractory relationships with other ones. Dissolving race as an outcome of some other factor or set of factors appears to produce "explanations," but ones which ultimately are always refractory to our original object of analysis. However, the tendency to produce sociological explanation by dissolving the entity in question against some other entity which is held constant is quite hard to abandon, grounded as it is in the deep structure of European intellectual traditions. These tend to invest closed or bounded models of social relations with the status of the creative, instituting forces underlying all forms of human intercourse, regardless of history and geography, emptying local legitimating ideologies of their specific efficacy: ideas of "society" and "ethnic group" or even "mode of production" and "class" (Marx's "classes for themselves") all involve the idea of a stable, bounded, complex structure which is generalizable across cases. One consequence of this tendency to think in terms of stable, collective wholes is that many attempts to explain the origins and development of racial sentiment start off by assuming the prior existence of distinctive groups which act as "raw material" for the process of racialization. A more radical procedure – not always apparent because of the "racialized" basis of sociological thought – is to examine the processes which make it possible to identify groups at all. Thus, rather than choosing to make racial ideology or other natural hierarchies the *explanandum*, and thereby imputing a particular causal ordering which accords an exogenous explanatory factor with its own autonomy and integrity, it is necessary to approach racial ideology and other social facts as conjoint. There is no warrant for the assumption that "race" or "racism" can be explained by other social relations which are implicitly regarded as causally prior instituting forces.

Such an approach offers some clear advantages, but is not without its problems. One advantage, in relation to the orthodox Marxist privileging of class, is that it draws attention to the way that "class" too possesses particular modalities of meaning which people deploy in a variety of ways in everyday life. We therefore confront an opposition between, on the one hand, class and race as cultural schemes deployed contextually in social classification and, on the other, an encompassing system of – in the Marxist view – the labor process within which they are located. The advantage of focusing on the former is that it enables us to appreciate the specific and nuanced modalities of race or class as lived experience, rather than treating them as "incidental" or – still worse – merely negating them, since – as I have already argued – a serious sociological approach to race demands that we render these modalities analytically in their full complexity. However, if we *only* focus upon these cultural schemes it becomes impossible to appreciate the way that they function in and are constituted in more broadly systemic ways. One would not, after all, wish to argue that the racial categories of eighteenth-century Jamaica were just a cultural scheme for social classification, without referring to the economic logic of the plantation system. At the same time, we relinquish much of our understanding if we render this broader system as simply *determinant* in some singular way, as with the argument that these categories were functional to the requirements of plantation production. The difficulty, then, is in holding together analytically both the specific cultural conceptions of social relations and the systemic forces within which those conceptions are related as factors bearing upon the course of social life in a way which, rather than reducing one to the other, maintains the sense in which they are moments within an encompassing structure. We will address ourselves to this difficulty by considering the development of the idea of "structure" in contemporary social theory, and then by abstracting from this discussion some theoretical propositions which, I will suggest, permit the historical comparison of different modalities of natural hierarchy.

Structure

Different intellectual traditions have produced different understandings of the creative forces shaping the social order. A well-known distinction is between "idealism," in which consciousness is modeled as the creative force of the social, and "materialism," in which the social emerges from the conditioning effect of the world or action in the world upon consciousness, reaching beyond its limits. In general, sociological theory has attempted to steer between strongly idealist and materialist positions, since the former elides that which is external to consciousness while the latter succumbs to the problem of exogeneity in making such external forces wholly determinant. Dan Sperber (1996) describes this kind of materialism as "self-contradictory" because it involves the assumption that factors external to human intentions (like the physical environment) determine the structure of those intentions such as are to be found in politics, culture, or religion. The problem with this is that the former are arbitrarily privileged over the latter as determinant "material" forces, implying that some things (like politics or culture) are less material than others, which would seem to be incompatible with the initial postulate of a fully material basis to social reality.

Another kind of materialism that Sperber finds wanting is what he calls "empty materialism," in which it is conceded that there is a material basis to social reality, but that basis is not made the ontological axis of the explanation, an approach which allows the analyst to defer the charge of idealism while avoiding any commitment to a fully materialist theory. Of the exit routes Sperber identifies from these problems, one is to give up materialism and proceed from the idea that the social world has its own autonomous and irreducible reality. This argument is close to the neo-Kantian foundations of German social science, which have been especially influential upon sociological and anthropological theory via Weber and Boas respectively. The emphasis here is upon the interpretive character of social science, which is especially evident in much anthropology. When, for example, anthropologists study witchcraft beliefs in a particular society, they are not concerned with whether witches "really" exist so much as with the way ideas about witchcraft are deployed and are socially consequential. But there is a constant temptation to fall back into self-contradictory materialism and to argue that the belief in witches merely conceals a "real" underlying principle such as social control or the distribution of wealth, thereby reducing cultural phenomena which appear inexplicable to the eye of the "rational" observer to the status of slightly deluded elaborations of a latent rational principle. In the sociology of race, this kind of argument is especially evident in vulgarized forms of Marxism (e.g. Cox, 1948; Bennett, 1969) which suppose that racial ideologies are a kind of smokescreen to conceal economic exploitation and/or to divide the working class. The problems with this are manifold: it implies the teleological proposition that the cause of racism lies in its effects, the corollary of which is that the effects of racism are also its cause, producing a logical circularity (Miles, 1982). It is also not actually materialist in the sense described by Sperber, because it fits into his definition of self-contradictory materialism where certain phenomena – like racist ideologies – are relegated from the domain of the material, while others – like economic rationality – bear the full onus of material explanation. Above all, it conforms to that class of theories examined above where the burden of explanation is merely displaced onto the trope of "nature," thereby avoiding the question of how "nature" creates an ideological alibi for the proposed utilitarian grounding of the race concept. Thus, vulgar materialism purports to explain an "irrational" institution – race – in relation to the "real" principle of economic reason, without perceiving that both are the products of a deeper structure of thought.

I want to suggest that some of the most familiar attempts to steer between idealism and materialism which have influenced more sophisticated versions of sociological theory nevertheless succumb to similar problems of exogeneity. Let us begin with Marxism. Marxist versions of materialism purport to resolve the antinomy of idealism's sovereign consciousness and materialism's external, objective reality through a dialectic of practice, in which human action in pursuit of material need transforms both the world of objects and, in its train, human consciousness. This thesis was set out most explicitly by Marx and Engels in their *German Ideology* (1845), where they posit an initial self-consciousness of human separation from nature in the knowledge of a livelihood which is actively *produced* from the world around it, that is, from nature (Marx and Engels, 1975–96: V, 31). Here, production or practice constitutes both the entry point and the subsequent dynamic of a dialectic between the form of society and its relation to nature, in which "nature" itself is no longer a purely contingent limit or force in the "natural" struggle for human existence, but is progressively humanized or socialized. In relation to the philosophical debates of the day, this idea of production as an active historical process which creates human society was of crucial theoretical importance to Marx in opposing both Hegelian idealism and the contemplative materialism of Feuerbach, whose point of departure already assumed a distinctive human subject with an identity formed through its subordinate reaction to the exigencies of an external world. Feuerbach, according to Marx and Engels,

> does not see that the sensuous world around him is not a thing given direct from all eternity, remaining ever the same, but the product of industry and of the state of society . . . the result of the activity of a whole succession of generations, each standing on the shoulders of the preceding one, developing its industry and its intercourse, and modifying its social organization according to the changed needs. (Ibid.: V, 39)

For Marx and Engels, then, neither "nature" nor "human nature" has a fixed or eternal quality. Rather, they are constantly transformed by human practice. The alternative to Feuerbach they offer is a socialized nature which is a consequence of human practice. However, the socialized character of nature is apt to go misrecognized as such and to be treated as an external force acting upon humans; in other words, socialized nature is reified as natural nature. This reification is a force for human alienation which is nowhere manifested more strongly than in the capitalist mode of production, where people are separated from the things that they produce and labor power is separated from the activity of production, a separation which produces a characteristic general form of value in relation to the commodity. Labor power is not simply labor, or work; its peculiarity is that it is a thing whose use (in work, the production of other things) yields more than is lost or used up in its deployment. This is only so, however, when labor power is put to work to produce commodities with exchange value, in other words when it is part of a process of capitalist production. Thus, labor power and capital presuppose each other. Marx resolves this duality by invoking primitive accumulation, "the historical process of divorcing the producer from the means of production" (ibid.: XXXV, 705–6) as the process which created this relation, thereby displacing a question of origin onto a question of process (Spivak, 1996: 117), a move characteristic of the later structuralist thought which his own writing influenced. The key point for present purposes, however, is the idea of labor power as a substantial quality which emerges in Marx's work. In fact, for Marx, the capitalist predication of labor power is *the* substantial quality around which all the myriad forms of social organization and cultural representation must ultimately condense. What emerges more broadly from his theory of value, then, is not a critique of a unitary essentialism through arguments about the "relational" character of social life, but on the contrary an argument that the plurality of social life emerges from a process inherent to the unitary essence or substance of labor power.

Let us now return to the critique of Feuerbach, and the idea of "changing needs" which impel and are impelled by the "state of society." There is an ambiguity in Marx's concept of "needs" which is brilliantly dissected by Sahlins (1976). On the one hand, Marx recognizes that the "needs" or practical interest from which the "sensuous world" emerges are not objective properties which apply invariantly to all human beings, but are themselves socially produced. In this sense, his theory of practice is also implicitly a theory of the symbolic – that is, under-determined – constitution of meaning. Herein lie possibilities to mediate idealism and materialism through recognizing the objective constraints upon human thought and action occasioned by the cumulative achievement of prior thought and action, a point I shall later pursue. And yet, on the other hand, in the elements of his historical materialism Marx seemingly does posit a process of determination whereby the social ordering of the sensuous world stands in an essential or necessary relation to a material logic beyond the compass of human action. So, for example, Marx and Engels advocate a materialist method which consists,

> not of setting out from what men say, imagine, conceive, nor from men as narrated, thought of, imagined, conceived, in order to arrive at men in the flesh; but setting out from real, active men, and on the basis of their real life-process demonstrating the development of the ideological reflexes and echoes of this life-process. The phantoms formed in the human brain are also, necessarily, sublimates of their material life-process, which is empirically verifiable and bound to material premises. Morality, religion, metaphysics, and all the rest of ideology as well as the forms of consciousness corresponding to these, thus no longer retain the semblance of independence. They have no history, no development; but men, developing their material production and their material intercourse, alter, along with this their actual world, also their thinking and the products of their thinking. It is not consciousness that determines life, but life that determines consciousness. (Marx and Engels, 1975–96: V, 36–7)

In this schema, the socially produced character of human conception is all but exchanged for an invariant concept of its material determination; the transformed world now stands as a determinate actuality outside human conception. As Sahlins (1976: 128) puts it, "social order and thought are sequitur to a practical teleology of production," and it is the unmediated logic of production which invests the social order. By thus making human practice or labor the fulcrum of his social theory Marx revealed the continuity of his thinking with the bourgeois ideology he otherwise opposed, universalizing a historically specific conception of work or agency (Baudrillard, 1975). This, according to Jürgen Habermas (1971), has to do with Marx's insufficiently reflexive epistemology which, though establishing historical materialism as critique and not natural science, assimilated it to the model of natural science and thereby neglected the lesson of Hegel in appreciating the contingent basis from which critical knowledge constructs the conditions of its own possibility. Such objections too can be leveled at sociological projects which define the grounds for their critique of natural hierarchies beyond the ambit of the social forces which constitute them rather than within those forces themselves. This would apply, for example, to Robert Miles's argument for a "scientific language which allows the deconstruction of the idea of 'race'" (Miles, 1989: 73), or to Michel Wieviorka's distinction between sociological analysis and "the discourse and consciousness of social actors" (Wieviorka, 1995: 34). In another book, Miles neatly summarizes the standard critique of idealism in arguing that it "implies both an infinite regress (ideas lead to ideas which lead to ideas, etc.) and the determination of socioeconomic structures and processes by ideas" (Miles, 1982: 89). He invokes the authority of the *German Ideology*, with its "real, active men" and its "real ground of history," to support his refutation of these tenets of idealism. But we have already seen some of the problems involved in this account of "reality"; at the same time, the view that social life is constituted through ideas is not without a philosophical rationale (Peirce, 1932; Wagner, 1986). These points will be developed in more detail later in the chapter.

On the basis of the preceding discussion we should perhaps introduce some distinctions into the concept of human agency. At a certain level, sociological analysis is necessarily committed to the view that human agency is the creative force of the social. Race and caste ideologies, for example, can only be seen as stemming from the things that people have said and done while "standing on each other's shoulders" in more ways than one; they cannot be seen as mystical, extra-human forces – the work of devils or cosmic sacrificers, as the quotations at the start of chapter 1 would have it – or else sociology becomes coterminous with the cosmologies it takes as its object. But Marx's theory of human agency is a much stronger one, making agency itself the instituting force of the social while reducing it to a very specific logic of material production as its fundamental ontological axis. This is a much more problematic proposition. We will return to this question of agency later in the chapter, but in order to do so we shall now consider a rather different tradition of structural analysis which emerges from the anthropology of Claude Lévi-Strauss.

In *The Savage Mind*, Lévi-Strauss (1966) develops the argument that the categories of the social world have grown untrammelled and haphazardly, like a field of "wild pansies," which is an alternative meaning of his book title in the original French. Yet, like Marx, this growth reveals for Lévi-Strauss an implicit order. Let us develop this point through considering the place accorded "nature" in his thought.

In his early work on kinship first published in the 1940s, Lévi-Strauss (1969) suggested that prohibition of incest was a universal feature of humanity which established the rule of exogamy (marriage outside the group). He located incest prohibition within the distinction between nature and culture, and it is this distinction which requires some elaboration for the present argument. For Lévi-Strauss, human beings are inherently "natural" or biological beings. Their capacity for differentiating themselves from the rest of nature by constructing themselves as cultural beings is not therefore a mystification of their "true" biological nature, but is a particular manifestation of that nature. For Lévi-Strauss, the incest taboo (and not Marx's production of livelihood) constitutes the originary moment of this process. It is "where nature transcends itself" and "sparks the formation of a new and more complex type of structure" (ibid.: 25). This new type of structure is human culture itself, whose defining feature is, in Lévi-Strauss's somewhat Hegelian conception, a consciousness of a differentiated and thus an organized unity or "self," which the incest prohibition achieves by preventing arbitrary relationships. Thus, for Lévi-Strauss, the definitive feature of culture is the fact that it *creates* difference. In a society composed of two exogamous moieties, for example,

> a woman, like the moiety from which she derives her civil status, has no specific or individual characteristics . . . which make her unfit for commerce with men bearing the same name. The sole difference is that she is *same* whereas she must (and therefore can) become *other*. Once she becomes *other* (by her allocation to men of the opposite moiety), she therefore becomes liable to play the same role, *vis-à-vis* the men of her own moiety, as she originally played to the men of the opposite moiety. . . . All that is necessary on either side is the *sign of otherness*, which is the outcome of a certain position in the structure and not of any innate characteristic. (Ibid.: 114)

This formulation can be criticized both for its reductionism and its androcentrism – since it makes nothing more of people and, above all, women than markers of groups – but its profound influence upon contemporary sociological approaches to the differentiation of "self" and "other" is nevertheless apparent. Rather than an evolutionary model of branching "speciation," Lévi-Strauss postulates a discontinuous series of arbitrary or "socially constructed" self–other differentiations, which are nested in the ultimate differentiation of culture from nature. A significant way in which difference is created is by modeling human relations after natural relations, a point which is discussed with particular clarity in the fourth chapter of *The Savage Mind*. Here, Lévi-Strauss reveals a concern for the characteristic structures of human thought fundamentally opposed to the program of the *German Ideology*, and in which "nature" occupies a critical place. Rather than Marx's social relation transformed by practice, Lévi-Strauss posits a "conceptual scheme" which renders socialized nature as a model for human relations. This point is developed through a discussion of the "transformation" between totemism and caste, not in the sense of a particular historical change from one to the other as modes of social organization, but in the structuralist sense of structures as systems of transformations.

In this spirit, the purpose of his chapter is to show that there is a common logic underlying the apparently antithetical systems of totemic and caste organization. Totemism, found predominantly among the so-called "primitive" societies, refers to the division of people into several groups modeled after species of animals or plants. Each group typically observes specific dietary and ritual practices, usually associated in some way with the totemic species, but practices exogamy. Lévi-Strauss's key insight was to see that totemism could be represented through two homologous series in nature and culture, as illustrated in figure 2.1. The critical relation in totemic organization is not an analogy between the human group and its totemic species, but a *homology* where the relations between human groups are modeled after the relations between totemic species. This yields the characteristic structuralist formula "group 1 differs from group 2 as species 1 differs from species 2." That one series of differences (in nature) provides the model for another series of differences (in culture) depends upon the absolute separation of nature and culture as discrete wholes; if some human groups could be classified as animal species or some animal species as human groups, there could be no homology. Thus, while totemic organization constructs differences between people in terms of their group identity and specific totemic practices, it also constructs a cultural unity of people in contradistinction to nature, a unity which is manifested in the practice of exogamy. Diversity is therefore indissolubly coupled with unity, and what Lévi-Strauss calls "endo-praxis" and "exo-praxis" (Lévi-Strauss, 1966: 118) entail each other mutually.

For Lévi-Strauss, caste organization represents a transformation of totemic organization. It is hard to describe what is entailed in this with any more clarity or economy than Lévi-Strauss does himself in the following passage:

> When nature and culture are thought of as two systems of differences between which there is a formal analogy, it is the systematic character of each domain which is brought to the fore. Social groups are distinguished from

Culture	Group 1	$\neq$	Group 2	$\neq$	Group 3

Nature	Species 1	$\neq$	Species 2	$\neq$	Species 3

Figure 2.1   Totemic relations
(*Derived from Lévi-Strauss, 1966: 115*)

one another but they retain their solidarity as parts of the same whole, and the rule of exogamy furnishes the means of resolving this opposition balanced between diversity and unity. But if social groups are considered not so much from the point of view of their reciprocal relations in social life as each on their own account, in relation to something other than sociological reality then the idea of diversity is likely to prevail over that of unity. Each social group will tend to form a system no longer with other social groups but with particular differentiating properties regarded as hereditary, and these characteristics exclusive to each group will weaken the framework of their solidarity within the society. The more each group tries to define itself by the image which it draws from a natural model, the more difficult will it become for it to maintain its links with other social groups and, in particular to exchange its sisters and daughters with them since it will tend to think of them as being of a particular "species." (Ibid.: 116–17)

Thus, for Lévi-Strauss, caste organization can be represented as in figure 2.2. Here, the natural unit itself is the model for the cultural unit rather than the relations between units, so that each social group is regarded as a complete natural entity. In such circumstances, marriage is necessarily endogamous. Caste is therefore based upon a natural *analogy* rather than a homology, as in totemism. Nevertheless, the model remains a figurative one: castes are *like* natural species, they are not actually species. The separation of cultural and natural domains therefore remains intact in caste organization, a point which Lévi-Strauss attempts to demonstrate with elaborate formal logic in terms of the counterposed endo- and exo-praxis of castes *vis-à-vis* totemic groups, as, for example, in the case of occupational differentiation in caste society, such that the endo-praxis of marital alliance is counterbalanced by the exo-praxis of occupational service to other castes.

Lévi-Strauss's analysis has not attracted much interest from theorists of caste, probably because it is compatible with neither Dumont's notion of encompassment nor with "radial" caste models. It is, however, compatible

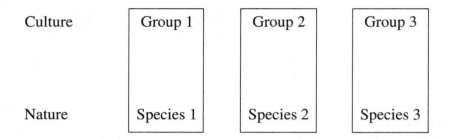

Figure 2.2   Caste relations
(*Derived from Lévi-Strauss*, 1966: 117)

with the model of ranking hierarchy set out in chapter 1 and therefore perhaps models rather better the character of racial thought, with its idea of social groups "naturally" differentiated under the sign of an undifferentiated nature. In this view, racial hierarchy rests upon an analogically transformed homologic relationship in which the ranking of human groups follows the model of an extra-human "natural" order. One implication of this is that insofar as racial ideology – or at least a particular version of it – can be traced to the emergence of egalitarian political thought, this is not because it legitimates a *de facto* inegalitarian state incommensurate with egalitarian ideology, as Malik (1996) has argued. It is more deeply rooted within a particular model of egalitarianism where the body politic is seen as a bounded, organic unity necessarily differentiated from "others" and constantly threatened by disorder through the possibility of absorbing alien elements, with the idea of race serving as the boundary marker for this differentiation. The integrity of this schema for racial hierarchy depends upon its projection from an exterior principle, that of *nature* which, moreover, permits the possibility of an absolute ranking (see also chapter 5).

The significant point here is that "nature" is already a cultural classification. The world is not inherently divided up into particular categories of animal, plant, and object, but is so divided according to culturally derived precepts. We therefore confront a kind of circularity in which the natural is made an object standing outside the cultural, is ordered and classified, and is then reappropriated as a model for ordering the cultural. This is suggesting something rather more specific than the familiar sociological refrain that some particular social domain is "socially constructed." It is suggesting that the *real* differentiation from nature established by the incest prohibition founds two classificatory series which are ("socially") constructed in relation to each other.

Thus, by contrast to Marx's labor theory of value, Lévi-Strauss offers the incest taboo as the "value" which differentiates the domains of nature and culture, and creates the latter out of the former in order "to ensure the group's existence as a group, and consequently . . . to replace chance by organization" (Lévi-Strauss, 1969: 32). His emphasis on the incest taboo now seems at best contrived (see also chapter 5), but any kind of sociological theory of ideology (including ideologies of natural hierarchy) which is committed to the view that they are systematically structured leads back to the problem of exogeneity discussed earlier if it lacks an analogous value-producing conception. In such a case, sociological explanation of self–other categories can only be approached by projecting them from some origin or phenomenon which cannot itself be constructed and which therefore "works" through standing in an exogenous relationship to the categories concerned, which is the strategy of idealist or materialist accounts of the social. The origin is transcendence or reality itself. Alternatively, the existence of single value-constituting phenomena may be rejected – the strategy of much poststructuralist writing – but the problem then lies in how to account for the systematic and patterned character of social life.

From this discussion, I infer that folk models of natural hierarchy involve a sense of natural diversity balanced by the unity of nature, but that it is an insufficient theoretical move to oppose the idea of natural hierarchy merely by privileging the countervailing term of unity. It would seem better to treat each term as folk categories whose mutual entailment requires an explanation of the social analyst rather than a choice between the preferable term. A common sociological procedure is to approach hierarchy from the point of equality, and thus to see in the trappings of political power an attempt through a calculated symbolics of obfuscation to justify a coercion which can have no final justification, a procedure which, in Joan Dayan's memorable phrase, can "reveal the blur at the heart of hierarchy" (Dayan, 1995: xx). Yet there is no logical reason why one could not "reveal the blur at the heart of equality" by approaching it from hierarchy to unravel transcendent claims towards equality in nature. Just as it is hard to sustain any transcendent argument for hierarchy, so it is hard to sustain any transcendent argument for equality, a point neatly made by the libertarian philosopher Robert Nozick (1974). This reveals that we are discussing structurally opposed types projected from an underlying "natural" principle. One problem – at least for those of us who, unlike Nozick, do not believe that the lack of an ultimate argument for equality constitutes sufficient justification for an inegalitarian status quo – is to adduce the normative implications of this point. I address this question in chapter 7 although, as I shall argue, I believe it is quite beyond the compass of sociological theory to answer it. The more significant point here is the lesson of Lévi-Strauss's thought, which lies less in its claim to provide a universal analytic method than in its unwitting but elegant summation of a particular ideology, that of a ranking hierarchy projected from the domain of nature. The theoretical problem is how to find the grounds from which this ideology itself can be constructed sociologically on a comparative basis.

A key theoretical step in Lévi-Strauss's argument is the reduction of particular cultural phenomena or acts to a generative system by emptying them of any specific content and emphasizing their arbitrary character in a system of differences. He does this through an orthodox, dualist reading of the structural linguistics of Ferdinand de Saussure (1857–1913). The remainder of this section will offer a particular characterization of Saussure's thought which will be used in subsequent pages. This is a most necessary digression, first because Saussure's is one of several philosophies of language which, in turning away from the question of consciousness, promise to overcome the antinomy of idealism and materialism (Habermas, 1992a: 44), and second because overly simplistic critiques of Saussure have too often been used as a warrant to assert the indeterminacy or contingency of everyday life in ways which very questionably deny the possibility of providing more systematic structural accounts of phenomena such as race or caste relations (e.g. Raheja, 1989: 80–1).

Saussure's linguistics were famously predicated upon two distinctions. First, he decomposed language into two elements; *langue* – the language system which speakers draw upon to formulate their acts of speech – and *parole*, the acts of speech themselves through which langue is instantiated. Furthermore, *langue* consists of a system of *signs* which involve a distinction between the *signified* or mental concept of a real world referent and the *signifier* or word sound which denotes it.

For Saussure, signifier and signified are not to be thought of as a means for rendering reality in language through a merely arbitrary or conventional relationship. The meaning of a word like "cat" emerges through a systematic set of relations of difference with other signs (like "dog," or "furry," or "animal"). Mutual comprehension between competent speakers is a corollary of the fact that there is a stable relationship between the components of the sign and between the elements in the system of signs, a relationship which exists independently of the many possible contexts in which a sign is invoked. The relationship is described by Saussure as the *value* of the sign. Signs are "arbitrary" (or, to use Saussure's less confusing synonym, unmotivated) insofar as they do not evince necessary correspondences to their extra-linguistic referents, but sign values impose an order upon the world of objects which constitutes the determinate "reality" of that world of objects.

Criticism of Saussure (and, concomitantly, Lévi-Strauss), has focused upon this apparent reification of *langue* as the ordered, generative plane of *parole*, and the scission or dismemberment of the sign which accords a privileged role to the signifier as an arbitrary unit within a system of differences. Paul Thibault (1997) has, however, opposed this dualist reading of Saussure. Part of his argument lies in the suggestion that Saussure does not suppose that *parole* is merely the instantiation of a unitary *langue* in speech acts by autonomous individuals. In fact, Saussure distinguishes the individual from what he calls "the speaking subject," the latter being the outcome of relations and tensions between the various subsets of the language system (dialects, subdialects, semantic registers, etc.). For Saussure, then, *langue* and *parole* are mutually entailed moments of a language system which is not a functional whole but is conceived as a "complex and uneven unity" of intersecting speech communities or speaking subjects (Thibault, 1997: 28). Significant linguistic change entails systemic transformation, but one that is lodged at the subsystemic level in the context of systemic continuity. Part of the reason for this is that mutual intelligibility demands singular norms, for as Vološinov (1929: 56) has argued, there can be no "tragedies" in language: a norm cannot exist with another contradictory one.

There are, of course, dangers in comparing culture with language. For example, while it may be true that norms cannot exist with contradictory ones in language, this is less obviously the case with culture. Indeed, according to one influential account, culture is inherently "tragic" in this sense (Simmel, 1968). But what seems useful in Saussure's account, if only by analogy, is the model it provides for understanding culture as a scale or density of systematically related representations, instead of either a wild plurality of conflicting ones or ones which are wholly unified by a singular creative principle.

This point can be pursued in two directions. First, the richness and subtlety of language (and of culture) lies in what Saussure called "associative relations," whereby words which have something in common are associated together in the memory such that a particular word invokes the trace of other, absent words and meanings (Saussure, 1983: 121–5). Perhaps it is the multiplication of this ambiguity which lends works of literature their richness and aesthetic appeal. By the same token, it is the attempt to disassemble and explicate the system of signs and its associative relations which makes sociological writings so tedious (I make no claims for exemption here). But the problem is not that literary works are more interesting than sociological ones. Rather, it is that the associative richness of cultural and political symbolism is of incomparably greater social force than a rationalist agenda of symbolic deconstruction. There is perhaps some force to the arguments of hermeneutic philosophy that any program of analytical exegesis in relation to such symbolism involves a reductionism incapable of rendering its meaning, a position that need only be conservative if it is further assumed that the extant system of signs is thereby non-ideological, or that the signs are the "right" ones. Thus, while it can persuasively be argued that cultural representations like race or ethnicity cannot be regarded as empty vessels whose content is explained by recourse to "the mysterious power of symbols" (Bentley, 1991: 175), sociologists would do well to retain some sense that symbols can indeed be both mysterious and powerful.

Second, Saussure's approach is grounded in the idea of socially intelligible speech acts and in the idea that reality is appropriated by the system of signs. Critiques of both these ideas have emerged in later writers and have strongly influenced contemporary social theory. Vološinov regarded Saussure's linguistics as an example of "abstract objectivism" which, placing the interpretive burden on the relation between sign and sign rather than sign and reality, constructed a theoretical space which was systemically closed to the ideological character of language (Vološinov, 1929: 58). Vološinov's emphasis, by contrast, was upon *parole*. For him, the very neutrality or arbitrariness of words gives them an indexical quality through which they can assume an ideological function in use or dialogue (ibid.: 14). An important aspect of Vološinov's approach is his opposition to views of language as a finished edifice in which words have a central, constitutive meaning: his emphasis, rather, is upon the comprehension of speech as a dialogic process in which the word is matched with a refractory counterword, though in the light of the foregoing discussion this is perhaps not as remote from Saussure's approach as is sometimes supposed. However, in Vološinov there is no counterpart to Saussure's concept of *langue*. Although this anti-structuralism is today enjoying something of a theoretical vogue, it begs several questions about precisely how patterned ideologies are consistently produced in language, or culture (Thibault, 1997). It is to this question that we now turn.

Culture, Practice, and Symbol

In the previous section, the trajectory of our discussion of structure from Marx to Lévi-Strauss and Saussure was aimed at suggesting that the dynamics of social life might be modeled after a conception of immanent structural transformation rather than transcendental human agency, as in Marxism. However, it was also suggested that the specific grounding Lévi-Strauss gives structural transformation through the nature–culture distinction reflects, despite his universalist claims, a culturally specific conception of the social world, even if it is one which by that very token is especially useful for understanding the basis of racial ideologies. Let us develop the implications of these two points.

Whereas Lévi-Strauss offers a universalist theory of culture whose opposition to nature is ultimately subsumed in the latter, Marx proposes a dialectical theory of practice which energizes the relation between the two. Here, then, an idea of culture as a functioning, organic unity confronts an idea of culture as a mode of organization which continually prods itself into higher levels of unity through the conflicting actions of its parts. Lévi-Strauss's genius was to produce a supple culture theory which could extend from local particularities to universal coordinates, but with a grandiloquent universalism so uncompromising that he was able to regard the anthropological study of native myths as itself another myth, revealing the way that both natives and anthropologists are simply the vehicles through which structures speak (Lévi-Strauss, 1970: 13). This reprises the legacy of Enlightenment universalism in an especially obdurate form. Most contemporary anthropologists have, by contrast, preferred to approach their material with a more ambivalent sense of cultural specificity, without perhaps always making its implications for the epistemological grounding of their analyses explicit.

One way of broaching this issue is in relation to the culture theory of Franz Boas (1858–1942), the pioneer of US anthropology. Boas established an anthropology framed in the tension between culture areas or cultures and the manifold individual units, traits, or representations which not only comprised but also transcended these larger regularities, changing his theoretical approach from a diffusionism consonant with one of the major schools of contemporary thought to a new appreciation of cultural diversity. Indeed, as Stocking (1968) has pointed out, it is only with Boas that the idea of *cultures* in the plural emerges from the nineteenth-century notion of a singular *culture* as civilization, whose degree within different populations was projected onto a chronological scale and read back as an index of "development." Consistently opposed to the theories of racial inferiority much in favor among his contemporaries, the concept of culture in Boas's later work emerged in the context of an attempt to break the link between biological race, language, and culture upon which such theories depended. Yet a tension persisted in his thought between the idea of culture as a chaotic accumulation of diverse elements which crossed all boundaries of race, language, and collective identity, and a more organic model of cultural difference in which these elements were "adapted and changed in form according to the genius of the people who borrowed it" (cited in Stocking, 1968: 214).

The idea of a people's "genius" may now seem redolent of a problematic cultural essentialism which betrays the origins of Boas's thought in the German Romantic movement and its *Kultur* concept. It was tamed anthropologically through derivative ideas like the notion of the "culture area," where particular regions were described through the exigencies of specific cultural complexes. But even this now seems problematic, because of its tendency to overemphasize cultural integration in relation to regionally specific characteristics. The idea of the "Indian caste system" is an obvious example. However, although there has been a move away from positing culture areas, the idea remains implicit in a good deal of anthropology, perhaps because of the need to characterize the particularities of local social processes after the fashion of the model derived above from Saussure; on a scale of more-or-less localized cultural representations which evince a systematic internal organization not simply reducible to the dynamics of some universal cultural or value-creating process.

In this spirit, I argue for a return or reappropriation of the idea of cultural difference, yet without reifying it as a "genius" particular to a specific "people." Perhaps the linguistic analogy drawn from Saussure overstates the sharpness which actually obtains between cultural "boundaries," but the idea of a scale of different cultural units or cultural communities which, through their affinities and antipathies, intersect within and constitute the uneven unity of a cultural metacontext, captures something of the idea I wish to propose. Because there is more than one cultural representation, and because they are not all perfectly consonant in their force or reach either geopolitically or among different kinds of people within a given geopolitical unit, cultural boundaries are inevitably nebulous and insecure, and can be drawn in different ways according to the focus of the analysis. More generally, while there may be many different mechanisms and rationales for the communication of representations, these are always already predicated on other sets of representations. Cultural representations, in other words, have specific effects which mediate the incorporation of other ones.

This poses at least two problems: how is the plurality of cultural representations mediated into coherent worldviews or ideologies, and how do these change? The reading of Saussure in the previous section can help answer these. Saussure's view of *langue* as a non-harmonious unity in which a manifold of intersecting subcomponents meet provides the basis for positing a varying density of more or less integrated cultural representations which provide the *a priori* or cultural metacontext for new representations or a new alignment of forces, not least as a result of the particular tensions or aporia manifested in the metacontext. Khare's (1984) discussion of "Indic" values in relation to the conflict between Brahmanic and Untouchable representations of social reality would be one example of this idea. Other examples might focus upon the continual articulation of tensions around the idea of political legitimacy in medieval Christian thought, or the ability of Vaishnavism to assimilate local religious cults in the Indian subcontinent (see also chapters 3 and 6). The idea of a cultural metacontext is also open to the possibility of major changes, as with the impact of European colonial projects in India or upon enslaved Africans in the Caribbean (see chapter 6). However, not only are these changes shaped in determinate ways by the prior metacontext, they also engage different groups of people (or "subjects") in different ways according to mutual affinities or dissonances.

The foregoing discussion is not offered as a theory of race or ethnicity but as a theory of cultural process which can construct the ground conditions or cultural metacontext through which cultural phenomena like racial, ethnic, national, or caste ideologies become manifest. Therefore, it does not necessarily conflict with an approach to ethnicity such as Barth's (1969) argument that ethnic processes construct cultural boundaries rather than the other way around, but it does not elevate this insight ontologically to suppose that these processes constitute the generative plane of cultural distinction in general. Other precedents for the kind of position proposed here also exist, for example in Talcott Parsons' norm-oriented systems theory, or in practice-oriented structural Marxism. Like my own approach, both of these kinds of theory attempt to strike a balance between, on the one hand, complexity and contingency and, on the other, order or systemic integration. There are, perhaps, two major differences between my own approach and these ones, one of degree and one of kind. Both of the other approaches incline towards closed system models, whereas the cultural representations I have postulated obey no inner necessity. Human ideas are under-determined by the reality they confront, constructing the latter in many different ways, and it is impossible for the sociologist to provide ultimate explanations of meaning, such that we can understand why some particular representation or its broader context emerged here or there. However, it is insufficient to go to the opposite pole of a completely chaotic proliferation of under-determined representations. The affinities and tensions between different representations produce an emergent but always insecure ideological patterning. The lineaments of this patterning are contained in the culture area idea, but the porousness of any cultural "boundary" must always be borne in mind. In this respect, the culture theory offered here emphasizes what Spivak (1996) has called "analogical" cultural relationships rather than involving her preferred emphasis upon relationships which are "attributive and supportive" of a particular ideological organization of forces. But it *is* a question of emphasis rather than an all-or-nothing choice between analogue and attribution (or "consensus" and "conflict"), a point which the particular reading of Saussure offered above is intended to establish.

The other difference has to do with the tendency to invoke meaning, practice, or agency as exogenous qualities which power system change and system integration. In my view, theories of agency can too readily essentialize their own understanding of practice as a quality which renders systemic integration when counterposed to the "essentialism" of culture theory. This would be particularly true, for example, of Marx's understanding of labor, where the revolutionary practice of the proletariat seems to be derived more as an *a priori* entailment of a particular structural account than from an empirical analysis of working-class people's behavior. It imports as well a good deal of Christianity's moral baggage, whereby the poverty of the proletariat invests them with a transcendental capacity, much as the life of apostolic poverty brings the mendicant closer to God, so that it is not poverty per se but the functional capacity of its conception to produce social change that is emphasized in the theoretical model (cf. Turner, 1974: 265). Concomitantly, despite the persisting influence of strongly anti-humanist French structuralist traditions (from Lévi-Strauss through Althusser to Foucault and Derrida), in the latest pendulum swing away from structure, recent social theory has emphasized a more humanistic conception of agency in terms of the capacity of people to act upon and change their world. This is particularly true of anthropology, perhaps inevitably so in view of its ethnographic methodology and its concern to describe the practices of everyday life. But without denying the gains achieved by such approaches, it is worth sounding a note of caution about too universalistic an appreciation of human agency. In a sense, this reflects an idea which is deeply rooted in Western thought via classical and Judeo-Christian traditions, namely the capacity of human beings to transform inchoate nature through their art or skill, described by Aristotle as *techne* (Pagden, 1995: 6). It is something of an irony that this idea, which in early modern Europe was so often used as a prop to underline the superiority of European colonizers against the "barbarism" of the colonized, should now be universalized in sociological theory under various guises in order to criticize the ethnocentrism of "Orientalist" or cultural relativist approaches which supposedly lock people within the trajectory of particular cultural forms (e.g. Fabian, 1983; Inden, 1990). It is not that these authors succumb to a "humanism" of the kind rejected in the structuralist tradition. Nor, as I argued earlier, is it possible to dispense with some conception of human agency in sociology. But it should not be assumed that an elevation of the human capacity to act upon and transform the world to the status of a universal ontological proposition renders a truer and less ethnocentric picture than an emphasis upon the cultural particularity of the ways in which the world is experienced and acted upon. The advantage of the Saussurean approach described above, albeit against the grain of conventional readings, is that not only does it retain an emphasis on pattern or system without implying stasis or closure, it is also quite open to systemic change on the basis of differentially enabled "agents" pursuing "interests," but on the basis of immanent contradiction rather than a transcendental conception of agency which rests upon a universalist conception of human practice.

There are, of course, wider conceptions of practice available in sociological theory. Pierre Bourdieu, for example, has espoused a theory of practice which interposes between the idealist–materialist antinomy described above, arguing in characteristically opaque prose that,

> The construction of the world of objects is clearly not the sovereign operation of consciousness which the neo-Kantian tradition conceives of; the mental structures which construct the world of objects are constructed in the practice of a world of objects constructed according to the same structures. The mind born of the world of objects does not rise as a subjectivity confronting an objectivity: the objective universe is made up of objects which are the product of objectifying operations structured according to the very structures which the mind applies to it. The mind is a metaphor of the world of objects which is itself but an endless circle of mutually reflecting metaphors. (Bourdieu, 1977: 91)

In this passage, Bourdieu relaxes some of Marx's assumptions about the nature of practice, constructing a more satisfactorily non-reductionist materialism, which is thereby more open to the material and constitutive grounding of ideas or dispositions. But he still invokes practice – "the practice of a world of objects" – as a kind of *deus ex machina* which provides the exogenous hinge to resolve the antinomy of subject and object in his "dialectic of objectification and embodiment." His dialectic involves the inscription or embodiment of structures into the unconscious routines of the human body by "the hidden persuasion of an implicit pedagogy" (ibid.: 94). There are at least two problems here. First, the whole approach is subsumed within a theory in which social meaning is constituted through competition over material and cultural resources or marks of distinction. As Dreyfus and Rabinow (1993) have charged, this constitutes a reductionism which, in the final analysis, is arbitrary and not, as Bourdieu would have it, "scientific." Second, Bourdieu's approach to embodiment leads to a psycho-philosophical problem which Stephen Turner (1994) has identified: how do people encode, transmit, and decode this implicit pedagogy of practice? If we reject explanations which depend upon the capacity of the mind to order an infinite number of representations then we have to postulate a metapractice which must also be transmitted. This leads to a "Russian doll" model of reproduction which is clearly problematic (practices must be transferred, together with the routines to decode them, together with the routines to decode the decoding routines, etc.). Turner pushes his argument to its logical conclusion: the reason pedagogy (or, more conventionally, "reproduction") seems implicit or hidden, he suggests, is that it does not exist. There are *no* collective cultural representations which are reproduced; there are merely a multitude of private "habits" whose routinized surface manifestations can inculcate a social response. Turner insists that his argument does not vitiate the idea of culture as such:

> Nothing I have said here denies the existence of culture in the sense of a body of observances, performances and the like – public things – and a body of habitual learnings, perhaps different in various ways for each individual, but which can collectively amount to a stick which it is more advantageous to hold on one end than another. (Ibid.: 112)

To turn this into an anthropologically useful theory requires that something is made of the apparent regularities in public culture which nonetheless seem to evince change as well as continuity and which vary across "culture areas," as defined above. The philosophy of Charles Sanders Peirce (1932) offers one resource for doing so. For Peirce, transformation occurs through the open-ended process by which reality is elicited by minds, but where "reality" and "minds" are parts of "mind" more generally. This theory of "habits" resembles Bourdieu's "habitus" in many ways, but whereas Bourdieu tends to fall back into a duality of structure and practice which evinces dialectical resolutions and material groundings, Peirce offers a more uncompromisingly monadic ontology, thereby also bestowing "habit" with more systemic properties than is entertained in Turner's understanding of the term. It is difficult to invoke agency in sociological theory without at some level conferring it with an utterly autonomous creativity, however hidebound by structure (indeed, recovering such creativity is the explicit aim of some writers), yet it seems to me that Peirce's approach provides the lineaments of a more satisfactorily sociological theory of practice, predicated on the elicitation of structure rather than the structuring of structure (as in amendments to the structuralist tradition of the kind undertaken by Bourdieu) or the creation of structure through the free play of creativity. It is at this level, I would argue, that we can recover "structure" as a universal social process, and not at the level of putatively universal structural phenomena like the problem of political authority, even if comparative sociological research which proceeds from such problems (e.g. Milner, 1994) can produce very plausible accounts of different social dynamics in relation to such phenomena. Sperber (1996: 9–31) shows quite convincingly how such accounts efface their specifically interpretive grounding, but whereas he uses this as the springboard for a naturalistic social theory, the argument I have developed in this chapter is directed at embracing this interpretive grounding more fully. Thus, I would advocate a sociological theory grounded in an understanding of the general way that specific and specifically communicated cultural representations invest social orders. It is never possible to provide so complete an account of these as to render fully what Raheja calls the "circumstantiality of everyday life" (Raheja, 1989: 81), but it does seem to me that one can model some representations which are powerfully consequential for social life, and relatively enduring. The conceptions of exchange, polity, and person considered in subsequent chapters as the basis for natural hierarchies are examined in this light. Similar ideas, grounded in Peircean theory, have been deployed empirically for comparative purposes, for example in Daniel's ethnography of South India, where it is argued, "the signs that constitute a culture are regnant and generative signs of habit" (Daniel, 1984: 24). Another anthropologist, Roy Wagner, has described the specificity of what he calls the "Western core symbol" in a parallel fashion which involves several Peircean undertones. Let us turn, then, to these ideas concerning "core symbols" as a way of pursuing a comparative historical sociology of natural hierarchies.

In his book *Symbols That Stand For Themselves* Roy Wagner (1986) provides several suggestive intellectual contexts for appreciating the way that racial ideology and its critique can be regarded as part of the broader historical development of what he terms the "Western core symbol." We will organize our discussion of this in relation to three topics: the elicitation of meaning, the logic of time, and the dialectic of relations and substances.

Wagner's general aim is to show how human thought and action is organized by tropes – that is, figurative elicitations of meaning – which are not reducible to some externality beyond themselves such as the "value" which provides the "ground" of structuralist ideas of system. Very briefly, he argues that tropes close upon themselves to constitute their own ground conditions. For example, metaphor is a trope which establishes a relation between two entities. In metaphor, it is as if "X" is "Y." This establishes the possibility of "back metaphor," whereby the "is" of the conventional denotations of X and Y can become metaphorical "as ifs." This is what Wagner calls "the second-order trope of figure–ground reversal, by which a perception can be inverted with its perceptual 'ground'" (ibid.: 33). Figure–ground reversal is a special case of the more general dialectical process through which meaning is created by means of an array of substitutive metaphors, a process which Wagner terms "obviation." For Wagner, meaning in a specific context works through the view of an actor, and it effects obviation by the changes it makes in that view. In his words, "when this flow of perceptual change becomes an instance of seeing vital antitheses as

differential perspectives through the same basic points of orientation, then
. . . the difference [becomes] . . . figure–ground reversal" (ibid.: 68).

Wagner gives several examples of figure–ground reversal. The relevant
one for present purposes relates to medieval understandings of the Christian sacrament of Eucharist, in which the devotee is connected to the divinity by the consumption of bread and wine which elicit the body and
blood of Christ. Here, we should note that there is already a differentiation
between the divine and the human, which is mediated by the Eucharist.
The differentiation conforms to the mediated ranking hierarchy discussed
in chapter 1, whereby the divine stands over and against the human. This is
illustrated in figure 2.3. An obviational format is generated if we now consider the mediations established between the points which are, as it were,
the "objects" created by the three prior entities. So, God creates "nature"
which mediates between "man" and the sacrament through the natural
matter comprising wine and bread which is transformed in the Eucharist;
"man" creates "society" in the form of the institutional hierarchy which
controls the administration of the Eucharist and thereby access to God
(namely, the church); and the Eucharist creates the "symbolic" relationship between "man" and God. For Wagner, these two formats are inversions of one another which constitute a figure–ground reversal. Whereas
the Eucharist represents a hierarchical mediation of the human and the
divine (establishing a relation in which God stands above humanity), its
obviation represents an egalitarian conception of societal "codes for conduct" which are reconstituted into the domain of nature through a symbolic mediation which, in the work of David Schneider (1968; 1977) on
contemporary American kinship, is viewed as the flow of biogenetic substance or "blood" between particular kinds of kinsfolk (see also chapter 5
on Schneider's work). This is not wholly dissimilar from the point noted in
chapter 1, where we encountered both a relational egalitarian critique of
hierarchical essentialism and an essentialist egalitarian critique of hierarchical relationality.

Wagner argues that the two mediations shown in figure 2.3 are mutually
entailed or implicit in one another, and it would be quite possible for them
to be manifested simultaneously, perhaps in ritual forms which often provide the medium for expressing antithetical perspectives. However, in the
case of this "Western core symbol" the figure–ground reversal proceeds in
linear historical time, a point Wagner substantiates by tracing a medieval
and a modern cycle of figure–ground reversal. The medieval cycle proceeded through a series of controversies and debates about the Eucharist,
in which an "egalitarian realist" view of the Eucharist as the actual body
and blood of Christ represented an internal resistance or obviation of the
dominant, hierarchical view that it was the figurative or "mystical" point at

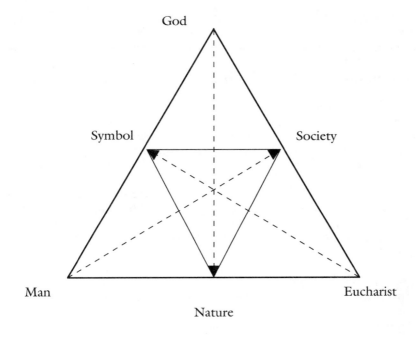

Figure 2.3 Symbolic mediation
(*Derived from* R. Wagner, *Symbols That Stand For Themselves,* Chicago: University of Chicago Press, 1986: 97)

which the human order was reconstituted into the divine. By the early thirteenth century, under the hierocratic papacy of Innocent III, egalitarian realism had been elaborated into the doctrine of transubstantiation: things possess perceptible qualities or *accidentia* which enable them to be differentiated from others of their class, as well as an inherent, universal, and invisible type-essence or *substantia*. In the Eucharist, the *accidentia* of the bread and wine remain unchanged, but the *substantia* change to that of Christ's body and blood. This differentiation invites a figure–ground reversal which rejoins essence and accident, a reversal which Wagner detects in the argument of John Wycliffe (*c.* 1320–84) that the Eucharist established an "indwelling" of Christ in the soul, while Christ's essence and accident remained resolutely in heaven. Wycliffe's thought, drawing on the rather one-sided late medieval interpretation of Augustinian philosophy, emphasized a Christian community united by the grace of God rather than a divine law mediated by an institutional church, and for this reason has often been taken as a precursor of Protestant Reformation theology (Cameron, 1991). As I shall argue in chapter 4, something approaching the modern conception of race later emerged from the philosophical debates that the Reformation was to provoke in early modern Europe. For his part, Wagner, too, sees the Protestant Reformation as the end point of the medieval cycle, for in the Reformation,

> *Accidentia* was discovered as nature . . . as a new, secular ground of being, in the very epoch in which *substantia*, the presence of God, was determined by Luther and others to be a function of human faith. Thus the epoch of the Reformation was the point at which Western culture, not having a stabilizing ritual, fell through its figure–ground reversal. (Wagner, 1986: 111)

In Wagner's view, the Reformation and the age of scientific discovery associated with Copernicus and Galileo and also with Columbus, Magellan, and the explorer pioneers of the first imperial age were therefore dual entailments of this figure–ground reversal, whose irresistible force he strongly underlines:

> Medieval civilization was a continual reform movement, motivated against the perceived secularization of its internal resistance – nature, society and reason, and production. Only after Wycliffe had articulated the union of *substantia* and *accidentia* . . . did the first mechanical clocks appear. (Ibid.: 111)

Thus, the Reformation marked the start of the "modern" cycle in which egalitarian realism formed the dominant movement, whose internal resistance was hierarchical trope or mysticism. Wagner traces this modern cycle through the Reformation, Enlightenment rationalism, its reversal via an internalization in the philosophy of Kant and Hegel from the civil reason of the Enlightenment to the nineteenth century in which "an internalized rational mandate made enlightenment itself a despot" (ibid.: 115), through to contemporary metaphors of production and nature.

The implication of Wagner's argument is that the obviation of the core symbol in the medium of historical time does not permit a symbol and its reversal to be entertained simultaneously but involves a monological discourse which proceeds by *critique*. Thus, Berengar of Tours, who asserted the figurative character of the Eucharist at a time in the eleventh century when its reality was the prevailing orthodoxy, was forced to recant among his fellow ecclesiastics with the ordeal of the hot iron in prospect. The modern discipline of the social sciences has found less excruciating measures for silencing its heretics, but one can imagine an analogous fate for a contemporary sociologist who proclaimed the essential character of race. Yet Wagner's analysis suggests that the antithesis of essence and accident (or "essentialism" and "relationality") has moved together through historical time and that, from a certain perspective, the standard sociological critique of essentialism represents but one more reversal in this cycle. The argument is richly suggestive for a historical sociology of race. The discovery of *accidentia* as "nature" in the modern cycle potentiated a whole series of possible oppositions between "natural equality" and "natural difference" which properly require a much more detailed and systematic analysis than I am able to provide in this book, although I begin the task in the next four chapters by considering the "natural" legitimacy of political rule, the conjunction of person and thing, and the construction of the person as a natural unit.

A somewhat frustrating aspect of Wagner's argument is his circumspection about its historical implications. He takes considerable pains to suggest that his model of historical obviation does not constitute an explanation for the course of history. In his words, historical obviation

> is by no means to be identified or confused with history itself . . . and it would be a mistake to imagine that it either explains or determines history. History, in the fullest sense in which its "actuality" is conceived by modern scholarship, suffers neither explanation nor determination. . . . However, certain aspects of it can be effectively modeled, and if the limitations of the model are kept in mind, a limited advantage can be realized. (Ibid.: 99–100)

The caveat is well taken. Certainly, it would be inappropriate to argue teleologically that historical obviation of the core framework of Christianity led inevitably to the Reformation, the age of discovery, capitalism, racism, and other modern scourges, as if through the unfolding of a plan in which they were already present in outline. As Wagner (ibid.: 121) puts it, tropes are *elicited* and not determined, and one cannot posit the historical obviation of the Western core symbol as an underlying causal force impelling history. Indeed, Wagner's analysis is conceived in part to rebut the idea of such grounded bases for sociological analysis. This enables him to mount strong anti-foundational arguments concerning the way that symbols constitute their own ground conditions which, in my view, can be convincingly adduced against the superficiality of a sociological anti-essentialism with respect to topics such as race, which trades upon the implicit and untheorized "ground" of structuralist conceptions of value. Relationality is the ground from which the essentialism of race as a thing is projected; recuperation of the former can therefore provide a critique of the latter, but the critique leaves exogenous that which holds them together and is therefore susceptible to a negation in which the ground and its projection are reversed, so that the relational appears as a projection of the essential. It thus becomes difficult to read a writer like Wood (1995) in his discussion of race as a "disease" or a "toxic by-product" in the minds of Europe's Renaissance colonizers without a sense of the analytical vapidity of the argument, even if one might now endorse the political sentiment. Against the tendency to regard the sociological critique of racial ideology as unsullied by essentialism it seems preferable to think of race rather as Lévi-Strauss approaches myth, as the sum of all its versions. Thus, analytical works such as Wood's function in the classificatory struggles which are constitutive of the concept of race, and which offer us a particular version of what race "is." Wagner's project is apposite in enabling us to deconstruct this entire discourse but, from another perspective, it seems legitimate to ask historical questions about how representations like race were instantiated in particular circumstances and evinced a particular historical trajectory. For while Wagner can show how figure–ground reversals occur in ways which have no obvious sociohistorical implications – as in the essentially scholastic debates about the Eucharist – his discussion is nevertheless replete with asides concerning apparently related historical phenomena (like the association between literalization of the sacrament and the church's move toward hierocratic monarchy, or the association between the closure of the medieval cycle in the Reformation and the inception of the Age of Discovery and the first imperial age). Moreover, Wagner never properly defines the "West" in his "Western core symbol" or adduces the historical implications of the fact that this core symbol is *not* the core symbol of other places. In this respect, I would argue that his approach can be incorporated into the kind of cultural theory I outlined earlier – to which it is perhaps in many respects otherwise opposed – as an account describing a specific Western core symbol as a metacontext or density of cultural representations which establishes a historically enduring problematic or aporia (and a specific kind of historical sensibility).

Let us pursue some aspects of this somewhat more positivist appropriation of Wagner's argument. Durkheim (1965), precursor of Lévi-Strauss and Dumont, first proposed the analytical utility of a domain distinction between the everyday "profane" world of human affairs and a suprahuman world of the sacred, often objectified in ideas of god or the divine. The significance of the Reformation as described by Wagner in this respect is that it initiated a reversal which began to establish the idea of the sacred as a secular rather than a divine quality. As we saw in chapter 1, in the work of contemporary writers like Habermas (1987) this secularization is viewed as the defining characteristic of that peculiar epochal self-consciousness generally described as "modernity." Whereas a sense of the sacred as divine seemed to establish unambiguously that codes for human conduct were knowable through recourse to the divine – even if much human argument was entailed in determining how that recourse could or should be achieved

– secularization undermined this certainty. Nevertheless, as Wagner's obviational format suggests, the secularization of the sacred called forth a countervailing sacralization of the secular, particularly in relation to ideas of "nature" and of "society" as a bounded organic unit transcending the individual person.

In later chapters, I shall discuss the way that the political theories and colonial actualities associated with early modern Europe provided a framework for the emergence of the modern discourse of race against this background. Here, I want to suggest that this secular reversal established a peculiar dialectic of equivalence and difference which acts as its deeper cultural context. My basic argument is that there are two features of the "Western core symbol" which were to prove especially propitious as the grounds for the elaboration of racial ideology, one a principle of separation (the sacred from the profane) and one a principle of connection (of persons to other persons). On the first point, Christian cosmology emphasizes the absolute, qualitative difference between the sacred – God – and the profane world of humanity. The degree of this distinctiveness has varied in different Christian traditions: from the Calvinist view of God as an unknowable "other" who, even for the elect in heaven, is always absolutely separate from the human, to the Catholic view in which humans through good works are able to participate in a little of God's sacredness, becoming saints for example. However, there is never any sense within Christian thought in which the divine and the human are regarded as manifestations of an underlying unity, as is the case with Hinduism. This denial of monism makes the relation between classes of entities an often problematic one, because a simple logic of encompassment is explicitly rejected. As a result, the distinction between persons and things emerges as a complementary domain distinction to that between persons and the divine. The ferocity of medieval debates over the Eucharist was, in part, a consequence of the fact that it was the point at which these three differentiated orders of entity – the divine, the human, and the material – ran into one another.

The obviation of these domain distinctions has led to one of the cornerstones of modern Western thought, namely the idea of the individual person as a subjectivity confronting a world of objective, external things. One development of this idea has been the logic of utility as a mediation of people with things, a position elaborated with increasing precision and sophistication by economic thinkers from Mandeville to Marx (Dumont, 1977). For Marx, as we have already seen, the relationship between people and things is increasingly abstracted and universalized until, in the capitalist mode of production, a general process of human embodiment in the object through labor emerges. The separation of persons from things as given entities is what gives capitalism its special pathos in Marx's thought, because people lose part of themselves through labor into objects without recuperating anything from the process except their own now alienated sense of self. Cognizance of this alienation is, however, also the medium for redemption via the revolutionary overthrow of capitalism. Both alienation and redemption rest upon a universalized sense of self beyond any specific context. As Marilyn Strathern has commented:

> In losing control over commoditized labor or action, the person is recreated as a complete, bounded entity. . . . We perceive of relationships between persons through concepts of control, rights, access to resources – all of which turn on the possibility that the things a person does or makes may be conceptually separated from him or her. At the same stroke this proposition creates the idea of an object whose value is not constrained by the social source of its production – the commodity – and simultaneously creates persons as totalized entities. (Strathern, 1985: 206)

This idea of the person as a transcontextual entity differs from the equilibrated flows of substance between persons conceived not as autonomous "individuals" but as fungible "dividuals" as described by Marriott (1976) in relation to Indian categories of the person. It establishes the possibility of seeing people as being fundamentally and inherently of a particular kind, whatever else they might be or do. In this context, Strathern mentions the generalization of identifications such as gender and race. Without this transcendent sense of identity, it is possible to consider persons through overlapping and context-specific identities. For example, gender differentiation might only be germane in certain specific contexts – sexual relations, for example – while in most other contexts people might not be regarded as differentiated in this sense. The fact that people *always* confront one another as male or female represents the transcontextual generalization of this identity (corresponding to our definition in chapter 1 of ranking hierarchy as opposed to encompassing hierarchy). This generalization also provides the context for political struggles of a particular kind which advocate an absolute emancipation of an entire class of people as against another one: female from male, black from white, proletarian from bourgeois, and so on (and of a "class" politics which attempts to inculcate these identifications, thereby in a sense further entrenching and generalizing them). One obviational trajectory of this generalized distinction between persons and things is its converse, that people can be treated *as* things. As Strathern puts it, "the terms of what is propositionally held separate (a person is never a thing) provide their own context for collapse – the possibility that persons may be treated as things, that is, as not-persons" (Strathern, 1985: 204). This, I shall argue in chapter 4, is part of the logic of American racialized slavery, albeit within a fairly specific historical context.

Race, gender, and other generalized identifications cannot, however, be derived as logical entailments of the distinction between persons and things alone. Their form is shaped by other kinds of ontological commitment. One that I want to suggest here is the second issue mentioned above, namely a principle of connection between persons, which Strathern (1992) has also elaborated. This has to do with the metaphor of blood or natural substance which is regarded as connecting particular kinds of people, especially in the irreversible movement of continuous, linear time. Blood is an invisible type-essence which flows from parents and is substantialized in their offspring as an amalgam of traits, to be sublimated once again as the offspring, in turn, procreate (Strathern, 1992: 80). The idea is central to the domain of relationships which are rendered in Europe as "kinship," precedents for which predate the modern period even if there have been significant changes in kinship ideology over time (Flandrin, 1979; Goody, 1983; Stone, 1990; Lazarus-Black, 1994). Moreover, transformations of the same symbol invest the idea of a human relation to the divine (or the natural), and to the idea of political rule.

From the preceding discussion, we can derive a number of propositions about some core symbols of European, Christian thought which emerge in particular from the separation and mediation of God, persons, and things. We have noted an obviation of the divine order, now expressed in "nature." We have noted an idea of natural substance connecting people conceived as autonomous organisms, a substance which flows irreversibly downwards through time, and a transformation of this conception in relation to the idea of legitimate political rule (i.e. the state metaphorized as a family, leading to strong tendencies towards essentialist rather than civic forms of nationalism). And we have noted the commodity logic which flows ultimately from the separation of persons and things. Each of these points is developed over the course of the next four chapters.

Together, these constitute cultural representations which evince a variety of incompatible or antithetical meanings or perspectives, and which may potentiate figure–ground reversals. But this does not alter the durability of the conception. Consider, for example, two opposed representations of eighteenth-century colonial slavery. One is Moreau de Saint-Méry's typology of racial types in the French Caribbean colony of Saint-Domingue. Moreau divided blood into 128 parts of "whiteness" and "blackness" to produce a proliferation of intermediate types between the "pure black" and the "pure white," including the *sang-mêlé* or "mixed blood" – 126 parts white and 2 parts black. Although his typology was largely hypothetical it nevertheless expresses the logic of blood as racial type-essence in that particular colonial society (that intimations of purity were *always* some-what suspect among colonials is suggested by a contemporary's mischie-vous corruption of Moreau's name to Moreau *dit* Saint-Méry). The other representation is Josiah Wedgwood's famous design for the seal of the Anti-Slavery Society, depicting a supplicant slave beneath the slogan "Am I not a man and a brother?" As a result of hard-fought struggles, few people today would, I imagine, demur at Wedgwood's slogan, whereas Moreau's typology now seems both absurd and offensive. But both develop out of the same structural logic which we have examined in this chapter concern-ing the unity and differentiation of human types as flows of substance in lineal time, a logic quite capable of producing and "naturalizing" both egalitarian and hierarchical conceptions of what it is to be human. In this respect, perhaps we can at last appreciate the sense described by Kenan Malik in which race acts as a context for changing relationships (see chap-ter 1). That it can do so reflects the fact that "race" is but one modality of a deeper core Western symbol system which evinces a set of interconnected ideas about the person, the polity, the divine, and the object world. These ideas have underpinned the peculiar conjunction of race and capital in American history, but are traceable to some characteristic features of Euro-pean politico-religious ideology which have also provided the means for their sociological and political critique.

I will not dwell at length on the Indian counterpart to the "Western core symbol," partly because I organize the discussion in the next three chap-ters – including the discussion of India – through the sociological catego-ries I have just derived from the Western core symbol. But, to anticipate my argument, I will suggest that there is no precolonial Indian counterpart to the Western aporias of nationalism – another modality of the Western symbol system to which the concept of race is related – aporias grounded in a root concept of nature as a system of differences which require homog-enization to form political communities. In this respect, there is some force to Dumont's view of caste as an encompassing hierarchy in which particu-lar entities are distinguished from and ranked in relation to a whole, though it is a view which can be expressed through the idea of essences or sub-stances (the compartmentalization of Brahman; cf. Marriott, 1976; Dan-iel, 1984) just as readily as through relations (Dumont, 1980). And against Dumont's basically unilineal view of the hierarchical order, I will suggest – following the logic of Wagner's argument – that the obviation of this core symbol does not proceed, as in the West, through linear time as a series of redemptive revelations or revolutions, but occurs in simultaneity through a plurality of legitimate claims to be the "real" brahman, or ascetic, or king, a plurality which in a sense constitutes the aporia of the Indian core sym-bol, of which caste is a manifestation. Perhaps this comes close to the Orientalist stereotype of India as a static and politically fragmented region, forever locked in internecine struggles within the endless cycle of the *yugas*. I hasten to add, then, that this "Indian core symbol," as with its Western counterpart, is constantly and dynamically elicited within changing circumstances whose dynamic is, moreover, not simply reducible to the logic of a single symbolic constellation. Nevertheless, even in a work explicitly devoted to refuting the stereotype of cyclic time in Indian tradition, Romila Thapar (1996: 33) concedes that the linear time through which the early Indian polities organized their rule did not have the sacred foundation it possesses in the Judeo-Christian tradition underlying Wagner's Western core symbol. It is worth tracing the implications of this point.

History

Earlier, various ways in which race or hierarchy have been deconstructed as an object of sociological analysis against the "ground" of social relations were criticized, and an argument for a historical approach to the phenomenon was made. Here, we will attempt to draw out from the preceding discussion what such a "historical approach" might mean. This is a necessary step in the argument because of the somewhat Janus-faced orientation to a historical approach in much contemporary writing on race and hierarchy, where recourse to history is made in order to upset the idea that any chronically enduring identity has been sustained in relation to such concepts, even as the very recourse to history is criticized as a mystification which is actually bound up with these concepts. A significant problem with both strategies is their tendency to account for hierarchy as merely determined within some particular sociohistorical conjuncture, while exempting their own analyses from the same limitation.

Perhaps this reflects some broader problems in the troubled relationship between sociological theory and history, which has undergone several swings of the pendulum over the years. The effacement of history in the dominant functionalism and structuralism of the earlier twentieth century was later rejected, particularly under the influence of Marxism, by approaches which emphasized the chronic development of social forms. More recently, poststructuralist theory has posed serious questions about the possibility of such approaches, although it remains common to advocate the need for a "historical" approach in sociology. But it is not always easy to appreciate quite what claims are involved in opposing an "unhistorical" sociology. The problematic relationship between social theory and history stems from the fact that social theory, as we have already seen, has tended to approach the conduct of social life by explaining it in relation to the dynamics of some underlying concept of order, structure, or system. History, understood as contingent event, disrupts the ordered relations implied in these constructions and therefore in a sense disrupts sociological explanation itself.

Of the various responses to this problem in sociological theory we might mention historicism, which postulates that apparently contingent event in fact constitutes the unfolding design of underlying structure over time, as in the deterministic moment of Marx's theory of practice. Alternatively, there is the view that contingent event is wholly absorbed by underlying structure, as in Lévi-Strauss's structuralism. Here, structures are not changed by contingent events; the latter are neutralized by structure, although there have been several attempts to reconcile structuralism with the idea of social change. Another argument is the currently fashionable view that the events of past "history" actually represent an appropriation by the contemporary social order, such that what we understand by "the past" is really a projection of the present, an idea whose own history goes at least as far back as Voltaire's aphorism that history is a pack of tricks which we play upon the dead. This argument possesses "weak" versions, particularly where deployed in essentially vulgar Marxist theories of ideology (e.g. Hobsbawm, 1983) and "strong" versions in much poststructuralist writing (e.g. White, 1973; Lyotard, 1984), though there are some interesting "hybrid" arguments (Foucault, 1977). In the rest of this chapter we will assess these different arguments in a little more detail in order to develop an approach to historical analysis which will be used later in the book.

Although Marx famously opposed the morality of capitalism, his historicism was such that – much like Hegel's idealist grand narrative of human history – he regarded the capitalist modernity which he located in Europe as a necessary stage on the path to human liberation. This led him to a marked if ambivalent enthusiasm for European colonial projects, such as in his article on the British rule in India (1853). Even if, for Marx, England "in causing a social revolution in Hindostan was actuated only by the vilest interests, and was stupid in her manner of enforcing them," the question was nevertheless whether humankind could "fulfil its destiny without a fundamental revolution in the social state of Asia?" If not, whatever may have been the crimes of England she was the unconscious tool of history in bringing that revolution (Marx and Engels, 1975–96: XII, 132).

This apologia for colonialism as the key which was needed (and which therefore came) to open the door onto progressive history for a people trapped by stagnant tradition reinvents the Aristotelian motif of *techne* as the measure of civility, here in a form which reveals the thoroughly bourgeois grounding of Marx's thought in his doctrine of "man" as the "sovereign of circumstances" (ibid.). This entertains a suspicious continuity with that strand of bourgeois, liberal capitalism in its imperialist guise which reassured itself of its own superiority by counterposing the credulous benightment of "natives" shackled to cruel and unchanging superstition with its own progressive liberation from the chains of custom and tradition. In Marx's theory of history, then, perhaps we can once again locate two "moments." On the one hand, the externalization of nature from mind which emerges in Marx's critique of Hegel leads – as we saw earlier – to a sophisticated anti-essentialist materialism whose synthetic movement has been described as "the both empirical and transcendental accomplishment of a species-subject that produces itself in history" (Habermas, 1971: 31). On the other, we encounter a crude logic of historical transformation which, when assimilated to a project of ethnological comparison as in Marx's writing on India, can readily be used to deny the historicity and thereby the morality of people who stand outside the putative moral progress of a linear time anchored in Europe. This, essentially, is the tactic of Orientalism which is merely inverted in its antithesis, primitivism, where non-Western peoples are used to represent a sense of ancient wisdom, innocence, or lost wholeness. In both cases an "other" is used as a screen to project a particular sense of the Western "self" without regard to its own complexities or contradictions.

But let us quote Marx in his more sophisticated mode, here in a claim about history from his *Eighteenth Brumaire of Louis Bonaparte* (1852), which is perhaps the most famous of all his pronouncements:

> Men make their own history, but they do not make it just as they please; they do not make it under circumstances chosen by themselves, but under circumstances directly encountered, given and transmitted from the past. The tradition of all the dead generations weighs like a nightmare on the brain of the living. (Marx and Engels, 1975–96: XI, 103)

A bad way of interpreting this is through the bourgeois sense of freedom from history, so that people are regarded as free agents making their own history who are merely constrained by the starting point bequeathed them by "inherited circumstances." Marx's idea of a subject produced empirically *in* history better captures the sense in which the "tradition of the dead generations" actually creates the possibilities of historical transformation conceived in and constitutive of the "brain of the living." As we saw earlier in the chapter, however, Marx conceives labor transcendentally – and problematically – as the unique world-constituting force.

Against this, Lévi-Strauss's structuralism postulated the "conceptual scheme" of underlying structure, which tends to annihilate historical change as mere appurtenance upon the transformation of structures. This led him to a thorough denunciation of the compatibility between the projects of anthropology and history (Lévi-Strauss, 1966). But he was only able to defer history by concentrating upon what he called the "cold societies" of "primitive" peoples which lacked the historical dynamism created by class conflicts in modern "hot societies," a distinction which now seems to neglect not only the production of "cold societies" through the tides of history which rendered them marginal to larger and more stratified polities, but also the historical changes within them, albeit ones which do not always conform to Western perceptions of change or history. Other writers have attempted a more thorough reconciliation of structuralism with history. For example, Sahlins (1985) has attempted to show how contingent event has a transformative effect upon the conceptual scheme even as it is rendered meaningful in the latter. Another formulation of the problem is found in the work of Pierre Bourdieu, who more clearly reappropriates Marxian theories of practice into the continuist history of structures:

> The individual or collective classification struggles aimed at transforming the categories of perception and appreciation of the social world and, through this, the social world itself, are indeed a forgotten dimension of the class struggle. But one only has to realize that the classificatory schemes which underlie agents' practical relationship to their condition and the representation they have of it are themselves the product of that condition, in order to see the limits of this autonomy. (Bourdieu, 1984: 483–4)

Both of these writers offer versions of structuralism reconcilable with a plausible interpretation of the historical subject which invests Marx's thinking in the *Eighteenth Brumaire*. They nevertheless involve a continuist account of structure as an *a priori* constraint upon practice which therefore projects the present from the past. Let us now consider some approaches which adopt the opposite strategy.

The idea of an *a priori* determination of the present by the past examined above is complemented by the idea of an *a posteriori* determination of the past by the present. In this view, history is made in the present through narrative constructions which have the past as their object. And, in one of its modalities, it returns us to the familiar sociological preference for synchronicity or the domestication of history, a preference readily amenable to further functionalist or materialist reductions. This is the case with Eric Hobsbawm's argument in his influential collection *The Invention of Tradition*. Although the volume contains some exemplary analysis of the way that nationalist and colonial regimes secure their legitimacy by elaborating connections with a distant past, Hobsbawm's theoretical distinction between these "invented" traditions and what he calls "custom" (that is, implicitly, "real" traditions or historical continuity) is a weak one which, in enabling the analyst to show how "invented traditions" function instrumentally in relation to the interests of the elite, is redolent of the vulgar materialism criticized earlier. As with vulgar materialism, the problem is in explaining *how* ideology – here invented traditions – succeeds in its act of concealment. Traditions may indeed be invented, but the basis upon which they are invented is not itself invented on the spot. A further analytical step is required to explain why notions of historical continuity serve these ideological ends.

Other arguments are more strongly anti-historical, including Lyotard's (1984) influential critique of "metanarratives." In Lyotard's view, what he calls "customary knowledge" is based upon narratives – stories – which legitimate themselves. There are many such stories. Metanarratives like "scientific truth" or "historical causation" involve claims to possess objective criteria by which such narratives can be evaluated, thereby refashioning the different stories through which people narrate their world to a single, transcendent story. Lyotard's point is that this reduction is an illegitimate one. Drawing upon Wittgenstein's concept of "language games" he argues that the legitimating criteria of different narratives are incommensurate, and the claim of scientific metanarratives to determine the validity of such narratives founders upon this point. The implication here is that the ability of the historian to determine what the events of the past actually meant rests, above all, upon the sheer power to pronounce authoritatively, based upon an institutional rather than an epistemological warrant which detaches the historian from his or her own historical conditioning. Pushed to its logical conclusion, this argument would suggest that history is only so many stories, narrative figurations made in the present with the past as their object (cf. White, 1973).

There are some obvious parallels here with the later work of Michel Foucault, although Foucault never said that the past is an invention of the present. His "genealogy of discourse" sought, rather, an account of the multiple events and representations through which different orders of knowledge were constituted, but without recourse to those metaphors of order, progress, or unfolding through which metaphysical projects produce knowledge claims (see also chapter 7). Broadly following Nietzsche's rejection of metaphysical claims concerning the possibility of objective knowledge, Foucault advocated a Nietzschean genealogy which "will cultivate the details and accidents which accompany every beginning" (Foucault, 1977: 143). The idea of "cultivation" here implies a radically different historiography to the one that we encountered earlier in standard critiques of the race concept, where the chronic reality of race is supposedly deconstructed by invoking history to describe the contingencies or accidents of its origins and transformations. Here, the discovery of these contingencies is held out to restore a lost truth of human unity. But this aim cannot properly be realized, for as Foucault puts it, "the origin makes possible a field of knowledge whose function is to recover . . . [truth], but always in a false recognition due to the excesses of its own speech" (ibid.: 143). For this reason, the desire so characteristic of Western thought for a return beyond the origins of hierarchy to a lost primal unity, which manifests itself in metaphors like that of racial thought as a "disease" (Wood, 1995), seems no more than a forgetting of its own historical entailment in hierarchical ideology itself as its counter-possibility.

For Foucault, the desire for a return to purity represents a modality of this redemptive characteristic of modernity. But his brand of history adopts a more austere path which eschews such comforts:

> We want historians to confirm our belief that the present rests upon profound intentions and immutable necessities. But the true historical sense confirms our existence among countless lost events, without a landmark or a point of reference. (Foucault, 1977: 155)

This is the modality of his own later historical writing. For example, as Clark (1990) has pointed out, in *The History of Sexuality* Foucault (1981) offers three different origins for the modern discourse of sexuality: the end of the nineteenth century, the seventeenth century, and the early thirteenth century, when the Lateran Council of 1215 codified the sacrament of penance. These wild discrepancies of periodization, together with the extraordinary precision of the latter date, seem designed to mock the pursuit of origins. Indeed, for Foucault,

> Genealogy does not pretend to go back in time to restore an unbroken continuity that operates beyond the dispersion of forgotten things; its duty is not to demonstrate that the past actively exists in the present, that it continues secretly to animate the present, having imposed a predetermined form to all its vicissitudes. Genealogy does not resemble the evolution of a species and does not map the destiny of a people. On the contrary, to follow the complex course of descent is to maintain passing events in their proper dispersion. (Foucault, 1977: 146)

This idea of "dispersion" will be used later in the book as a way of examining how racial ideologies have undergone various processes of historical transformation, among the people objectified by racial discourses as well as those who objectify them (cf. Duara, 1995). At the same time, the argument has considerable force in pointing, rather more satisfactorily than Hobsbawm, to the way that universalist or progressive narratives of history

contribute to a conservative sense of social orders as fixed or rigidly en-
folded within layers of historical meaning, such that "historical analysis,"
far from providing the explanation for contemporary events, becomes their
profoundest form of legitimation as ancient conflicts gain new life through
providing models for new ones. Perhaps it also resonates with contemporary political realities such as the unheralded emergence of violent anti-
racist struggles in the USA during the 1950s and 1960s (McKee, 1993), or
the spectacular and blood-soaked progress of ethnonationalisms in the
former Yugoslavia during the 1990s, events contributing to a sense that
the fixing of the social order is much more provisional and less historically
secure than was thought in classical sociological theory. As Bette Denich
has argued in relation to Yugoslavia,

> The ethnographic observation of disjunction on this scale calls for a grasp of
> history that defies the expectation of processual unfoldings and evolutionary
> progression that have dominated social sciences. Instead, it is the Nietzschean
> vision, as updated by Foucault, that is relevant, focusing not on predictabil-
> ity, but on chance, the random constellations that create opportunities for
> those who lurk off-stage with alternate scripts. (Denich, 1994: 369)

However, we do not necessarily need to leap from the idea of singular
historical determination to the idea that there is no historical determination at all, that "random constellations" potentiate "alternate scripts" of
ill-defined provenance. This, it seems to me, is a problem with importing
too hastily into sociological analysis the anti-metaphysical tendencies of
contemporary philosophy, which can readily destabilize the postulation of
transcendental structure but at the cost of providing a more mediate sociological account of the way that structures are implicated in existing social
dynamics. Instead, we might profitably enquire into the basis upon which
such "alternate scripts" are themselves invented or systematized. For his
part, Foucault elevated an empiricist conception of power to an almost
transcendental status, consistently seeking to delineate the concordance of
knowledge with power. In ways not dissimilar to Bourdieu, he thereby
drew attention to the pervasiveness of power as a multiplicity of force relations (Foucault, 1981: 92), immanent in and constitutive of every kind of
social relationship or representation. But, as many critics have argued,
Foucault's concept of power seems *too* pervasive, *too* diffuse, making it
difficult for him to explain how relations of power are shaped into the
persisting, institutionalized forces construed in his empirical analyses of
sexuality, medicine, criminality, and so forth (e.g. Habermas, 1987: 287).
His clearest argument on this point – that the unintended consequences
of local and contingent power struggles become the stuff of a supra-local

condensation of forces (Foucault, 1981: 94–5) – would seem insufficient to the task. In this respect, there are perhaps certain advantages to the more traditional account of structure I have advocated.

The preceding discussion has suggested that it is necessary to appreciate the sense in which "history" becomes a medium through which contemporary cultural representations are given concrete form – as in nationalist ideologies – while at the same time maintaining a "historical" sense of the way that those representations are determined in history. Among the most sustained attempts to do so in recent theoretical writings is Paul Ricoeur's *Time and Narrative*, which we will examine to conclude the present section.

Ricoeur rejects the totalization involved in the grand narrative of Hegelian history, but does not simply replace singular metanarrative with a plurality of narratives, thereby rejecting totalization as such. Against the tendency to see history as a mere narrative of the present, Ricoeur postulates the materiality of the "trace" of the past – in documents, monuments, artefacts – which imposes a limit upon the kinds of narrative refigurations of the past possible in historiography. Thus, against the somewhat narcissistic logic of the argument which posits "the invention of the past," Ricoeur cautions that,

> the concern for "returning history to its origins in the literary imagination" must not lead to giving more weight to the verbal force invested in our redescriptions than to the incitations to redescription that arise from the past itself. (Ricoeur, 1984–8: III, 154)

Instead, Ricoeur attempts to recuperate the status of the present as a kind of horizon or frontier between past and future:

> Nothing says that the present reduces to presence. Why, in the transition from future to past, should the present not be the *time of initiative* – that is, the time when the weight of history that has already been made is deposited, suspended and interrupted, and when the dream of history yet to be made is transposed into a responsible decision? (Ibid.: 208)

Thus, Ricoeur seeks to preserve the notion of a historical agent, but not a transcendent one. Borrowing from Gadamer's idea of "being exposed to the efficacity of history" he posits a dialectic which "proceeds from the tension, at the very heart of what we call experience, between the efficacity of the past that we undergo and the reception of the past that we bring about" (ibid.: 220). This dialectic enchains another one, between what Ricoeur calls the "space of experience" and the "horizon of expectation" which expresses the transformative, but historically mediated, capacities of human agency in a way which renders the due of Marx's concept of history in the *Eighteenth Brumaire* by neither erasing nor transcendentalizing human agency. In other words, the kind of futures potentiated in the human capacity for directed agency are a consequence not only of the "conscious" sense of historical continuity through which that agency grounds itself, but also the "unconscious" effect of history upon the very terms of that agency. At the same time, the argument offers no warrant for reading into the idea of the efficacity of history or the notion of historical continuity any commitment to hierarchy as an essential or historically transcendent condition.

These arguments can be linked to Wagner's idea of "elicitation" discussed earlier. Both positions capture the efficacity of past representations while avoiding historicist assumptions about their contemporary force. They also carry certain implications for sociological theory, which itself must be conceived as being within these dialectics of the present. One implication is that sociology is incapable of predicting how things will turn out, because there are many possible modalities through which the past, in its efficacity and in the subject's consciousness of its efficacity, can run into the future. In this respect, Ricoeur's metaphor of the horizon is apposite. The actuality of the past does not impel us towards the future as some fixed point on the horizon from the present, but only towards the horizon itself as a kind of arc of possibilities. Miller (1994) develops similar arguments to suggest that the historicized structuralism associated with writers like Sahlins and Bourdieu invokes what he calls "the legacy of the *a priori*" which, in anthropological contexts, preserves the emphasis on prior cultural difference by showing how new cultural forces (such as the "globalization" involved in capitalist "modernization") are given shape by older, culturally specific representations. Against this he posits the logic of the *a posteriori* by which, in this example, distinctively local cultural forms are created out of the putatively homogenizing forces of global consumer culture. The point is well taken, though Miller tends to write as if the perspective of the *a posteriori* is analytically *better* than the perspective of the *a priori*, whereas a fuller picture might result from finding a way to incorporate both of them. To a degree, this is my aim in subsequent chapters, where I discuss the transformation of race and caste relations in various postcolonial nationalist contexts, though I agree with Miller's comment that this plotting of historical transformation is only possible with what he calls "the *déjà vu* of the contemporary perspective" (Miller, 1994: 307).

Armed with this *déjà vu*, and with the philosophical space opened up for the present by the work of writers like Ricoeur and Wagner, we can perhaps approach the concept of race as a particular kind of tension between past and present social orders in which all social actors – including sociologists – participate, through their constructions of what the past means in the present. It is for this reason that purely synchronic definitions of race in sociology – for example, as the social construction of difference on the basis of somatic characteristics – always seem incapable of accounting for the force and complexity of the phenomenon, and it is for this reason also that it is hard to find definitions of race which do not need tautologously to invoke the idea of race itself. Race represents the embodiment of particular histories and political struggles in history which are inherited contemporaneously not only as an actual socioeconomic legacy – for example, in the poverty which is the disproportionate lot of the most "African" segment of the population throughout the Americas – but as an implicit or potential context for relationships between people of different "races" in accordance with a particular model of the flow of substance between persons. Race, in other words, is constituted in relation to knowledges of what race has meant in the past, and of how the past is linked to the present in people's bodies. Sociological analysis has tended to construe this process of historical embodiment in particular ways: as the political economy of colonialism, or as the discourse of racial essentialism, for example. As we shall see in chapter 6, there are other, subaltern discourses of "racial" history, in India as well as in Euro-American contexts, all of which might be regarded as constituted in relation to Ricoeur's dialectic of experience and expectation. It makes no sense to deny any of them the status of a "true" reckoning of the meaning of race although, as I suggest in chapter 7, it may be possible to suggest in a very particular way that some of these reckonings are better than others.

Conclusion

In this chapter, I have tried to establish an appropriate basis in sociological theory from which to construct a comparative historical sociology of natural hierarchies. This has involved a double engagement with structuralist thought, which has been used to illustrate the ideological underpinnings of racial sentiment as well as develop a model for the broader theoretical analysis of natural hierarchies, as perhaps is fitting for a culture which has produced both racism and sociology. This, I would argue, confers certain advantages over those poststructuralist approaches which reject structural accounts of social process in favor of positing multidimensional sets of social objects with no logical ordering. Perhaps this move has to do with the reflexive dynamic of modernity to which many writers have pointed, where the self-legitimating character of explanatory models becomes increasingly evident, so that the metacontext framing explanation itself invites an epistemological negation. However, the strategy I have pursued in this chapter seeks an alternative accommodation with this turn to reflexivity by fully incorporating epistemological claims within a specific culture history, enabling them to be mobilized knowingly as such. In contrast to the tendency towards an epistemological involution in certain poststructuralist positions, this has the advantage of being able to model the social worlds framed by different cultural metacontexts as ones which are systematic, but in different ways. A potential disadvantage is the possibility that this approach will merely reinscribe long-exhausted models of societies as unitary, bounded, and static. A good deal of discussion in the present chapter has been aimed at avoiding this error. At the same time, I would argue that my approach is better able to model a sense of social life as both contextual or circumstantial *and* structured than anthropological accounts such as Raheja's (1989), which invoke contextualism to criticize structure while making implicit recourse to structure via specific culture-historical conceptions of exchange relations. The approach developed here does not assume stasis or a bounded societal consensus predicated upon structuralist ideas of a unified "conceptual scheme." This has several analytical and normative implications which will be clarified in subsequent chapters.

3 | Economic and Political Formations

Introduction

In this chapter and the three that follow it, we will pursue the approach to the analysis of natural hierarchies set out in the previous chapters through a historically grounded discussion of political economy, state formation, and conceptions of the person in relation to the formation of race and caste identities. In doing so, I want to suggest that the distinction between modernity and premodernity which has traditionally been invoked to explain the distinctive features of these identities has serious limitations. It is a distinction that has been employed in various ways. In the first place, modernity has been linked with the development of capitalism – which is often regarded as a uniquely European socioeconomic phenomenon – wherein the logic of race is located as a form of labor exploitation in the capitalistic plantation economies of the early modern European colonies, while, second, modernization has been considered the decisive factor in the transformation of Europe from the hierarchical political structures of feudalism, which are sometimes regarded as akin to the Indian political formations underlying caste relations (Cox, 1948; Dumont, 1986; Jha, 1987; Baechler, Hall, and Mann, 1988). In relation to the first point, I will argue in this chapter that there is nothing uniquely European about capitalism. It also figured in the history of precolonial India, although its manifestation in each place had a particular local accent expressive of deeper sociopolitical differences which partly underlie the distinctiveness of race and caste relations. And in relation to the second point, I will argue that the "premodern" polities of Europe and India possessed distinctive features that vitiate any simple analogy between them. I will try to demonstrate this later in the chapter through a detailed analysis of these polities which, I suggest, undermines not only Dumont's conception of a premodern hierarchy common to India and Europe mentioned in chapter 1, but also theories of "Indian feudalism" which have drawn parallels between the two cases insofar as strong, centralized structures of imperial authority (in Europe, the Roman and subsequently the Carolingian empires; in India, the Mauryan and subsequently the Gupta empires) crumbled during the medieval period into the "parcelized" sovereignty of smaller regional polities, and into a network of vassal relationships.

Despite these limitations to the way that the concept of modernity has been used, I do not wish to deny that both race and caste identities are dynamically related to social circumstances and have in certain respects been of recent origin. By way of introduction to this chapter and the one that follows, then, I briefly summarize below the main features of an alternative accounting for the continuities and changes evinced in these phenomena.

When we consider race in American contexts it is apparent that its history is inseparable from the colonial projects of European polities, the development of capitalism, and the emergence of slavery, bringing Europeans and Africans together with their creole descendants and also American Indians into a set of more or less (but mainly more) conflictual relationships with one another. In some strands of scholarship – particularly Marxist, but also in some non-Marxist writings – the relationship between colonialism, slavery, capitalism, race, and political organization is straightforward. Colonialism in America represented a "capitalistic" phase of primitive accumulation by centralizing European states, using coerced forms of labor such as slavery which in turn created racial or ethnic differences within the workforce and, in the end, also created the conditions for the emergence of full industrial capitalism in Europe and its associated political forms such as nationalist class societies (Williams, 1944; Cox, 1948; Wallerstein, 1974). However, in this chapter I will argue that the relationship between these different entities is more refractory and harder to pin down analytically than this, and that it is a mistake to view capitalist development and racial ideologies in a causal relationship running from the former to the latter. Rather, without denying the crucial links between racial ideology and economic forces, I suggest that Europe's racial ideologies and its self-propelling forms of capitalism were entailed in a deeper cultural context. In its essentials, my alternative argument is that the developing nexus of racism, slavery, and colonialism in the Americas has to do with an economic logic grounded in a longer term sociocultural order, ethnocentric judgments about the peoples living beyond established political boundaries, compounded by a particular structuring of European polities which has persisted across the putative rupture of modernity, an emerging organization of American colonial societies in response to these imperatives, and, finally, new forms of political discourse which emerged in relation to the foregoing. Caste relations were also grounded in a complex of economic and political arrangements, but of a determinately different kind, until they were given new force and direction by the English colonial regime from the late eighteenth century. To put the matter as simply as possible, my argument will be that the political formations underlying caste relations involved the *incorporation* of heterogeneous groups of people, whereas race relations emerge from political formations which involved the *delimitation* of territory around a homogeneous political community.

European colonial projects have been distinctive, if not perhaps entirely unique, in turning particular categories of political inclusion or exclusion into actual groups on the basis of indelible, "natural" criteria. This is what distinguishes racism from ethnocentrism – a historically much more pervasive phenomenon – whereby a defined group of people is judged negatively against a set of culture-specific criteria concerning "civilized" behavior, as for example in many of the accounts by Europeans of Asians, American Indians, and particularly Africans from the fifteenth to the eighteenth centuries. Although there is perhaps a "racializing" proclivity in the Judeo-Christian traditions underlying European political thought – with their tendency to turn spiritual commitment into corporeal essence (cf. Schneider, 1977) – the major dynamic of racialization in European history occurred, I argue, in the early modern period associated with the first imperial age. This had to do in the first instance with a particular confluence of nationalism and colonialism. I do not propose to enter the debates over when to locate the origins of nationalism, debates which are probably as fruitless as corresponding ones concerning the origins of race, and for much the same reason (see chapter 1). Nevertheless, while it may be possible to agree with "modernist" writers like Gellner (1983) that forms of cultural nationalism fully coordinated with the state and its legitimation projects only emerged in eighteenth- and nineteenth-century Europe as a corollary of the formation of industrial class society, there are good reasons for suggesting the slow emergence of forms of national cultural identification – forms distinct from the state, but which gradually became entwined with it – over a much longer time period, perhaps from as far back as the early or high middle ages, at least in Western European countries like England, France, and Spain (Castile), which in fact were the countries principally involved in American colonization (Smith, 1991; Llobera, 1994; Johnson, 1995). As we shall see, part of this trajectory of nationalism in Europe had to do with the contest between regional monarchies and the residual imperial claims of the Holy Roman Emperors and the papacy, leading to a distinction in political thought between a limitlessly expansive *imperium* on the Roman model, and territorially delimited monarchies (or even republics, as in the Italian city-states) quite tightly integrated with their subject citizenries. In the colonial expansion of the first imperial age, this breach between *imperium* and citizenry – unknown in the classical period – provided a first model for the racialization of social distinctions. Racial distinction was given further shape in American colonial societies themselves as they achieved greater definition, particularly as their indigenous European-origin elites struggled against their role as political and economic satellites oriented to their European metropolises (Canny and Pagden, 1987). And then racial sentiment began to take on something of its recognizably contemporary mantle in the emerging political discourse of modern Europe as it sought a secular moral foundation for social and political life. Most intellectual histories of the race concept develop this point in relation to the enchantment of "nature" in the eighteenth-century Enlightenment, and then in nineteenth-century movements like Romanticism. Here, I want to suggest the importance of antecedent thinking, particularly in the development of "natural law" ideas in sixteenth- and seventeenth-century thought.

All this is, of course, to take a very "Eurocentric" approach. The people who were objectified and externalized by European racial thought, like American Indians and African-origin slaves, were also very active participants in forging the meaning of race in colonial societies, working with the European categories but also transforming and subverting them. This is something we will consider much more closely in chapter 6. For the present, a "Eurocentric" approach is perhaps to the point in emphasizing the sense in which the discourse of race precisely captures the involution of European thought, the entailment of race in Europe's dialogue with itself, the very construction of Europe as a self-conscious – though never fixed or impermeable – entity. But, of course, Europe was hardly without its own internal tensions, and a major axis of early modern political debate was in the conflict between Reformation and Counter-Reformation accounts of the basis for political society, accounts which invoked colonial societies and the emerging category of race to wage their own more parochial battles, giving further shape to the race concept in the process. At the same time, the ferocious religious conflicts of sixteenth- and seventeenth-century Europe drew upon the quasi-racial categories of a prior exclusionary discourse (concerning the corrupted body and blood of Jews and heretics) to stigmatize the Protestant or Catholic enemy (Burke, 1978; Moore, 1990). Perhaps this lends some support to the frequent assertion that racial sentiment was generated in Europe's internal tensions and applied to its own internal "others" (Miles, 1993; Stoler, 1995; Malik, 1996). However, while we can identify various points in European history where this seems to be the case – for example, in the persecutions of twelfth-century Western Europe and sixteenth-century Spain (Elliott, 1963; Moore, 1990), the religious wars of the sixteenth and seventeenth centuries (Burke, 1978), and the liberal "biostates" of nineteenth-century England and France (Drescher, 1990; Stoler, 1995) – these tensions have generally been resolved or mitigated in ways which scarcely occurred in colonial contexts, except through the complete rupture of successful anti-colonial struggle, and perhaps not even then. In 1648, the Peace of Westphalia effectively brought to an end the politico-religious struggles that had ravaged Western Europe for much of the preceding century and entrenched the conception of the undivided, sovereign state as the basic political unit, without, however, broaching questions concerning the political status of European overseas colonies. At much the same time in many of those colonies, plantation agriculture was beginning a takeoff which was to draw in millions of enslaved Africans over the next two centuries, even as European intellectuals began to theorize the boundaries of political community defining the emerging nation-states of Europe. If it is true that the working people of late medieval and early modern Europe were despised, excluded, and exploited by elites it is nevertheless also true, I will argue, that they were a part of these emerging political communities and were not subjected to the chattel slavery through which medieval elites had yoked many people from their own local populations. So, while it is important to emphasize the expedient economic character of colonial plantation slavery rather than simply its putatively "racial" aspect – and important, too, to consider slavery not simply as distinct from freedom but as part of a continuum of labor coercion in colonial America within and without the plantation complex – I will nevertheless suggest that non-economic explanations for the pervasive enslavement of African-origin people over and above other sources of labor in colonial America are crucial for an understanding of the modern discourse of race.

The polities of modern Europe have not been the only ones in history involved in conquest and territorial expansion but, as I suggested earlier, they have been unusual in the way that they have drawn such firm "natural" boundaries around the communities making up the political order, or, in other words, in the way that they have mobilized discourses of racial difference. The example of India has been introduced in this book partly in order to provide a comparative contrast, since here we find an alternative cultural logic of natural difference which has been associated with the formation of very different kinds of political community. Mention might also be made of Islam, which stands not only as the geopolitical bridge between Europe and India after expanding from its Arab heartlands during the medieval period, but has also been, as it were, the interlocutor of community formation in both regions. As we shall see, Muslim slave-trading in sub-Saharan Africa provided one of the contexts for the European colonial slave trade and though, unlike the European colonies, black Africans were far from being the only people reduced to slavery in the Muslim world, they quickly became archetypically associated with it, enjoying few of the routes to upward social mobility that were available to other slaves (Lewis, 1971; Evans, 1980; Phillips, 1985). But, however entrenched, the impediment remained lodged at an "ethnocentric" level, and was scarcely elaborated as in Europe to a doctrine of racial difference. This returns us to the point made in chapter 1 concerning the monadic character of Christian political discourse and its tendency towards the closure of political communities around a single, transcendent source of political authority. Outside Christendom more plural forms of political authority have been entertained, not least in India, where Islam itself came to be integrated within political and social structures in ways unparalleled in Europe for this very reason. It would be wildly inaccurate to suggest that the Islamicization of India carried out from the eighth century onwards by Arab traders, Sufi saints, and Turkic raiders from the North with their Persianized Islam, was an entirely peaceful process, but – rather ironically in view of the communal tensions in contemporary India examined in chapter 6 – it was not initially, I would suggest, a process as handicapped by colonial boundaries and communal definitions as was European territorial expansion. Thus, as many scholars have recently argued, Islam in India did not progress through the "syncretic" blending of different religious traditions, but through certain affinities between Islam and Indic religious tradition in terms of the way they constitute political communities (Bayly, 1986; Wink, 1990; Khan, 1994; van der Veer, 1994). Although something of the same potential can be seen in colonial mission Christianity (particularly of the Catholic variety), European Christianity was never able to transcend its political monism, and the cultural, then proto-racial, identifications associated with it. Thus, although the temptation to read a racial dimension into the harshness of plantation slavery is probably better resisted in favor of an appreciation of the way that specific forms of production like sugar cultivation demand their own forms of labor discipline, this cannot account for the pervasive forms of racial hierarchy which obtained more generally in colonial America.

The structure of the subsequent argument can now be outlined against the background of this rather lengthy introduction. First, we consider the cultural logic within which the social relations of production in Europe and India were located as a context for understanding the economic basis of race and caste hierarchies. We then move on to discuss the development of politico-religious ideologies in Europe and India, building upon the points made above and in chapter 1, to assess the significance of their respective ideologies of political rule and religious transcendence for their distinctive conceptions of natural hierarchy. This leads into a discussion, one that closes the present chapter, of the different kinds of political community associated with these ideologies, which I characterize as European "nations" and an Indian "scale of citizenries," again bearing upon an understanding of the respective formation of natural hierarchy. We then leave the Indian case aside until chapter 5 and, in chapter 4, pick up the nexus of race, colonialism, nationalism, and slavery mentioned earlier in relation to the European colonial empires, a nexus which lacks any Indian parallel. Here, we develop an analysis of the historical trajectory discussed earlier, towards the increasing elaboration of racial discourse in colonial society and in metropolitan political thought, as the antecedents of a contemporary understanding of racial sentiment.

European Capitalism, Indian Capitalism?

Michael Mann (1988: 6) has written of a "European miracle" involving a massive economic development which occurred nowhere else in the world, and which began its takeoff in the high middle ages. In this, he builds upon the classical sociological theories of Marx and Weber, with their different explanations for the development of capitalism in Europe. Marx distinguished between forms of merchant capital – found in various historical societies – where mercantile profit accrued from the circulation of commodities produced under various social circumstances, and capital itself, where commodity production is generalized to the extent that labor too is commodified as labor power. Whereas, for Marx, merchant capital is static and contained within the extant social relations of production, capital responds to the dynamic law of value, whereby the returns from increasing surplus value draw more people into capitalist relations of production as capitalists and wage laborers. Approaching capital in terms of the production of labor power as a commodity implies an understanding of labor power as an individual, private property right, so that the presence of free wage labor becomes a defining feature of capitalism.

These points are of concern to us for two reasons. First, given a dynamic tendency to proletarianization, it becomes necessary to explain why free wage labor did *not* readily develop in some places that were linked to the emerging European capitalist economy, the most important among them for our purposes being the slave plantations of the American colonies. This point will be addressed in chapter 4. Second, the view that the "miracle" of an indigenous capitalism was restricted to Europe alone suggests a special structuring of the social order that did not occur in other places. In examining the circumstances surrounding the production and circulation of goods in precolonial India, I wish to suggest that the specificity of capitalism to Europe has been very considerably overstressed by Marx and by contemporary writers like Mann. Nevertheless, there are important differences between the two places in the way that production is embedded within a wider structuring of social relationships which will enable us to develop an understanding of how race and caste ideologies are sustained in relation to the production of goods. Let us examine these points.

In describing the conditions of possibility for his "European miracle," Mann (1986; 1988) talks of a "multiple, acephalous federation" of economic, military, and ideological power networks in the Europe of the high middle ages, which – due to the rise of the feudal institutions that had broken the economic grip, but not the political legitimacy, of monarchical and ecclesiastical authorities – combined extensive local rights in private property with a broader, normatively regulated market. Invoking Weber's notion of Europe's "rational restlessness" as its dynamic principle, Mann argues that this permitted the widespread capitalization of agriculture and merchant trading networks without being stifled by revenue exaction from centralized political authority, thereby paving the way for a later capitalist transition.

An interesting point about this analysis is its remarkable parallels with Indian economic history. So, for example, in India too merchant guilds possessed considerable autonomy from political rulers, enabling them to sustain extensive long-distance trading networks in bulk goods as well as precious items (Bayly, 1985a; Inden, 1990; Subrahmanyam, 1994). Extensive private property rights were held, if not necessarily in land itself then at least in the product of land, permitting local reinvestment which fostered increasing agrarian surplus and monetization (Bayly, 1983; Kumar, 1985; Washbrook, 1988). Industrial production by specialist urban workers had developed by the seventeenth century to the extent that in some instances, notably the textile trade, it threatened the nascent industrial base of Europe (Wolf, 1982). And all this was sustained by normative political regulation which essentially conformed to Mann's definition of a "multiple, acephalous federation." Although something of these points could perhaps have been constructed from Mann's own analysis of "Hindu caste" (Mann, 1986: 348–63), the opportunity is missed through reversion to stereotypes of a stultifying "Oriental Despotism" and a popular "mystical acceptance of the social order" (ibid.: 398) which have been endlessly recycled in European writings on India since the seventeenth century.

Of course, my own argument is a very considerable generalization from the long and complex history of the subcontinent during the millennium from roughly the seventh to the eighteenth century. Nevertheless, much of the foregoing would apply to Indian polities as different in time, place, and style as the Rashtrakutas of the medieval Deccan, the Cholas of later medieval South India, and the Mughals of early modern North India, perhaps suggesting a pan-Indian process of agrarian expansion and political development (Chattopadhyaya, 1994). Without rehearsing the various debates on "Indian feudalism" (Jha, 1987; Chattopadhyaya, 1994; Kulke, 1997) I would suggest, following the prevailing orthodoxy of scholarly suspicion towards the applicability of "feudalism" to India, that in this respect the Indian case differs from the European one inasmuch as its "multiple" and "acephalous" character was not a consequence of an undermining "from below" of centralized economic control as in the European case, but was actually entailed in the very logic of political rule. I will pursue these points in more detail later in the chapter; for the present, let us consider some of the implications for an understanding of capitalist development and the socioeconomic structures that sustain it.

In his historical ethnography of the Nakarattars, a South Indian merchant caste, David Rudner (1994) has shown how the Nakarattars have combined the systematic pursuit of wealth with an ascetic lifestyle, a point which echoes Weber's (1930) famous thesis on the ascetic Calvinist ethic underlying capitalist development in Europe, whereby the doctrine of predestined salvation leads to an emphasis on this-worldly asceticism as a mark of divine grace which potentiated the accumulation of capital as an end in itself. Even though this briefest of summaries traduces some of the complexities of Weber's argument, his thesis rather founders on the fact that an ascetic and accumulative ethic could be found in Catholic Antwerp or the Italian city-states as much as in the zones of Calvinist influence (Pagden, 1990; Duplessis, 1997). Indeed, Pagden has argued that perhaps what really counts is an ethic of "classical republicanism," common to the politico-religious traditions of both Calvinist and Catholic trading communities, which emphasized commitment to a broader social collectivity devoid of any further discriminations of status. In a sense, this represents the completion of the modern, egalitarian order as described in chapter 2 in relation to the work of writers like Roy Wagner and Louis Dumont, where "there is no real, no ontological intermediary between the individual man and mankind at large" (Dumont, 1970: 34). However, as Rudner shows, the situation was quite different among the Nakarattars; for them,

> actions were directed toward the good of specific social groups to which they belonged: their joint families, lineages, villages, clans, business associations operating out of specific localities, and the caste as a whole. (Rudner, 1994: 105)

Thus, Rudner argues that collectivism or communalism is not an impediment to capitalism, as has been argued in classical Western sociology, but is the very basis of Indian capitalism. Nevertheless, a distinction can be made between Indian and European forms of capitalism. While Indian capi-

talism went very considerably beyond the kind of static and inherently limited economic forms described under Marx's conception of merchant capital, it was not perhaps generalized in quite the same way as was to be the
case in Europe. In this distinction we can discern different Indian and Euro-
American predications of the person which partly underlie caste and race
hierarchies.

Let us examine the generalization of capitalism in the European case.
Here, I want to suggest – rather against the grain of Weber and of more
recent orthodoxy in comparative historical sociology (e.g. Baechler, 1988),
but perhaps in keeping with Dumont's comparative sociology – that certain affinities exist between the logic of capitalism and Christianity more
generally, rather than within particular schismatic tendencies within it. Perhaps this requires some explanation in view of biblical associations between
money and evil, and the contempt in which merchants and moneylenders
were held within medieval Christianity. Parry (1986) has argued that the
status of Christianity as an "ethicized salvation religion" (as described in
chapter 1) establishes a logic of this-worldly renunciation or asceticism (the
profane world is irredeemably spoiled as against the world to come) which
is manifested in disinterested gift-giving (alms) and, more generally, in a
radical separation of the person's true, inner being from the profane things
of the world. This separation between persons and things is a prerequisite
for the truly detached market transactions of the kind implied in Pagden's
republicanism, where the complete alienation of substances demands that
substances are not implicated with the self. Thus, despite the anti-mercan-
tile bias of medieval Europe there is an implicit affinity with the logic of
market transaction in Christianity which, through long and painful historical processes beginning with the marketization and monetization of the
manorial economy in the twelfth century, became an empirically manifest
reversal. Part of the "pain" of this transformation was experienced by Jews
and heretics who bore the brunt of increasing persecution from around the
same time. On the one hand, this can be explained in relation to elite
discourses which attempted to restore a firm ranking hierarchy as the basis
of the social order at a time when the monetization of the economy was
calling this hierarchy into question (Moore, 1990). At the same time, the
persecution of Jews in particular was responsive to a popular anti-semitism
stirred by the same uncertainties and informed by millenarian, laicized forms
of Christianity which drew upon images of inherently defective bodies and
blood (Cohn, 1957; Poliakov, 1974; Burke, 1978; Lynch, 1992), while
the idea of Christian community was elaborated into an identification of a
Christian populace with the monarchical state (Kantorowicz, 1957; Canning, 1996). Here we encounter a second dynamic of transformation, towards forms of nationalism which conceived a body politic in terms of

religious (Christian) exclusivity. These two transformations from the medieval social order are extremely important in relation to the later history of European colonialism and racism.

The separation of persons from things which we have just suggested is bound up in the Christian logic of salvation has also been a fundamental feature of sociological theory, where it has appeared most characteristically as a loss or aporia. For Marx, as we have seen, the pathos of capitalism lies in the radical separation it creates between the worker and his or her product. And for Marcel Mauss – whose essay on *The Gift* (1922) was the progenitor of anthropological economics – this separation represented a disjunction in modern societies which was not to be found in noncapitalist or "primitive" societies where people and things were inseparably combined.

Parry (1986) argues that anthropologists have tended to decompose Mauss's theory into two parts. On the one hand, gifts or prestations of artefacts (usually between groups of people in given circumstances like marriage ceremonies) are regarded as eliciting a counter-gift, and thereby establishing solidary political relationships between the protagonists to the exchange. This idea of the gift as a kind of implicit social contract which works to the mutual benefit of the protagonists has received much favor. On the other hand, Mauss suggests – most notably in his famous discussion of the Maori concept of *hau* – that the gift actually represents the "spirit" or part of the person, an argument which has generally been dismissed for its complicity with the mysticism of indigenous representations concerning exchange. Parry criticizes this dualistic reading, arguing that in some circumstances the "social contract" aspect of Mauss's analysis is less to the point than his approach to the "spirit" of the gift. This is of particular relevance to the study of gift exchange in India, or at least with the significant subset of religious exchanges – which can include marriage – known as *dana*. Unlike the gift that demands a return, the key point about *dana* is that it must *not* receive a return, for it represents the sin or impurity which, inevitably, the donor's actions in the world have created. This impurity is concentrated in *dana*, so that in passing *dana* to a recipient the donor restores their own purity, an alienation of self constituting the "poison in the gift" (Raheja, 1988). If the gift of *dana* provoked a counter-gift, the flow of impurity away from the donor would immediately have been reversed; complete alienation without sublation is required.

The model of alienation implied in Parry's discussion of *dana* seems diametrically opposed to the one invoked by Marx. Whereas, in the one case, the unrestored alienation involved in the gift of *dana* recuperates the self, in the other, the unrestored alienation involved in the commoditization of labor fragments the self. Rather than indicating a different conceptual basis for exchange, however, perhaps this reflects the different basis of the "self" in the two cases. Although for Marx the commoditization of labor tends to make the human self object-like, he in fact retained a strong distinction between human and object. As we saw in the previous chapter, the idea of alienation in capitalism makes sense only if the person is recreated as an autonomous entity which has "lost" something of itself through commoditized labor (Strathern, 1985: 206). By contrast, the logic of *dana* implies a "self" with looser boundaries, a point given its clearest formulation in Marriott's ethnosociological argument that persons in India are generally thought to be "dividual" or divisible rather than "individual," acting, as it were, only as nodes in a flow of substance (Marriott, 1976: 111). From this view, Marriott derives an account of the *varna* scheme in terms of transactional strategies, with brahmans as "optimal" transactors who give but do not receive, *kshatriyas* as "maximal" transactors who both give and receive, *vaishyas* as "minimal" transactors who neither give nor receive, and *shudras* as "pessimal" transactors who receive but do not give. This can also be related to the broader Hindu cosmology in which, ultimately, social action is directed at transforming substance. Although this conforms to an underlying unity, substance is contextually varied, and Marriott suggests that different strategies attend the transfer of "gross" and "subtle" substances. Developing these points, Rudner (1994) argues that the transactional order of the male merchants from the Nakarattar caste is based upon maximizing transactions in gross substances like money, and minimizing transactions in the subtle substances which have to do with the reproduction of their own persons, like women as wives and the "seed" of their descent lines. He thereby gives a communal twist once again to his understanding of Indian capitalism, by contrast to orthodox theories of capitalist relations of production which emphasize their solvent effect upon particularistic identities. This touches upon the somewhat paradoxical way in which a monism in Indian thought establishes the possibility of differentiating substance, whereas the binary thought of Christianity places emphasis upon its singularity. Something of the particularity of race and caste as hierarchies secured in nature can be located in this distinction. The autonomous individual conceived in European racial thought presents itself as a complete realization or "copy" of one of the variant human forms which reflects part of the diversity created in the singular domain of "nature." By contrast, the dividual conceived in Brahmanic universalism is a temporary container which manifests some of the undifferentiated pure substance of nature.

Parry (1989) argues that there is no counterpart in Indian history to the suspicion with which money and mercantilism have been held in Christianity. The reason, he suggests, is because within Christianity there is a founding belief in human autonomy and autarkic production for one's own use which is compromised by commoditized exchange. The caste order of India, by contrast, is based upon the idea of an interdependent division of labor at every level from the household upwards and (notwithstanding Orientalist stereotypes to the contrary) there has never been any ideological emphasis on economic autarky in India. In this sense, the fulminations of Marx and Mauss against the alienation of capitalism at the ontological level can be seen as representative of one pole of an immanent contradiction within the economic logic of Western or Christian thought; sublated, autarkic production for use as against the alienated logic of utility and production for exchange. This point can be developed through considering the influential reading of Mauss's text provided by Marshall Sahlins (1974). Pursuing the idea that Mauss's theory of the gift is a theory of social contract, Sahlins draws out the parallels between his theory of exchange in "primitive" societies and the political philosophy of Thomas Hobbes. In his *Leviathan* (1651), Hobbes provided a contractual theory for the emerging secular sovereign state, whereby people engage in a "mutual surrender" to the state of some part of their autonomy of action in recognition of its superior ability to vitiate the "war of everyone against everyone" that results from complete autonomy of action, a "state of nature" in which life, according to Hobbes's famous description, was "nasty, brutish and short" (Hobbes, 1968: 186). Sahlins shows that Hobbes's "war" is not, however, best thought of as a condition of complete disorder or anarchy, but rather as a condition in which wholly autonomous action is socially recognized as a legitimate possibility. This situation of plural sovereignty is, I would suggest, somewhat akin to the caste order of India, which might be described as a kind of institutionalized "war," if not of "everyone against everyone" then at least of one caste against another, undergirded by an ideology of *jati dharma*, that is, of a code for conduct which is appropriate for one's caste, within an encompassing cultural order. But Hobbes was unable to countenance such a solution because of the essentially monadic conception of political legitimacy which, I have argued, has been an enduring feature of Western, Christian thought; there is no parallel to *jati dharma* within the universalist categories of Christianity. Hobbes's solution was therefore constituted through the idea of a "surrender" to the state. This is uniquely susceptible to individualist conceptions of the autonomous individual who submits to some superordinate entity, which might be the kind of community described by Pagden's classical republicanism or, as in Hobbes's thought, it might be the sovereign state. In the latter case, this creates an aporia or contradiction between individual autonomy and political subordination that can be resolved through nationalist ideologies which construct special affinities between particular kinds of person and the states which are the "natural" repository of their interests. I shall argue in chapter 4 that in this respect Hobbes's thought gives expression to the "nationalist" context within which early modern ideologies of colonial racism were to emerge; for present purposes, the important point is that in India *jati dharma* and the particular communal institutions which intercede between the person and the "community" at large provided a check of a kind that barely existed in Europe to the generalization of the cultural logic of capitalist accumulation. Thus, we might suggest that the universalist logic of Christianity, once detached from the more specific antipathy to money and mercantilism, provided grounds for a society-wide radicalization of capital accumulation which were not present in India.

Rudner (1994) argues that studies of Indian caste relations have suffered from an overemphasis on castes involved in agrarian production at the expense of merchant castes. Nevertheless, in a general sense, recent debates about the so-called "jajmani system" pertaining to agrarian castes have established an understanding of the communal structuring to social relations underlying caste society which is similar to Rudner's distinction between Indian and European capitalism. The jajmani system refers to customary relationships at the village level in rural India between castes in accordance with the "radial" caste model described in chapter 1, relationships which could be regarded as Maussian "total social phenomena" combining domains of action normally separated as "political," "economic," "social," and so on in Euro-American thought. Traditional scholarship, however, has emphasized the economic aspects of the jajmani system, particularly with regard to the relationships between dominant, landholding castes and service castes like potters, carpenters, and agricultural laborers. In return for the services of these castes, especially during customary occasions such as life-cycle rituals, the dominant caste pays them, usually in kind with grain or other agricultural produce. The jajmani system has therefore been regarded as a kind of integrative counter-tendency to the divisiveness of caste reckoning; where service castes are inferiorized as "other" by the dominant caste, here they are reabsorbed as "one's own" service castes in an organic village economy. Needless to say, this is a somewhat idealized perspective which reflects above all the kind of view articulated by members of the dominant caste (Lerche, 1993). Moreover, recent scholarship has attempted to undermine the notion that the jajmani system represents a long-term, stable economic order at the level of the village. For example, Fuller (1977; 1989) has argued that what has been described as the jajmani system is the remnant of a much more ramifying system of Mughal imperial (and, later, British) revenue collection based originally on prebendial grants to land revenue, where the grant holders or *zamindars* were intermediaries of agrarian redistribution between local cultivators and elites, and higher

level state treasuries. Although acting to some degree as customary landlords playing a local status game, the *zamindars* were not isolated from the
vicissitudes of the market economy and nor, indeed, were the local cultivators. In fact, *zamindari* rights were themselves a tradeable commodity. In
pre-British India, state revenue collection was based upon the idea of a
proportionate share in the harvest and not upon a land tax, but by the
sixteenth century this customary right had often given way to fixed cash
payments. Thus, what was once seen as a village-level economic system is
now regarded as part of a broader economic order, which perhaps was
concealed hitherto from anthropologists working under the "Orientalist"
misapprehension of the Indian village as an autarkic economic unit.

Other writers have argued that the idea of the jajmani system conflates
several distinct forms of economic relationship which vary across India, but
take forms like village-level patron–client relationships of different kinds
depending upon the castes involved, vertical economic obligations of the
sort described above, and more market-oriented transactions. But against
the implication of some recent critical writings that the literature on the
jajmani system conflates or reifies different kinds of economic relationship
as an all-India "system," it can be suggested that generalizable forms of
monetary and nonmonetary economy did and do exist in India which are
grounded at the geopolitical level of the village (Bayly, 1983; Miller, 1986;
Lerche, 1993). In his account of the political economy of eighteenth-century India, Bayly goes so far as to reverse the derivation of the jajmani
system from higher level economic concerns that is implied in critiques
such as Fuller's, arguing,

> The aspect of Hindu caste practice which was most appropriate to the flex-
> ible political economy was the *jajmani* system. . . .We are used to seeing this
> operate mainly at the level of the village. But in . . . [the eighteenth century]
> whole kingdoms – even kingdoms with a formally Islamic constitution – can
> be seen as extended sets of *jajmani* relations. . . . Emerging classes and do-
> minions were most secure when they adjusted themselves to the theories of
> "sharing" and redistribution which were prevalent among the mass of the
> Hindu and Muslim population. (Bayly, 1983: 50–1)

From this, Bayly infers that "Hindu and Islamic theory were flexible
enough to accommodate many varieties of political practice" (ibid.: 50),
and we shall pursue this idea that kingdoms or polities can themselves conform to a jajmani model in more detail below. But one conclusion for
present purposes is that, notwithstanding considerable levels of coercion
by ruling elites against cultivators, the more pluralist logic of agrarian relations in the Indian case – the relative autonomy of the labor process among
cultivators – did not potentiate, as in Europe, a wider process of agricul-

tural capitalization and the "liberation" of rural workers from customary tenures which emerged from, and helped ramify, the generalizing and binary dynamic of European class struggle familiar from Marxian analysis (cf. Mukhia, 1997; Duplessis, 1997). This does not mean that there was no social change in India but only that it remains possible to ground an understanding of an interactional order – one partly constitutive of what scholars have understood as "caste" – within a particular and enduring cultural metacontext of specifically local relationships which were politically and economically tractable to higher levels of geopolitical organization in ways that are analogous to, but different from, the case of Europe.

Eisenstadt has argued that in India "the restructuring of economic activities did not lead to the development of more autonomous economic roles, to the definition of the arena as a distinct, symbolically autonomous one, or to principles of control over access to markets and of conversion of resources" (Eisenstadt, 1997: 47). Although this is perhaps an overstatement, our analysis in the preceding paragraphs of the structure of mercantile and agrarian activities in pre-British India lends some support to this argument. Thus, it is probably fair to say that the economic ideologies of Europe lacked some of the moderation that obtained in India. For example, the *jati dharma* of Indian merchants reflected a minimally transacting, ascetic, *vaishya* lifestyle which abjured the excess and conspicuous consumption of the optimally transacting *kshatriyas*, but merchant wealth was often channeled into religious patronage. Indeed, Bayly (1983) suggests that merchants who were noted for their ascetic lifestyle were often followers of Vaishnavism rather than the more ascetic Shaivite cult because the former enabled them to participate in lavish acts of religious patronage. This constituted a resolution to the aporia of asceticism and accumulation in a way which was not available to the European merchant capitalists described under Weber's rubric of the Protestant ethic. Likewise, Bayly shows that the pursuit of profit was never the single and fundamental motivating factor in Indian mercantile enterprise, though it was certainly one motivating factor. And, in contrast to the largely secularized economic order of Europe which had been well established by the eighteenth century, temples were themselves major economic players. These features of the cultural milieu are not, however, set in stone, as is perhaps the implication of Eisenstadt's position. Susan Lewandowski (1985) has shown how Indian merchants found different politico-economic outlets over time as their dominance and autonomy increased during the eighteenth and nineteenth centuries, first indulging in the temple patronage of time-honored *vaishya* tradition, then engaging in a more aggressive program of temple dedication which increasingly assumed the *kshatriya* mantle of the kings who had been usurped through the monopoly of political power claimed by British colonial government, and later developing secular caste associations. These would prove to be the breeding-ground for the nationalist, anti-colonial politics which ultimately succeeded in ousting the British. Whether or not this represented an "indigenous" ideological development is probably the wrong question to ask, but perhaps it is possible both to concur with and to generalize from Bayly's comment that caste and religion provided the "building blocks" for Indian mercantilism and urbanism in the colonial period (Bayly, 1983: 175) by suggesting the existence of an Indian cultural metacontext conjoining aspects of economic and communal domains of action which, however, evinced a variety of transformations before, during, and after the British colonial period in relation to contemporary political and economic exigencies.

Political Formations

One can debate the similarities or the differences of specific political formations almost endlessly, and in ways that after Said's (1978) critique of Orientalism now seem to be loaded with normative implications. In the comparative scholarship of European and Indian polities, an earlier emphasis on similarities supposedly engendered by a common "Indo-European" cultural inheritance was replaced by Orientalist readings of difference, to which Dumontian orthodoxy contributed, even if Dumont himself never sought to make difference absolute. More recently, this has given way to scholarship which emphasizes similarity, either as a deliberate corrective to Orientalism (Inden, 1990) or in exercises which update the concerns of classical sociological theory to show how the European and Indian cases can be explained in terms of different empirical combinations of universal political factors (Baechler, 1988; Quigley, 1993; Milner, 1994). This is the implication of Milner's (1994) analysis of the fourfold status order, discussed in chapter 1, which can generate most of the salient features of both medieval Europe and India. So, in both places, we find an emphasis on sacred kingship, a somewhat complicated nexus of relationships between kings and priests, renunciative religious traditions which emphasize a less worldly and more uncompromising path to spiritual transcendence and, concomitantly, a particular institutional framework mediating the intersecting claims of kings, priests, and renouncers. However, in medieval Europe, the picture was complicated by the competing claims to secular political authority of "ethnic" forms of sacred kingship originally associated with the pagan traditions of Rome's barbarian usurpers, and the Roman model of limitless imperial authority which was bequeathed to the Roman Catholic Church and personified in the pope, but also later in secular imperial office, introducing a further tension into the Caesaro-papalist model itself. The institutionalization of these contests in a fully Christian medieval European ecumene leant a distinctive shape to medieval Europe's political traditions. I shall argue that this contest is not paralleled in Indian political traditions which have articulated different kinds of tension. Thus, while I will draw from more universalist sociological approaches in placing emphasis upon common processes such as status maximization and closure, the following discussion of "premodern" European and Indian political formations will remain attentive to the consequences of the culturally specific ways in which status claims are mounted in the first place. This leads to a discussion of the differences between Europe and India, both in conceptions of political authority and in the way that this authority is located within wider social structures, wherein, I suggest, an incipient logic of race and caste formation can be discerned.

Europe

In this section, I will argue that despite tensions between royal, imperial, and papal authority in medieval Western Europe, European political thought rested upon a monadic conception of political rule, conforming to the Christian cosmology of ranking hierarchy discussed in chapter 1. This came to be linked with a proto-nationalist territorial delimitation of a people around a royal line within a broader Christian ecumene which was to form the context for colonial racism.

But let us begin with tensions within the Caesaro-papalist model itself, between the papacy and imperial Byzantium which, in AD 494, found notable expression in *Duo Sunt*, the letter of Pope Gelasisus I to the Byzantine emperor. In the context of the Acacian schism, wherein the emperor had exceeded his authority from the perspective of the papacy by intervening in entirely religious matters, Gelasisus wrote,

> There are two things, August emperor, by which this world is chiefly ruled, the consecrated authority [*auctoritas*] of bishops and the royal power [*potestas*]. Of these, the bishops bear a burden which is so much the weightier as they must render an accounting in the divine judgement even for the kings of mankind. You know, most clement son, that although you surpass the human race in dignity . . . yet you devoutly bow your neck to those in charge of divine things, and you seek from them the means of your salvation. And hence you recognize that in the reception and proper administration of the heavenly sacraments, in the sphere of religion . . . you must be subject, rather than rule. . . . So far as the sphere of public order . . . is concerned, the bishops themselves know that the imperial office . . . has been conferred on you

by divine disposition, and they obey your laws lest they seem to oppose your authoritative decision in worldly matters. If so, with what zeal, I ask you, is it fitting and proper to obey those who have been charged with the administration of the revered mysteries? (Cited in Benson, 1982: 14)

But if it is tempting to conclude from this that Gelasius thinks of priestly *auctoritas* as superior to royal *potestas* it becomes clear from his other writings that he did not regard kings or emperors as depending for their legitimacy upon the clerical mediation of the divine and it is also clear – not least from the emperor's actions – that secular rulers were not regarded and did not regard themselves as being so dependent, so that secular and clerical authority are regarded as separate and autonomous, if interrelated, offices (Benson, 1982; Canning, 1996). As Louis Dumont puts it, "we must understand Gelasius as saying that, if the Church is *in* the Empire with respect to worldly matters, the Empire is *in* the Church regarding things divine" (Dumont, 1986: 48). Dumont detects in this situation evidence for much the same hierarchical complementarity between secular power and priestly status that he has identified in the premodern ideology of Indian caste. Yet, just as in the Indian case, he undermines the subtlety of his own understanding by insisting on the ultimate superiority of clerical authority, such that "priests are superior, for they are inferior only on an inferior level" (ibid.: 46). According to Dumont, it was this premodern hierarchical conception which, in Europe but not in India, was to be swept away by the advent of modern individualism, although he seems uncertain as to when this decisive rupture occurred, singling out the eighth century, when the popes dignified the rule of the Frankish kings (ibid.: 49), the late eleventh century, when imperial and papal power directly confronted each other in the "Investiture Contest" between the emperor, Henry IV of Germany, and Pope Gregory VII (ibid.: 68), and the sixteenth century, when the Reformation theology of John Calvin all but dissolved the church into a conception of a this-worldly participation in God (ibid.: 53–6). If, instead, we accept the logic of Dumont's argument for hierarchical complementarity then we might regard the Gelasian doctrine and its later appropriations as part of the story of two different kinds of authority whose confluence and divergence in the claims of theocratic secular and hierocratic clerical monarchies impelled much of the political discourse of medieval Europe. Thus, when in AD 754 Pope Stephen II extended his blessing to Frankish royal claims by anointing Pippin III, the first of the Carolingian dynasty, and when Pippin's son Charlemagne was crowned emperor by Pope Leo III (a coronation that the latter did not entirely welcome, or need) this did not represent a "glaring contradiction to Gelasius' doctrine" as Dumont (ibid.: 50) argues, but simply one twist in the medieval story of temporal and spiritual power. However, I want to argue that whereas in India there was a genuine complementarity between royal and priestly authority, the Christian cosmology of Europe recognized only one source of authority. Thus, while it was possible for secular and clerical political institutions to coexist by representing themselves as different aspects of transcendent authority, the inherently monadic character of that authority predisposed them to contest the right fully to appropriate its mantle to themselves. It is thus possible to agree with Dumont when he writes:

> The two agencies or realms are unified while their distinction is relegated from the fundamental to a secondary level, as if they differed not in their nature but only in degree. The distinction is henceforth between the spiritual and the temporal, as we have known them ever since, and the field is unified, so that we may speak of spiritual and temporal "powers." It is characteristic that the spiritual is conceived as superior to the temporal *on the temporal level itself*, as if it was a superior degree of the temporal. (Ibid.: 50)

This, however, was not some modern breach of medieval hierarchy, as Dumont argues, but was always present in medieval Christianity, where the "dualist" idea that secular rule enjoyed transcendent authority independently of the priesthood was never without currency (Canning, 1996). In this respect, Dumont's argument that the hierocratic case for papal dominance outshone the dualist case for royal authority around the time of the Investiture Contest (Dumont, 1986: 68–9) is misplaced. On the contrary, there were strong arguments in favor of royal precedence in the political discourse of the time which had to do with approaching monarchy and priesthood through the idea of Christ's dual nature as both divine and human, so that priests were understood as the human custodians of divine truths while kings were understood after the model of Christ's divine rule itself (Kantorowicz, 1957; Canning, 1996). Thus, in the words of Georges Duby, "the culture of the high middle ages culminates in the person of the sovereign as the image of God" (Duby, 1968: 8; cf. Canning, 1996: 104–5).

Let us pursue some of the implications of this idea of the divine king in the medieval period. Before they were Christianized, little is known about the political organization of the barbarian tribes which had gradually usurped the Roman empire by the fifth century AD, but they subsequently espoused strongly Christian notions of kingship as grounded in divine authority. It was for this reason that Pope Stephen II's anointing of Pippin III, mentioned above, was of some use to the Carolingian king in wresting the Frankish monarchy from the Merovingian dynasty. But the more important contribution of Roman Christianity to the Carolingians was to provide an ideological and institutional infrastructure for their imperial ambitions. Establishing Christian dominion over the wreckage of the Roman empire, but without Roman conceptions of territorial jurisdiction, the Carolingians developed an interpretation of Gelasian doctrine which elaborated a notion of the church as the corporate body enjoining both clerical and secular rule, using the clerical authority structure to check the autonomist impulses of the local nobility (Benson, 1982; Ertman, 1997). But they scarcely respected the autonomy of the church itself, and they did not abandon the lineaments of sacred kingship which conferred royal rights of priestly investiture, so that the church became a fundamentally lay institution. The empire, however, proved to be short lived, partly because of the difficulties of dynastic succession which fractured it into several kingdoms. In this respect, the transcendent authority attributed to secular rulers in the early medieval period can be thought of as one attaching to individual persons. This was to change in the high middle ages when, in Ernst Kantorowicz's words, "the centre of gravity shifted . . . from the ruling personages to the ruled collectives" (Kantorowicz, 1957: 193), a shift given considerable impetus by the eleventh-century reforms of the church which increasingly asserted its autonomy from lay control. The Eucharistic controversy that we touched upon in chapter 2 was in part a reflection at the conceptual level of this change. In the Carolingian period, a figurative view was taken of the Eucharist; the locus of Christ's passion was *corpus Christi*, his "proper and true" or human body, whereas the Eucharist was his *corpus mysticum* or "mystical body." But for the reformers of the eleventh century, the "true body" of Christ was identified with the Eucharist, and the *corpus mysticum* was identified with the body of the church which thereby took on the shape of a complete corporate, political entity. However, as Kantorowicz (1957) points out, a transformation in which the church asserts its institutional autonomy and secular political authority invites a complementary tactic of secular rule to encompass the church institutionally and assert its divine authority, which was roughly the issue at stake in the Investiture Contest and in other later medieval conflicts between secular rulers and the papacy. The "mystical body" of secular rule readily became a corporate body politic comprising a people with a king at their head. This conception resonated with the emerging nationalist discourses of the late medieval period, which celebrated loyalty and even martyrdom for the secular *patria*. More generally, the thirteenth century witnessed a new, desacralized sense of nature as an autonomous entity. This, however, was readily appropriable within the nascent political nationalism; feudal ties of fealty were described as the "natural" basis of the community and, increasingly, the word was used to describe the relationship between the ruler, the ruled, and their country (Guenée, 1985).

In this respect, the claims of hierocratic and secular monarchy were nourished by different biblical traditions. On the one hand, the Old Testament describes the "chosen" nation of the Israelites, united by blood or common substance and subject to the rule of a patriarchal line. Although this bio-genetic criterion is relaxed in Christianity – unlike the Judaic principle, one does not have to be born to a Christian mother in order to be Christian – it is, as Schneider (1977) has argued, refigured as a heavily substantialized commitment to spirituality over matter. Thus, Christian commitment to a code for conduct assumes the quasi-natural character of a spiritual substance which triumphs over natural matter, thereby preserving the Judaic logic of substance over conduct. This Christian substantialization of spirit was re-fracted through the Old Testament model of the nation to connote a kind of spiritual unity of the people. By contrast, the New Testament describes a world of many "nations," none of which is divinely "chosen." Indeed, the only uniting force now sanctioned through the divine is the church itself, which did not correspond to contemporary political boundaries. Thus, whereas older forms of sacred kingship and the newer medieval nationalism looked to Old Testament models, the votaries of hierocratic monarchy looked to the New Testament for its model of the church as the institutional basis of the contemporary order and the pope as the bearer of Christ's legacy through his succession from St Peter (Lynch, 1992; Hastings, 1997). Nevertheless, as we have seen, the position of Christ as a "royal" man-god figure was pregnant with possibilities for secular political appropriation. Indeed, the motif of an older sacred kingship based upon the idea of a divine race of kings with superhuman "blood" was reinvented through a Christian framing, in which dynastic succession continued a sacred line established by Christ himself (Kantorowicz, 1957: 330–3; Battaglia, 1962), but now increasingly associated with the sacred places of the emerging nation (Hastings, 1997).

Some other implications of the secular position can be adduced by a more direct analysis of the *corpus mysticum* conception, traced through by Kantorowicz to the work of Thomas Aquinas (1225–74), the founder of the "Thomist" doctrines which, as we shall see, were to be of some significance in later debates over colonial policy. The social order, understood in relation to the *corpus mysticum*, was metaphorized as a single rather than a collective body; the collective aspect was instead expressed through the medium of time. Hence,

> one constructed a body corporate whose members were echeloned longitu-dinally so that its cross-section at any given moment revealed one instead of many members – a mystical person by perpetual devolution whose mortal and temporary incumbent was of relatively minor importance as compared to the immortal body corporate by succession which he represented. (Kantorowicz, 1957: 312–13)

On the one hand, this solved the problem of the continuity of the body politic in the idea of the king who never really dies, while on the other it expressed the temporally expansive nature of the "mystical body" comprising the community of believers, which would grow to encompass Pagans, Jews, and Muslims outside the contemporary fold. Thus, in addition to territorially delimited, proto-nationalist monarchy, we encounter the idea of a limitlessly expansive religious *imperium*.

The thirteenth century marked the high point of hierocratic monarchy; its sovereign pretensions were broken in the succeeding century by a series of conflicts with secular rulers and within the church itself. Much the same fate befell secular imperial rule, whose claim to be the sovereign fount of law within the domain of Roman Christendom was increasingly appropriated by territorial monarchies according to the dictum that "the king is emperor in his own country" (Spruyt, 1994; Pagden, 1995). This paved the way for an increasing fetishization of kingship, later culminating in the ideology of absolutist monarchy and, in England, convoluted attempts to conflate ideas of the king's "body natural" and "body politic," which Kantorowicz describes as a "monistic formula" of an "ultra-fanciful" kind, implying the king's incorporation with himself (Kantorowicz, 1957: 438–9). But following our model of ranking hierarchy set out in chapter 1, and with the eclipse of hierocratic monarchy and imperial rule, the logic of such ideas can be discerned in the idea of the king as Christ, an embodiment of God and the sole mediator of the ranking hierarchy, drawing the profane order up into his divinity.

Much of the preceding discussion, of course, has operated at the level of the political ideology of kingship rather than the deeds of actual kings, which often fell very obviously short of the ideal in the eyes of their subjects. At the same time, kings were very much a part of the social order and their political success or failure lay not so much in relying upon their putative divinity but in their gifting and generous patronage of political factions gathered around the royal court (Duby, 1968). Nevertheless, the notion of the sovereign as the image of God was the idiom of political discourse, so that even within popular culture belief was sustained in mythic hero-kings of the past who, after the model of Christ, would return to right the wrongs of the present venal incumbent (Burke, 1978). From a contemporary perspective, it is tempting to see this as a conservative ideology sustaining royal domination which began to be eroded in the medieval and early modern period through checks on royal authority like *Magna Carta* and later through hitherto inconceivable acts like popular regicide. Yet while the program of much medieval political discourse was perhaps inherently limited in this way, I will suggest – in keeping with my general argument for structural transformation – that the same flavor of political sacrality has merely been reproduced in a transformed state in modern ideologies of popular democracy, the agency of the people or formulas like "the rights of Englishmen." Indeed, Pagden (1987) has argued in similar vein that eighteenth-century revolutions, including the anti-colonial struggles of white creole elites in Mexico and the United States, extemporized around the refrain "long live the king, down with bad government" (cf. Pagden and Canny, 1987), and the parameters of this model are not much upset if "the people" or "democracy" is substituted for "the king."

A good deal of the inspiration for these early modern political experiments came from Reformation theology which, as we have seen in the work of Wagner and Dumont, merged the medieval cycle of clerical reform with the political theory of secular rule. It is in this context that Burke (1978) speaks of a reform movement that spanned the medieval and early modern periods – also excellently analyzed by Bakhtin (1984) – whereby the "godly" reformers asserted an absolutely distinct and deeply serious sacrality against its implication in profane affairs, not least through the struggle to transform popular festivities in which kings and nobles were also active participants. This is the context in which we can turn to the question of renunciation in European Christendom.

There are two strands of asceticism through medieval Christianity. On the one hand, the program of institutional reform within the church which emerged in the eleventh century and culminated – albeit with diametrically opposed political implications – in the Reformation involved an asceticism which sought to differentiate itself from the gross categories of everyday life and recover its sacrality. This is one way of understanding clerical reforms such as the prohibitions on priestly marriage and simony (sale of ecclesiastical offices), although these also emphasized the institutional distinction of the church in the context of its struggles with secular authority. On the other hand, there was a long tradition of a much more individualistic renunciation of worldly things as a path to the divine which recovered the ideal of apostolic poverty or the proto-egalitarianism of the prelapsarian Christian origin myth. It can be traced in early Christian monasticism, in twelfth-century movements like Catharism and Waldensianism, in the religious cosmology of late medieval pauper crusading or peasant rebellion (as captured in the famous refrain from the English peasant revolt of 1381, "when Adam delved and Eve span, who was then a gentleman?"), and in early modern movements such as Anabaptism (Cohn, 1957). This exemplifies a tension between hierarchy and egalitarianism in Christian thought, one perhaps in keeping with the logic of ranking hierarchy (Lévi-Strauss's "diametric structures') which permits both an egalitarian complementarity and, as we saw in chapter 1, a transitive hierarchalization (cf. Guenée, 1985: 43). But in medieval Europe it was the institutional asceticism of the hierarchical church which prevailed, while individualistic or egalitarian asceticism was repressed as heresy by a battery of institutions established to police it such as the Inquisition and the Dominican order. This, again, indicates the affinity of Christian thought with monadic resolutions to its own internal tensions whereby we encounter, from the medieval to the modern period, a series of different but always sovereign and monadic claims to mediate the transcendental. There is an instructive contrast here with the understanding of heresy developed within the *bhakti* orthodoxy of medieval South India, where heresy was viewed as a teaching of the gods which disturbed the cosmic order in its very foundations, rather than representing a heterodoxy of human provenance (Shulman, 1984: 28).

Although the preceding discussion has sought to accent continuities rather than ruptures in the history of European political formations, there is no denying a historical transition between medieval polities and the modern territorial nation-state, upon which there is an extensive sociological literature (e.g. Mann, 1986; Tilly, 1990; Spruyt, 1994; Ertman, 1997). In favoring an account of political ideology over the broadly materialist tone of this literature, my analysis risks an idealism or a historicism in implying that this transformation was inscribed in the very logic of European political categories. Some pains were taken in chapter 2 to show how such an assumption can be avoided within my theoretical enterprise, and I reiterate here that there was nothing preordained about the transformation, which also responded to a series of more or less contingent political and economic factors. There is neither space nor necessity to describe these factors in detail, but it is perhaps worth commenting briefly on certain aspects of them in order to underline the preceding argument.

Spruyt (1994) has suggested that various forms of political organization in Europe coexisted in the early modern period, such as city leagues, city-states, secular empires, and territorial nation-states. These forms had emerged from medieval polities as a result of a variety of conflicts and alliances between emperors and the papacy, kings, nobles, city merchants, and so on. But, he argues, it was ultimately the undivided, sovereign, territorial nation-state that predominated. And, as Ertman (1997) has shown, it was more specifically bureaucratic–constitutionalist states (like late seventeenth-century England) rather than patrimonial–absolutist states (like late seventeenth-century France) which finally prevailed, because their administrative efficiency lent them a competitive advantage that led to their eventual adoption throughout much of the European region. In France, the emerging nation-state was an achievement of the Capetian (and then the Valois) royal dynasty, despite its fiscal and military weakness *vis-à-vis* other political agents for much of its monarchical tenure. This success was built on the wreckage of the Carolingian empire, which – along with its ecclesiastical institutional

structure – had been predicated upon "feudal" ties of bilateral fealty between patrons and their vassals, in which service of various kinds by the
vassal was reciprocated, often by military protection or – in the case of
aristocratic military service – by the grant of lands as fief. The decline of the
Carolingian empire can be traced to the inability in the long term of its
leadership to keep its side of this bargain, and to the depredations of non-
Christian raiders from the north, east, and south of the European heartlands
who insinuated themselves into the resulting discord. In the wake of the
empire there arose in the eleventh century local castellanies or "banal lordships" which were predicated upon the ability of local strongmen to arrogate territorial control to themselves by force of arms. This resulted in an
intensification of the net exploitation of dependent rural cultivators, but it
also resulted in the elimination of chattel slavery through the equalization
of peasant status, and a certain accommodation between peasants and banal lords within distinct territorial domains (Duby, 1974; Davies, 1996).
In France, the Capetian monarchy which had succeeded the Carolingians
with papal blessing in AD 987 was extraordinarily weak at this time, and
barely possessed authority outside its ancestral domains. However, it was
able to assert an increasing hegemony over the succeeding centuries by
legitimating peasant rights against the arbitrary demands of local lordships
and developing a proto-absolutist bureaucracy. Moreover, it could call upon
the legacy of theocratic kingship as a weapon in this process. As Heesterman
(1997) among others has argued, West European rulers had to reconstitute small, local territorial units which viewed themselves as exclusive areas
of peace into broader political domains, and their success in this respect
reflected the superior legitimacy of their political claims as well as more
pragmatic considerations of material interest on the part of the urban citi-
zens and subject peasantry who allied themselves with the monarchy. If
this success was later to lead to the fetishization of state power in absolutist
regimes which became strong enough to abrogate more variegated customary rights within their dominions in ways that provoked significant social conflicts and disturbed the coordination of national identity with the
sovereign state, their hold on the core ideological element of a monadic
political legitimacy enabled them in the longer run to stabilize national
allegiance around their territorial political claims. Although they were never
completely successful in this, as the later history of European ethnonationalist
movements testifies, it is significant that these movements have almost invariably conceived their counter-claims in terms of secession, thereby preserving the same monadic political logic.

We can therefore identify three broad trends in the political developments around the late medieval and early modern periods. First, a rough
territorialization of political identities at various levels of inclusiveness, from

the domains of the local lord, to those of territorial kingships and thence to the whole of European Christendom modeled after the Roman empire. Second, particularly in relation to the monarchical unravelling of local aristocratic power, a conscious sense of the distinction between government and community, or what we might now call state and society. As Joseph Strayer puts it, "Government was something separate from the folk-ways of the community, and a realization of this separateness was an essential ingredient in state-building" (Strayer, 1970: 18). Third, there was an idea of unitary political authority embodied in the office of the secular king which represented a transformation of Christian politico-religious thought. This was conducive to the emergence of the sovereign, nation-state. My argument here is that the victory of this mode of political organization over countervailing forms of power was not just to do with its superior efficiency – though this was assuredly a factor – but also because of the proto-nationalist consensus about the character of legitimate power which had been embodied in the king's office and its transformation into the idea of representative secular government. The implications of this for the emergence of racial and colonial ideologies will be examined in chapter 4.

India

We now turn to the case of India in order to provide a parallel argument about the development of its political categories from the ancient to the early modern period. Indian state formation, I suggest, has differed from European forms insofar as it has been characterized by a plurality of overlapping political centers, but one integrated within a more overarching and systemic structure of political organization. Ronald Inden (1990) coins the term "imperial formations" to refer to this, which captures something of their character. Unlike sovereign monarchies or nation-states, land empires do not have clear territorial boundaries. They are inherently (if not always actually) expansionary, attempting to encompass greater territory. Since imperial rule imposes itself over large areas admitting to great variability in the social organization of local elites and subjects, empires are also characterized by a series of internal frontiers in relation to the intermeshing of imperial and local power (Embree, 1977). In Heesterman's words, they show "a resilient multicentric pattern geared to expansion on the basis of horizontally dispersed and dovetailing power" (Heesterman, 1997: 106), though quite how dispersed and multicentric Indian empires have been has proved a controversial topic. Thus, as suggested above, the imperial model is based upon the *incorporation* of heterogeneous groups of people, whereas the sovereign model is based upon the *delimitation* of territory around a homogeneous political community. However, when applied to India, the term "imperial" imports many misleading connotations from its European context. In the present section I will examine some of the other attempts to describe the ideal-typical character of the Indian state in the extensive scholarly literature on the topic (e.g. Stein, 1980; Heesterman, 1985; Tambiah, 1985; Dirks, 1993; Quigley, 1993; Kulke, 1997), and draw upon aspects of Tambiah's concept of the "pulsating galactic polity" to grasp the character of the systemic integration (or, using the terminology developed in chapter 2, cultural metacontext) which Inden wishes to emphasize.

We will begin by considering briefly a specific empirical example, namely Burton Stein's (1980) influential, if controversial, analysis of the Chola empire in medieval South India, which flourished from c. AD 850–1300. Through a consideration of Stein's approach, we will draw out some more general postulates about the character of Indian state formation which we will then subject to further analysis.

The cornerstone of Stein's argument is that, against earlier scholarship which viewed it as a geographically extensive, centralized, empire, the Chola state must be understood as a large regional polity assembled from smaller geopolitical units which functioned as autonomous political entities, so that the authority of the central ruler is manifested almost entirely in ceremonial or ritual rather than in political or economic terms. Although there might appear to be parallels here with analyses of feudalism in medieval Europe which emphasize the "parcelization" or "downward allocation" of sovereignty from the apical point of the monarch to integrated local domains of politico-economic relationships (Anderson, 1974: 148), Stein does not generate the political order of Chola society at large through any such disintegration from an apical point. According to him, although the Chola king possessed a ritually integrative capacity of often exceptional territorial reach, his political and economic control was very geographically limited; such control was vested in the localized territorial segments (*nadus* in the Chola polity) of an essentially autonomous agrarian or peasant society, so that attempts at state-building by aggregation from below or by political imposition from above were limited by the continually fissiparous nature of the fundamental sociopolitical order. For Stein, the *nadu* was the "natural unit" of South Indian society which persisted well into the modern period. Thus, unlike the attempts of later rulers such as Tipu Sultan and the English East India Company to break down the complex set of local communal structures through vertical integration, the Chola state worked with this fractured, horizontal sovereignty by extending only a ritual suzerainty over the localized political segments. Drawing upon the distinction made in the early Brahmanic texts of the *Dharmasastras* between *kshatra* and *rajadharma*, Stein argues that the South Indian political system admitted to multicentric sovereignty; at the local level, there could be many "little kings" exercising secular authority after the *kshatriya* model, but there could only be one *raja* with ultimate ritual authority. Thus, local chiefs paid ritual obeisance to the king, while exerting full economic and political control within their own rather limited dominions.

Stein's analysis is mainly restricted to the Cholas, but he makes clear his belief in the pan-Indian implications of his model. And, although there are grounds for arguing that he understresses the extent of Chola political centeredness (Subbarayalu, 1982; Heitzman, 1997), the general theme of differentiated, shared sovereignty recurs throughout analyses of Indian polities from quite different regions and periods. This, arguably, constitutes *prima facie* evidence for the view that these features of the political landscape represent part of a pan-Indian cultural metacontext which, quite to the contrary of the monadic sovereignty we have traced in the European case, is predicated upon readily partible or shared conceptions of political authority. This is effectively the view taken by Jan Heesterman (1985; 1989), who elevates it to a fundamental and enduring tension in Indian society by reconstructing it in the earliest pre-classical texts of ancient India and tracing it through even to the eighteenth-century Mughal successor states. Let us appraise this argument as a context for our broader analysis of state formation in India.

Heesterman (1989) examines the character of the disjunction between *kshatra* and *raja* mentioned by Stein in the *varna* scheme of the classical Vedic literature. Here, the king (*raja*) is almost completely subsumed within the category of warrior (*kshatriya*), such that kings are conventionally regarded as *kshatriya*. Heesterman argues that the *raja* then emerges as an essentially sacral or priestly figure in contradistinction to the *kshatriya* as ruler/warrior. This establishes a complementary opposition. On the one hand, the *raja* is the numinous figure of the settled sacrificer who brings into being the order of the world. On the other, the *kshatriya* wanders the margins of the world, yielding to nobody in his unstinting vocation as a fighter. The distinction is represented in the Vedic ritual of the horse sacrifice, where the warrior lets loose his horse for a year, fighting anyone who challenges its wanderings, thereby establishing a territorial domain in which he settles thereafter. Kings are therefore both the foundation of a social order and predatory figures beyond the stable boundaries they establish, a point which conforms to the identities in Indic thought between kings and bandits, from whose obscure ranks new kings frequently emerge. In a comparative analysis of kingship, Geertz (1983) identifies these two forms of kingship – the sedentary, sacral king and the peripatetic, martial king – as structurally differentiated types, contrasting the hierarchical numinosity of the Indic kingship in medieval Java – "ruler over rulers of the world, spirit of the spiritual, unconceivable of the unconceivable" (ibid.: 130) – with the ceaseless activity of the king at a later period in Morocco, whose constant martial perambulations through his domain were constitutive of his sovereignty. But here (and, arguably, in Geertz's Indonesian case too; see Tambiah, 1985: 316–38) both conceptions are brought together in a Vedic complementarity of *raja* and *kshatriya* as symbolics of power; figuratively or actually, the numinous king moves through his domain, consecrating it through temple dedication and sacrifice. Yet he enjoys no ultimate authority, and the martial predation of rival would-be *rajas* is part of an ideology of power with conflict among equals at its very core. Thus we might say that, perhaps ironically, the dualistic cosmology of European Christendom has affinities with a monadic conception of political sovereignty, whereas the monadic cosmology underlying Indic kingship is more open to the possibility of plural political authority. But we need to examine more closely the character of this plurality and, more specifically, the way in which claims to authority are sustained within it through recourse to the transcendent.

Heesterman (1985) proposes three historical stages in the social relations pertaining to the transcendent order. In the first pre-classical stage associated with the transhumant pastoralist lifestyle of the Aryan-speaking peoples, the transcendent order was approached through rituals of agonistic sacrifice between two parties, a prototype whose trace is apparent in later writings such as the fratricidal war described in the epic poem the *Bhagavad Gita*, whereby the god Krishna assures the doubtful warrior Arjuna of the war's compatibility with the proper order of things. The purpose of sacrifice in this primordial order was to assure the victory of human life over death by removing the impurity of death from the patron of the sacrifice, the *yajamana* (or jajman). In contrast to later ideas of purity as a transcendent ideal, purity and impurity figure here as complementary opposites. Impurity or "evil" had to be passed from the "winning" patron of the sacrifice to the officiant in order to be converted into purity or "auspiciousness," which then had to be reappropriated by the patron from the officiant, a treacherous transaction in the context of agonistic sacrificial exchange. Indeed, the whole sacrificial order was suffused with the possibility of danger, violence, and death, and therefore with what Heesterman (1989) describes as an "awesome sacredness."

The outline of three kinds of person which were later to be more sharply differentiated are incipient in this primordial sacrificial order, namely the *raja*, *kshatriya*, and *brahman*. As we have seen, Heesterman contrasts the initial pair as respectively the sacrificer-king of the sedentary political community who underwrites its viability, and the ascetic, unyielding warrior who traverses the wilderness beyond established communities and is, as it were, the nemesis of the king. It is not difficult to see in these categories echoes of everyday life for a pastoral people cycling between an itinerant and sedentary existence, not least in the context of dynastic intrigues which must have deposed settled kings and brought in new ones. However, as Heesterman (1989) argues, these echoes are elevated in sacrificial ritual to the status of cosmological principle. In this respect, the renunciatory asceticism of the warrior provides a model for transcendence which is central to the third category, the *brahman*.

Heesterman's second stage, associated with the classical writings of the Vedic literature, represents the overcoming and, in a sense, the "domestication" of agonistic sacrifice by Brahmanism. Instead of a combative ritual transacted between equals, the *yajamana* is the single patron of the sacrifice, and the *brahman* the ritual specialist who acts as its officiant. Conquest is eliminated from the sacrifice, and violent sacrality replaced by detailed ritualistic prescription. Thus, the incipient categories of the preclassical stage are concretized into the *varna* scheme of caste hierarchy. In the classical stage, the *raja* threatens to disappear from view. No longer a sacrificer, the king's ritual role appears as a generous donor or patron of sustaining rituals whose custodians are the *brahmans* (cf. Shulman, 1985). In this respect, it seems that the king has surrendered his transcendent, numinous capacities to the *brahman*, much as in the Dumontian formula of the king's "power" submitting to the *brahman*'s "status." Although the *brahman* now possesses a protective layer of ritualism from the violent transcendence after the pre-classical model, he nevertheless assumes the full mantle of transcendence which is compromised by any participation in the mundane order of everyday life. Thus, in each case we can contrast, as it were, the "ideal" and the "real" person. The ideal king is the *raja*, the self-sufficient ruler whose access to the transcendent order seals his actions with authority. The ideal brahman is the renouncer, the self-sufficient sacrificer whose access to the transcendent order is not compromised by any extraneous dependencies. Both ideals are unrealizable. The "real" king holds political society together through his patronage and martial prowess rather than through any special authority, and the "real" brahman is the priest, who officiates at royal ceremonies and purifies the king by taking on his impurity. Herein lies the insoluble contradiction between the mundane and the transcendent orders. For the king to assume the mantle of legitimate rule, he requires perfect access to the transcendent order which he can never achieve. For the *brahman* to achieve his desired transcendence he must eschew all dependence on others, yet to do so is an impossibility. Thus, "real" kings and brahmans try to complete themselves by connecting with their ideal "alter-egos" of the raja and the renouncer, but cannot properly do so. The situation does not correspond to the all-or-nothing secularization of the king's power by the *brahman's* status which is central to Dumont's theory, so much as the defective sacrality of both parties.

For Heesterman, recognition and endorsement of the classical ideal of purity has remained widespread in India up to the present day, but so too has recognition of the impossibility of the path to transcendence adumbrated in classical texts and the problems entailed by their substantial failure to pronounce upon codes for conduct in the mundane world. Thus, in Heesterman's third post-Vedic stage, the classical texts occupy the strange position of being both central (in theory) and peripheral (in practice) to extant conceptions of appropriate conduct. Arguably, however, while post-Vedic developments such as *bhakti* devotionalism and the Vaishnavite and Shaivite movements have extemporized around classical themes, later Hinduism has not rearticulated conceptions of the state or political order into the transcendent order, and Indian states almost up to the present day have been faced with the same ambiguities over the legitimation of hierarchy (Rudolph and Rudolph, 1985).

For example, Burghart (1996: 35–58) discusses evidence from the Hindu kingdom of Nepal at the turn of the nineteenth century which shows how the king, brahman, and renouncer each articulated a different model of hierarchy, attempting to encompass and subordinate the others on the basis of their respective models. But relations between the three were characterized predominantly by recognition of the other's superiority within their own domain, and delicate efforts at mutual avoidance. We thus encounter separate models of authority whose relationship is ambiguous and complicated.

The Brahmanic model is neatly encapsulated in the *Vedic* hymn concerning the division of Purusha which was cited at the start of chapter 1. The Brahmanic world is an organic hierarchy of differentiated ritual function, with the highest status accorded to the purity of the *brahman*. Other functions are incorporated into the Brahmanic model in subordinate capacities, including that of the *kshatriya* ruler. In the Brahmanic law of the *Dharmasastras*, a model of social incorporation is articulated which retains the organic, hierarchical separation of function; communities coexist peaceably as functionally distinct entities integrated into a larger cosmological order (Rudolph and Rudolph, 1985). Royal power constitutes one such entity, whose function is to preserve the encompassing order. Thus, in the Brahmanic version of royal power the good king is not a usurper of the extant social order but its greatest protector, and the ephemeral earthly power which is wielded by any particular king in his expansionary political aims is subordinated to his conservative cosmological function. In this respect, the ideal realization of Brahmanic universalism eschews identification with any territorially bounded state.

Kingship, on the other hand, is often based upon dynastic models of patrilineal succession which attempt to appropriate Brahmanic authority by assuming the *kshatriya* mantle (see also chapter 5). This provided a ready model for the legitimacy of a would-be ruling lineage, which – with some judicious elaboration of genealogies – was thereby able to come into local caste society as high status *kshatriya*, despite frequently obscure origins. Brahmanic ideology permitted a divinization of the king as the protector of cosmic order. At the same time, the king attempted to secularize Brahmanic authority by incorporating *brahmans* as servants to royal *jajmans*. Thus, hierarchical models of Indian society involve the double apex of the brahman and the king, each professing the ability to incorporate the other. This, I would suggest, better conforms to the logic of Dumont's conception of encompassing hierarchy than his own argument that royal power is encompassed by priestly authority. At the same time, it differs from the European discourse of sovereignty which we traced in the previous section from Gelasius onwards, and which never departed from an essentially monadic conception of political authority.

Let us develop the implications of this point a little further. In the previous section, we examined the career of the sacred king in medieval Europe, whose prototype was Christ. In fact, the idea of the sacred king with similar properties occurs quite widely in different cultures. In one modality, the king is a kind of *primus inter pares* who, despite some claim to transcendent authority, must nevertheless act principally as a secular agent who establishes and maintains dominion through military or political skill. In another, the king mediates the human with the sacred worlds. Here, according to Sir James Frazer's (1922) classic analysis, he acts as a sacrificial object whose annihilation establishes this particular connection. Although, as Gillian Feeley-Harnik (1985) has shown, the argument is steeped with Christian tradition – Christ, the embodiment of an omnipotent god, is killed by human hands in order to reconstitute the human order in the domain of the sacred – it is easy to spot parallels in Indian tradition, such as in the myths concerning the kings Rama, Vena, and Prthu. For example, Pollock (1984) and Heesterman (1989) have shown in analyses of the *Ramayana* epic that King Rama represents a liminal figure, neither man nor god (a peculiarity of status rendered in his identification as an avatar of the god Vishnu), who is regarded not only as simultaneously abominable and sacred but also, like Frazer's sacrificial object, as beholden to external agency. However, in Christian political thought the sacrifice provides ideological closure – a complete model for reconstitution into the sacred – even if the legitimation of authority was never quite as straightforward as this for actual Christian kings, as we have seen. In the Indian case, on the other hand, there is no completely secure way of stabilizing political authority even at the ideal level.

This can be illustrated with reference to the theme of kingship in the recurrent Indian myth of Vena and Prthu, which I abridge from Shulman's account (1985: 75–88). Although one must of course take care not simply to assume that such myths reflect political reality, the advantage of describing them here is that they provide a lapidary statement of tensions which historical sources do seem to suggest were actually manifested. In the myth, Vena is the paradigm of the evil, violent king who spurns all attempts at Brahmanic mediation of his authority on the grounds that he is himself the complete embodiment of divinity so that, like the *Rig Veda*'s Purusha, he professes to combine in his person the subject, object, and context of the sacrifice (cf. Heesterman, 1985: 231). Because, through his arrogance, he unwittingly appropriates the role of a person-dissolving, world-creating renunciation, the *brahmans* take him at his word and kill him. But the kingdom, now without a king, succumbs to complete disorder. The *brahmans* are able to restore the kingdom by creating out of Vena's body a homunculus which absorbs his evil and becomes the ancestor of the "wild tribes" beyond the civilized realm, and then the two "pure" figures of King Prthu and his sister/wife Arcis. Prthu restores order by acting as the focal point of redistribution and, unlike Vena, as the patron of Brahmanic sacrifice thus validating the dyadic relationship between kings and brahmans rather than attempting to subvert it, as Vena's monism did. But in doing so he reprises the original problems faced by the "real" king and brahman as they contemplate their "ideal" counterparts. In this respect, the myth's source in Brahmanism need not throw its dramatization of the insecure basis of authority into question.

A key message of this myth seems to be the denial of monism. The king must *not* incorporate himself, or create the kingdom out of his putative divinity, but must act as the secular patron in dyadic exchanges, most crucially with the brahmans. This, of course, contrasts with the ideologies of kingship in European Christendom which we examined in the previous section, and we can draw several broader conclusions from the Vena/Prthu myth which underscore the distinction. First, in the Indian case, we encounter a more genuine differentiation of function *vis-à-vis* the transcendent order in the role of the king and the brahman, rather than simply the rival claims to the same transcendence we encountered in the conflict between the representatives of secular and clerical authority in Europe. But these functions are shorn of the ability to make any final claim over transcendence, precipitating an instability in their respective domains of action which has at least two important consequences. First, it establishes an inherent danger of collapse in political structures. This is dramatized in the spellbinding myth concerning the King of Maturai in the pre-Chola Tamil poem, the *Cilappatikaram*, also analyzed by Shulman (1985). When it is revealed that the king has mistakenly convicted and executed the story's

innocent protagonist, he immediately loses all semblance of royal authority, indeed becomes a caricature of the pretension to that authority, and
then dies. The story dramatizes the thinness of the line between authority
and mere violence or political muscle. Thus – and this is the second point –
such political conceptions in theory render appropriation easy by those
who would profess the ability to be kings or brahmans through the very
recognition of the impossibility of ever being a proper king or brahman.
Again, this contrasts with the European situation, which is well summarized by Baechler as follows:

> The polities set up by the Barbarians to succeed the Roman Empire remained
> *virtually* remarkably stable. Cases of usurpation of the throne are astonish
> ingly few, which indicates a very deep faith in the idea of monarchical legiti
> macy. . . . In vain were the kings reduced to the political role that was allowed
> them in their power as lords: over all their rivals they benefited from one
> decisive advantage. Whereas the conquered are eliminated from the game,
> the kings can lose every battle (Baechler, 1988: 43)

And, indeed, as we have seen, while the aspirations to political control of
kings in medieval Europe often received scant respect or reward, this did not
affect their grip on sovereignty. The situation could not be more different in
India, with its innumerable succession of rulers vying over a political authority which seems to be inherently exiguous. The motif of an unattainable
transcendence also bears upon the "urge to transformation" which was remarked in chapter 1 and which is evinced in the textual sources by a fascination with, but also an abhorrence for, transgressive categories like the warrior
brahman or the king as clown or renouncer, a point to which we shall return
below. At the same time, it lends a certain credence to Stein's analysis of the
Chola polity insofar as the king's greatness is measured by his ability to confer resources upon others, and therefore comes at the expense of his own
self-aggrandizement. Drawing these points together, Shulman postulates

> a system of delicate balance in which a heavy surplus of evil flows outward via
> the Brahmin priests, under the watchful eyes of a weakened arbiter, the king;
> in which royal splendor . . . can only be extracted from the sacrifice, hence
> from an unending circulatory process that created the Brahmin–king inter
> dependence; and in which control over this process is always threatening to
> break down as both the major figures, saddled with impossible ambivalence
> toward each other and toward themselves, cling reluctantly to the thin life
> line of their common . . . distaste for disorder. (Shulman, 1985: 88)

Shulman's argument is broadly in keeping with that of scholars like
Dumont and Heesterman whose work has recently been criticized for its

Orientalist assumptions. As I suggested earlier, however, one of the problems with the recent critiques of Orientalism is their somewhat paradoxical tendency to elide a critique both of the exoticism which overstates cultural "difference" and the reductionism of sociological explanations couched in the familiar categories of Western social science or historical experience, leading to forms of theoretical obviation which propound a countervailing reductionism (by affecting to provide the "real" explanation for the Indian social world hitherto concealed by Orientalist distortions) or a hyper-exoticism, in neither case appreciating more reflexively the mutual implication of Western social science with the discourses it takes as its object and their historical grounding. By moving on to an appraisal of some of these critiques, then, I hope to offer a way of understanding Indian political categories which steers between these pitfalls.

Let us begin by considering a sharply critical review paper of Heesterman's 1985 book by Ronald Inden (1986), and some of the alternative arguments mounted in Inden's later book (Inden, 1990). Inden lodges three related objections to Heesterman's position. First, he criticizes Heesterman for essentialism in the idea of a single Indian "tradition" which imposes an inexorably determining logic throughout the whole vast history of the subcontinent. In his words,

> To assume that India has an essence is to devalue the actions of the transitory agents of India's past (and present, too). Acts ranging all the way from the performance of Vedic sacrifices to wars are construed not as the acts that have made India and Indians what they are at a particular moment or over a period of time, they are simply assumed to be expressions of (or temporary departures from) the underlying essence of the civilization. (Inden, 1986: 774)

Second, Inden criticizes Heesterman's Weberianism and the associated condemnation of Indian political thought implied in the "irrational" disjunction of authority Heesterman posits. And, third, he gives examples of enduring and successful solutions to Heesterman's supposed "problem" of royal authority in Indian history, notably royal land grants for the establishment of brahman villages (*brahmadeyas*) within the royal domains which enabled kings to partake of brahmanic authority, and the theism of post-Vedic religious traditions such as Vaishnavism and Shaivism which, in Inden's view, could and did provide kings with the same theocratic warrant for secular power that we encountered in medieval Europe.

Now, we have already devoted much attention in earlier chapters to questions of essentialism and historical determination. While Heesterman can certainly be accused of a rather one-dimensional gaze over Indian history, Inden's appeal to the mystique of human practice in his "transitory agents" of history does not, in the light of our foregoing critique, constitute an especially convincing alternative. Inden's second point does, however, highlight Heesterman's debt to Weber's unfortunate conflation of rationalization as a peculiarity of European state formation with a normative sense of its "rationality" (Weber, 1946: 298–9). But perhaps Inden does not give full due to Weber's ambivalence about rationalization, nor to the peculiar disjunctions with which it has been associated in the West, a point Heesterman himself addresses (e.g. Heesterman, 1985: 157; 1997: 115). This underlines another issue which Inden somewhat neglects: the fact that political ideologies contain particular aporia or contradictions does not mean that they are incapable of achieving stability or "success." This should be clear enough from the long history of European triumphalism about its own political forms despite the violent contradictions they have entailed. Thus, the mutuality between kings and brahmans expressed via the *brahmadeyas* – even if it does circumvent the problem of the brahmanic gift, which is debatable at the very least (cf. Shulman, 1984) – does not necessarily constitute evidence for the absence of a contradiction. Moreover, whereas Inden detects the pejorative inference of "irrationality" in the theme of disjunction which writers like Heesterman and Shulman emphasize in Indian political discourse, quite the opposite assumption could be made. One should perhaps resist the temptation to confer upon Indians superior abilities as sociological ironists, but the fact that the political discourses we have examined emphasize rather than efface the impossibility of legitimating power could just as well be taken as evidence of a sophisticated "rationality," if it were ever possible to stand outside the consequential effects of the very modes of thought being compared.

Inden's reference to the legitimating potential of Vaishnavism and Shaivism raises different issues. It is undoubtedly true that Heesterman ignores these religious traditions and their role in legitimating political power, but it is less clear that in this role they entirely circumvent the "conundrum" of the king's authority. The clearest formulation of the problem has come in analyses of the relationship between royal authority and temple-based Vaishnavism and Shaivism, mainly in South India but also elsewhere (e.g. Appadurai and Breckenridge, 1976; Stein, 1980; Appadurai, 1981; Shulman, 1985; Peabody, 1991a; Dirks, 1993; Inden, 1995; Schnepel, 1995). Medieval South India comprised a set of cross-cutting locality communities on the basis of territorial, lineage, and cultic loyalties which were more or less successfully stabilized around sectarian temples. The deity of Vaishnavite temples was conceived as a king who presided over a kind of jajmani structure of local redistribution, rather than of exclusive territorial control (Appadurai and Breckenridge, 1976). Actual kings, on the other hand, typically emerged from successfully expansionary warrior chieftaincies and were therefore essentially territorially delimited *primus inter pares* who often sought legitimation through temple patronage. There is a certain amount of expert disagreement concerning whether royal authority was dependent upon or was merely augmented by temple legitimation (Appadurai, 1981; Dirks, 1993). In the British colonial period temples gained in power at the expense of kings, but in medieval India one can say more safely that locality societies which were integrated around temples coexisted with sacral kingship.

Perhaps the crux of the issue lies here. On the basis of Vaishnavite texts, Inden (1995) has discussed the way that the paramount "king of kings" in medieval India performed or constituted his power through ceremonial royal procession in which the king embodied Vishnu, not as a transcendent godhead but as a specific form immanent to the context of the procession. Thus, we might say, god is embodied or contained as a king in the king's person. This contrasts with the situation in medieval Europe where, as we saw earlier, the king's person is an embodiment of god. In the former case the king – even though he is an exceptional, paramount king – never embodies the complete transcendence of the deity, as is the case in the Christian conception. And less superior kings are even less able to dissolve rival claims to transcendent authority, as when they lose control of temple objects which embody the deity's divinity either through capture by rivals or, more tellingly, bestowal by sectarian leaders who thereby indicate their autonomous authority (Peabody, 1991a; Schnepel, 1995). A different limitation occurs where the king turns to the ascetic Shaivite cult in order to warrant his authority, since this culminates in the king adopting the guise of the renouncer, and thus neglecting his royal duty. For this reason, as Shulman (1985) explains, the texts enjoin the king not to engage in doomed attempts to transcend his violent, secular agency. This underlines once again the point made earlier that – unlike Europe – the political discourse of medieval India created genuinely different foundational ways of constituting the social order, but within the same cultural metacontext, so that instead of simple conflict between competing versions of the right social order we encounter a complex articulation which permits each version to encompass the others within specific contexts (Malamoud, 1981; Peabody, 1991a). Here, I have dwelled upon the irresolvable contradictions which are brought to the fore in this mode of political discourse in order to distinguish the Indian case from the European one, where a series of categories – like the *corpus mysticum*, or the nation, or race – has been invoked to make good the contradictions involved in supposing a single order of transcendence. But – and here I agree with Inden – this need not imply that social arrangements in medieval India such as the relation between kings, brahmans, and temples were unable to underwrite or unify a particular kind of perduring social order.

This becomes a significant point when we turn to examine Declan Quigley's theory of caste, which is based on a somewhat different appraisal of the disjunction between kingship and locality societies. Quigley criticizes Dumont's view of a Brahmanic preeminence based upon purity, highlighting on the contrary the ambiguity of Brahmanic status through its association with the absorption of impurity. Drawing upon the earlier work of Hocart, Quigley seeks to make kingship central to caste relations, since – before British colonialism interceded by eliminating kings and elevating *brahmans* – it was above all the purity of the ruler to which ritual action was directed. He thereby draws out the implications of the "radial" model discussed in chapter 1, with its plurality of political centers, for a theory of caste, showing how a pattern of divided sovereignty of the kind described above creates a set of overlapping centers whose position in status terms is ambiguous and contextual. The pervasiveness of the concern with purity in caste society is explained as a replication of "royal" ceremonial in these circumstances, where each caste unit seeks to purify itself and gain restitution from the inherent evil of its actions, just as the king does. However, whereas I argued in chapter 1 through recourse to Lévi-Strauss's analysis of dual organizations that this situation of plural sovereignty could be encompassed as a specific conception of political authority, Quigley suggests that it results from the ineffective centralization of kingships which would otherwise be more unified, so that plural sovereignty emerges from a tension between politically centralizing kingship and the fissiparous tendencies caused by kin relations as an alternative basis for corporate political organization in the context of kingship's relative failure. In his words,

> Constant internecine conflict and the always available option of moving to another kingdom, another administration, or to virgin territory, turned precolonial India into a collection of fragile patrimonial states, endlessly crumbling and being rebuilt. On the other hand, there was little alternative but to strive for centralization. . . . Caste results when kingship attempts to assert itself against kinship but ultimately fails because the conditions do not allow for stable kingdoms. Put another way, caste results when the retention of power and the imposition of stability through kingship are continually under threat and there is no option but to fall back on kinship. (Quigley, 1993: 129–30)

Thus, Quigley posits a different kind of political instability to Heesterman which is predicated upon the idea that Indian states have been weak, a situation explicable ultimately by the environmental contingency of low population density relative to habitable land in precolonial India, such that cultivators were always able to escape political encapsulation.

Quigley's analysis represents a self-conscious attempt to mediate between idealist and materialist approaches by understanding caste in relation to kingship as a particular form of political authority which, in caste systems, is weakened by exogenous material factors. He invokes Hocart as an appropriate precursor for such an attempt, but there is an ambiguity here which is worth emphasizing. As we saw earlier, Frazer's original anthropological formulation of sacral kingship drew upon a specifically Christian understanding of transcendent authority. Yet, as Feeley-Harnik (1985) shows, this context was increasingly sundered from the anthropological framework, most notably by Hocart (1936) and then Evans-Pritchard (1948), who presented a secularized understanding of kingship as a social-structural position and saw regicide as a feature of weak polities rather than a particular representation of the cosmological order. Rituals of kingship can then be seen as attempts to transform an individual person into the bearer of a political office functionally derived from universal social-structural forces, and their specificity is thereby denied. Alternatively, Feeley-Harnik stresses the "culturally specific ways in which abstractions are created out of homely materials" such that people, always "intensely human," are made into things and ideas "both more or less than persons" (Feeley-Harnik, 1985: 279-81). Hocart indeed recognized this point in his conception of ritual as world-ordering practice directed at effecting human intentions (Hocart, 1936: 69), but the question here is the extent to which the objective constraints upon these intentions are – as in the two moments of Marx's practice theory discussed in chapter 2 – best located in the historical accumulation of human practice or in material factors of an entirely extra-human kind. Quigley (1993: 134) is alive to the former possibility in endorsing Hocart's emphasis on the institutional tensions at the heart of caste society, but to my mind, as with Marx, this produces an explanation predicated upon a notion of value which is better encompassed in a theory of the metacontext (see chapter 2). Moreover, Quigley goes on to accord purely exogenous environmental determination considerable causal significance. On this point, while there is no denying that social forms vary with and are affected by environmental factors, I would argue that this relationship is likely to be less straightforward than Quigley suggests (cf. Sinha, 1965) and the evidence for material disjunctions between levels of political encapsulation in precolonial India seems doubtful at best, except perhaps for the early medieval period (Sinha, 1965; Fuller, 1989; Habib, 1992; Subrahmanyam, 1994). Thus, although he usefully turns the understanding of caste towards a comparative political sociology, Quigley's approach risks understressing some of the more culturally specific features involved in conceptions of political authority and concepts of the person in India within which, I would suggest, caste relations can be located, and which are not amenable to a materialist account of ineffective political centralization, or perhaps even to so singular an emphasis upon kingship.

My argument, then, is that the political categories of precolonial India are not at root the result of a tension between centralized political rule (kingship) and acephalous, decentralized corporate organization (kinship) occasioned by the weakness of the former, but are intrinsic to specific conceptions of political authority, although this does not entirely preclude the role of weak kingship or kin-ordered political organization. Indeed, it remains important to link an understanding of broader structures of political authority with their instantiation in local contexts where kinship constructs do act as organizing principles in social life, an issue to which we shall return. But the point I want to emphasize here is the specific "plural" character of political authority which transects different levels of political inclusiveness. As Stein has argued,

> The capacity of chiefs, *as well as kings*, to centralize resources is an important historical fact that is easily overlooked or trivialized because the simultaneity of enhanced power and authority by lesser and greater lords does indeed appear like a denial of centralization, as some critics charge. But this seems to me to essentialize central authority, forcing all historical kingdoms into the mould of the absolutist states that historians see in sixteenth to eighteenth century Europe, as well as in parts of southern and western Asia, where increased central authority always appeared to come at the expense of lesser lordships. (Stein, 1997: 139–40)

This centralization of political authority in Europe was not, however, a novel feature of absolutism but was also an implicit feature of earlier medieval political thought in Europe, as Stein recognizes in his definition of European feudalism as "a form of prebendalism based upon a high degree of political centredness" (ibid.: 137). Stein's analysis would thus seem to exemplify Heesterman's thesis on the ideological disjunction at the heart of Indian conceptions of political authority. The disjunction is not between the secular power of the king and the transcendent ritual authority of the brahman, as Dumont would have it, nor in the disjunction between brahmanical and royal authority analyzed earlier, but between different levels of what might be glossed as the "royal" authority of little kings or dominant castes on the one hand and the paramount king on the other. The apparent weakness of Indian polities is then seen to be an artefact of the analytical assumption that the legitimation of secular power must be a total one that flows from a single, transcendent source. In this respect, sociological approaches which emphasize the "weakness" or "instability" of political authority in India tend to derive their understanding of the situation from the particular history of political objectification in Western Europe, so that the plural, shifting, and contextual basis of political authority in India is wrongly taken as evidence for the inadequacy of stabilizing political institutions. Thus, while it is possible to agree with Mann (1986) that caste is almost the opposite of a Christian ecumene, it is extremely misleading to argue that Indian political history furnishes evidence of a perduring feudalism (Baechler, 1988), or of a weakness and instability which led to stagnation and foreign conquest (Hall, 1988); indeed, one might just as well say that it furnishes evidence of a supple and adaptive set of social institutions which were able to accommodate themselves to different historical contingencies, by contrast with the involution of the European ecumene. Although Stein's formulation of the Indian "segmentary state" avoids this pitfall, it still carries something of its flavor in the contrast between the ceremonial status of the paramount king and the politico-economic status of locality rulers, implicitly taking the latter as the "real" mark of authority.

This is not a novel criticism, and we shall shortly conclude this section by looking to approaches which have gone beyond Stein's rather problematic distinction. But let us first point to some implications of the preceding argument. Although our analysis of Indian political categories has suggested that attempts to determine which category of person sits atop the social structure may be to misunderstand the "radial" and contextual character of caste relations, this need not entirely undermine a more traditional concern with hierarchy. As Eisenstadt has suggested,

> To assume that Brahman cannot be hierarchically preeminent while being, at the same time, in some ways equivalent to Barbers, Untouchables, and other recipients of gifts from the ritually central jajmani, is to fall prey to an unnecessarily reified and concretized notion of social structure and social order. The order lies not in one fixed or internally consistent ranking, but in a pragmatically constituted set of shifting meanings and shifting configurations of castes. (Eisenstadt, 1997: 41)

Rather as Dumont (1980: 71–2) asserts the superiority of brahmanic purity "in theory" even when it submits to power "in fact," it may be possible to discern in Eisenstadt's argument traces of a brahmanic ideology seeking to establish its unassailable superiority even in the face of all evidence to the contrary, which Quigley (1993) has aptly criticized as the basis for a sociological theory of caste. Nonetheless, the argument is suggestive of one context I have tried to bring out in this section, namely a widespread recognition of the ultimate validity of brahmanic *ideals* – and not necessarily the superiority of *brahmans* – as a mode of connection to the transcendent order. As Heesterman (1985: 42) puts it, the question is not so much whether the *brahman* is superior or not, but of who the true brahman really is. In this respect, it is better not to think of *brahman*, *kshatriya*, and other categories as actual groups of people with an enduring historical presence so much as *brahman*ism, "*kshatriya*-ism," and, indeed, "*vaishya*-ism" and "*shudra*-ism" as particular models for behavior which actual groups of people are – with a greater or lesser degree of difficulty – able to appropriate. Srinivas's (1956) concept of "Sanskritization" is a generic expression for this process, for which endless historical examples could be provided. Even in contemporary times, the discourse of Hindu nationalism which otherwise seems to bear so little relation to precolonial politics can be seen in part as reviving Brahmanic discourses of "purity" within the novel framework of the nation as a political object (Hansen, 1996a; see also chapter 6). But as well as emulating Brahmanic mores, it is also possible to emulate *vaishya* ones or, as with the "right hand" castes of medieval South India, *kshatriya* ones (Heesterman, 1985; Stein, 1997; though see Subbarayalu, 1982). At the same time, there are considerable incentives towards forms of collective closure around these categories, because if they were too readily appropriable by anyone their status-enhancing capacity would be lost (Milner, 1994). So, for example, it is not in practice usually very easy to turn oneself into a *brahman*. In this respect, the logic of caste categorization may be amenable to standard Weberian sociological analysis. Over and above this, I have argued that the "radial" model of caste can be understood as being encompassed in a direction which points to a more unitary and apical sense of political authority, so that there are definite limits to the "shifting configurations of castes" described by Eisenstadt, and strong proclivities to recuperate royal and brahmanic preeminence.

In effect, then, it can be argued that a set of cultural representations is superimposed on the *varna* scheme; these representations provide particular models for social action which can be appropriated by different people in different circumstances. This is the context for Stein's argument that South India, if not indeed the subcontinent more generally, has seen the blending and interaction over several millennia of political and cultural representations from disparate sources into a single cultural system (Stein, 1980: 5–6). Thus, even where autonomous entities such as the Chola *nadus* exist, they nevertheless participate in a broader construction of cultural meaning. As Stein suggests,

> In being the socio-economic foundation of that medieval metasociety these locality societies should not be thought of as isolated or complete in themselves; all were part-societies, linked to more extensive formations in ways

dictated by historical contingencies in relation to their own attributes. Communities or localities were thus linked by political and cultic affiliations to the protection of great or small kings and gods and, increasingly, in later times, by commercial ties to even quite distant places in India and beyond. Still, as part-societies these communities of pre-modern South India retained historic identities and the capability to act with considerable independence regarding their internal constitutions and their external linkages. (Stein, 1997: 161)

Similarly, Chattopadhyaya describes caste formation in medieval India as a process in which a dominant *varna* ideology "drew widely dispersed and originally outlying groups into a structure which allowed them in a large measure to retain their original character except that this character was now defined with reference to the structure" (Chattopadhyaya, 1994: 203), a conception of shared sovereignty *oriented to* an apical point that again is clearly different from the "parcelized" sovereignty of European feudalism which *disintegrated* from an apical point (Anderson, 1974). In this respect, while it is doubtless correct to argue that no premodern state of any kind possessed the resources to achieve the thorough penetration of the civil order which occurs in the modern nation-state (Mann, 1986), it is nevertheless worth stressing the fact that conceptions of political authority in some premodern states, but not others, were effectively built upon this premise, even if the ubiquity of the modern state in everyday life so well analyzed by Foucault was nowhere envisaged, at least until after the Reformation. The premodern Indian states described by Chattopadhyaya were predicated on quite different assumptions, but in order for the processes of cultural unification he describes to prosper, a cultural metacontext propitious for such a situation of "ordered heterogeneity" was necessary. It is in this sense that Brahmanism and its later variations can be thought of as a set of cultural representations immanent in longer term "core symbols" in Indic thought in the sense defined in chapter 2, which have exerted a unifying force in the Indian subcontinent. Thus, while one can concede with Ainslie Embree and others that "Hinduism" has possessed no unifying political character in Indian history in the sense that it has not, as has been the case with European politico-religious thought, brought the transcendental into a direct relation with the mundane to provide a mandate for a singular political sovereignty which orients people's fundamental sense of being to an identification with the state (Embree, 1985; Rudolph and Rudolph, 1985; Eisenstadt, 1997), we can nevertheless appreciate the sense in which Brahmanism has been politically and culturally unifying. It is not that an essentialized group of actual people – "the *brahmans*" – stamped their culture upon a chaotic social order and thereby established their hegemony over it, but that Brahmanic ideology as a system of representations has done so in determinate ways which, however, admit to considerable contestation. Here we have traced one such arena of contestation in the problem of or ambiguity over the king's legitimacy.

My argument nevertheless contains the danger of propounding an essentialism which makes one particular context definitive of a "culture" and neglects the complexity of the relations between its constitutive representations. This point is made by Inden (1990), whose position suggests that even if it were possible to see India as anything other than an intellectual abstraction, its people must be understood as producing different political and social forms over space and time. These include the one I have abstracted as a European archetype, the single territorial polity united under a supreme rulership, which Inden sees in the recurring Indian category of the universal king or *cakravartin*, and finds manifested in the Rashtrakuta imperial formation of the central Indian Deccan from the eighth to the tenth century AD. Other writers, conversely, see the *cakravartin* model as an unrealized, even utopian, abstraction (e.g. Gonda, 1969; Thapar, 1992; Chattopadhyaya, 1994), or as the centerpiece of a more diffuse conception of political authority:

> The *cakravartin*'s rule was not absolute; it was best expressed in the formula "king of kings," a term which implies the existence of lesser kings over whom the *cakravartin* presided. The lesser kings, once they recognized the supremacy of the center, were allowed to remain the heads of virtually autonomous vassal states. Hence, the polity could be represented as a center-oriented arrangement wherein satellite principalities or provinces of various magnitudes revolved around the central domain. The satellites reproduced the features of the center on a decreasing scale in a system of graduated autonomies. (Tambiah, 1985: 323)

This constitutes the mandala structure of what Tambiah refers to as the "galactic polity," whose several features include a dynamic of expansion and contraction from exemplary centers – the seat of the *cakravartin* – according to the ability of the paramount king to incorporate outlying polities and preserve them within the ambit of his authority on the basis of religious, political, and economic motivations which Tambiah conceives as inseparably combined. In this respect, Inden's quasi-sovereign model of the *cakravartin* might be viewed as one modality of the pulsating dynamism inherent to the galactic polity which also encompasses, at the other extreme, the radial model of political authority. But, as Tambiah shows, there is a constant replication of the exemplary center even in lesser centers beyond its ambit, suggesting a unified field of political values. This, I would argue, casts some doubt on approaches to caste which place the burden of explanation upon ineffective political centralization. A similar point would apply *mutatis mutandis* to writers who wish to do away with the concept of caste. For example, in research on Bengal in the early modern period which subsequently led him to reject the idea of caste, Inden (1976) finds that the proliferation of the endogamous, ranked *jatis* later taken to be definitive of caste emerged in the context of Muslim conquest as a means of establishing rank in the absence of a world-ordering Hindu king and in the face of polluting contact with the new rulers. This argument may be plausible, but it still invokes a prior and very particular emphasis on kingship, rank, and purity.

Tambiah formulates his analytical model through a procedure he calls "totalization," attempting to steer between various familiar explanatory frameworks in sociology which privilege some particular quality of the social world – culture, the economic or ecological "base," power, and so on – as an exogenous explanatory factor:

> I have tried to show that the geometry of the galactic polity is manifest as a recurring design at various levels that the analyst labelled cosmological, territorial, administrative, politico-economic, but that the accurate exegesis is that this recurring design is the reflection of the multifaceted polyvalence built into the dominant indigenous concepts, and of the traditional idea of a simultaneous convergence of phenomena in a *mandala* pattern. A corollary of this demonstration is that the cultural model and the pragmatic parameters are in concordance and buttress one another, and cannot be disaggregated. (Tambiah, 1985: 280)

Thus, Tambiah attempts to show how a political order, the mandala pattern, generates a particular structure of socioeconomic relationships while simultaneously showing how that order is structured by socioeconomic factors, such as the organization of rice agriculture. By foregrounding the analytical assumptions he brings to the empirical account within his mode of analytical exegesis, he is able to avoid the problem of exogeneity which, I would argue, still attends the efforts of a writer like Quigley to transcend the antinomy of idealism and materialism, but he does so by invoking the idea of mutual constitution at the base of a causal account in a way that seems ultimately evasive. Rather than invoking conjointly a "materialist" explanation from the agrarian base or periphery and an "idealist" explanation from the politico-religious superstructure or center, a better extension of his approach might be to provide a historical account of the metacontext framing both kinds of explanation. This would be in keeping with the theoretical model outlined in chapter 2, although I would not claim to have achieved such an account at the rather general level of analysis undertaken in this book. It should also perhaps be added that while Tambiah has generally limited his galactic polity model to analysis of Buddhist Southeast

Asian polities, others have suggested its wider applicability (Seneviratne, 1987). However, while concurring on its relevance to India, I would argue that my foregoing analysis of medieval Europe calls into question Seneviratne's (1987: 154) view of its "near universality . . . as a pre-modern political formation."

Another example of attempts to create a sovereign territorial polity in precolonial India is provided in analyses of the political use to which the Indian epic poem the *Ramayana* has been put, especially by contrast to the other great epic, the *Mahabharata* (Thapar, 1989; Pollock, 1993). The central theme of the *Mahabharata* is fratricidal struggle for dominion, to which the only response can be a transcendental turn to unity at a higher level. This approximates the model of fractured sovereignty and transcendent unity which I have pursued as definitive of Indian tradition in this chapter. The *Ramayana*, on the other hand, describes the vicissitudes of King Rama's life in terms which evince a much more territorialized and sovereign understanding of political authority, thereby permitting its appropriation in particular historical periods to create a sense of an exclusive political community. Thus, it was used in the eighth century AD as a warrant for the conquest of forest tribes by Brahmanized monarchical states, and in the twelfth century as a model to define and fix a "Hindu" political community against a disparaged "other" in the form of Muslim invaders from the north. In the latter case, it is significant that the ideological response to present uncertainties was to invent a unitary political community legitimated in relation to the past, an "invention of tradition" familiar from the example of nationalisms in modern Europe and which, as we shall see in chapter 6, now haunts contemporary Indian politics. However, these elaborations of the Rama myth did not constitute the fabrication of a *post facto* tradition foisted on an extant political order in accordance with some practical exigency, as is generally the implication of the "invention of tradition" literature. On the contrary, the elaboration was the very construction of such an order. One is reminded here of Kafka's extraordinary story *The Great Wall of China*. We imagine the wall to be constructed by an empire, already unitary, in order to protect incursions at its boundaries. Instead, we learn that the construction of the wall was actually the construction of the unitary empire itself, the process of organizing a massive workforce and of signifying external threat being constitutive of political order. But if the foregoing analysis is accepted, it could be argued that this represents a particular obviation of extant conceptions of political authority which were capable of expansion in order to create an encompassing sense of geopolitical community, and not necessarily a directly parallel Indian version of monadic sovereignty. As suggested in chapter 2, this is not to suggest that competing representations of the social order cannot coexist. It is the tension between these representations that creates the dynamism of political tradition, in India as much as anywhere else, and contingent events can have a determinate role in shaping the particular choice or repertoire of cultural representations. But when the caveats enumerated in chapter 2 about the boundaries of "civilizations" are borne in mind, we can nevertheless argue that "civilizational categories" exist which act as a kind of hysteresis in this process, shaping the contest of cultural representations at the marginal point of historical transformation and, indeed, persisting in their effects beyond the transformed social state (cf. Mauss, 1979).

Nations and Citizenries

The previous section concentrated upon the structures of political authority in medieval Europe and India, but this necessarily implies a consideration of the social context within which political authority operates, and which scholars have often referred to as "civil society." By placing a slightly different emphasis upon some of the material presented earlier, in this section we will briefly consider the predication of "civil society" in relation to the character of political authority in our two cases in order to inform our subsequent analysis of race and caste hierarchies.

Jürgen Habermas has discussed the development in modern Europe of what he calls a "bourgeois public sphere," defined as "the sphere of private people come together as a public" (Habermas, 1989: 27), an institution whose zenith he locates in the seventeenth and eighteenth centuries, but whose origins he traces to the high middle ages. A prerequisite for the emergence of this public sphere was the eclipse of the more particularistic identifications of locality, lineage, or status group as the principal motivators of interested social action. Earlier, we identified this as a feature of the political process in the high and late middle ages which was caused by several factors. Changes in political organization from imperial to feudal, and thence to sovereign, territorial state structures led to the elimination of chattel slavery and consolidated the peasantry as a dependent and more or less undifferentiated class. Forms of territorial identification gradually came to be coordinated with the life of the polity, particularly in relation to the body of the sovereign. Distinctions between different local communities and between local communities and the political elite were eroded, not least through the ministry of a literate and educated clergy. Alongside these forms of proto-nationalism was a discourse of kinship as a relation through blood, which came to be extrapolated in the early modern period as a metaphor of inclusion and exclusion in this wider social body across other distinctions of status, as for example in the deprecation of converted Jews and

Muslims as against "Old Christians" in imperial Spain. And, in the medieval period, an increasingly monetized economy eroded some of the more elaborate forms of local status discrimination.

In many respects, these processes were accompanied by intensified exploitation of the less privileged, and the increasing popularity of egalitarian millenarianism among them was one result of this. However, the increasing bureaucratization of secular and clerical authority both informed and made possible the repression of such counter-practices, through the quashing of popular violence and heresy. The result was an emerging class society that conformed to our depiction of ranking hierarchy, with "lower" and "higher" classes who were opposed but also integrated complementarily within a unified structure. A common way of viewing the dynamism of this structure more recently – for example, in the thought of Hegel and Marx – has been through the idea of an agonistic or oppositional conflict, in which the negation of the opposite leads to a new structure (cf. Dumont, 1980: 243), the characteristic formulation of class struggle. This has provided contemporary analysts with one way of examining medieval political discourses of the kind to be found in popular festivities such as carnivals, with their ritual subversions, inversions, and comic mockery of the extant status order, which can plausibly be read as models for class struggle, so that a judgment can be made concerning their "success" in effecting an enduring transformation of the social order when the carnival is over. Here, the *content* of the performance matters only with respect to its consequences for transformation, except that when such a transformation is not deemed to have occurred the charge of a derivative or inauthentic popular culture is invited. On the other hand, one can view carnival as a popular counter-project to the extant order which encompasses it creatively. As Bakhtin has put it, "the people's ambivalent laughter . . . expresses the point of view of the whole world; he who is laughing also belongs to it" (Bakhtin, 1984: 12). The accent here is on a continuous creativity which destabilizes and obviates the transitive order of ranking hierarchy within which it is articulated, but not in any necessary, transformative, or dialectical respect. Yet both ways of reading carnival point to the reproduction of the structure of ranking hierarchy itself, by supposing categorical oppositions which fully transect a social universe that is bounded at some level. This, as I argued in earlier chapters, has been the intellectual context for the emergence of both racial categorization and sociological theory.

There was nothing in Europe that paralleled the sovereign, territorial nation-state from classical antiquity until the high middle ages. Under the Roman and early medieval empires it was recognized that different "peoples" following different law codes shared the same territorial space, albeit within a wider imperial ambit, but this changed through the territorialization of legal jurisdictions during the feudal period and then under the increasing centralization of royal power in the high middle ages (Hazeltine, 1968). These elevated the broader distinctions of foreigner, citizen, and slave that had always been made to the key distinctions of political life. As we have seen, the category of "citizen" encompassed a bounded polity completely transected by class distinctions, which have formed the basis of Marxist sociology. But in order to undertake class analysis of this sort one must first assume a social order so constituted; Bakhtin's analysis has the merit of instilling an awareness of the way in which this possibility depends upon the prior constitution of a particular kind of civil society. A different situation obtained in precolonial India, I shall argue, requiring different modes of analysis.

A basic unit of early Indian political organization was the *janapanda*. In his critique of Orientalism in Indian historiography, Ronald Inden (1990) argues that the *janapanda* refers to the idea of a territorially based citizenry connected to the rulership of a polity, a conception which in his view has been "Orientalized" through the idea of local dominant castes delinked from broader political rule. Other writers, however, have argued that the *janapanda* should *not* be regarded as territorially bounded but as territorially located political centers which are in no way closed to the accretion of new people (Heesterman, 1985; Thapar, 1992; Chattopadhyaya, 1994). In fact, Inden himself introduces a series of qualifications to his argument which work against his notion of territorial sovereignty. For example, he describes castes as a *scale* of more or less inclusive citizenries which can be contrasted to the simpler European situation of citizen, slave, or foreigner (Inden, 1990: 218–19); he suggests that brahmans and merchants can be regarded as separate societies, distinct from the royal courts, over which the latter had no real control (ibid.: 227). He concludes:

> India . . . was neither a unitary administered polity, an empire or nation-state, nor a system of atomistically conceived, formally equal sovereign states. As an imperial formation, it consisted (as did the other imperial formations of the time) of one (or more) empires and a number of other kingdoms. It was a scale of polities, of rulerships that overlapped one another. (Inden, 1990: 267)

But, as our preceding discussion of Tambiah's "galactic polity" model was intended to suggest, this scale of overlapping polities is not readily assimilable to a general model of plural sovereignties in an imperial context. Two particular features of Tambiah's approach are its orientation to a center-focused rather than a territorially bounded political geography and the replication of the galactic structure at the level of the lesser entities (so that they, in turn, act as centers to still lesser satellites). The implications of this are several. First, it suggests that while the structure is characterized by a "pulsating" dynamism driven by conflicts between its parts, these do not correspond to "class conflict" in the Marxist sense because of their overlapping, concentric, or particularistic character. Nor, Marx's unwarranted teleology aside, is there any reason to suppose that they should necessarily coalesce into more "diametrical" forms of class conflict. This is not to say that certain recurrent features of conflict between, say, cultivators and local land controllers were absent or were incapable of generalization in such a way that they can usefully be modeled as class struggles (Palat, 1986). But since no identification transected a unitary structure it is barely possible to generalize such conflicts to suggest systemic transformation from a more "encompassing" form of hierarchy towards ranking hierarchy. Second, the compatibility of the mandala conception with a jajmani-type structure is apparent, perhaps suggesting – as we saw earlier – that this structure is not best derived "downwards" as a remnant from Mughal or British imperial structures of revenue collection, but refers to a more deeply rooted indigenous conception. It is, moreover, an indigenous conception that reappears in various guises throughout very different ecological, economic, and historical contexts in South Asia. Thus, third and finally, the conception is consonant with our emphasis on the way regimes of power are instantiated through a cultural metacontext. As Nicholas Dirks has put it, "culture . . . is and can be contested; but at another and more fundamental level culture is the abstraction of discursive and institutional sites which contain contest, define its antipodes, seal its interpretations, and configure its possible resolutions" (Dirks, 1989: 43). In this respect, I would argue, the struggles of precolonial Indian caste society evince Inden's conception of a "scale of citizenries" which was structured rather differently to the civil society of medieval Europe.

The foregoing points are not intended to suggest that political structures of this kind have always obtained everywhere in India, as if they were some essence of an original and pristine mode of political organization. On the contrary, their emergence can probably be linked roughly to the historic progress of Brahmanism and Buddhism in South and Southeast Asia. Resistance to such progress can readily be discerned, for example, in the persistent but nebulous tension between "caste" and "tribe" in Indian history. However, it can be suggested – very much in keeping with the contemporary view of "tribal" societies as ones produced *within* the ambit of broader and more stratified political structures, rather than "primitive" throwbacks standing outside them (e.g. Kuper, 1988) – that tribes and castes are generally better seen as part of a continuum of political organization (Sinha, 1965; 1997; Unnithan, 1994). Moreover, it can also be shown that the distinction was greatly inflated by British colonial "divide and rule" policies (Skaria, 1997). Indeed, one might argue that the galactic polity is inherently capable of absorbing, containing, and synthesizing resistance of this kind within the modality of a pulsating "radial" structure in ways that have determinate implications for the social order, just as sovereign, territorial, Christian polities in Europe found very different methods for containing their negations.

4 | Race, Slavery, and Colonialism

Introduction

The previous chapter discussed the character of late medieval and early modern European polities and the development of European capitalism as a context for understanding the emergence of racial categorization in the European colonial societies of the Americas. This question is the focus of the present chapter.

Let us begin with a very brief historical overview of the colonization process. The first imperial ventures of West European states were those of Portugal and Spain. Despite some early experiments with sugar cultivation in the Caribbean based upon models imported from the Mediterranean and longer-lasting industrial mining enterprises, the enormous Spanish American empire was for a long time built largely around scattered urban outposts based upon an extensive, manorial economy and tribute-taking from indigenous Amerindian populations. More than a century elapsed after the initial Spanish conquests before other European powers were to move into the American colonial theater. In the Caribbean, the English occupied Barbados and some of the Lesser Antillean islands in the first part of the seventeenth century, capturing Jamaica from the Spanish in 1655. They also occupied several colonies on the North American mainland at much the same time. Contemporaneously, the French occupied parts of the North American mainland, particularly around the St Lawrence and Mississippi Rivers, and in the Caribbean took possession of some of the Lesser Antillean islands, while gaining control of the Western part of Hispaniola (which was to become French Saint-Domingue) at the end of the seventeenth century. The Dutch were also active in the Caribbean and the South and North American mainlands. Originally, these forays were mainly private ventures, but were increasingly incorporated – not always without resistance – under metropolitan control and drawn into European political conflicts (Greene, 1986; Canny and Pagden, 1987). The newer colonial powers initially attempted to harry the Spanish in their imperial dominions and to avail themselves of its specie, but increasingly in the seventeenth and eighteenth centuries as the Spanish star waned they devoted themselves where possible to intensive plantation production of tropical produce like tobacco, indigo, cotton, coffee, and, above all, sugar, a process which articulated with consumer demands from growing urban populations in Europe (Mintz, 1985). In the eighteenth century, American colonial plantation societies were at their zenith in British Jamaica and Virginia, French Saint-Domingue and Dutch Suriname, all employing African-origin slave labor.

This highly summary account raises two issues which will be pursued in this chapter in order to understand the development of racial categorization; namely, the extension of European polities into new territorial dominions and the employment of African-origin slave labor. On the first point, while the colonial dominions are sometimes described as the "satellites" or "periphery" of the European metropolises, they were not satellites in the same sense as were the political formations incorporated into Tambiah's Asian "galactic polities." The logic of the contest between metropolitan and colonial political authority in the extended polities of the European colonial powers was not a "pulsating" one, a point with very significant implications for the way that the people comprising colonial polities were able to imagine themselves as political communities. We will pursue this later in the chapter, but let us begin with an appraisal of the second issue, concerning slavery.

Slavery

Slavery is usually defined as a social status where the person and their labor power is owned as a thing by another person who has more or less complete rights to dispose of them as a capital asset. However, the tendency to read off an entire mode of being from the legal distinction between slavery and freedom can obscure both the variation and the degree of continuity in forms of labor coercion, discipline, life opportunity, and lifestyle across the distinction. One only has to contrast the situation of those slaves in Santo Domingo whose owners were, in 1659, unable even to discover their whereabouts when their labor was sought (Hoetink, 1973) with the pervasive and rigorous disciplining of "free" industrial workforces in nineteenth-century Europe to appreciate this point. Nevertheless, although not all slavery was plantation slavery, American slavery was in general an economic institution geared to maximizing output on plantations which were essentially agricultural "factories" designed to provision the European metropolis (and whose work regimen indeed provided a model for later industrialization) at the expense of the dignity, wellbeing and, ultimately, life of the slave. The underlying dynamic to the vast growth of the colonial plantation economy from the seventeenth to the nineteenth centuries reflected the economic imperatives of European capitalist development. But this does not fully explain why the general form of plantation labor rested upon enslavement, and in particular the enslavement of Africans. The novelty of the American colonial situation was not the existence of slavery as such, which had been familiar in Europe from antiquity to the high middle ages in Northern Europe and had persisted through to the contemporary period in Southern Europe, albeit in less intensive forms than those that were to emerge in America. Rather, it was the specifically "racial" character of slavery which was new. Although many societies have reserved slave status for "outsiders," they were not usually so discriminating about precisely which outsiders to enslave as were Europeans in the Americas, and nor did they build such impediments to the incorporation of people descended from slaves as full members of civil society. Almost without exception, the slaves of the American colonies originated from Africa, and the development of the idea that these Africans and their creole descendants were especially fitted to a degraded and inferior status was to have inestimable consequences for the subsequent elaboration of racial ideology.

In contrast to the tenor of the preceding discussion, Hoetink (1973) has argued that slavery is not radically distinguishable from other forms of labor coercion in American history and that there was little relation between the character of American slave systems and their socioracial structure. In his words, "only gradually did American slavery become the reflection of the total socioracial structure; it adjusted itself to it and was not its forerunner or model" (ibid.: 57). For Hoetink, the dynamics of slavery in the history of different American societies have, overall, barely coincided with changes in the context of the racial categories through which those societies have understood themselves. His arguments help us to see why, for example, the early colonial legislation of the English and the French placed considerable emphasis on regulating the boundaries between slave and free, without initially understanding these in "racial" terms by mapping the distinction onto African and European, or black and white; and why, later on, the significance of racial categories did not just respond to the dynamics of slavery but to the total political, economic, and social forces which affected American colonial and postcolonial societies. On the other hand, Hoetink's view of a "socioracial structure" pre-established at the "historical baseline" of each society artificially severs connections at a more general historical level, first between the proto-racial context of American slavery in its over-whelming reliance upon specifically *African* labor, and then in the way that the deployment of racial categories in American colonial and postcolonial societies corresponded more broadly to some of the characteristic features of European political thought that we have examined over the longer term, a point to which we shall return later in the chapter, and in chapter 6. But to address the African character of slavery requires some understanding of questions concerning the development of capitalism in relation to colonial slavery.

While there is little controversy about the broad historical outlines of American slavery as described above, its place in the history of European capitalism has proved to be a much thornier issue. Purist definitions of capitalism based on free wage labor obviously exclude slavery from their purview, but then seem rather inflexible and abstract exercises of the ideal-typical sort in the face of the manifest coordination of European empires based upon emerging capitalist wage labor at home and labor coercion abroad (Mintz, 1978). This has led to extensive debates within Marxist historiography about the "articulation of modes of production" to account for the coexistence of different forms of labor exaction within a common capitalistic economy. If these debates seem needlessly convoluted to non-Marxists who have no pretensions towards a "scientific" social theory based upon a transcendental and historicist theory of labor, the coexistence of these different forms of labor exaction nevertheless presents itself as an anomaly which requires explanation, particularly if any credence is given to Marx's theory of value. From within the Marxist tradition, Robert Miles provides one point of departure:

> Forms of unfree labor can be explained as both *anomalous* and *necessary* to the reproduction and spread of the capitalist mode of production. . . . They are *anomalous* when viewed in relation to the tendency for the emergence and increasing dominance of free wage labor, and yet they are *necessarily* introduced and reproduced because historical conditions obstruct the uni-versalization of wage relations of production. (Miles, 1987: 197–8)

A standard argument of economic history holds that these "historical conditions" relate to the specific ecological requirements for the mass pro-duction of crops like sugar, which demanded that plantations be sited on coastal lands in the tropics where, in the Americas, land was abundant but local labor scarce, such that labor had to be imported and coerced into remaining on the plantations (Mintz, 1977). Yet while this might conceiv-ably explain why slavery proved a superior form of labor exaction, it does not explain why enslavement was limited almost exclusively to Africans.

There were, to be sure, many non-Africans involved in coerced plantation labor at various times and places in American history, not least the indentured European "servants" who were employed mainly by the English at an early stage in the development of their Caribbean and mainland colonies. But, as I shall argue shortly, although the servants were often subjected to much the same harsh labor discipline later meted out to African-origin slaves, their legal status was never assimilable to that of the slave, and attempts to account for this incipient "racial" difference in terms of economic or "rational" rather than cultural criteria (e.g. Handlin and Handlin, 1950; Morgan, 1972; Wallerstein, 1974; Fields, 1990) usually founder on assuming the very thing that needs to be explained, namely the "difference" between Europeans and Africans.

One way of approaching this question is to return to the idea of the slave mentioned above as the property of another person in law (see Davis, 1966; Patterson, 1982; Phillips, 1985; Miles, 1987, for a variety of more detailed discussions). To this simple definition, Temperley (1996: 147) makes an intriguing addendum. In his view, slavery is also characterized by some recognition of the *illegitimate* nature of the slaveowner's power. If slavery is illegitimate, but not necessarily illegal, then some recourse must be made to an idea of "natural" justice. To understand the logic of slavery is thus to understand how some people are denied this natural justice, or alternatively of how some people have access to it. This establishes two ways of approaching the racial logic of American slavery, even if they are only different sides of the same coin. The first, which has been predominant in the literature, is to consider how it came to be Africans and their descendants in particular who suffered this denial of natural justice. The second is to consider how other people – and particularly Europeans – were *not* denied this natural justice. This, ultimately, will help us to understand the idea of "natural justice" itself, wherein I suggest lies the logic of race and racialized slavery.

Let us briefly consider this point in relation to the so-called "origins debate" concerning the racial character of English colonial slavery as it emerged particularly in the Chesapeake colonies of the American mainland (Virginia and Maryland) during the course of the seventeenth century. At its bluntest, the debate has concerned whether "racist" prejudice against Africans was a consequence of their enslavement, or whether their enslavement was the consequence of a prior European prejudice (and it is worth immediately noting the tendency to conflate racism with a rather narrow conception of social prejudice on both sides of the debate). In the debate's opening salvos, the former position was associated with Oscar and Mary Handlin (1950) and the latter with Carl Degler (1959), whose critique of the Handlins led to some acrimonious exchanges. Although subsequent research has interpolated between the Handlins' and Degler's positions, scholars often continue to align themselves within the broad terms of the debate. Here, I provide a brief critical appraisal of Barbara Fields' (1990) neo-Handlinian analysis, which is especially clear in adducing the underlying implications for a sociological approach to race.

Fields' analysis focuses upon seventeenth-century Virginia, which during this period was increasingly given over to plantation based export agriculture, at first primarily employing English indentured labor. These indentured laborers or "servants" fulfilled a fixed term of indenture – typically four to five years – during which time they were subject to much of the harsh disciplining of labor later associated with African slavery. The supply of indentured labor declined in the English colonies towards the end of the seventeenth century, mainly as a result of colonial policy and socioeconomic changes in the English countryside. Although opinion is divided about the social mobility achieved by freed servants (Morgan, 1975; Horn, 1994; Allen, 1997) it seems clear that short terms of indentureship were significant in creating a high demand for labor, and despite the fact that indentured servitude in the Chesapeake represented an intensification of labor exploitation by comparison with the coercion of unskilled labor in England during the same period, Chesapeake planters were unable or unwilling significantly to increase the standard period of indentureship. But by around 1660 Africans, who had some presence in the colony for most of the century, began increasingly to replace the servants on the plantations. At the same time, their legal status was regularized. A law passed in 1661 indicated that "negro" servitude was lifelong, a status which came to be inherited from the mother. Laws against sexual and marital relations between free women and slave men quickly followed, in order – so Fields contends – to protect the capital embodied in the person of the slave. Fields quotes from a 1664 law passed in Maryland, which stated:

> forasmuch as divers freeborne English women forgettfull of their free
> Condicion and to the disgrace of our Nation doe intermarry with Negro
> Slaves by which alsoe divers suites may arise touching the Issue of such woemen
> and a great damage doth befall the Masters of such Negros for prevention
> whereof for deterring such freeborne women from such shamefull Matches.

Similarly, a 1691 Virginia act denounced miscegenation as "that abominable mixture and spurious issue," while in the Caribbean a law had been passed as early as 1644 in Antigua against "Carnall Coppullation between Christian and Heathen" (Jordan, 1968; Dunn, 1972). In support of her argument that racial thought remained inchoate in seventeenth-century Virginia, Fields points out that the Maryland legislation mentions "freeborne

English women" and not *white* women, though she does not point out that the slaves who are mentioned are *negro* slaves, a term which had been current in English for around a hundred years before the seventeenth-century development of the slave society she describes. Nevertheless, in these events Fields discerns race in the very process of its creation. "Race," she contends, "is not an idea but an ideology. It came into existence at a discernible historical moment for rationally understandable historical reasons and is subject to change for similar reasons," and she is sharply critical of the view that "having arisen historically" race "takes on a life of its own" for its "latter-day version of Lamarckism" which expels the concept from its contingent historical origins (Fields, 1990: 101). Instead, she prefers a view of ideology as "help[ing] insiders make sense of the things they do and see – ritually, repetitively – on a daily basis . . . [and] not a material entity, a thing of any sort that you can hand down like an old garment, pass on like a germ, spread like a rumour, or impose like a code of dress or etiquette" (ibid.: 110).

For Fields, then, ideologies are not handed down. They appear as radically contemporaneous manifestations of a vanishing calculus of material interest, misrecognized in the mindless practices of the everyday. This is apparent in the reading of the miscegenation laws as nothing more than a means to maximize exploitable labor. Yet here one might lodge two objections. First, the dramatic language of "shamefull matches" and "carnall coppullations" seems to touch a different register to that if utilitarian interest were all that was at stake. Second, if social categories merely follow practical needs, one might also question why the planters did not opt for the same super-exploitation of European servants later applied to Africans. On this point, Fields argues that the terms of the contest between servants and planters had already been established "in the long history of negotiation and contest in which the English lower classes had worked out the relationship between themselves and their superiors," whereas Africans "enter[ed] the ring alone" (ibid.: 104).

At this step of the argument, Fields implicitly abandons her synchronic view of ideology, making English servants and planters heirs to a long tradition denied to Africans. Here, then, ideology *does* seem to be handed down like a garment, and class, if not yet race, has indeed "taken on a life of its own." Consider the following passage:

A commonplace that few stop to examine holds that people are more readily oppressed when they are already perceived as inferior by nature. The reverse is more to the point. People are more readily perceived as inferior by nature when they are already seen as oppressed. Africans and their descendants might be, to the eye of the English, heathen in religion, outlandish in nationality, and weird in appearance. But that did not add up to an ideology of racial inferiority until a further historical ingredient got stirred into the mixture: the incorporation of Africans and their descendants into a polity and society in which they lacked rights that others not only took for granted, but claimed as a matter of self-evident natural law. (Ibid.: 106)

The idea in the latter part of this passage that racial ideology is predicated upon the subordinate incorporation of people who are seen as deeply different into a particular political economy can serve as a useful working definition, which others have also touched upon (Comaroff, 1987), but it clearly contradicts the first part of the passage. The subordinate incorporation of Africans is accounted for in relation to difference, their different history, their lonely entry into the ring of English relationships; it cannot be, then, that their difference is a *result* of their subordination. Like many writers on race, Fields vehemently denies the reality of racial ideology but implicitly assumes group distinctions – here between Africans and English – which then become racialized. To a large extent, this simply displaces the question of racial ontology onto this construction of group difference. Part of the explanation for the emergence of early forms of European racism does, I would argue, rest upon the perception of African difference in the context of a self-absorbed and essentializing European Christendom which was increasingly articulated around ideas of national homogeneity, particularly with its transformation into secular ideologies of political community during the early modern period. Fields captures this, albeit somewhat ingenuously, in her origin myth of feudal hierarchy in which the superiority of the nobility, "more powerful than their fellows through possession of arms or property" (Fields, 1990: 106) was naturalized. Although this point raises many problems, not least in its implicit, and perhaps implicitly Christian, appeal to an original, pre-feudal egalitarian state of nature, it does capture the sense in which the colonial expansion of early modern Europe took place against the background of the stabilization of sovereign, territorial polities in Europe in the late medieval and early modern periods which we examined earlier. But this vitiates the notion that Africans were ever perceived as similar or equal to Europeans in early modern Europe. In fact, in the English case, although the early colonial period furnishes evidence of "racial" alliances which would have later been unthinkable – albeit often ones expedient to intra-European colonial rivalries – this "feeble structure of racial morality" (Sanders, 1978: 219) was readily undermined by prior cultural imperatives, and not just by the emerging economic character of colonial societies. Indeed, research on seventeenth-century English colonies suggests that Africans were from the outset always debased in relation to even the rudest among indentured servants (Dunn, 1972; Vaughan, 1995).

Thus, the view that American exploitation of Africans was facilitated by the latter's "difference" is not implausible, but it requires the recognition that "differences" had already been constructed. If race was created at a "discernible historical moment," this was not it, for in the English colonies of seventeenth-century America, a good deal of symbolic work had already been done. As Alden Vaughan (1995) has argued, what can be seen in seventeenth-century Virginia is the invention of a language to express a racial ideology, and not the invention of racial ideology as such.

A good deal of the heat that has been generated in the origins debate stems from the fact that its protagonists believe it carries implications for contemporary race relations. The Handlins did not broach the matter, but the political implications of their argument in the 1950s that whites and blacks had once enjoyed an equivalent status in a country then gripped by the civil rights struggle were not too deeply submerged. Allen (1994: 2–3) is more explicit, and tendentious, in suggesting that to consider racial prejudice an antecedent of slavery in the seventeenth century necessarily implies a commitment to the view that it holds an intractable contemporary grip. This, to be sure, is the position set out by Degler (1971), who purveys the rather extreme and problematic argument that color distinctions which place white over black (as day to night or milk to dirt or European to African) are intrinsic to human thought, and he therefore offers a much more pessimistic appraisal of the prospects for contemporary race relations. And, in more measured tones, Vaughan also concludes gloomily,

> The interpretation put forward by the Handlins . . . is implicitly more optimistic about a speedy end to racial prejudice and eventually to race as a functioning concept in human relations. But I go where the evidence takes me. In this case it went in a depressing direction, one that suggests the future of race relations may be more drawn out and contentious than people of goodwill had hoped. (Vaughan, 1995: 174)

My own argument, based upon the perspective on history outlined in chapter 2, is that whether racial prejudice preceded slavery or not in the English colonies of America in the seventeenth century has absolutely no implications whatsoever for contemporary race relations in America or anywhere else and, in a certain sense, the conviction that it does among the protagonists to the origins debate is indicative not of the intractability of racial prejudice but the grip of historicist assumptions in Western intellectual frameworks within which racial ideologies, among other things, are grounded. But I would nevertheless take Degler or Vaughan's side of the argument that prejudice did precede slavery, and I would argue that while this prejudice does not equate with racism as such, it was one entailment of the "Western core symbol" within which racism can be located, and which has continued to influence the course of contemporary social relations. Thus, in turning to consider the racial character of American slavery we are able to perceive one moment in the trajectory of this symbol, but we are unable to draw any contemporary inferences from it.

Why, then, were the peculiar handicaps of plantation slavery reserved almost exclusively for Africans and their descendants, and why slavery? Broadly, three kinds of explanation might be offered. First, it can be suggested that the enslavement of people from the African continent offered several practical advantages over the enslavement of people from elsewhere. In this view, slaves could have come from anywhere but were drawn from Africa for purely expedient reasons which simply happened not to hold for other people. Second, African enslavement could be regarded as a corollary of the fact that Europeans defined Africans (as well as themselves) as a distinctive group which they placed lower than themselves and other groups according to specific ethnocentric criteria, therefore regarding Africans as particularly appropriate for the degraded status of slavery. And third, African enslavement could be viewed as a corollary of the political contexts within which Europeans encountered – and understood themselves to be encountering – the peoples of the African and American continents. There is probably some value in all of these arguments, which we shall now review in more detail. Nevertheless, I shall argue that greatest weight should be accorded to the third.

Curtin (1990) sets out one "practical" argument for African enslavement, suggesting that there was a grain of truth behind the racist stereotype concerning the special "fitness" of Africans for plantation work, inasmuch as Africans possessed greater immune resistance to tropical and Old World infectious diseases, resulting in lower mortality rates in the Americas than either Europeans or Amerindians. Other writers have argued that Africans were less able to escape to kinsfolk and familiar territory than Amerindians enslaved in their native lands, and easy to recapture because of the visible color difference.

We will leave an evaluation of such "practical" arguments aside for the moment and move on to the issue of ethnocentrism. One can perhaps discern two tiers of ethnocentrism in early modern Europe. At the most inclusive level was the view that *all* peoples outside the geopolitical scope of European Christendom were inferior and suspect, a view accompanied in the sixteenth and seventeenth centuries by pervasive narratives concerning the inferiority and degeneracy of non-European peoples and an antipathy to miscegenation, particularly among the English (Boxer, 1965; Jordan, 1968; Walvin, 1973; Zuckerman, 1987). Certainly, the racial categories which were deployed were much more fluid and much less grounded in a sense of an inherent natural rank than was to be the case in succeeding centuries, but the prototype for these ideas is evident in the earlier period. There was, however, a second tier of ethnocentrism which distinguished between different kinds of non-European "others," such as Amerindians and Africans, judging the latter more harshly. Various explanations for this could be provided. Europeans were from the outset attuned to the supposed "blackness" of Africans; distinctions between African "blackness" and the "whiteness" of Europeans began to be made in the sixteenth century, well before the major expansion of African-origin slavery in the colonial plantation system (Jordan, 1968; Walvin, 1973). One argument is that this blackness became associated with the broader negative connotations of "blackness" in Christian cosmology. Another focuses upon the so-called "Hamitic myth" derived from the Book of Genesis, in which black Africans were – on the basis of several highly tenuous arguments – defined as the issue of Canaan, the son of Ham who was condemned to be a "servant of servants." It would, however, be unwise to argue that the Hamitic myth and other such stories had much significance other than as *post facto* justifications for slavery. But, as I shall argue later, deeper affinities exist between Christian cosmology and racialized slavery than these examples of explicit recourse to biblical authority. More generally, English, French, Dutch, and Portuguese accounts of early contacts with these non-Christian West Africans in the fifteenth and sixteenth centuries almost invariably describe them negatively, as uncivil peoples on the thoroughly ethnocentric grounds of such things as their semi-nakedness (associated with excessive sexuality), body decoration, unintelligible languages, and so on (Jordan, 1968; Sanders, 1978; Cohen, 1980; van den Boogaart, 1982). Such accounts evince a European concern with "civilization" viewed through the Aristotelian lens of *techne*. And, in this context, while it is now evident that sub-Saharan Africa taken as a whole was quite as technologically "advanced" as any other part of the world, this was perhaps less obviously the case among most of the West African coastal societies with which Europeans came into direct contact.

Another factor that made Africans suitable for enslavement in the ethnocentric worldview of Renaissance and early modern Europe was their lack of Christianity. European incursions from the fifteenth century onwards along the west coast of Africa brought Europeans into contact with African peoples who were neither Christian nor Muslim. This provoked a certain debate in Europe over the religious status of Africans. Contemporary thought drew a distinction between *heathens*, those previously unaware of Christianity who were ripe for conversion, and *infidels*, those such as the Muslims who consciously eschewed it, and who were ripe for extirpation, though there was a strong tendency to essentialize Christian commitment around particular territorially identified "peoples." The non-Christian status of Africans in any case constituted a convenient, if always tenuous, justification for the slave trade. Similar arguments were applied to Amerindians, but never with such force. The main reasons for this have to do with our third category of explanation, the political contexts of colonial encounters, to which we now turn.

It has become commonplace to think of the history of the early modern period in terms of an "Atlantic world" linking Europe, Africa, and America (Morgan, 1997) but, useful though this concept is, it can obscure the very different social relationships entered between Europeans, Africans, and Americans on these respective continental soils. Parenthetically, much more could be said about the predication of race and colonialism in relation to the geopolitical separation of seaborne empires, particularly when contrasted with the land empires of Asia (for some suggestive discussions along these lines see Braudel, 1972–4; Greenblatt, 1991; Stinchcombe, 1995; Benítez-Rojo, 1996; Heesterman, 1997). At any rate, the basis of the initial encounter between Europeans and Africans on the coasts of West Africa was such as to enable fairly readily a transfer of Africans into the hands of the Europeans, a factor facilitating the later and much more extensive Atlantic slave trade. Indeed, this availability of Africans for enslavement provided one justification in European eyes for their enslavement, in view of the fact that they were traded by other Africans to Europeans *as* slaves. As Robin Blackburn frames the argument,

> African slaves . . . were found living in societies organized in states, with their own laws, and participating in commerce. The captive purchased on the African coast was legitimately a slave, some argued, because he or she had been produced as such by the coastal slave trading or slave-raiding complex. (Blackburn, 1997: 63)

Since European slave trading was based largely upon coastal contacts with African intermediaries who drew their human merchandise in from a hinterland about which Europeans knew quite little until the colonial expansion of the nineteenth century – well after the cessation of the legal slave trade – this undoubtedly was a genuinely held, if ideologically self-serving, belief. But it conceals a more complex reality. What made the West African slave trade possible was not so much the prevalence of strong states willing to trade in people, but on the contrary the weakness of political institutions in the interstices of the great sub-Saharan states. Relatively few of these states subjected their local populations to the depredations of the slave trade (and therefore retained civil institutions which made them especially refractory to later European efforts at colonial domination), but the

West African peoples most subject to enslavement lived in zones of linguistic, cultural, and political fragmentation between them. These proved unable to mount large-scale resistance, first to the slave trading linked via the interior states to the trans-Saharan Arab slave trade, and then to the slave raiding states which arose in response to the trans-Atlantic European trade and which increasingly augmented the fragmentation by breaking down and reorienting the extant politico-economic order (Evans, 1980; Ekeh, 1990; Klein, 1999).

To understand the Atlantic slave trade, then, requires an analysis of the interaction between West African economic systems and the European slave trading powers, initially the Portuguese and then the English, French, and Dutch, who tapped indigenous trading networks, rather than attempting extensive territorial conquest. Partly, this was an expedient choice since such conquest was blocked through the military strength of the polities they encountered. This is one reason why Africa long remained outside the "world system" that the European colonial powers built around their Atlantic empires (Wallerstein, 1974). However, as we have seen, it was not simply a case of the Europeans encountering strong, unitary polities but of the interpenetration of the such polities with smaller coastal societies. Thus, one context for the emergence of the European trans-Atlantic trade was the fact that people from coastal West African societies were already subjected to slavery (albeit slavery of a different kind to the sort that was to develop in the Americas under the aegis of European capitalist development), which the Europeans were able to tap, but only across the strong political boundaries established between themselves and their African trading partners.

Indeed, it is this insuperable political barrier that needs to be brought out here. The argument will be recalled from Barbara Fields' comparison between European indentured servants and African slaves that African labor in the Chesapeake colonies was not subjected to any special handicaps *vis-à-vis* European labor until late in the seventeenth century, when changing economic and demographic factors in Europe and Africa began to create a divide on the continuum of labor exploitation which disadvantaged Africans. Fields argues that planters were constrained in their ability to exploit indentured laborers only insofar as news of American working conditions would return to the source of labor and stifle its flow, whereas this did not happen in the African case. Even if we fully accept this argument – and there are considerable grounds for doubting it (cf. Horn, 1994; Vaughan, 1995) – it already points to a major difference between Europeans and Africans: the one-way flow of people and information in the latter case indicates the colonial character of European slave trading in Africa, in which sale of people into slave status at the European coastal enclaves constituted an explicit and irredeemable transfer between two different sociopolitical systems. But in fact Fields understates the extent to which Europeans did make a qualitative distinction between servitude and slavery, reserving the latter status for non-Christians and non-Europeans. This bears not only upon the question of relative intensity in the exploitation of European and African labor in the Chesapeake (on this point it seems clear that European servitude was the forerunner of slavery and exceeded accepted degrees of labor exploitation in England, and yet remained formally quite distinct from lifetime and hereditary bondage). It also has a bearing on the degree to which these forms of labor came to be included or excluded from a political community anchored in the metropolitan center, regardless of the degree of coercion to which they were subjected. Herein lies a deficiency in those approaches which account for the enslavement of Africans purely in terms of a class logic of labor exploitation or social control (e.g. Fields, 1990; Allen, 1997), both in privileging class identification as the fundamental constituent of social identity and in making the *a priori* assumption of a manifest "difference" between Africans and Europeans which could be incorporated instrumentally into the logic of labor exploitation.

What, then, established this absolute ontological boundary between Europe and Africa? Instead of seeking to account for the specific "difference" of Africans, David Eltis (1993) has instead drawn attention to Europe's sense of its own integrity which vitiated the enslavement of Europeans. His understanding of American slavery is implicitly utilitarian; enslavement was the most "rational" form of labor exploitation from the slaveowners' point of view because it maximized output. The question then becomes why, with the opening of the American colonial frontier and its new economic opportunities, the votaries of profit-creation in Europe did not enslave their own local populations, as had their medieval forebears. This would have eliminated costly and dangerous expeditions to the African coast and thereby enhanced the economic rationality of American slavery. Eltis's argument is essentially that this did not happen because a sense of a pan-European common identity grounded in a proto-egalitarian materialist individualism had arisen in early modern Europe, the same ideology, indeed, which underpinned the capitalistic plantation enterprise. As Eltis points out, those residents of Europe who did not fit in with its incipient nationalisms – like the Jews of Spain or residents of the "Celtic fringe" in the English-dominated British Isles – were killed or expelled and sometimes pressed into coerced labor, but they were not enslaved in the sense of being consigned to hereditary bondage in conditions more or less lacking legal restitution. In this respect, slavery was a fate worse than death which could only be countenanced for those outside the common European firmament (Patterson, 1982), and some of the reasons given above which apparently made it more "practical" to enslave Africans than others fall rather by the wayside, because the enslavement of non-Africans was never actually contemplated.

Robin Blackburn (1997) has recently contested Eltis's interpretation. Blackburn is not convinced that Europeans in America were unwilling to enslave other Europeans, and argues with some plausibility that funneling the supply of European labor into American slavery would have been counterproductive to European economies (cf. Klein, 1999). Indeed, in his view, the enslavement of Africans was not especially rational either, and he highlights the free wage labor principles underlying the organization of the shipping industry which sustained the Atlantic colonial enterprise as a counter-possibility to the economic organization of plantation slavery. But there is evidence to suggest that Europeans in America *did* on the whole think of other Europeans in a qualitatively different light to Africans and were unwilling to enslave the former (Dunn, 1972; Vaughan, 1995). While there are good "rational" economic explanations for the organization of the shipping industry rather than, say, sugar production on the basis of predominantly free wage labor (Stinchcombe, 1996), the fact that colonial planters did not contemplate this possibility suggests that they did not need to contemplate it precisely because they could entertain modes of labor coercion for Africans which were unacceptable for Europeans, even if there were also more directly economic reasons vitiating the enslavement of the latter. The enslavement of Africans may, in the long run, have been economically inefficient but such a view risks an unwarranted presentism in its construction of the economic choices facing colonial planters. Indeed, the efficiency of free wage labor principles was perhaps a lesson of Europe's industrial revolution which, it could be argued, represented the paradoxical dynamic of an expansive capital investment due to the very limitations upon the direct coercion of local labor, even if this was to result in the proliferation of working conditions little less repressive than on the slave plantations themselves (Curtin, 1990). Perhaps this suggests that the question of African "difference" does have some bearing upon American colonial slavery. Indeed, Orlando Patterson (1977; 1982) has offered a sustained critique of the economic argument for enslavement, arguing that slavery is always a relation of authority – "the permanent, violent domination of natally alienated and generally dishonoured persons" (Patterson, 1982: 13) – which is in the last instance established politically. In this context, I suggest that the development of African slavery in early colonial America represented a moment of racialization which preceded the predication of race in the rather complex climate of eighteenth- and nineteenth-century liberalism.

One political context for African enslavement, then, is the nature of the relationships between Europeans and Africans in West Africa in the early colonial period. Another is the differences between Africans and Amerindians imputed by Europeans. Although Amerindians were enslaved by Europeans in the Americas just as Africans were, they were not enslaved to the same extent, and – as we shall see in the following section – their treatment more generally was accompanied almost from the outset of the European presence in the Americas by a moral debate in Europe which did not occur in relation to Africans until the late eighteenth century. Again, these differences may owe something to practical expedients like the need to placate Amerindians where, unlike enslaved Africans, their military strength threatened the wellbeing of the colonies, or to the different kinds of ethnocentrism alluded to above. However, a more significant factor was the different geopolitical coordinates which Africans and Amerindians represented within the political discourse of Europe. Let us expand upon this point.

In retrospect, it is difficult not to suppose that the "discovery" of America must have had astonishing and revolutionary consequences for the intellectual universe of early modern Europe. Perhaps in the longer term this was indeed the case, but for a long time – stretching into the much later period of English colonial expansion – the "discovery" was assimilated into the prior worldview of early modern Christianity, which in the words of Michael Ryan was "oriented to a mythic past [and] whose members fulfilled themselves in relationship to a divine reality outside time" (Ryan, 1981: 523). In this context, Europeans had greater intellectual difficulties with the discovery of vast new land masses than they did with the fact that these land masses contained hitherto unsuspected peoples. On the one hand, the Americas became a place where Europeans projected prelapsarian images of natural perfection (Davis, 1966). On the other, they were viewed through the anti-primitivism of early modern Christianity which strongly demarcated the boundaries between the human and the natural – particularly the animal – world (Thomas, 1984). Unpopulated and untilled land was "wilderness" to be feared, and a principal difficulty in coming to terms with America was therefore what Pagden (1993) has called "the principle of attachment," whereby civilized Europe could extend itself into the American wilderness. Thus, America became a screen upon which various representations of early modern Christendom were projected, and in which the most general and serviceable model for the Indians was the distinction between Christian and heathen or infidel. During the first period of Hispanic colonization the missionary hope was expressed of Christianizing the Amerindians and it was often thought, in the eschatological climate of the time, that success in this respect would bring forth the day of judgment. Indian recalcitrance to conversion and resistance to conquest elicited the more somber projection of the infidel. Similar conceits were expressed by

English colonists of the seventeenth century, though with considerably less zeal (Sanders, 1978; Zuckerman, 1987; Vaughan, 1995). As we have seen, the same nexus of Christian–infidel–heathen also attended European contact with Africans in the early colonial period, but whereas the Indians were part of an American landscape wholly new to the European imagination and therefore more amenable to any number of fanciful projections, Africa and black Africans were fixtures on the periphery of Christian Europe which had been known about there – even if only in a sketchy, semi-legendary fashion – more or less continuously from antiquity (Davis, 1966; Cohen, 1980). They therefore lacked some of the protection afforded Amerindians via the principle of attachment, a point to which we shall return below.

Still more important is the way that Amerindians became, as it were, pawns or images in debates within Europe about the proper political structure of the metropolis–colony relation, whose treatment in theory if not in fact was contingent upon the way these debates were settled, whereas no such complicating factors applied to Africans of "alien" origin. We will consider this point in the following section. But when all the various factors touched upon here are added together – the development of labor-hungry capitalist agriculture in the American colonies, the political involution of territorial European polities, the incorporation of coastal West African societies into an Atlantic capitalist system, ethnocentric judgments concerning the culture, religion, and appearance of Africans, and European geopolitical sensibilities which differentiated Amerindian autochthons from imported Africans – the context for the enslavement of Africans and the essentialization of an inferior "negro" identity becomes clearer. Later colonial projects were to construct other groups through the multiplication of similar ideologies of inferiority, but perhaps rarely with such a dramatic historical effect. If the various rationalizations for enslavement were never fully accepted in Europe, and never accepted at all by enslaved Africans who, as we shall see in chapter 6, produced their own creative responses to their circumstances, Africans and their descendants in the Americas nevertheless long remained their singular victims.

Race and Colonial Society

In the previous section we traced the incipient racialization that was an inextricable component in even the very earliest movement of European empire-building in the Atlantic world. This process was to be reinforced by later colonial developments which we shall briefly enumerate here. These include political tensions in the metropolis–colony relationship, particularly in association with the emergence of colonial "creole" societies which engaged their local populations in social structures characteristically corresponding to a ranking hierarchy, and the vast extension of colonial plantation economies in the eighteenth century. In this section we will examine these dimensions of colonial society before concluding the chapter with a closer look at the way that the political discourse of early modern Europe helped solidify emerging conceptions of racial difference.

There were significant differences in the constitutional basis of Spanish, French, and English colonization in America. The Spanish and French adopted stronger forms of monarchical absolutism which made universalist claims over political authority throughout metropolis and colony, in contrast to the more confederate basis of English arrangements (Canny and Pagden, 1987; Pagden, 1995). But in practice none of the metropolitan powers could fully sustain their claims for a variety of reasons, including the material disjunction of the Atlantic Ocean, the unprecedented character of the American "discovery" for the contemporary political discourse of Europe, and the fact that for all of them, though to different degrees, a very considerable proportion of settlers were deliberately seeking to distance themselves from metropolitan political control. The situation led to enduring conflicts between the metropolitan powers and colonial elites in all the European Atlantic empires over issues like trade, legal liberties, local political autonomy, and rights to land or labor coercion. These conflicts ebbed and flowed between metropolitan "center" and colonial "periphery" until they were largely decided in the course of the late eighteenth and early nineteenth centuries in favor of the colonial elites in the mainland Spanish and English colonies by way of secessionist revolution and in favor of the metropolitan powers in much of the Caribbean, with the major exception of Saint-Domingue, where a slave revolt ultimately succeeded in despatching colonists and metropole alike. Perhaps the finality of these revolutionary solutions betokens the underlying character of the conflicts in the ultimately impossible task of balancing inherently monadic conceptions of political authority between the different parts of geopolitically divided polities that could never really be united. The conflict and, ultimately, violence between metropolitan "core" and colonial "periphery" was therefore of a very different character to the conflict and violence associated with the pulsating dynamism, by turns unitary and plural, of Tambiah's incorporative Asian "galactic polities." Even in the Atlantic empire least wedded of all the European powers to a monadic conception of sovereignty, the English one, the colonial view that the English parliament constituted a kind of exemplary center which colonial assemblies replicated in making themselves "an epitome of the house of Commons" necessarily called forth the countervailing metropolitan view that local legislative autonomy was a derivative power granted "from the Grace and Favour of the

Crowne alone" (Greene, 1986: 31–4). This situation reflects the monism I have identified at the core of European politico-religious philosophy from the medieval period onwards, a point well captured by Anthony Pagden:

> Ultimately, the image of God as father to the human family made the idea of a multiplicity of cultures, and by extension a multiplicity of states within the *Imperium*, difficult to accommodate. (Pagden, 1995: 25)

The transformation in the early modern period of this divine image to a correspondingly secular monism underlay the conflicts between metropolis and colony described above. It was also associated with colonial social structures which, for whatever other reasons, could not incorporate cultural "others" such as Amerindians or Africans as "castes" in the subcontinental Indian sense, but only as "classes" in a ranking hierarchy. For example, in the Spanish American empire status distinctions proceeded downwards from peninsular Spaniards to creole Spaniards, *mestizos* ("mixed race" Indian and Spanish), Indians, *mulattos* ("mixed race" black and Spanish) and finally black, a status order which roughly conformed to the legal distinctions enshrined in the *Sociedad de Castas* ("society of castes"), although sometimes subject to practical ambiguities (Mörner, 1967; Pagden, 1987; Lewis, 1995). The term "creole" here refers – as throughout this book – to that which is indigenous or locally born to the Americas, including the descendants of Europeans. In this sense, the idea of Spanish or "European creole" seems almost a contradiction in terms. It is a contradiction for which the idea of "race" represents one kind of solution. Thus, although colonial racial categories drew from prior conceptions concerning the heritability of "blood" and other cultural factors (see chapter 5), they were more fundamentally engaged with a particular construction of political community.

Such constructions were especially problematic in zones of plantation production – paradigmatically, the sugar islands of the eighteenth-century Caribbean – where murderously exploited African-origin slave populations outnumbered the free population by as many as twelve to one. Earlier, it was suggested that, initially, colonial legislation made more of the distinction between slave and free than between black and white. However, with the major expansions in the scale of the slave plantation system these two dichotomies began to coincide, so that "race" increasingly marked the absolute disjunction between slavery and freedom in the harsh and bipolar order of the colonial plantation. As the Saint-Domingue planter Hilliard d'Auberteuil, writing in the late eighteenth century, remarked,

> In Saint-Domingue, interest and security require that we crush the black race under so much contempt that whoever descends from it should be covered with indelible scars until the sixth generation. (Cited in Trouillot, 1982: 361)

The instrumental character of a racism which invokes "interest and security" is plain enough, even if d'Auberteuil is willing to invoke "the black race" rather than simply "slaves." Nevertheless, there is evidence to suggest that from early on in the European Atlantic empires people of African origin were accorded a debased status, and were sometimes regarded as barely human at all (Pagden, 1987; Zuckerman, 1987; Vaughan, 1995; Schwartz, 1997). At the same time, however, their substantial presence in colonial societies was such that they were active participants in the forging of these societies and not just objects of intellectual contemplation, as was more often the case in Europe. For example, drawing on the distinction made by Foucault between the systems of "legalities" and "illegalities" through which people negotiate a *de facto* social order in relation to official legal discriminations, Mindie Lazarus-Black has shown how the African-origin slaves of Antigua "regularly used legalities to resist the power wielders' attempts to stray beyond the legal limits they set for themselves, to check the elites' assumptions about the social world, and to demand a 'justice' born of their own experiences" (Lazarus-Black, 1994: 10). In this way, they helped forge creole societies of a distinctive character, but nevertheless ones in which racial identification figured in a determinate ranking hierarchy.

The pervasiveness of a racial ranking hierarchy in colonial and indeed postcolonial America was also associated with a European political and cultural involution which we shall examine in more detail in the following section. It was manifested in part by processes of colonization which, despite the autonomist impulses of many of the colonizers, were characterized by attempts to replicate European social orders in the Americas. Early Spanish experiments in creating a *mestizo* aristocracy aside, these processes were accompanied with a general fear of parochialism, degeneration, miscegenation, and "going native" (Canny and Pagden, 1987). Thus, the ethnocentrism of white creole elites, their status concerns in the context of political relationships with the metropolis, and the socioeconomic structuring of colonial societies, all contributed to the fixing of racially stratified social orders in colonial America.

As we have seen, the character of the conflict between European "core" and colonial "periphery" culminated in revolutionary solutions to creole autonomism. This autonomism was underwritten by premodern conceptions of effective local autonomy so that the extension of more "absolutist" forms of colonial governance from the metropolitan centers in the eighteenth century informed an elite anti-colonial discourse of "liberty" grounded in these conceptions, albeit couched in the modern language of the Enlightenment (Pagden and Canny, 1987). This was particularly true in the English and Spanish mainland colonies, where discourses of "natural community" were mobilized which attempted to create distinctions from the "mother country" of the metropolitan power. In the Spanish case, these involved white creole claims to authenticity articulated mainly around identification with a mythologized Aztec or Inca past rigidly distinguished from existing Indians, a project which, in Anthony Pagden's words, was "poised forever on the edge of absurdity" (1990: 10). The principal axis of creole anti-colonialism in the English case was a white class alliance defining an exclusionary public sphere which dramatized the essentially Lockean theme of the "rights of Englishmen," although – as in Jefferson's famous equivocations over race and slavery – it also claimed, grudgingly and partially, a wider constituency of Indians and blacks, establishing tensions which were to rock the postcolonial United States, in many respects to the present day (Morgan, 1975; Zuckerman, 1987; Blackburn, 1988; Appiah, 1996). As we shall see in chapter 6, the problems of white creole anti-colonialism were much more acute in the Caribbean sugar islands, with their massive preponderance of black slaves, but the point raised in this discussion which I wish to focus on for the remainder of the chapter is the way in which Amerindians and Africans were represented in European political discourse. In this respect, eighteenth-century creole nationalisms partook of a much longer tradition which, I shall argue, continuously frustrated openings to a more genuinely civic and republican order.

Race and Political Thought in Early Modern Europe

In this section we turn to early modern Europe itself to see how the incipient racialized structures of the Atlantic empires came to be amplified and directed through political discourses into recognizably "modern" forms of racial sentiment. In its essentials, my argument is that these racialized structures were exacerbated by the way in which colonial rule was constituted through systematically closing the possibilities of bilateral participation in the political process. This occurred in two ways. First, by the elaboration of arguments, albeit for different reasons and in several different ways, that the political communities comprising the colonies were, above all, communities of Europeans, and second by a particular fetishization of nature. We will consider each point in turn.

To understand how Europeans came to think of the Americas as a theater into which they could extend themselves – though never without costs or transformations – requires an appreciation of the way that they represented their encounters with the Amerindian peoples who lived there. Although it might be possible in this context to invoke ethnocentric European judgments based upon observation of particular Amerindian lifeways, just as

this was suggested earlier as one of the issues shaping relationships between Europeans and Africans, the point is better subordinated to consideration of the way the encounter was modeled among the Europeans in
political terms. Indeed, as was suggested earlier in relation to the enslavement of Africans, the difference of the Amerindians from the Africans lay in
the unprecedented character of European contact with the former, so that
whereas other cultural encounters were anticipated and therefore open to
the possibility of "porousness" or bilaterality, this was not the case in the
American context (Greenblatt, 1991: 54–5). Moreover, the initial moment
of colonization was essentially a Castilian scheme imbued with a Christian
cosmology which assured itself of its own divinely ordered geopolitical centrality, taking as its model for the conquest (if not the subsequent colonization) of peripheral lands the Christian "Reconquest" of Spain from the
Muslims, which had helped turn politico-religious identities into territorial
ones (MacKay, 1977; Elliott, 1984; Greenblatt, 1991). This is the context
in which Pope Alexander VI could, with his papal donation of 1493, confer the whole of the Americas to Spanish and Portuguese sovereignty, and
in which Christopher Columbus could perform the famous ritual by which
he took possession of the first American island he encountered and, calling
it San Salvador "in remembrance of the Divine Majesty, who has bestowed
all this," half-knowingly erase its Amerindian name of Guanahani. Stephen
Greenblatt (1991) argues persuasively against the temptation to see
Columbus's carefully staged rituals of possession as a mere charade mask-
ing the purely instrumental power of the vast colonial onslaught it pres-
aged. For him, the rituals followed the model of a baptism in which the
name is erased and substituted for one which partakes of divinity, but is
here applied to an entire geography, and whose real spectators were not
the Indians but other European powers who might contest, but were thereby
made witness, to the construction of a limitless empire centered upon Castile.

In this respect, even as the Castilians appropriated for themselves the
model of a smoothly expansive Christian *imperium*, they implicitly recognized its core European region and the rivals therein who they attempted
to disarticulate ideologically as well as militarily. But it was not only these
rivals who contested the grounds upon which the Castilians claimed imperial authority; they were also questioned in the political discourse of Castile
itself, albeit for somewhat different reasons. Indeed, there are many examples of official concern with the moral authority of colonial policy during
the sixteenth century. Often, it is possible to discern a pragmatic basis for
it. For example, the Crown's New Laws of 1542 sought to protect the
Indians against the worst excesses of colonial enslavement and labor coercion, but against the background of the demographic catastrophe that had

already largely exterminated the Indians of the Caribbean islands and therefore deprived the colonies of labor. The New Laws encouraged the search for fresh sources of labor through slave raiding in the American periphery of the Spanish colonies, the enslavement of "rebellious" Indians, and the purchase of African slaves. Nevertheless, the significance of the Crown's attempt to protect Indians within its dominions went beyond the purely instrumental, and it is ironic that the New Laws were to stimulate the trade in enslaved Africans who never found a champion among Spanish elites in the way that the Indians did. Perhaps the best known of these latter champions and dissenters from the practice of Spanish imperialism in the Americas was Bartolomé de Las Casas, firsthand witness to the Spanish devastation of the Indies, who famously debated the morality of the enterprise with Juan Ginés de Sepúlveda at Valladolid in 1550 upon the invitation of the Crown in order to settle questions concerning colonial policy (Hanke, 1959). For our purposes, however, it is more useful to contrast Sepúlveda's position – if only summarily – with the rather more clearly systematized thought associated with the neo-Thomist theology at the University of Salamanca pioneered by Francisco de Vitoria.

Sepúlveda's defence of Spanish imperial policy was based upon an Aristotelian argument concerning the category of the "natural" slave which was placed within a Christian framing to vindicate the just enslavement of the ungodly. But for the neo-Thomists of the Catholic Counter-Reformation this represented a dangerous opening to the Lutheran or Calvinist heresy which had developed a mistaken interpretation of Augustinian philosophy. Augustine (354–430) had been interpreted during the medieval period as arguing that only the church comprising the body of committed Christians could form a truly just community. Luther and Calvin developed the Augustinian position into the idea of an active, divine grace which was withheld from the ungodly. The neo-Thomists countered this through their adherence to the doctrine of a universal natural law, divinely ordered but humanly instituted, as the basis for all human community. But if the Protestant doctrine of grace emerged from a misinterpretation of Augustine, it culminated in a highly Augustinian indifference to a secular political rule shorn of any special access to divine legitimation. At the same time, however, since the church was now regarded as having no greater access, Protestantism involved a kind of limited *de facto* warrant for secular political rule. Indeed, because it largely broke with the idea of Christ as a mediator between the divine and the secular it provided something of a mandate for an unlimited or absolutist secular power (Skinner, 1978). But this was of a radically different kind to that envisaged by Spanish Christian imperialism, because papal authority was absolutely denied, and the turn against papal universalism helped foster forms of local territorial nationalism by emphasizing vernacular translation of the Bible, local lay clergies, the moral relevance of the Old Testament as a political model and, as we shall see, in the longer term the political sovereignty of the community of individuals. Thus, the Protestant polities of Northern Europe opposed the papal donation both because of the military threat posed to their own dominions by an expansive imperial Spain and because they rejected the whole basis upon which papal authority claimed to rest. But the Spanish neo-Thomists were no more comfortable with the papal claim over the power to settle questions of American sovereignty. On the one hand, they rejected papal pretensions to secular authority because it undermined their view that political authority was based upon natural law. This was not the case with the secular power of a figure like the Habsburg Charles V, who inherited the Castilian crown in 1516 and became Holy Roman Emperor in 1519. However, the neo-Thomists argued against universal empires because there was no justification from natural law principles for arrogating secular imperial authority other than the capacity to do so, a dangerous warrant for the victory of sheer might in the context of rivalries between the European powers. Further, they linked secular political authority to territorial occupation sanctioned by humanly instituted tradition, for which their primary geopolitical model was the Roman empire. To extend political authority beyond the territorial borders of the empire, they argued, required consent from the people living there of a kind which was not countenanced either in the Protestant doctrine of grace or in the shallow legitimations for conquest practiced by the Spanish *conquistadores* (Pagden, 1990; 1995; Greenblatt, 1991). This anti-imperialist countercurrent in Spanish political thought was increasingly to be marginalized by a combination of factors: the rise of a more bullish Jesuit defence of conquest which built upon Vitoria's defence from natural law principles of the Spanish presence in the Americas, if not its associated conquest and exploitation of the Amerindians; the growing hegemony of Protestant humanism which, in developing a language of "natural rights," dispensed with some of the safeguards against colonial exploitation implied in the natural law theory of neo-Thomism; and the institutionalization of the Spanish American empire such that the image of Amerindians as the sovereigns of their territory increasingly became an intellectual abstraction (Pagden, 1987; 1995; Tuck 1993; Tully 1993). Nevertheless, it recuperated the same sense of a European "core area" – here modeled upon Rome – that attended the colonization process, albeit that in this case it was associated with an anti-imperialist position.

The political ideology of English colonization differed in important respects from the Spanish, and this – together with its later occurrence and the political geography of a colonial project undertaken in a more sparsely populated and less immediately remunerative environment – affected the character of relationships with the Indians. English colonization was, much more than the Spanish, an achievement of various different groups of people who had gone to the Americas as settlers with a large measure of autonomy from state control and, indeed, often precisely to escape it. If it is not therefore possible to generalize too widely about English relationships with the Indians in the different mainland colonies (Jacobs, 1969), there is perhaps some force to Pagden's claim that the religious beliefs of the English were broadly Calvinist (Pagden, 1995: 36). This amplified a tendency in their colonial project to try to exclude rather than incorporate the Indians which was to be systematized by John Locke. In his *Second Treatise of Government* (1690) Locke engages in elaborate arguments which justify English colonial intervention in America through an early prototype for the labor theory of value which vested political authority in the hands of individuals whose membership in the political community was contingent upon their productivity as laborers, and not through any recourse to customary authority. Since such membership was abrogated by Amerindians living within the natural economy of a primordial American "wilderness," this became a justification for its expropriation by English colonists (Hulme, 1990; Parekh, 1995). In the same work, Locke also notoriously justifies the enslavement of Africans despite having rejected slavery as the basis for English political society in the *First Treatise* (Goldberg, 1993). In this respect, although Locke's *Two Treatises* can be read both as a liberal theory of government which replaces the discourse of sovereignty with an agonistic conception of rulers and ruled holding each other in mutual subjection, and as an allegorical work of advocacy for an emergent capitalist ideology in England against an unproductive landed aristocracy (Tully, 1993), in both cases geopolitical limits are drawn around participation in this political society which, as in the Westphalian system, effectively excluded non-European political societies. This is equally apparent in Locke's contributions to the question of poor law reform, where his advocacy for the moral disciplining of the English laboring classes at home and abroad constituted them within a project of national regeneration, from which Amerindians and African slaves were effectively excluded. Thus, in an American context it provided a warrant for colonial domination marked by a sense of ethnopolitical closure.

In summary, despite considerable differences between the European powers in their American colonial projects and their accompanying political ideologies, they evinced a common tendency to construct a kind of political meta-community around Europe – variously defined according to the parameters of Christendom, Rome, or "civilization" – making it a core region which could act as the source but not the destination for the impress of political authority seen as final and absolutely constitutive. Thus, even though the Catholic as well as the Protestant political theology of the sixteenth century began to undermine aspects of the medieval Christian transcendentalism which had made "royal" claimants to Christ's mediative mantle the central figures of a polity, their most fundamental political conceptions retained a monism which could scarcely tolerate cultural plurality. At the same time, they began to undermine an antecedent universalism. One approach to the medieval myth of Prester John – a Christian king sought by medieval European explorers among the pagans at the edge of the world – is that it expressed a soteriological model of expansionist Christian globalization, an "*Orbis Christianus*" where the pagan world was rounded up "between the center of Christianity and its lost periphery in order to bring it back into the confines of the flock guarded by the Divine Shepherd" (Fabian, 1983: 26). But this was transformed in the equation of religion, territory, and citizenship or personhood first worked out in the context of the Spanish Reconquest and later radicalized in the colonialism of the Protestant nations. Now, Christianity was itself contained within a model of territorial expansion which recuperated the subordinate difference of the conquered even in the face of conversion. To return to the seventeenth-century Chesapeake context discussed earlier, it is perhaps significant in this regard that a Maryland miscegenation act described marriages between English women and "negroes" as a disgrace "not only of the English *butt allso of many other Christian Nations*" (cited in Jordan, 1968: 79–80; emphasis added). This is a wording readily transformable into conceptions of a superior, white European region and an inferior, black African one. At the same time, the preceding discussion helps establish a major reason for the rather paradoxical process by which territorial conquest in the Americas provoked a moral debate in Europe about the rights of Indians which was almost entirely lacking in the case of Africans, through differing emphasis on the political boundaries which established people as autochthons or chattel. If this was ultimately to be of sadly little relevance to the violent subjugation of both groups, it nevertheless helps explain how they came to be constituted as "groups" in the first place, with consequences which are highly relevant to the shape of American colonial societies.

Let us now turn to questions concerning the fetishization of nature in early modern political thought, which began to emerge in the materialist philosophies of seventeenth-century Europe. Although the conflict between Reformation and Counter-Reformation thought in the previous century had moved conceptions of political authority away from a reliance upon divine transcendence, their engagement with the Augustinian and Thomist traditions nevertheless still relied upon recourse to the supernatural as the determinate point of a complete ontology. In seventeenth-century thinkers such as Descartes, Hobbes, Locke, and the votaries of "natural religion," such reliance was undermined by making the dynamics of the actual, material world bear the stamp of the eternal (Westfall, 1970; Foucault, 1970; Taylor, 1989). This represented another move in the direction of secularization, dispensing with the notion of God or Christ as a mediating presence in the world or a moral judge in the afterworld, and paved the way for the forms of secular universalism which emerged in eighteenth-century thought. In contrast to the unremittingly pessimistic view of a human nature "bonded to sin" associated with Luther and Calvin, such thinking made it possible to conceive of a human agency with the capacity to achieve this-worldly redemption through historical action, the forerunner for the Enlightenment ideal of "progress" whose ambivalent implications in both liberating and intensifying forms of disciplinary power and, perforce, racial identification has been the focus for much contemporary social theory (Foucault, 1981; Stoler, 1995).

Here, I want to suggest something similar in relation to the thought of Thomas Hobbes which, I argue, provided an opening to conceptions of racial difference. It did this by retaining a sense of ranking hierarchy as its model of the social order, even if the sacred was now replaced by secular nature, and divine mediation between the human and the sacred was replaced by the authority of the secular ruler. Such thinking makes possible closure around the idea of political communities as "natural types." As we saw in chapter 3, Hobbes contrasted a "state of nature" with a political community in which people surrendered their capacity for legitimate autonomous action to the state as the supreme arbiter of human conflict. In this we see an attempt to provide justification for a political rule which is fully secular and instrumental. Hobbes's writing – his appeal to "all helps and advantages of Warre" outside the contractual state – has sometimes been read as an apologia for brute conquest in the historical context of European imperial expansion, and thus as a precursor for racism (Arendt, 1967). But one must tread carefully here. In general, brute conquest is precisely what Hobbes is seeking to excise; it is the "invisible adversary" of *Leviathan* (Pasquino, 1993: 81; cf. Sahlins, 1974) whose problematic is not political power but political *order*. Here, mutual surrender to the state implies an ethical commitment to authority which is always understood as human artifice, a "cultural plane of peace" as it were. Arendt's argument is that such commitment takes place within given geopolitical boundaries and therefore warrants an abandonment of ethics outside them, and thereby a construction of race as absolute otherness, the "antonym to politics" mentioned in chapter 1. But, in Hobbes's state-centered worldview, this would apply to any other polity, including local European ones, as much as to peoples beyond Europe; indeed, his writings can be read as a manifesto for the mercantilist antagonisms of seventeenth-century European states (Colella, 1982). This does not in itself provide a rationale for racism.

Notwithstanding this point, there is a sense in which it may be appropriate to read Hobbes as providing such a rationale, since his thought articulated a contractual theory of a state with an authority which supervenes over individuals, equal in nature, and whose only claim to legitimacy can therefore be that its authority is grounded in the will of the people. This idea was later to be elaborated in the hands of thinkers such as Rousseau and Herder, forming the eighteenth-century nationalist backdrop to the increasing biologization and mystification of national identification in the century that followed. This reflects a tension associated with the secularization of European thought, whereby the desacralized politics of egalitarian individualism confronts the persisting sacralization of sovereignty. In Bruce Kapferer's words,

> Among nation-states formed within the conditions of egalitarian individualism the issue of legitimacy has an enduring problematic specific to it. This is so because the individual autonomy preached as a central part of egalitarianism potentially conflicts with the loss or surrender of this autonomy to others, specifically agents of the state. One resolution, part of the fury of Western political philosophical discourse from the seventeenth century on, is precisely the argument that the state embodies the pure spirit of the people and is the guardian of this spirit. (Kapferer, 1988: 166)

Kapferer (ibid.: 16–17) suggests that the tendency sociologists have inherited from Max Weber to consider the closure of status groups as a universal phenomenon – and, indeed, to consider Indian caste society as its most extreme expression – may in fact be a peculiarity of the ethnic closure entailed in these egalitarian ideologies. Thus, the aporia of the modern European state is its tendency to a mystified or "hyperenchanted" nationalism or racism. Although this particular implication of Hobbes's thought commands little scholarly respect today, other aspects of his philosophy remain strikingly influential. In particular, Hobbes precisely identified the problem of legitimacy in a political context of secular, egalitarian individualism, and the intellectual framework he deployed to solve it of a disenchanted human order (or, in other words, human agency) has been fundamental to sociological explanation. But perhaps it is now easier to see that a philosophy or a sociology which starts from the assumption of individual subjects and then seeks to justify or account for the exercise of sovereign power over them will inevitably fall short of its goal. Certainly, recent theoretical work has tended to focus on what Foucault calls "the fabrication of subjects rather than the genesis of sovereignty" (cited in Pasquino,

1993: 79), though the ethical implications of these different projects remain debatable (see chapter 7). Nevertheless, in chapter 5 questions concerning the "fabrication of subjects" will also form a significant part of our effort to provide a sociological critique of racial ideology.

The present chapter and the preceding one have traced some of the ways in which European political thought from the medieval to the early modern period has provided grounds for the elaboration of racial ideology. We will leave our chronology at this point, where many intellectual histories of the race concept begin their narrative, first in order to pursue questions concerning the relationship between hierarchy and the person and then in order to examine the colonial legacy in the contemporary political discourse of once-colonized countries. But it is worth casting a glance forward to consider some of the implications of the preceding argument for an understanding of a later racial ideology. I have suggested that the racial ideologies associated with the first European colonial ventures were stabilized by an early modern philosophical discourse which expressed new forms of political closure around the concept of sovereignty. In this respect, the argument perhaps effaces differences between nationalism and racism which should be made more visible. George Mosse (1995) has argued along these lines in distinguishing between nineteenth-century nationalisms grounded in civic identification with the state and nineteenth-century racisms based upon a concern to make political community contingent upon the attributes of the human body. If, like Mosse, one restricts the definition of racism to an ideology of the eighteenth and especially nineteenth centuries then the distinction is undoubtedly important, but it seems to me more useful to regard these as inflections of a process both more enduring and more unitary in which the idea of political community was established through somatic markers in the colonies as well as in the European core region, and in which forms of civic identification always struggled against a more organic sense of political closure. The point also bears upon the way that race figured within European anti-slavery movements of the eighteenth and nineteenth centuries. This is, of course, a vast topic in its own right, but one could perhaps cite Seymour Drescher's conclusion that "the entire abolitionist process altered the path of racism very little" (Drescher, 1990: 442). The intellectual force of European abolitionism came from an accent on the secular, universalistic aspects of modern thought highlighted earlier whereas, paradoxically perhaps, many of its activists were drawn from a skilled manual workforce facing the solvent, universalizing forces of an emergent industrial capitalism which threatened to "enslave" them, and who therefore extended a kind of class alliance to the actual slaves of the British colonies (Davis, 1966; Blackburn, 1988; Holt, 1992). But although abolitionism was associated with an opening towards a more humanitarian and genuinely universal political discourse, in many ways it was the vehicle for a specifically metropolitan political radicalism directed to the local context (Blackburn, 1988), and one in which class "alliance" was made largely *by* the metropolitan working classes in relation to this context. Indeed, contemporary working-class radicalism could just as easily be ill-disposed to abolitionism and identification with black slaves (Hollis, 1980). In these respects, then, there remained continuities with the political closure described above.

5 | Race, Caste, and the Person

Introduction

In this chapter, we turn our attention from the form of the state or polity and its relationship to the construction of hierarchies to consider the form of the person and the way that the relatedness of persons to others correspondingly affects the construction of hierarchies, partly through the way that it is coordinated with political structures. The chapter has two broad aims. The first is to suggest that the construction of the person in the Euro-American and Indian cases roughly corresponds, with differences in "core symbols" of the kind analyzed in previous chapters which distinguish race and caste from one another. The second is to suggest that, notwithstanding this difference, there are certain similarities in the two cases, especially insofar as the group identifications they entail seem to be reproduced through the principles of group endogamy (people take their spouse from the same group) and group heritability (people pass their group status on to their offspring). Thus, I will argue that both race and caste hierarchies evince ideological parallels which turn upon commonalities in gender differentiation and conceptions of lineality and which underpin a common structure of inherent hierarchy.

However, we will have to qualify this view in several ways during the course of the chapter. A starting point here would be Dumont's work, which understands endogamy in the Indian case to be an intrusion of hierarchical caste principles, requiring fixed but not essential or material points of separation, into kinship. Thus, for Dumont, "caste endogamy, as oriented to the whole, is the opposite of racist endogamy, for 'race' is in this respect the individual substance made permanent" (Dumont, 1965: 91). The first part of this argument no doubt succumbs to some of the more general problems with Dumont's hierarchical conception of caste. There is more merit in his characterization of the situation pertaining to race, but common understandings of the reproduction of racial identifications have focused inordinately upon systems of "racist endogamy" of the kind typifying the postbellum states of the US South, where a bipartite status order was constructed through the idiom of racial separation or purity. This can obscure a more complex dynamic of race and status, such as can be found in many Caribbean societies. Later in the chapter, we will examine some of these societies in order to suggest that the predications of the person within them represent particular transformations of the Euro-American symbolic logic within which we have located the construction of racial sentiment. Likewise, we will consider the predication of the person and the relatedness of persons through some Indian examples in order to develop an analysis of its relationship to the logic of caste reckoning described in earlier chapters. First, however, we attempt a broader characterization of these logics in relation to an understanding of kinship and the construction of the person.

Race, Caste, and Kinship

The discussion in this chapter takes us into the traditional anthropological domain of kinship. Once at the heart of the discipline, kinship theory has since the 1960s been increasingly subsumed within other concerns, and indeed many of its core propositions from an earlier period have more recently been subjected to severe criticism. One of the reasons for this is the assumption of earlier theorists that some discrete domain of "kinship" could be readily detached from the broader flow of social relationships, an assumption which now seems to speak more to the ethnocentrism of anthropological models implicitly based upon the folk categories of Euro-American kinship constructs than to any universal principles of social life. More recent studies have deconstructed "kinship" as a discrete domain against other social identifications, like gender or labor. Nevertheless, in this chapter we shall proceed from the rather traditional anthropological domain of kinship because it can help render visible certain aspects of hierarchy. In doing so, however, we will need to turn our deconstructive gaze back onto the integrity of kinship as a domain that permits such illumination. Thus, as the argument develops, the chapter moves on from kinship to a consideration of gender, labor, and questions concerning political incorporation or nationalism which were broached in chapter 4.

Let us first review some elements of traditional kinship theory and its later reformulation. This will be used as the basis for a contrast between the construction of the person in race and caste ideologies, the implications of which will then be examined through analysis of historical and ethnographic data from India and the Caribbean.

The domain of kinship was a principal topic for research in British social anthropology from the 1930s to the 1960s, and unilineal descent systems were its paradigmatic focus. *Descent* refers to the reckoning of social relationships traced through a common ancestor. A distinction can be made between *cognatic* descent (where the descent rule allows links to be traced through either the male or female line) and *unilineal* descent (where links are traced through one or other line only; *patrilineal* descent referring to links through the male line, and *matrilineal* descent to links through the female line). Lineage systems are typically based upon a rule of exogamy. Thus, within a given patrilineage, the men take wives from other groups; the offspring are part of their father's lineage, but female offspring will eventually marry outside the lineage and *their* children will be part of their husband's and not their own lineage. The offspring of male children, however, will remain part of their father's lineage. These practices are typically accompanied by descent ideologies which focus upon how people are related to their parents, an issue referred to as *filiation*. Often, strongly patrilineal systems emphasize the male role as genitor, as for example in the Brahmanic idea that the man provides the "seed" of the child and the woman acts only as the "ground" or container for it. Such ideas are described as *patrilateral filiation*; other descent ideologies are *matrilateral* or – as with Euro-American kinship constructs – *bilateral*, positing the equal inheritance of human substance or "blood" from both parents. However, descent and filiation can rarely be described as fully unilineal or unilateral in any particular case. This element typically varies in degree across different social contexts, and there is always an element of cognatic or bilateral reckoning even in strongly unilineal systems (Goody, 1983). As we shall see, this is an important point when we come to consider the reproduction of caste distinction.

In unilineal descent systems, a segment or "sub-lineage" of the larger lineage may split off over time to establish a new descent line, but the important point is that the people comprising the new segment are lineally related to the larger whole through ties to some common ancestor. The descent system as a whole is "segmentary" in the sense that each of its constituent parts is a segment or miniature replica of the larger system. For this reason, there need be no hard-and-fast rule about the point of segmentation, but different levels of segmentation can be defined in terms of successively more inclusive segments tracing themselves to an increasingly distant common ancestor. Beyond this level, the word *clan* has been used to define a group which believes itself to possess a common ancestor but is unable to trace the genealogical connection.

Anthropologists working mainly in Africa from the 1930s to the 1960s claimed that the descent rules of the societies that they studied corresponded closely to the theoretical model described above, perhaps the most famous example being Evans-Pritchard's (1940) study of the Nuer in Sudan. According to Evans-Pritchard, lineage segmentation among the Nuer corresponded to the territorial basis of "tribal" organization, descent thus being seen as an idiom of political relations. In Evans-Pritchard's famous formulation, people within different lineages at a relatively minor, local level might oppose each other in a feud, but would unite in a feud against people from more distant lineages, and so on up the segmentary tree beyond the level of the clan or tribe (ibid.: 143–4). The reckoning of unilineal descent is a necessary condition for this corporate, political function of lineages, because there can be no exclusive, unambiguous group membership in a cognatic system where kinship ties multiply as one ascends each generational level.

The formulation is compellingly neat, but later analysis of the Nuer data suggested that the lineage as a corporate group conjoining kin and political relations bears rather little resemblance to Nuer conceptions or behavior. In particular, it appears that the Nuer did not make a sharp conceptual distinction between lineage and territorial organization, nor did lineages operate as corporate groups in any concrete situation; rather, as Evans-Pritchard himself conceded, the Nuer thought in terms of extant relationships between kin groups within territorially based communities (ibid.: 202), and lineage ties often appeared to be elaborated as a rationale for locally based relationships, constituting a kind of idiom for the latter. Thus, as Kuper pithily observes, "even the Nuer are not like *The Nuer*" (Kuper, 1988: 201). Such observations led to a thorough critique of segmentary lineage models.

Why, then, did lineage theory so pervade the writings of a generation of anthropologists? Kuper and others have suggested that the answer has to do with its ability to resolve longstanding problems in sociological theory that Evans-Pritchard and his colleagues inherited from their nineteenth-century forebears. Imbued with modern European political philosophy of the kind we examined in the previous chapters, these writers had raised the problem of how "primitive" societies lacking a strong centralized state were able to maintain political order, and – concomitantly – of how kinship was related to territorial identity, or in the more evocative terms of the nationalist ideologies which constituted one of the intellectual contexts for the problem, of how "blood" was related to "soil." Evans-Pritchard's lineage model neatly solved these puzzles, constituting descent as the political idiom of "stateless" societies guaranteeing an "ordered anarchy."

The segmentary lineage model reflected the distinctive Euro-American conception of political order in terms of a single, sovereign center or apex which we examined in chapter 3, supplying a unitary principle of political organization for societies apparently lacking a centralized agency in which sovereignty was invested. At the same time, the model and some of its attendant assumptions about the character of "primitive" society drew attention away from aspects of the societies under scrutiny which *did* evince political centralization and from the historical emergence of such societies in the interstices of more centrally organized states. For these reasons, the segmentary lineage model was later subjected to severe criticism. Nevertheless, the idea that unilineal descent constructs model representations of the social world which constitute particular kinds of social action in some societies should not perhaps be entirely disregarded.

The hold of lineage theory over the anthropological imagination had begun to break down during the 1960s under several different influences. These included the structural anthropology of Claude Lévi-Strauss (1969), which interposed the issue of marital alliance into the model of lineage identity, suggesting that it was the exogamous practice which tied lineages together that provided the key dynamic of the system. Another influence was US cultural anthropology, particularly David Schneider's (1968) "cultural account" of American (that is, US) kinship. According to Schneider, there is an underlying logic to American kin terms which distinguishes between an "order of nature" and an "order of law" and through which people are related respectively according to either "natural substance" or a "code for conduct." A person is related by indissoluble bonds to certain categories of kinsfolk with whom they share substance – a "natural," biogenetic substance whose dominant symbol is blood and which is imparted through a process of procreation which derives from sexual intercourse. Other kinds of relationships are relationships in law governed by a code for conduct, of which marriage between men and women who do not share substance is one example. Sexual intercourse between husband and wife creates a unity of substance with their offspring. Schneider distinguishes a "pure domain of kinship" defined around the single symbol of intercourse, from a "conglomerate domain" which constructs the person as a particular social being in relation to other symbol systems such as age and gender (Schneider, 1977: 68). For Schneider, American kinship operates in general around the symbol of "love"; sexual or "conjugal" love creates substance through the union of a genitor and genetrix differentiated in nature, while "cognatic love" constitutes the affective relations between those united in nature through blood, as are parents and children. Together, the symbols of American kinship converge upon solidary or affective relationships which are diffuse (that is, not organized around the execution of specific tasks or duties) and enduring.

Schneider's approach is of interest to us here for two reasons. First, it has been extremely influential in the comparative study of kinship, not least in studies of caste and kinship in India associated with the "ethnosociological" school of Chicago anthropologists, which we shall examine below. Second, the symbolization of "diffuse, enduring solidarity" is not, according to Schneider, restricted to kinship but also applies to other cultural units such as religion and nationality. This, of course, brings us close to the topic of the present book, but the theoretical implication is that different cultural domains can entertain a similar structural logic, making the distinction between categories like "kinship," "ethnicity," or "nationality" problematic, a point carried further in Schneider's (1977) later work.

Schneider's focus on the nature–law distinction on his home turf of the USA contributed to a growing sense that aspects of orthodox kinship theory involved the inappropriate universalization of specifically Western conceptions of social order. The developing body of anthropological research among societies of the South Pacific also contributed to this trend. Here, it was found that kinship was commonly articulated around ideas of patrilineal descent in the context of political decentralization, as had earlier been found in the classic African studies. However, a smooth transfer of African lineage models did not prove fruitful because in the South Pacific patrilineal and nonpatrilineal kin mixed without corporate distinctions at the level of the local community, and people appeared to articulate their kin relations around several different dimensions which vitiated any regular segmentary principle (Holy, 1996). Here, an "ancestor" was not used to constitute an unambiguous collectivity but to create a name or socially differentiated entity through which the flow of human relations could be modeled as an analogue, a flow which could also be modeled after other differentiations.

Wagner (1977) has developed this idea into quite a radical reformulation of earlier approaches to kinship, not least Lévi-Strauss's. Opposing the tendency in kinship studies to define the initial problem in terms of how individuals are bound into groups, Wagner starts with the proposition that all human relationships are analogous to one another, and that the production of relationships involved in the structuring of kinship therefore involves acts of differentiation. The argument explodes the concern in descent theory to construct the culturally specific ways in which people – conceived metaculturally as social persons who are always coextensive with the autonomous human biological organism or "body," as in Euro-American constructions of the person – are linked to one another through particular ideologies concerning the transfer of human substance. It does so because it entertains a much more monadic conception of substance or essence as that which is differentiated in order to produce order, of which one particular resolution is indeed the Euro-American idea which identifies persons as individual, autonomous human bodies and, moreover, ones which are intrinsically gendered. Thus, the argument departs from the tendency in lineage theory to view kinship as a set of offices (mother, son, etc.) which are given or differentiated *a priori*, and are then bound together in systemic ways which vary cross-culturally. The logic of the argument is that in order to explain "kinship" one should not proceed from an analysis of individuals already assumed to be marked or differentiated by kin relations, a point which resembles Foucault's substitution of the fabrication of subjects for the genesis of sovereignty which we encountered in the previous chapter. The same point can be made *mutatis mutandis* for explanations of ethnic or racial group formation which proceed by assuming the existence of individuals organized into groups.

Wagner advocates this "analogic" approach to kinship over the "homologic" approach dominant in traditional kinship theory, which we can illustrate in relation to Lévi-Strauss's model of totemic relations (see chapter 2). For Lévi-Strauss, the collective differences created in totemic relations are constructed as cultural homologues of natural differences between species. Wagner argues that the same homologic model is implied in the distinction between naturalized kin "offices" like "father," "mother," or "son," and their accompanying codes for conduct ("paternal solicitude," "maternal solicitude," "filial solicitude"), as is shown in figure 5.1 (a). This homologic approach makes the empty spaces between the boxes in figure 5.1 (a) problematic. How does culture relate to nature? How is the relationship between the cultural code for conduct which is associated with a natural kin office made manifest? For Lévi-Strauss, of course, the answer is the incest taboo, which establishes the distinction between culture and nature and the correct kind of intendedness between conduct and nature. Thus, people learn to accommodate their conduct to the natural kin offices they inhabit; a woman displays maternal solicitude to her son and conjugal solicitude to her husband. To display conjugal solicitude to her son would be "unnatural" and incestuous.

Wagner rejects this approach to the problem, proposing instead the analogical approach which is displayed in figure 5.1 (b). The problem of relating nature to culture or of "natural" kin types to kinds of solicitude is thereby abolished, because it is subsumed within the analogic relationship which postulates an identity between the two. The problematic area now becomes the relationship between the analogic boxes in figure 5.1 (b), which correspond to different natural kin types, a problem which, according to Wagner, is addressed by the flow of analogy or similarity between kin relationships. This flow is always directed by an arbitrary or contrived interdict which partitions and creates order out of the formless resemblances

(a) Homological relations

Culture
Code for Conduct
"Man"

Nature
Kin Office
God

(b) Analogical relations

Culture
Code for Conduct
"Man"

Nature
Kin Office
God

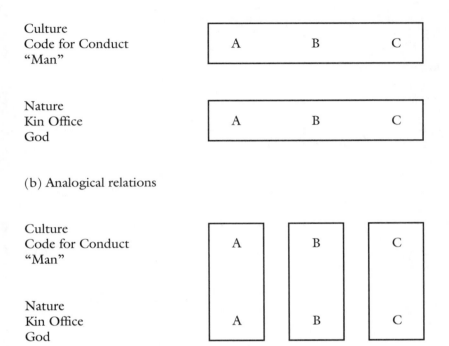

Figure 5.1 Homological/analogical relations
(*Derived from Wagner*, 1977: 625. Reproduced by permission of the American
Anthropological Association from *American Ethnologist* 4: 4, November 1988. Not
for further reproduction.)

of things, of which the nature–culture distinction or the incest taboo are
perhaps merely culturally specific manifestations.

Surprisingly, Wagner omits to mention the part of Lévi-Strauss's work
which gives most explicit attention to the kind of analogic approach he
favors, namely the discussion in *The Savage Mind* of caste as an analogic
transformation of homologic totemic relations, which we examined in chapter 2. There I argued that Lévi-Strauss's analogic model of caste – still
predicated upon the distinction between nature and culture – in fact better
typified race relations than caste relations, a point which is perhaps supported by Wagner's view that constructions like Lévi-Strauss's putatively
universal nature–culture distinction represent a specifically "Western" approach to the problem of creating relatedness. If this is so, it may be

(a) Ranking hierachy

Culture
Code for Conduct
"Man"

Nature
Kin Office
God

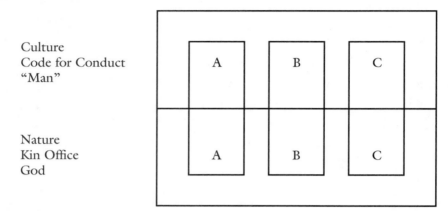

(b) Encompassing hierarchy

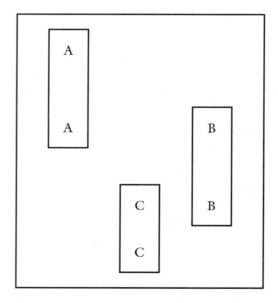

Figure 5.2   Analogical relations and hierarchy

instructive to view this analogic model of race derived from Lévi-Strauss as a special case of Wagner's universal analogic schema. It is then possible to locate them within our two models of Western ranking hierarchy and Indian encompassing hierarchy which, in chapter 1, we derived from Dumont, yielding figure 5.2.

Figure 5.2 (a) indicates what an analogic model of race relations might look like when it is considered as a modality of ranking hierarchy, of the kind we have constructed as a Euro-American archetype. Here, instead of totemic groups or kin types we might substitute the idea of distinct races – let us say, following a Caribbean colonial example, of whites, blacks, and mulattos – whose absolute distinctiveness is established by their "analogic" differentiation in a secularized, essential nature. Once so concretized, it is a simple matter to rank these groups according to any number of possible criteria so as to produce a hierarchy which, in our historical example, elevated whites above blacks. But whereas in Wagner's kinship examples the "problematic" space between the analogic boxes is addressed by the flow of similarity between kin relationships, with the example of race, ideological emphasis is placed upon the need to maintain the absolute distinctions between races as groups which have been established as different in nature (cf. Williams, 1995). Perhaps this explains the tenor of the early colonial legislation concerning interracial sex cited in chapter 4, with its language of "shameful" matches, "abominable" mixtures, and "disgraceful" conduct. Such matches and mixtures were nevertheless entered into, producing the mulatto or "mixed race" group which, we might expect, could logically be ranked as somewhere in between black or white, assimilated to one or other category, or alternatively viewed as an "abominable" degradation of both black and white type-essences. There is evidence for all of these views in colonial Caribbean history (the etymological derivation of "mulatto" from "mule," the sterile offspring of the horse and donkey, points to the latter interpretation, one which was not easy to sustain in the face of the facts, although this did not prevent prodigious efforts to do so in Caribbean colonial societies). But whatever the case, we can expect on the basis of this model interdiction or at least problematization of some kind to apply to interracial sex (thereby making gender relations an especially prominent concern), and not a smooth analogic "flow" of relatedness. We can also expect certain political problems if the model persists in a postcolonial context. Instead of finding a common national public or citizenry constituted by a bloc of equal individuals as we scan across the upper or "profane" part of figure 5.2 (a), we now find several blocs of incommensurate groups who need to be homogenized if the standard idea of a culturally unified nation discussed in chapter 3 is to be realized. Such ideologies of nationalist homogenization immediately spring to mind in American contexts, as with the various metaphors of admixture and blending to be found in ideas like the famous "melting pot" metaphor of the USA, Frederick Jackson Turner's (1894) "frontier hypothesis," or the Jamaican national motto "Out of many, one people." We shall examine this issue in more detail in chapter 6.

A somewhat different situation results when an analogic representation of caste relations is placed within the model of encompassing caste hierarchy, as in figure 5.2 (b). Here, castes figure as subsets of the broader hierarchical unity. In this model, we might conceivably expect similar kinds of problems to arise over intercaste sex–gender relations (cf. Tambiah, 1985: 212–51), but there is no parallel with the political problem of creating a nation (because there is no "nation").

The culture theory of both Wagner and Schneider involves a kind of closure which Wagner (1986) later elaborated in his idea of symbols which "stand for themselves." Here, nothing lies beyond the generation of meaning other than the process itself. In an outstanding analysis of systems of racial and caste classification, Brackette Williams (1995) has recently criticized both Wagner and Schneider on this account. Whence comes Wagner's arbitrary interdict? How, for Schneider, does blood come to invest the family and the nation? Williams radicalizes Wagner's argument that the generative symbolism of social categories is never a completed process by invoking "history" as the missing term in the cultural account, such that "culturally constructed persons embody the historicity of prior ideological formations" (ibid.: 232). Whereas Wagner and Schneider (and indeed Lévi-Strauss) attempt in their different ways to provide a self-contained analytical model, Williams is dissatisfied with their putatively idealist reduction of history to mere diachrony which, to take the example of Wagner's model of analogic flow, always proceeds from the same arbitrary interdict. In her words, "systems of ideology are not autochthonously produced and the world of practice sprung from their loins," but rather "the historicity of the invention of similarity and the differentiations it makes possible reveals intricate and inextricable connections between power differentials and the symbolic and ideological practices out of which these are naturalized in substance definitions and categorical deployments in classificatory system" (ibid.: 225). The point recalls Spivak's discussion of "attributive" rather than "analogical" relations as the fields of force within a nexus of cultural representations through which particular configurations of power (such as patriarchy) are advanced. As with our discussion of this point in chapter 2, there is a question of emphasis here; how much analytical weight should be put on attributive ("power") relations as the motor of social process and how much upon analogical ("cultural") relations? In inclining towards the former – the "naturalization of power" – Williams risks the kind of reductionism criticized in chapter 2, which would render the "historicity of prior ideological formations" as a continuity undergirded by elite self-interest, comprehensible through the ahistorical and universal dynamics of instrumental social power. But in fact she comes to a much more "analogical" understanding of the way that caste and race ideologies are enjoined:

> Brahma, as homologue for the body politic, was composed of partable substance that could be mixed and hierarchicalized. It could be hierarchicalized precisely because all variants of substance were ultimately thought to derive from or to have been absorbed into a unitary whole; each represented a more or less pure version of the original substance now bounded as a discrete unit of a type of pure impurity. Nature, as biological diversity and environmental variation, although acting on the common concept of *human*, did not provide a unitary whole composed of discrete units of purity. It could be said that each race of humans was made in nature's own image, but the fact that from place to place and from time to time nature's image was *variable* posed a problem for nationalism and nationalist ideologies' efforts to define, bound, and hierarchically arrange the biogenetic "races" of the body politic. . . . This problem was not shared by caste ideology and its employment of Brahma as source for the classification of a unitary, but stratified, social body. (Williams, 1995: 225–6)

Thus, likewise, my argument has been that racialized thought, and its broader context of political or "nationalist" closure, parallels the "analogic" moment of Lévi-Strauss's theory of caste, whereby social groups define themselves by an image drawn from a model of natural differentiation, but in circumstances where each "natural" group is conceived as part of a systemically ordered whole, under the sign of "nature." Here, we encounter units in a ranked series which necessarily transcend "all categorical divisions if . . . [they are] to be coterminous with the sociopolitical unit. Otherwise one has more than one social order occupying a single political unit" (Williams, 1995: 225). As we have seen, a plurality of social orders is something that *can* be argued with some plausibility to characterize caste-ordered societies, but not race-ordered ones.

Taking issue somewhat with Williams's point about Brahma[n], my own argument is that Brahman serves as a unitary metaphor for a divided social order, whereas in race-ordered societies nature serves as a divisive metaphor in a unitary social order which defines its own boundaries as a "natural" limit. Or, alternatively, we might say that the logic of Indian caste hierarchy is that unitary substance produces divided types in relation to the polity and the person, whereas the logic of European natural hierarchy is the production of unitary types from contextually divided substance, leading to a characteristic nationalist aporia.

Schneider's work and its appropriation in the ethnosociological approach to caste is an obvious influence upon this argument. There is, however, a certain irony in this tradition because Schneider's account of "American" kinship was explicitly restricted to the USA, and yet has received its most enduring attention from theorists who reject a comparative sociological approach in favor of an ethnosociology which seeks to understand "what is perceived by Indians in Indian categories" (Marriott, 1989: 1). While it is hard to accept this strong relativism, the code/substance distinction deployed in ethnosociological approaches remains useful in suggesting the difference between Euro-American cultural categories which are based upon an absolute distinction between codes for conduct and natural substance, and Indian categories based upon a monism in which code and substance interpenetrate.

It is perhaps inevitable that the hubris of Euro-American sociologists who seek to describe India in its own monadic categories should invite the nemesis of an Indian sociologist who identifies an encompassing monism in Indian *and* Euro-American culture. Such is the position of André Béteille, who argues that the "biological substantialism" diagnosed by Marriott as a peculiarity of Hindu culture is in fact a common feature of "Indo-European culture" (Béteille, 1990: 497). Assimilating the separability of substance and code to that of actor and action, Béteille (ibid.: 498–9) contends that in America just as in India, this separability does not hold in certain domains of social life. The arena of race is his principal example, for a central tenet of American racism has long been that blacks and whites act differently because they are different kinds of actor. They are people who differ *in nature*.

Valid though this point is, it is misdirected when it is used against Schneider or the ethnosociologists, as Béteille does. This is because there are several conceptions of "nature" at play here which Béteille tends to conflate. Understanding their different connotations will help us to put the construction of the person in its proper comparative context. The first conception relates to Schneider's code/substance distinction, which was originally formulated to characterize American kinship constructs. These do make a clear distinction between those people whose relationships are thought to be "natural" ones, ineluctably consecrated by biogenetic substance ("blood relatives"), and those which involve a socially sanctioned code for conduct, most notably that between spouses. Such a separation does not figure so sharply in Indian kinship constructs, even if it is possible to overdraw the contrast. But this is an entirely different sense from Béteille's suggestion – also true – that in America people who fit into particular social categories are subject to behavioral stereotypes grounded in an essentialism of "nature," as when black people or white people, men or women, young or old, rich or poor and so on, are thought "naturally" to possess some positively or negatively valued attribute. The point bears upon deeper constructions of the person in Euro-American culture which hold that whatever a person says or does, their "race" – or, indeed, these other identifications – remains the same (Strathern, 1985), constructions in which much anti-racist political activism also participates. This is quite different from the logic of caste categories in India of the kind described by Bayly when he says "there was no such thing as a creditworthy Kalwar family, but a Kalwar could become a creditworthy Jaiswal" (Bayly, 1983: 408). In America, by contrast, black people might generally be associated with uncreditworthiness, but it is nevertheless possible for any particular black person to be creditworthy. It is never possible for a black person not to be black.

Finally, there is a difference between Indian and Euro-American conceptions of "nature" in terms of the way that the relationship between persons and conduct tends to be constructed. In India, one's "natural" inclination is towards the conduct sanctioned in one's *jati dharma*, conduct which may go unrealized in practice because of societal pressures not to conform, whereas in Euro-American contexts one's "natural" inclination is towards egotistical or amoral behavior (as expressed in Hobbes's "state of nature," according to a common interpretation) which is checked by societal pressures to conform to codes for conduct (cf. Miller, 1986).

My reference to "America" in the foregoing discussion was left vague, but whereas Béteille (and, of course, Schneider) restricts his analysis to the USA, my own argument can, I think, be generalized to the broader American context of the Caribbean. In so doing, however, the idea of natural substance and its mutability will call for some further comment.

Louis Jean-Jacques Acaau, leader of the *piquet* peasant rebels in mid-nineteenth century Haiti, is said to have first coined the well-known Haitian saying "nèg riche cé mulat, mulat pov cé nèg" (a rich black is a mulatto, a poor mulatto is a black). The saying captures a dimension of social life in many Caribbean postplantation societies, and while it can appropriately be seen to articulate the class character of black poverty it also exemplifies a particular associative process. In these societies physical appearance is socially significant, and people are described in relation to various somatic norms which include – but are not limited to – skin color. But these are transformed by other systems of social classification, for example by socioeconomic status. Thus, a dark-skinned person might be described by a somatic term denoting lighter skin if they are wealthy or of high status. In this sense, a "nèg riche" might indeed be a "mulat." To account for this phenomenon, we can recapitulate the following aspects of our general model for Euro-American racial ideologies, whereby,

1   actions or codes for conduct are separated from "natural" substance;
2   conduct cannot change substance;
3   objectified things and qualities are related associatively.

There has been a persistent association in Caribbean history between wealth and color – in the polarized plantation order, to be white was to be wealthy, and to be black was to be poor. Thus, a wealthy person seems "white" but a black wealthy person cannot alter their blackness on account of their wealth. They become associatively or, in Saussurean language, syntagmatically, "white" (cf. Dominguez, 1977). In other words, if it is true that to be white is to be wealthy, it is also true through a chain of associative meanings that to be wealthy is to be white. The association is perhaps more salient for poor black people than it is for lighter-skinned people, whose status concerns are such as to incline them to deny the possibility that a black person could ever be anything other than black. But this does not mean that poor black people in the Caribbean are at all deluded about the true historical character of the association between whiteness and wealth, or that they bring no sense of irony to the idea that "money whitens." It means rather that in everyday life, somatic categories are used as a means to represent wealth or social status. Thus, somatic or "racial" categories in the Caribbean reveal their fundamentally social character; they act as one set of metaphors for the location of the individual within the polity. In this respect they contrast with Indian caste categories which might be seen as synecdoches of Brahman in the context of encompassing hierarchy, rather than as metaphors of social rank (Daniel, 1984).

It is necessary to make a final point about gender before moving on to consider some more specific historical and ethnographic material. In general, gender differentiation has been conceived after the model of ranking hierarchy in Euro-American thought, both in traditional anthropological theory and in folk consciousness. Wagner's is only one among several works which problematize this Western construction on the basis of South Pacific ethnography (cf. Strathern, 1988; Tcherkezoff, 1993). Tcherkezoff, for example, draws upon Dumont's discussion of encompassment to contrast the Western juxtaposition of male and female as fixed and exhaustive terms with the Samoan conception in which femaleness is the ontologically fixed ground encompassing maleness as an ontologically insecure domain of action within it, in ways that subvert complete identification between biologically male and female human organisms and "men" and "women" as transcontextual social actors. Femaleness above all connotes genealogical title, and the core relationship in Tcherkezoff's Samoa is not, as in descent or alliance theory, between parents and children or husbands and wives, but between sisters (as embodiments of title) and brothers (as their agents). Later on, I shall suggest that the natural hierarchies under consideration here necessarily incline towards a dualistic and not, as in Tcherkezoff's Samoa, an encompassing conception of gender.

Caste, Kinship, and Gender in India

In this section we will draw out some of the implications of the preceding discussion with a more specific analysis of caste, kinship, and gender in India. Let us begin by observing that whereas caste, variously understood, is usually thought of as a more or less pan-Indian phenomenon, ways of reckoning kinship vary widely across the subcontinent. Although we are unable to consider the many variants in their full complexity here (see Carter, 1973; Trautmann, 1981; Dumont, 1983; Uberoi, 1993), it is worth at least pointing to the most obvious distinction in Indian kinship, namely between the "Dravidian" forms of the south and the "Indo-Aryan" forms of the north.

The preferred form of South Indian kinship is traditionally called "cross-cousin marriage" by anthropologists. "Cross-cousins" refer to the offspring of different sex siblings, as opposed to the "parallel-cousin" offspring of same sex siblings, so that the cross-cousin marriage partner for a man could be his father's sister's daughter (patrilateral cross-cousin marriage) or his mother's brother's daughter (matrilateral cross-cousin marriage, the commonest Dravidian arrangement). Through an analysis of its kin terminologies, Dumont (1983) conceives the Dravidian system in terms of the establishment of affinal relations between two separate classes of same sex cross-kin, so that a man's marriage to his mother's brother's daughter confirms his affinal relationship with his mother's brother's son, just as – from the complementary gender perspective – a woman's marriage to her father's sister's son confirms her affinal relationship with her father's sister's daughter. These affinal relationships between classes of same sex cross-kin are replicated in succeeding generations so that, for example, a man "inherits" the affinal relationship that his father established with his male cross-cousin through marriage with his male cross-cousin's sister, by marrying the sister of his own male cross-cousin. Thus rooted in the theory of alliance which Lévi-Strauss counterposed to descent theory, Dumont's schema abolishes the need to appeal to the concept of crossness and thereby to invoke the idea of descent. It also demands, counterintuitively to Western notions, that a man's affinal links to his cross-kin are traced (in the matrilateral case) not through his mother but through his father, just as a woman's links are traced not through her father but her mother. In thereby making relationships between same-sex affines its central focus, the schema deflects attention from the very centrality of gender differentiation to the system (Trawick, 1990; Busby, 1997; see below).

In the Indo-Aryan systems of North India, cross-cousin marriage is prohibited and marriage is typically enjoined as an exogamous contract at some level of patrilineal segmentation, which usually involves circles of marital exchange of wider compass than in Dravidian systems. Thus, North Indian kinship systems would seem to be based upon principles of patrilineal descent and are less obviously predicated upon a logic of alliance. However, Dumont argues that such a logic can be discerned in the nature of the gifts or prestations associated with marriage. These apparently flow unilaterally from "wife-givers" to "wife-takers" in a status relation of inferiority to superiority which constitutes a man's kinsfolk, like mother's father, mother's brother, and wife's brother, into the subordinate class of "wife-givers" in relation to kinsfolk who belong to his own "wife-taking" patriline. This creates a tendency to open-ended ranking hierarchy, where marriage involves the unilateral movement of women "upwards" to higher status spouses (a practice anthropologists call "hypergamy," which, it will be noted, is consistent with the nonreciprocal logic of the "Indian gift" discussed in chapter 3). Its open-ended, nonreciprocal character – "generalized exchange," after Lévi-Strauss (1969) – contrasts with the "restricted exchange" associated with forms of cross-cousin marriage, which involve bilateral marital exchange over two generations, although the matrilateral cross-cousin marriage widespread in Dravidian systems is consonant with generalized exchange.

Parenthetically, in view of these different forms of Indian kinship, it is tempting to contrast once again the plurality of the Indian situation with the substantial unity of European kinship, which Goody (1983) has argued stemmed largely from the success of the church in limiting and controlling relations of conjugality and inheritance. This view has a "materialist" component in its suggestion of an effective centralization of ecclesiastical power aimed at directing a flow of resources to the church, and an "idealist" component in suggesting that the sectarian foundations of Christianity oriented it towards the dissolution of alternative collective bases of social organization. The contrast between Indian plurality and European singularity should not, however, be overdrawn in view of attempts to show the underlying commonalities of Indian kinship systems, as in Dumont's analysis outlined above (see also Carter, 1973; Östör, Fruzzetti, and Barnett, 1992). At the same time, since these attempts emphasize a particular logic of exchange, in a sense they underscore the difference between Indian and European "core symbols" discussed in earlier chapters. The more significant point for present purposes, however, is the relationship between caste and kinship in the Indian case.

A simple emphasis upon the endogamous character of castes or *jatis* must be supplemented with the recognition that exogamous principles exist within the caste prohibiting marriages of certain kinds, prohibitions which vary according to the different modes of kin reckoning alluded to above. Thus, it is tempting to seek the hard and fast boundaries which establish, on the one hand, the maximal endogamous unit and, on the other, the minimal exogamous one in order to define caste membership in terms of an unambiguously identifiable group of people who are all equivalent in status, thereby making the group boundary itself the fundamental manifestation of the hierarchical principle. But this is not how the system operates. First, although the *jati* has conventionally been taken as the basic endogamous unit, and thereby the building block of caste society, in fact it can prove to be either larger or smaller than the unit people routinely consider to be the one from which they take spouses. Larger, because a *jati* can be composed of several endogamous units, or "sub-*jatis*," and smaller because sometimes the logic of intracaste exogamy, and particularly hypergamy, creates pressures to break the boundaries of *jati* endogamy (a practice given guarded sanction in ancient Brahmanic texts such as the *Dharmasastras*, which entertained the possibility of hypergamous *anuloma* unions, but not hypogamous *pratiloma* unions, where it is men who marry higher status women). Second, hierarchy also suffuses relationships within the endogamous unit. For example, on the basis of research among the Rajputs of Kangra, Jonathan Parry (1979) shows that any unit which the analyst might be tempted to reify as a "real" corporate unit of marital exchange (or subcaste) can be further sublimated into a set of hierarchical relationships. In this sense, endogamy is not a fundamental principle underlying caste society so much as an entailment of hierarchy, which *does* constitute such a principle, and which tends to enjoin a logic of separation within the social domains it encompasses. This is effectively a statement of Dumont's theory of caste, and it underscores his view that kinship is analytically separate from caste (Dumont, 1980). Caste, rather, is the hierarchical principle which encompasses or suffuses kin relations.

There have, however, been several efforts to transcend this distinction and to demonstrate the connections between caste and kinship. In this category could be mentioned attempts to emphasize the grounding of both caste and kinship in the problem of creating political order (Fox, 1970; Dirks, 1993; Quigley, 1993); arguments – often developed within or against the ethnosociological approach – which have emphasized a common systemic structure to kin and caste ideology in India (Inden and Nicholas, 1977; Trautmann, 1981; Daniel, 1983; Raheja, 1989; Trawick, 1990; Östör, Fruzzetti, and Barnett, 1992); and Milner's (1994) ingenious attempt to account for Indian kinship through his neo-Weberian theory of status competition. Here, we will briefly examine some aspects of the first two of these three approaches. This will enable us to see how the conceptions of lineality, nature, and gender discussed earlier relate to caste ideology, while also helping to illuminate the homologous logic of political and kinship principles in caste relations.

Let us begin by considering Richard Fox's analysis of Rajput state formation in pre-British Uttar Pradesh (North India). Fox (1970) argues that the expansionary Rajput polities were built upon a ranked lineage structure comprising lineage centers, segmentary in nature, in which "cadet lines" split from the locally dominant lineage to form new, lower ranking and geographically dispersed settlement clusters. This partially accounts for the tension between isogamy (i.e. marriage to status equals) and hypergamy in North Indian kinship. Hypergamy was a strategy of status improvement and territorial expansion for the socially and politically inferior – but still relatively powerful – cadet lines, as they attempted to attach themselves to more powerful, territorially based lineages. By contrast, less dominant castes had no such leverage, and their isogamy reflected a strategy of the powerless to adapt to their situation by at least ensuring that those who were even less powerful could not encroach upon them (Quigley, 1993).

Arguably, the expansionary *kshatriya* ethic of Rajput social organization does accord quite closely with the classic model of segmentary patrilineages, with a patrilateral bias in ideologies of filiation which is consonant with the sanction for *anuloma* unions in the *Dharmasastras*. In a sense, this reflects the specific "tribal" organization of the Rajputs and the affinity of *kshatriya* ideology with a continuum between non-caste "tribal" status and processes of "Rajputization" through which kin-ordered polities within the caste order can be constituted (Sinha, 1965; 1997). There are, however, some further complications to Fox's model of Rajput state formation. As Stern (1977) has argued, the Rajputs were circumscribed by the authority of the ruling Mughal dynasty, and indeed served the Mughals as a client ruling warrior class; dominant political positions within the Rajput firmament could owe as much to this cross-cutting fact of Mughal patronage as to lineage dominance, leading not only to ideological tensions concerning the proper model for political organization among Rajputs, but also to a dissonance between ritual status – to which hypergamous strategies were directed – and political power (Stern, 1977; Ziegler, 1978). In this respect, politically dominant Rajput lineages did not necessarily hold the monopoly of status, and singular hypergamous strategies of marrying into politically dominant lineages did not obtain.

Whatever the merits of these positions, their difference from Dumont's theory of caste should be clear. Dumont makes hierarchy the transcendent principle of caste, and therefore denies that other principles of social reckoning are germane to an understanding of caste relations except insofar as they are encompassed by the hierarchical principle. So, for example, he turns locality identification into the principle of descent reckoning (Dumont, 1964), and turns descent reckoning into a principle of alliance which vitiates hierarchy among the parties to the marriage (Dumont, 1983). The advantage of the approach charted by scholars like Fox and Quigley is that it brings hierarchy down to earth by showing how it is articulated in kinship structures as a modality of competition for political power. A similar point could be made, *mutatis mutandis*, with South Indian examples such as the "little kingdom" of Pudukkottai, for which Dirks (1993) demonstrates the relationship between political centrality (kingship) and caste, understood as lineage ranking within the territorially defined polity (*nadu*). Dirks argues that Pudukkottai provides an especially clear exemplification of this political aspect of caste because royal sovereignty was never subordinated to Muslim or British overlords whose political dominance elsewhere provided the opportunity for a world-transcending Brahmanism to supersede royal authority. Nevertheless, this leaves open the predication of the little kingdom within the same "radial" model, and raises the same sorts of questions discussed in chapter 3 about the extent to which it can be understood in structural or cultural terms.

The preceding discussion has perhaps helped clarify the relationship between caste and kinship, but it does not explain the compatibility of different forms of kinship reckoning with caste organization. One way of approaching this question is to seek an underlying unity in putatively different kinship systems by identifying the basis upon which they are systematically oriented to conceptions of caste relations. To do so, we could begin by considering Stern's (1977) objection to Fox's model of Rajput state formation on the grounds that Fox overemphasizes patrilineal descent at the expense of intermarriage, with its implication of bilateral status reckoning, as a structural factor in Rajput social organization. In fact, it is only because of this bilateral component that marriage assumes such great importance in intercaste and intracaste status reckoning, since otherwise status could be vouchsafed through unilineal pedigrees (Yalman, 1963). In itself, this does not explain why hypergamy is preferred over hypogamy both in Brahmanic sources like the *Dharmasastras* and in contemporary and historical practice. Instead of simply assuming androcentrically that women rather than men are the vehicles for establishing relations between groups, as in Lévi-Strauss's kinship theory, or attempting to account for this in terms of a matrilateral bias in filiation (Yalman, 1963), it may be appropriate to consider the gendered character of marital exchange as part of a deeper cultural logic of exchange, a point which has been emphasized within the ethnosociological tradition.

According to Steve Barnett's (1976) South Indian ethnography, which is conducted in the ethnosociological vein, caste identification has to do with considerations of a bilaterally inherited purity which is commonly rendered in everyday life through recourse to ideas of blood, and its substantialization in persons through the mixture of male blood (in semen) and female blood (in breastmilk and the uterus) through which a new person is constituted from his or her parents. This "blood" is not fixed or immutable but is thought to be modifiable by action, and the idea of blood heritability therefore does not possess the hard "Darwinian" determinism of racial ideologies (or, in fact, Euro-American kinship ideologies more generally). Although it has been objected that such analyses involve the illegitimate superimposition of Western values (see, for example, Dumont, 1983: 156–8), this general approach enables us to posit the mixing and sharing of substance through marriage and other transformational procedures as a broader (perhaps pan-Indian) "core symbol." For the ethnosociologists, code and substance in India are not absolutely differentiated, as Schneider suggested was the case in American kinship constructs. Rather, the conduct of social actors can affect and alter the substantive qualities of the world of objects, and a good deal of everyday life in India is thought about in terms of the conduct requisite to achieve the appropriate mixture and balance of substance. Daniel's (1983) study of a village in Tamil Nadu is an exemplary ethnographic demonstration of this point, showing how in various everyday matters – sexuality, predicting and controlling the future, the spatial order of the house, and even the very concept of the "village" – there is a central concern with the properties of substances and their "ability to mix and separate, to transform and be transformed, to establish intersubstantial relationships of compatibility and incompatibility, to be in states of equilibrium and disequilibrium, and to possess variable degrees of fluidity and combinability" (ibid.: 3). In this schema, the position of the "individual" as the fundamental social actor – or, to put it another way, the identification of individual human organisms with "persons" – is much less secure than in the Euro-American milieu. This is the sense in which Marriott (1976) coins the term "dividuals" to emphasize the fluid parameters of the person in India. At the least inclusive level, the dividuality of the person inheres in gifts or *dana* of various kinds which it emits or alienates. At a different level, the dividual is subsumed in the idea of a collective "person" whose boundaries vary contextually. They might, for example, be drawn around some kin grouping in a way quite different from the fixity of the person as organism which, as we have seen, is articulated in Euro-American thought both in folk kinship constructs and anthropological descent theory. This Indian example, whereby all of the people related by sharing the body of the "patriarch" are in this particular context the same person, reveals the ethnocentricity of these procedures. However, the concept of personhood might extend more broadly to fellow *jati* members or even beyond (Inden and Nicholas, 1977). And, finally, the emphasis on release of the soul into Brahman within classical Hinduism represents the ultimate extension of personhood into the perfect and unlimited equilibrium of substance. Thus, as Daniel (1984) has argued, the infinite divisibility and combinability of substance in India is "person-centric" – whatever level we take the "person" to refer to. In other words, there is no universal *dharma* or code for conduct which is always correct for everyone; it varies according to a panoply of factors. In this respect, the emphasis on the divisibility and combinability of contextually variable substance and associated codes for conduct clearly fits with the Dumontian idea of encompassing hierarchy, but without endorsing Dumont's strongly concretized notion of power encompassed by status undergirding brahmanic dominance. This emphasis reveals a culturally specific conception of persons and things which underlies the common basis to the construction of exchange and kin relations. However, as Inden and Nicholas point out in discussing the Bengali idea of *kutumba*, which roughly connotes affinal kin,

> What marks off the gift and acceptance relationship of *kutumba* and distinguishes it from all others is that it is established by the "asymmetrical" or "nonreciprocal" exchange of a human body, that is, by the gift of a daughter (*kanya-dana*). Thus one feature that defines the *kutumba* relationship is the body of the daughter (*kanya*) who is given in marriage by her father and accepted by her husband. This daughter, whose body comes to be shared by persons of her husband's clan while continuing to be shared by persons of her father's clan, contains a particular code for conduct, *kutumbita*, that sustains and nourishes the *kutumba* relationship. (Inden and Nicholas, 1977: 16–17)

Thus, the transcontextual differentiation of gender appears as a regnant symbol underlying marital exchange through the idea, most clearly expressed by Inden and Nicholas, of a woman's body as the mediation of relatedness. Let us now examine this more closely.

Following Mauss (1922) and Lévi-Strauss (1969), marriage can be regarded as an exchange of persons establishing relations between the groups which have produced them as persons, a point acknowledged explicitly in Indian thought through the idea of marriage as a form of *dana*, involving *kanyadana* or "the gift of a maiden." There is some ambiguity in the literature over the status implications of this "gift." Some writers maintain that status inferiority accrues to wife-givers through their very capacity as wife-givers (Trautmann, 1981); others emphasize the existence of a status order grounded in political or economic power which forms a prior context for marital alliance (Quigley, 1993; Milner, 1994); while others distance themselves from the whole association between marriage and hierarchy (Raheja, 1988). But even Raheja argues, like Trautmann, that *kanyadan* is an example of inauspicious *dana* which participates in the logic of the unreciprocated

"Indian gift." This, however, can be questioned not only in relation to other ethnographic treatments which emphasize the auspiciousness of marriage and marital prestations (manifested, for example, in parts of the marriage ceremony replicating the structure of religious rites, where the bride is identified with a pure or auspicious gift "sacrificed" by her father to the groom identified as a god), but also by recourse to the debates over the character of the "Indian gift" which were examined in chapter 3, where the idea of the unreciprocated "poison in the gift" is contested by the view that prestations, in India as elsewhere, create solidary if asymmetrical relationships (Tambiah, 1985: 212–51; Hesse, 1996). For present purposes, the important points which we must pursue are first that the gift relationship of marriage prestations evinces a fundamentally gendered character, because it is women alone who embody *dana* in this context, and second that this relationship conforms to a deep logic of exchange, even if the character of that logic has been a matter of scholarly controversy.

Raymond Jamous (1992) has shown how the marriage ceremony among the Meo Rajput caste in North India operates as a ritual of status transformation which does not merely turn a man and a woman into a husband and wife, but in fact turns the unmarked and relatively undifferentiated coupling of unmarried brother and sister into man and woman. In this respect, his emphasis on the brother–sister relationship contrasts with the emphasis on parent–child relationships in descent theory and husband–wife relationships in alliance theory. The significance of a woman's status transformation through marriage is partly that she then assumes various ritual responsibilities within her *natal* family, particularly in relation to her brother's wife and children, while a man assumes complementary responsibilities for his sister's husband and children. Jamous calls these relations "metasiblingship," since they involve a relationship between brother and sister mediated by marriage.

This approach stands in critical counterpoint to the androcentrism of Lévi-Strauss's alliance theory, since here women figure as gendered persons who are agents rather than simply as tokens of exchange between corporate groups, although it may be more accurate to consider all persons as comprising bundles of rights which can be reallocated in context-specific ways (Goody, 1983: 225). The approach also emphasizes marriage as a ritual of (gender) differentiation and (sibling) conjunction, although it does not explain the basis of gender differentiation as such, since the undifferentiated sibling couple were already a boy and a girl inherently destined to become a husband and a wife (to different spouses). This forms the point of departure for Margaret Trawick's (1990) neo-Freudian approach to Dravidian kinship, which she explains in terms of an unconsummated sexual desire of brothers and sisters for each other sublimated by the marriage of their offspring. There is certainly a considerable articulation of connubial brother–sister relations in South Indian mythology, and to a lesser extent in North Indian mythology too (Shulman, 1980; Malamoud, 1992). This often takes form in ideas of an original wholeness, of a twin brother and sister sleeping together in the waters of their mother's womb before being born into the world. In a sense, the foundation of the human order is conceived as the division of this pair through marriage to different spouses, which vitiates their sexual capacity to form a pure or divine race out of themselves. In various contemporary Indian rituals, sisters are allotted roles in which they "tie" or "bind" their brothers, thereby acting as an encompassing female "ground" for male agency. Thus,

> the sister is preventing her brother from wasting himself and, notably, from wasting his virile energy; she is giving him the corporeal or ritual sewing which he needs to travel the pathways of life. (Malamoud, 1992: 45)

In this respect, conceptions of gender differentiation in India might be conceived after the model of encompassing hierarchy as discussed by Dumont (1980) and Tcherkezoff (1993), but this in turn would seem to be encompassed by the transcontextual differentiation of gender in accordance with the model of ranking hierarchy where the woman as wife is subordinated to male agency. Thus, the "encompassing" moment of Indian gender differentiation vitiates neither the separation entailed by birth and marriage nor the potential for the subordination of women this involves.

Trawick, on the other hand, partly conceives her argument against theoretical approaches to kinship which construct it as the execution of an underlying, unified structure. In her words,

> the continuation of a particular institution such as cross-cousin marriage may be posited, not upon its fulfillment of some function or set of functions, but upon the fact that it creates longings that can *never* be fulfilled. It is possible to see kinship not as a static form upheld by regnant or shared principles, but as a web maintained by unrelieved tensions, an architecture of conflicting desires, its symmetry a symmetry of imbalance. (Trawick, 1990: 152)

The advantage of the Freudian tradition invoked here rather than the Hegelian–Marxist or Durkheimian traditions is precisely this refusal of wholeness or completion. However, perhaps it does not undermine the idea of regnant principles as much as Trawick suggests, and indeed her argument – in supposing a social order created by desire across a complementary gender principle – readily fits into the other traditions mentioned, as for example in Marx's view of a social order created by labor across a complementary class principle. Thus, we might assimilate Trawick's argument to our broader discussion of core symbols through her view of gender differentiation as a key moment of elicitation in (South) Indian kinship. Indeed, she does much the same herself in criticizing ethnosociological explanations for social behavior based upon the rationalizations of local informants acting as "theorists" of their own social mores. The problem with this is that there may be any number of mutually incompatible local theories. Of the options available to surmount this problem, one is to provide a metatheoretical account which seeks to uncover principles bringing competing native theories into some kind of systematic relation with one another: in other words a theory of the cultural metacontext for which I have argued throughout this book. This is implicit in Trawick's approach, but is somewhat occluded by her substitution of "desire" for "structure." In a recent paper, Cecilia Busby is more explicit about this implication:

> There is no obvious homogeneity of cultural discourses around kinship and marriage across this area, or even within one community. Nevertheless . . . I believe that those discourses and practices which do exist are *predicated* on certain fundamental, implicit notions about gender and the person which in the first place create the conditions of possibility of Dravidian kinship and cross-cousin marriage. (Busby, 1997: 32)

For Busby, these notions hinge upon gender differentiation and in particular the absolute differentiation and complementarity of male and female substance. A woman transmits her femaleness to her daughters, a man his maleness to his sons. Parallel cousin marriage would therefore constitute an inappropriate involution of the selfsame substance. As one of Busby's male informants put it, "To marry my mother's sister's daughter – how could I do that? She is my own sister!" (ibid.: 35). Thus, whereas gender differentiation is the unmarked condition for Dumont's alliance theory, which assimilates crossness to affinity by taking gender differentiation as the point of departure for an analysis of relations between an already gendered ego, for Busby gender differentiation is the *sine qua non* of the system.

However, as Busby makes clear, gender differentiation is not simply the central fact from which the kinship system is derived. Rather, it is a regnant symbol in a chain of related axioms:

> It is good to marry a relative . . . yet you cannot marry too close a relative (a brother or sister); your parallel cousins are brother and sister to you and hence unmarriageable; your cross-cousins are the closest relatives who are "different" enough to be marriageable; hence the cross-cousin is the best spouse. (Ibid.: 38)

These axioms form something like implicational or associative chains and therefore admit to the inflections, reversals, substitutions, and elaborations of native exegesis, but gender differentiation remains a regnant, transcontextual symbol invested in the logic of the system. As we have seen, it is not necessarily quite the same as the kind of gender differentiation which occurs in Euro-American contexts, and it would certainly be possible to assess its particular developmental possibilities in terms of gender inequality. My predominant concern here, however, is with the structure of Indian kinship systems which we have discussed in relation to North Indian examples of segmentary patrilineal descent, South Indian examples of cross-cousin marriage, and the Brahmanic ideology of *kanyadan*. Unlike theories of human agency which attempt to generate the ontology of such examples through the action of some instituting principle like desire, work, or consciousness, I would argue that no such unitary principle can fruitfully be isolated, but it is nevertheless possible to see the way in which people try to incorporate these different structures within a broader cultural context, often very explicitly such as in Brahmanic writings which attempt to accommodate themselves to Dravidian kinship principles. In this respect, much as the work of scholars like Raheja (1988) emphasizes the identity between the transactional contexts of marriage and a deeper, more enduring logic of exchange, it can be suggested that the construction of the person in India is responsive to a cultural metacontext, which revolves around lineality and gender differentiation as the vehicles for collective identity.

Race, Kinship, and Gender in the Caribbean

There are, on the face of it, several similarities between the Indian case described in the previous section and colonial and postcolonial Caribbean societies in terms of the conjunction of marriage, gender differentiation, and hierarchy. These will form the focus of the present section. My argument will be that although there are structural similarities between the two regions which have been underemphasized by earlier comparative commentators, there is a major difference between them which follows the contours of the differentiation in political ideology examined in chapter 3. In general, the Caribbean exemplifies transformations of the monadic political cosmology which we have traced in European culture history. This has systematically oriented Caribbean gender and kinship constructs to forms of nationalist consciousness with characteristic territorial identifications, albeit in "elite" and "popular" forms of different compass.

Let us begin our discussion by examining one account of the structural significance of the "mixed race" unions mentioned in chapter 4, namely Verena Martinez-Alier's (1989) pathbreaking analysis of race and kinship in nineteenth-century Cuba. Cuba remained a Spanish colonial possession long after the Spanish American mainland achieved independence in the first quarter of the nineteenth century. Indeed, the colony gained in its importance to Spain during the century as a result of the loss of the other colonies, domestic political changes, and changes in the global economy. In particular, the nineteenth century saw a flowering of the Cuban sugar industry based upon African-origin slave labor, particularly in the western provinces. The plantation regime did not come to dominate the island as a whole, however, and even at the zenith of the sugar boom in the mid-nineteenth century whites were only barely outnumbered by the combined slave and free colored populations (the latter comprising many people descended from those already free when the plantation regime began its takeoff in the 1770s). Nevertheless, this period was accompanied by a hardening in attitudes to race, which, according to Martinez-Alier, was the basis around which the hierarchical character of the Cuban social order was constituted. In her view, this stemmed from slavery as both an economic and a social institution, which affected Cuban society in its totality by elevating color as a badge of status consistently referring back to a hierarchy of origins in the antinomy between freedom and servitude. In such circumstances, the major option for status improvement among non-whites was to "whiten" themselves and their offspring by contracting unions with a white or "whiter" partner. This, of course, undermined the emphasis on racial endogamy through which a rigid dualism in Cuban society between black and white was affected. However, it was a fact of Cuban life nonetheless. It manifested itself particularly in concubinage between white men and black or colored women, impelled on the part of the former, Martinez-Alier reports, largely by the demographic deficit of white women. This "color hypergamous" concubinage was a widely accepted practice in Cuba and in other Caribbean societies. However, interracial *marriage* was a quite different proposition, against which strong legal and social impediments were erected. The bulk of Martinez-Alier's analysis is devoted to those relatively few cases (some two hundred in the course of the nineteenth century) where a marriage license was sought for an interracial union. As Martinez-Alier shows, the resulting deliberations – and particularly the objections to the union often lodged by the white man's family – reveal much about the racial thinking of the protagonists.

For colored women, as we have already seen, a key advantage of union with a white man was status improvement for herself, and particularly her children. In this respect, the union can be regarded as a kind of exchange, in which the woman's sexual availability is traded for improved social status. This association between colored women and sexual availability – rendered in contemporary Cuban proverbs like "no hay tamarindo dulce ni mulata señorita" (there's no sweet tamarind fruit, nor a virgin mulatto girl) – may have gained succor from racist projections of female sexuality, but can also be seen as a structural property of the social system. For their part, white men suffered no loss in status when they entered into concubinage with colored women, but this did not hold true for marriage. Indeed, it was not only the man but also his relatives who lost in status when such unions were contracted, hence the frequent appearance of family members as petitioners against the marriage license in the court records analyzed by Martinez-Alier. What emerges from the analysis is, first, a strong sense of family honor which is contingent upon the proper conduct of all the members of the family, and second the ineradicable heritability of status. A family is – theoretically at least – forever compromised by dishonorable unions which undermine its status lineally. By the same token, low status people can never escape the disability of their condition. As one of Martinez-Alier's petitioners stated,

> A mulatto girl never has nor will be able to leave the sphere of this class of humble people, on account of her color in the society of that village, even if her complexion were white and her hair straight. (Martinez-Alier, 1989: 17)

The idea of the "transcendental stain" of slavery transmitted through the blood regardless of physical appearance or any other socially mitigating circumstances recurs throughout the petitions examined by Martinez-Alier. Thus, the fundamental bar to marriage was the heritability of low status associated with slave origins and symbolized by color. That this symbolization was imperfect is shown in the example of a white woman who, having agreed to marry, discovered from baptismal records that her suitor was not white (ibid.: 72–3). Obviously, the "color" in question here is of a legal rather than a phenotypical kind, a point to which we shall return shortly.

The corollary of these status concerns was that interracial marriage became less problematic where the white man and his family themselves were low in status. Here, there was a certain conflation of race and class identities, as in the court ruling which remarked that the racial difference between the couple was not so marked because "although the suitor is white he does not belong among those in society who are of a higher rank" (ibid.: 25). The quotation indicates that notwithstanding a clear definition of race in color terms, racial identification was transformed by social status. It also points to another general feature of the system. The ideological dualisms of black/white and slave/free at the heart of Cuban society were in reality compromised by a continuum of phenotype and status from one to the other. In these circumstances, fewer barriers stood in the way of union between individuals who more nearly approximated to one another on the continuum than between those who stood far apart. Sometimes, the union was explicitly or implicitly a trade on the basis of different status systems, as where a poor white man offered his "whiteness" to a rich colored woman in exchange for a share in her wealth (ibid.: 65).

The Cuban system described here was clearly disadvantageous to the status concerns of black and colored men, who had little to offer their female counterparts by way of either economic or social status and – in a society characterized both by an essentialist racial classification and patriarchal views of female honor – could command little respect in view of the sexual laxity of "their" women. This, according to Martinez-Alier (ibid.: 118), precipitated an instability in their own sexual relations.

Martinez-Alier's approach enables us to appreciate the structural logic of Cuban kinship as a society-wide system without making it epiphenomenal to something else. But it rests upon some exogenous postulates, which in this case – just as in our Indian examples – are to do with the gendered character of Cuban descent constructs and the hierarchical character of Cuban society. Let us examine these points in more detail.

For Martinez-Alier, the dynamic principle of Cuban kinship is status, inasmuch as the system emerges from people's attempts to improve or preserve their status. But this in itself is insufficient to explain why the result is a tendency towards endogamy offset by a countervailing hypergamous tendency, a fact which requires additional consideration of gender differentiation. In a system based upon unilateral filiation, there is no need for endogamy because the status of the family or lineage can, in theory at least, be maintained by unilineal pedigrees (Yalman, 1963). But in Cuba, filiation was bilateral, so the standing of the spouse was critical for the maintenance of family honor. The status concerns established by simple bilateral filiation would be consistent with isogamy (in order to preserve status) but with a countervailing tendency towards "anisogamy" (i.e. marriage between spouses of unequal status) as lower status people sought to improve their standing by seeking higher status spouses. This tendency could conceivably be manifested through either hypergamy or hypogamy, or both. Martinez-Alier explains the fact that the predominant anisogamous form was hypergamy and not hypogamy by arguing that in Cuba women were regarded as the true perpetuators of the lineage, and in corroboration she cites legislation which justified the harsher penalties for female as compared to male adultery on the grounds that "the woman can bring bastards to the marriage" (Martinez-Alier, 1989: 117). In this respect, then, there was a matrilateral bias to the sociolegal correlates of filiation, because it was only women and not men who introduced "bad blood" into the otherwise bilaterally reckoned family. Thus, the hypergamous tendency within the Cuban kinship system cannot simply be ascribed to the emphasis on female purity in the context of a patriarchal and hierarchical society. Rather, Martinez-Alier's argument depends on the exogenous postulate of bilateral filiation with a matrilateral bias, which is derived implicitly from the pre-existing cultural fact of Spanish kinship ideologies even though Martinez-Alier couches her own argument in terms of utilitarian motives and structural causes. As Raymond Smith (1978) has argued in a sympathetic critique, not only does she thereby downplay the significance of culture-history, she also tends to neglect class-specific kinship behaviors, a point to which we shall return below.

In Cuba, the offspring of interracial unions followed the condition of the lower status parent, a principle consistent with bilateral filiation strongly marked by a hierarchical social ideology which continuously attempted to restore the dualism at its heart. However, this ideological repair could not have been wholly successful, otherwise hypergamous union would not have been especially attractive to colored women. In this respect, one might view the social order of nineteenth-century Cuba as one held in tension by the mutually distorting effects of a dualistic principle of ranking hierarchy and a kinship system based upon bilateral filiation.

To characterize the Cuban situation through a tension between hierarchy and kinship seems to me preferable to Martinez-Alier's suggested tension between hierarchy and egalitarianism, which she draws out by contrasting Cuban hypergamy with Dumont's discussion of hypergamy in India. For Dumont, Indian hypergamy is but a consequence of hierarchy as the central value of the Indian social order, since hierarchy creates strong pressures for status improvement, towards which hypergamy is directed (Dumont, 1980: 124). For Martinez-Alier, on the other hand, Cuban hypergamy represented the intrusion of egalitarian principles into a hierarchical social order which otherwise rigidly enforced isogamy. This does not, however, explain why the *sine qua non* of hierarchy is hypergamy in the one case and isogamy in the other. Martinez-Alier argues that whereas in India there was only one kind of status, Cuban society was characterized by a more open status structure. But, as well as resting on a questionable view of caste hierarchy, this rather unconvincing distinction compounds the problem of explaining the strong barriers to social mobility in Cuba. Perhaps the issue is better framed through appreciating that egalitarianism, too, implies a form of hierarchy. The ideology of egalitarian individualism evinces a complementarity between a principle of differentiation (the difference between individuals which establishes their individuality) and a principle of association (the identity between individuals which establishes their equality), whose political resolution is a nationalism which postulates the state as supreme representative of a homogeneous people. I have also argued that individualism is predicated upon domain distinctions between persons and things which creates the transformative possibility that persons can be treated *as* things, or non-persons. American chattel slavery was one manifestation of this transformation. But it then becomes difficult to create the homogeneous polity demanded by nationalism in a society where some individuals are not fully persons or are "stained" by the heritability of that status. The Spanish solution of expelling these non-persons (Jews, Moors, heretics) was hardly practicable in Cuba, and so the aporia of colonial Cuba – in the context of its bilateral principles of filiation – was the de-generation of the nation. This seems to me the context within which to understand the distinction between phenotypic and legal whiteness mentioned above. Whereas Oliver Cox (1948) had argued that hypergamy was inimical to race-stratified societies because it blurred the phenotypic distinctions upon which the system rested, Martinez-Alier reaches a different conclusion on the basis of her Cuban material:

> The Cuban situation was thus not a "racial" situation, if by race we mean phenotype. Legal color shows that the basic criterion of social classification was social origin and not physical appearance, and that Cox is wrong in approaching hypergamy in purely "racial" terms. (Martinez-Alier, 1989: 137)

Her own view, as we have seen, is that race stands as a symbol for significant social cleavages, and that in Cuba this inhered in legal color for which phenotype stood only as a poor guide. Race, in other words, is not best understood only in terms of the construction of differences around somatic markers. The argument is largely endorsed in this book, but it is worth remarking how decidedly odd is a system of legal color in which a bride can suddenly "discover" that her groom is not white. Here, whiteness becomes a rather nebulous quality defining more a political category of national inclusion than an actual population group, and while the system is certainly workable – as Cuba's nineteenth-century history shows – it surely creates strongly countervailing nationalisms which indeed manifested themselves during the period and which Martinez-Alier does not perhaps incorporate into her model as much as she might. On the one hand, the nationalists who fought the Ten Years War against Spain mobilized under a banner of racial equality summarized in Maceo's slogan "no hay negritos ni blanquitos, sino cubanos" (there are no little blacks or little whites, only Cubans), which constituted one obvious solution to the problem of an egalitarian nationalism. But it was not a solution much to the liking of planters and other members of the Cuban elite, a point to which we shall return in chapter 6.

The features described by Martinez-Alier for marriage in nineteenth-century Cuba resonate with aspects of the pre- and post-emancipation situation in Jamaica, even if the relationship between kinship and political structures there is part of a very different history. The "color–class system" in Jamaica involves "hypergamous" unions between (white or colored) men from the upper and middle classes and (black) lower-class women. These often take the form of concubinage, as in the Jamaican practice of extramarital "outside" unions among middle-class men (Austin, 1979; Smith, 1996). Unions within the black working class tend, by contrast, to be more temporary and marriage occurs much later, usually as a consecration of a long-term consensual union which confirms the couple's respectability within their own milieu. In this context, "outside" connotes sexual relationships outside an individual's primary conjugal tie. Raymond Smith (1996: 59–80) argues that these class-specific practices should be regarded as features of a total system – the "dual marriage system" – which constitutes part of a distinctively Caribbean culture-history.

In the work of Diane Austin too (1979; 1983), the inside/outside distinction is expanded as a broader medium for expressing class relations in Jamaica (where, for Austin, "class" is understood in broadly Gramscian terms as a position in the relations of production associated with culturally specific representations which, at least potentially, figure in the dominant political articulation of the state). In family relations, "outside" unions produce "outside" children who are not stigmatized after the fashion of illegitimate children in the traditions of the European family, but may or may not enjoy the same rights to parental support and affection depending upon the class and conjugal status of their parents. Where the child is the offspring of a "hypergamous" outside union, he or she may enter into a client relationship with patrons from the higher status family, and this may enhance status in his or her own lower-class milieu. This is particularly so where there are color distinctions between the two families, as in the case of a woman discussed by Austin (1979), who – though the outside child of a woman who was herself the outside child of a white man – was able to offset her somewhat disadvantaged outside status against the advantages accruing from her white connections, thereby achieving respectability through early marriage.

The inside/outside metaphor also codes thinking about the house or neighborhood (the orderly middle-class house in which family activities are conducted inside in private, as compared to the working-class life of the street or the yard), and work ("inside" office work conducted by middle-class people with education – itself a major Jamaican class metaphor – as compared to the "outside" manual work of the working class).

In her earlier work, Austin's argument is essentially that the contemporary Jamaican class ideologies in which both the middle class and working class participate draw upon the historical dualisms of the plantation complex, such that the "incorporation of the past in the present gives Jamaican class relations a timeless quality which serves the plausibility of a conservative ideology" (ibid.: 507). The contention is convincing enough, and it could be illustrated with reference to a good deal of Jamaican ethnography. One example is the "hypergamous" color ideology among black working-class women, which tends to marginalize their male counterparts. Raymond Smith quotes the following comment from a black working-class informant concerning her maternal grandmother, "Aunt Ellie:"

> My granny did have flat mind. She live in the bush there and just like pure black nigger man. So that's why we now don't have better quality. Aunt Ellie did have flat mind man; she just go, go so, with any black man. (Smith, 1996: 89)

Although the same informant conceded that there are "plenty good black men" according to criteria of "refinement" and "education," thus transforming color with class identifications, the idea of the unrefined, outside "nigger" among the Jamaican working class could be taken as evidence for the replication of the historical dualism mentioned above. Moreover, working-class counter-ideologies which contest "outside" status often proceed by reproducing it in relation to another domain. For example, the tendency to derogate women in the patriarchal ideology of the working-class Rastafari movement can be seen as an attempt by its predominantly male adherents to reconstitute themselves in the fashion of middle-class men who are able to dominate the family as its patriarch while engaging in outside unions, a possibility which is largely denied working-class men in Jamaica, not least because of "hypergamous" sentiments of the kind expressed by Smith's informant (Austin-Broos, 1987; though see chapter 6). At the same time, the appeal of Pentecostal Christianity to working-class women reconstitutes *them* in relation to middle-class ideals of respectable female domesticity in contexts where their relations with men are too often disappointingly ephemeral (Austin-Broos, 1987; 1997).

In a sense, this updates an older gender motif in Jamaican society which emerged in the immediate post-emancipation period. Caribbean plantation slavery made no concessions to bourgeois ideals regarding the confinement of women and children to the domestic domain. Indeed, women were over-represented in the "great gangs" of field slaves engaged in the most backbreaking unskilled work, and in Jamaica the emancipation of 1838 was accompanied by a widespread withdrawal of women from field labor (Holt, 1992). This was considerably abetted by the designs of Nonconformist missionaries who replaced the planter's image of "Quashie," the stereotypically irresponsible and dim-witted slave, with their own image of the dignified "Christian black," degraded only because of the degradation inflicted by the plantation order (Austin-Broos, 1992). The missionaries' goal was to realize this image through sponsoring "fair" wage labor and sexual propriety, both understood after their own bourgeois model. The willingness of newly freed female slaves to conform, at least in part, to this model of female domesticity can be seen as an act of resistance to a plantation order which had denied women the possibility of any such respectability. Although it remained an unattainable ideal for most women, it nevertheless exerted a powerful ideological attraction. Here, one might remark upon a certain historical irony, for whereas feminist resistance to the logic of capital outside the plantation system has often turned upon opening up the world of work for women, the path of resistance for enslaved women lay in the opposite direction.

Against this background, Austin-Broos's argument that "Jamaica is a society shot through with different competing resolutions to the conundrum of race and morality; a conundrum which often finds its nexus in gender relations" (Austin-Broos, 1987: 32) has considerable force. The conundrum is also explicitly formulated in class terms. Here, the historical dualism is replicated in an ideology of the middle class which effectively denies its own origins in plantation slavery, displacing this onto the "negro" working class (Alexander, 1977; Austin-Broos, 1994), and concomitantly an ideology of the working class which demands redress from the contemporary middle class for this historical injustice. However, as we have seen, although in Austin's view the working class entertain class-specific valuations of their own dignity, these demands for redress turn upon a claim for middle-class acceptance and "inside" status (Austin, 1979: 504), so that the cultural categories of the working class can be viewed as a consequence of ideological domination, and their forms of consciousness represent a conservative or ameliorative "trade-union consciousness" of the kind criticized by Lenin. Austin's more recent work appears to modify this position somewhat, opposing the argument that Jamaica's cultural specificity inheres in its elevation of race to a timeless idiom of hierarchical social classification across all classes and arguing instead that both race and class are "historically emergent dimensions of a discourse of heritable identity that is characteristic of Jamaica" (Austin-Broos, 1994: 219). Particularly within the middle class, this manifests itself in the idea that both race *and* class are heritable statuses evincing hierarchies constituted in but modifiable through history, a point encapsulated by a middle-class informant's comment that "education" was something that had taken her five generations to complete, and could not simply be achieved among the working class by school attendance (ibid.: 218). This is an especially interesting point in relation to the broader contrast drawn earlier in the chapter between the nexus of race and nation in Euro-American forms of hierarchy and the predication of caste in Indian hierarchy (figure 5.2), because it would seem to represent an almost Lamarckian form of folk culture theory, which attempts to overcome the aporia of national ethnogenesis created by ideologies of racial difference through an encompassment of race and class into a single national bloc in which, however, the working class are subordinated to the middle class. By contrast, Austin-Broos reports,

> The Jamaicans who posit in their practice radically equal communities are also, often, lower-class people unable to engage with the rhetoric of class, or with the political rhetoric of nation. Unlike a section of the middle class, they are sceptical regarding individual achievement in the absence of spiritual support. . . . The discursive formation here described could be rendered as a "culture of race." (Ibid.: 222–3)

This working-class "culture of race" therefore seems to involve an acceptance or complicity with colonial racial categories insofar as it bases its view of Jamaican social distinctions upon enduring racial identifications and not upon class. However, in so doing it rejects forms of postcolonial nationalism which would attempt to incorporate the black working class as a subordinate component of the nation. Moreover, even the middle-class discourse of race evinces continuities with colonial categories. Partly this is because, as Jack Alexander has written, it shares their conception of race as a "very deep, given component of the person" (Alexander, 1984: 152), although it transforms this conception by regarding it simultaneously, and for this very reason, as an extraneous aspect of social identity for which no responsibility is taken. But more importantly, Alexander – like Austin – perceives a continuity insofar as this discourse of race and class invokes the historical dualisms of the plantation complex and thereby commits itself to "a view that sees the present as the result of a long process of mixture in which the two elements are always kept track of – because they have never really joined" (ibid.: 174).

A somewhat different "culture of race" predicated upon the colonial legacy has obtained in Haiti. The modern Caribbean republic of Haiti was born from the revolutionary overthrow of French colonial Saint-Domingue, at a time when the French metropolis was in the grip of its own revolution, through a complex and shifting set of alliances between republican forces, slaves, and *affranchis* (free non-whites who were mainly identified with the "mixed race" *gens de coleur*). With the rise of Napoleon in France, the *de facto* free dependency in Saint-Domingue carved out under the leadership of the former slave Toussaint Louverture was no longer tolerated, leading to a bloody war of independence which, despite Toussaint's capture, was successfully concluded under the leadership of the black former slave Jean-Jacques Dessalines, who named the new "black republic" Haiti in 1804. Tensions between the *ancien libre* faction of the *affranchis* and the *nouveau libre* faction represented by Dessalines, which found their idiom in color distinctions, culminated in Dessalines's murder and the dismemberment of the republic, most notably into the kingdom of the dark-skinned Henry Christophe in the north, and the light-skinned Alexandre Pétion in the south; the republic was reunited under the regime of Pétion's successor Boyer in 1818, but the underlying tensions were not resolved.

Late colonial Saint-Domingue featured an interpenetration of race and class similar to the one described by Martinez-Alier for Cuba, with relatively weak – though ever-strengthening – barriers against "color hypergamous" unions between *affranchis* and lower status whites. There was intense, but regionally variable, conflict between these *petits blancs* and the *affranchis* as the colony's would-be middle class, but marriage between indigent rural *petits blancs* and wealthy free colored women operated as a system of mutual status improvement which contributed to the emergence of a racially ambiguous class of self-styled *colons américains* who played a significant political role, particularly in the south, in the events leading up to the revolution (Trouillot, 1982; Garrigus, 1996). As colonial Saint-Domingue gave way to the postcolonial republic of Haiti, this "whiter" '*clair*' group with its roots among the colonial *affranchis* was able to secure itself as the new dominant class, although the anti-colonial *noiriste* legacy of the revolution made its legitimacy as such forever questionable. This transformation finds its corollary in a postcolonial Haitian color endogamy through which blackness and other "negro" physical traits have persistently been associated with lower social status. However, the dual status orders of color and politico-economic influence are such that the practice of "color anisogamy" obtains, in accordance with what Trouillot (1990) calls "social direction." Here, darker people (usually men) who are upwardly mobile in politico-economic terms are able to contract unions with women who are less well connected but lighter-skinned; perhaps this can be seen as an inversion of the colonial "color hypergamy" among the *affranchis*, but one with a similar logic. As Trouillot points out, in a country with a large black majority and no significant white presence since 1804, the very persistence of a lighter-skinned *clair* class testifies to the successful pursuit of color endogamy, but the somatic boundary of the *clair* identification has "darkened" over time. In his words, "it is the elasticity and resilience of this boundary – the fact that it always allows for the isolation of a category of people called *clairs* – that bears witness to the social reality of color" (ibid.: 119). This social reality is similar to the one described by Martinez-Alier for Cuba, though it figures in a very different history of contestation over the nation. Of course, these conceptions of social color are not "racial" in the same sense that colonial discourses of racial inferiorization were racial, and indeed there has been a general commitment in Haiti to anti-colonial views of human equality. But it does not seem useful to make a sharp distinction – as, for example, David Nicholls (1996) does – between "race" in colonial Saint-Domingue and "color" in postcolonial Haiti. The one emerged out of the other and if – as I have argued throughout this book – race is to be understood above all as a culturally specific and historically perduring way of imagining political communities, its salience in postcolonial Haiti should not be surprising.

In Haiti, opportunities for upward "social direction" among the black rural working class have been severely limited throughout most of the country's history, and the result has been a quite involuted peasantry evincing distinctive forms of sociocultural organization. A common term for the peasantry among the urban middle classes is *mounn andewo* or "outside people"; concomitantly, *leta*, the peasant term for the state ("l'état") also means "bully," which describes fairly accurately the character of the historical relation between the state and the peasantry. It is inappropriate to stretch this point into the image of a dual society characterized by entirely separate social blocs, but the Haitian peasantry has nevertheless remained much more "outside" the national political culture than is generally the case among rural working people elsewhere in the Caribbean. Indeed, while Caribbean "peasantries" have, quite obviously, never existed independently of world system forces, there has arguably remained a significant social cleavage not only in Haiti but quite generally in Caribbean life between peasantries and national "class society," even if it is one that has too often been mythologized and is now in any case considerably in decline (Mintz, 1974).

It is worth considering the forms of sociopolitical consciousness associated with this cleavage. To return to the example of Jamaica, in contrast to Austin's studies of urban populations, Edith Clarke's (1966) classic study of rural Jamaican communities in a somewhat earlier period did not report any "hypergamous" ideology or derogation of "outside" status among the rural working class. It is possible that this has to do with the different sensibilities of rural small landholders. Whereas the "inside/outside" discourse appears to be a transformation of colonial categories manifested in the hegemony of a postcolonial middle class, the social order based around these forms of rural tenure can be traced to quasi-peasant "counterplantation" adaptations where those oppressed in the plantation order were able to assert some modicum of authority. As with the slave cultivation of provision grounds, these were incipient before emancipation and they persist to the present day, although they have been much in decline since the mid-twentieth century (Mintz, 1974; Besson, 1992). Arguably, they reflect a political imagination relying less upon the abstractions demanded by nation-statist projects which attempt to homogenize a people with a territory, and more upon land itself as the reference point for the sociopolitical order.

The concept of "family land" associated with tenures of this kind has been quite widely reported in the non-Hispanic Caribbean (Besson, 1992) and seems to share several common features. These include the presence of a named ancestral figure as the founder of the land; rights in the land inherited bilaterally to all of the ancestor's lineal descendants; strong sanctions – often supernatural – against sale of the land by family members; supernatural and family-specific associations with its landmarks such as trees, fences, and rivers; the siting of family burial grounds upon it; and an ethic of non-residence, so that family members aim not to live upon it or rely upon it economically.

These features bear a striking resemblance to ancestor-focused representations of the land in West Africa (see, for example, McCall, 1995) and some scholars have suggested a historical connection (Carnegie, 1987). However, in perhaps the most comprehensive analyses of the institution – based mainly upon research in Jamaica – Jean Besson has argued that it represented initially a proto-peasant adaptation to the plantation order among slaves and has continued to function structurally as part of a counterplantation system in rural parts of the contemporary Caribbean still dominated by plantation-based agribusiness. One feature of family land that has baffled social scientists is that cognatic inheritance means a rapid and ever-proliferating expansion of people with rights in the land, quite beyond its capacity to support them economically. Indeed, it was the capacity of unilineal rather than cognatic descent groups to bound and limit kinsfolk into corporate groups which originally led anthropologists to invest so much effort – from a contemporary perspective, perhaps too much effort – in describing them. Cognatic descent groups are, by contrast, unpromising as a basis for defining a kin group with corporate political functions. Besson's (1979) argument is that the cognatic descent groups associated with Caribbean family land are corporate groups only in respect of the land itself, and that property-holding groups require no exclusive and unambiguous membership, as would be the case for groups organized around political or military functions. Moreover, although Besson argues that family land is explicable in socioeconomic terms as part of the counterplantation system, she stresses that it is what land *symbolizes* rather than what it produces which is significant. On the one hand – in keeping with an emphasis on cognatic rather than conjugal ties in Jamaican kin reckoning – family land "serves genera-tions," acting as a countervailing focus against the migratory dispersal of rural people in search of work in the cities or abroad. But, Besson argues, there is also a historical symbolism involved, insofar as family land owner-ship, however tenuous or unproductive, restores a subjectivity denied by slavery, in which people were kinless and propertyless adjuncts to somebody else's land (Besson, 1988: 44). The fixing of social identity in relation to the timelessness of family land and its ancestral spirits might be regarded as a strategy for achieving ontological security in a context where Caribbean colonial and postcolonial states have been unable or unwilling to provide it. However, by the same token the idea of inalienable rights to a property whose landscape objectifies one's genealogy, despite its possible African ref-erents, derives its very force from cognizance of an alternative, namely the disenchanted world of capitalist transactions in property and people. In this sense, the use of the landscape as an object system seems consonant with the predication of "private property" under capitalist relations of produc-tion and rather different from the various ways in which people objectify themselves in relation to the land reported by anthropologists in noncapitalist contexts (e.g. Munn, 1971). The emphasis on lineality as a form of political identity also participates in the construction of "race" as the contemporary medium through which the historical legacy of plantation slavery is under-stood by the descendants of those that it brutalized.

Rural Caribbean objectifications of land can also be manifested in gen-der relations. To take a Haitian example, as described by Lowenthal (1984), conjugality in rural Haiti appears as a specific mediation of sex and labor which are the principal domains in which men and women are differenti-ated from each other as such. To be in a union is to be *fè afè* (to make a deal), and the deal is essentially that a man will make a house and tend a garden for a woman while the woman will allow him exclusive sexual ac-cess. In this respect, women's sexual availability always involves an eco-nomic recompense. This is the context for the Haitian saying that "every woman has a *carreau* of land between her legs," and for women's refer-ences to their own genitals as "my money," "my capital," or "my land." Thus, albeit in a rather different sense to the object system of land and persons we discussed in the Jamaican case, we encounter in Haiti a particu-lar association of female sexuality with land and productivity which, while recapitulating the capitalist predication of personal and territorial autonomy, also constitutes a culturally specific transformation, so that it can rightfully be regarded as what Lowenthal calls "a peculiarly Haitian innovation in the world of male/female relationships" (ibid.: 29).

Peter Wilson (1969; 1973) has argued that it is gender differentiation above all which articulates broader political structures in the Caribbean, through the dualism of an egalitarian working-class discourse of "respect" associated with men, and a hierarchical discourse of "reputation" associated with women and with the values of the middle class or aspirant middle class. In his view, denial of opportunities for status attainment to working-class men leads to alternative forms of status reckoning, often in relation to activities which are illicit or at least offend against middle-class mores, such as fighting, drinking, gambling, smuggling, and banditry. Respect accrues to the Caribbean "man of words" not in accordance to his place as an actor within the social structure, but in accordance with his actions outside and against it (cf. Diaz-Royo, 1979; Abrahams, 1983). It is too tempting to refrain from pointing out the contrast here between Dumont's Indian "individual-outside-the-world" in the form of the renouncer given over to an ascetic and cerebral transcendence and Wilson's Caribbean "individual-outside-the-world" in the form of the working-class man given over to an egotistical and visceral transcendence (though in the next chapter we will see how the Rastafari movement in Jamaica has attempted to transform the latter into the former). Wilson contrasts this male "reputation" with the status concerns of working-class women which implicitly place them inside the "respectable" system of colonial values. However, although one can easily read the social order of many Caribbean societies in this light, his model displaces class relations onto gender relations, failing to appreciate how such particular domains are refractory to a more fundamental cultural dualism which has been identified by Miller (1994).

In the course of this discussion we have encountered various dualisms; of male to female, middle-class to working-class, "inside" to "outside," rural to urban, plantation to counterplantation, and land ownership to landlessness. Whereas Wilson tends to reduce such alternative dualisms to epiphenomena of class as a "real" ordering principle in Caribbean life, it may be better to follow Miller's suggestion that the sense of social order in the Caribbean is quite widely predicated upon dualism as a cultural category which can be expressed across any number of social dimensions, without any one being privileged as the primary generator of social meaning or distinction. But as Miller among others points out, it cannot be argued that the oppositions male/female, respect/reputation, equality/hierarchy are homologous, because – as we saw with the examples of post-emancipation domesticity and Rastafari – female respectability may evince resistance to colonial hierarchies, just as male reputation may evince conformity to them.

My general argument in this section, then, is that forms of postcolonial Caribbean elite and popular consciousness represent particular transformations of European cultural representations, and particularly the cultural nexus of capital and race which, historically in the Caribbean, revealed its most nakedly violent logic of alienation in respect of persons, land, and labor. The various popular appropriations of gender and territorial identities that we have encountered can be seen as transformations of this brutal colonial legacy. In this respect, my argument is consonant with Paul Gilroy's description of the "Black Atlantic" culture as a "counterculture" or "grand narrative" of modernity (Gilroy, 1993b). However, to my mind, Gilroy, like most contemporary sociologists, is overly keen to expunge the idea of race from analytic frameworks (cf. Gilroy, 1998). Racial identifications have emerged as a historical precipitate of Euro-American cultural categories which cannot be effaced or reduced to something else, though, as we have seen, they articulate with or run into many other dimensions of the socio-political order. Perhaps one might draw an analogy here with the concept of "history" as discussed by Richard Price (1985). Whereas for some of Price's Caribbean informants, the word "history" evokes only its hegemonic metropolitan meaning of a linear, national past marked by battles and dates, Price shows how such people possess other ways of rendering their pasts which scholars steeped in their own metropolitan historical consciousness too easily miss. Just as Price extends the compass of "history" as an analytic term to incorporate these alternative representations of the past, so I argue we might extend our conceptions of race to see why land or the cognatic family has mattered so much in the Caribbean. Here, "race" figures as an explicit cultural consciousness of racial oppression in history, constituting a contemporary source of pain which requires expiation (Brodber, 1987). But, as we have seen, it also figures as an implicit ordering feature of social life. Discussing the sensibilities of the devotee or "serviteur" in the Haitian peasant religion of *vodun* and its pantheon of spirits or *loa* (see also chapter 6), Gordon Lewis has commented,

> Vodun assures the *serviteur*, in sum, that all of nature and life is governed by a transcendental logic – an assurance that neither of the official institutions of his society, the Catholic Church and the secular political state, has been capable of making. It tells him that the past, present and future are all continuous and related moments in the passage of time, and that when the ancestors become *loa* – as they do all the time – the history of the race runs in his own blood as part of a unifying psychic heritage that is passed on from generation to succeeding generation. (Lewis, 1983: 192)

My argument is that the ideas referenced here like "race," "blood," and historical continuity should be retained analytically in their full ambiguity, as Lewis does. Only then will we have a sociological language that allows the construction of race in its full historical dispersal, rather than one which reduces it to its own objectivist categories, and thereby legitimates its own implicitly prescriptive claims about the character of the social world.

6 | Race, Caste, and the Nation

Introduction

In the preceding chapters I have argued that the political logic of race, at once unitary and exclusionary, was installed by European colonial powers with its full brutality in the Americas. Though not without their own brutalities, caste relations in India have, by contrast, manifested a much more differentiated sense of political order. It is a considerable irony, then, that when we survey the way these different kinds of natural hierarchy figure in the contemporary politics of the two regions we encounter something of a reversal. Much political mobilization in India today and the concomitant politics of caste have been oriented to a "nationalist" sense of a unitary if not primordial discourse of political sovereignty, first in the politics of secular anti-colonial nationalism and more recently in the politics of anti-secular Hindu nationalism and untouchable assertion. By contrast, despite an often invidious politics of race, the Caribbean – and perhaps the Americas more generally – has been spared the "blood and soil" nationalism which has claimed the allegiances (and often the lives) of many in Europe, and now India (Mintz, 1996). In this chapter, therefore, we will develop the arguments begun in the previous one concerning the relationship between models of the person and the polity in order to characterize these processes through our approach to the historical transformation of cultural representations. Here, I shall argue that aspects of both colonial and postcolonial Caribbean life represent a transformation or "creolization" of race, where people of black African origin participate in the construction of national political communities from which they were excluded in the first movement of European colonization. However, the path of nation-building has not been smooth, and the creole societies of the contemporary Caribbean are very far from eliminating the reproduction of a status order coded by racial distinctions. Aspects of the recent history of India, on the other hand, represent the "racialization" of caste, whereby categories derived from the caste order come to be perceived increasingly as essential attributes of persons linked to bounded political communities, so that brahmans can be described as "foreign" Aryan invaders in the south, untouchables as the "original" inhabitants of India, and Muslims as the "enemy within" throughout the country, although I shall argue that this reversal is not to be understood entirely as the importation into India of a derivative, Euro-American "modernity."

It is impossible to provide an extensive analysis of these processes here, but some of their main lineaments will be set out in this chapter, together with more detailed analysis of specific examples. This will not only complete our analysis of the historical course taken by ideologies of natural hierarchy in the two regions up to the present, but will also allow us to develop some concluding arguments in chapter 7 about cultural representations and their contestation, which bear upon the way that sociological analysis itself is immured in the contemporary politics of natural hierarchy. A subsidiary aim is to underline the argument begun in chapter 3 that the differences between race and caste-ordered societies inhere mainly in the different kinds of political community which were imagined on the basis of their distinctive cultural metacontexts, an argument which we will address by a historical comparison of state formation in parts of India and the Caribbean during the eighteenth and nineteenth centuries. We will begin, however, with an analysis of the creolization of race in the Caribbean.

Race and Creolization in the Caribbean

Earlier chapters have shown how the idea of "society" deployed in sociology is analytically problematic, reflecting in no small measure the peculiar sense of closure which has invested projects of racial exclusion and national ethnogenesis as well as sociological models. But in the postcolonial world, there have been few options for decolonizing countries but to create such national "societies." For the reasons we encountered in the previous chapter, the problems of constructing them in the Caribbean have been particularly acute and therefore particularly explicit in the thinking of intellectuals and political elites. They have also invested sociological approaches which, especially in the Anglophone Caribbean, have tended to fracture along the lines of three distinct approaches to the question, conventionally labeled the "plantation society," the "plural society," and the "creole society" theses. Let us briefly examine these approaches, with their different conceptions of race and politics, in order to illuminate the relationship between the racialized status order and national ethnogenesis.

We have seen that the plantation became a key form of socioeconomic organization in the Americas – although its centrality to any given territory and its reach over the people within it varied between times and places – and that the plantation is a type of monocrop agriculture which employs intensive techniques of cultivation and "industrial" labor discipline upon an unskilled or semi-skilled workforce. The social character of the plantation is typically bipartite: a socially dominant but numerically small metropolitan group and a large group of unskilled workers, often imported from elsewhere via a colonial nexus of labor coercion (as with slavery or indentured labor). In this respect, all the people comprising a plantation society usually come from somewhere else, so that the distinct ("racial") origins of the two groups coincide precisely with the class distinctions of plantation labor, a coincidence blurred when sexual unions between the two groups produce an indigenous group of "mixed" offspring.

The plantation society thesis essentially reads off a social order from the structure of this dualistic and dependent colonial economy, and it has allowed scholars to explain things like why the character of slave society in nineteenth-century Cuba or Puerto Rico looked much like the character of slave society in eighteenth-century Jamaica or Saint-Domingue, and why colonies such as Trinidad and Guyana which were developing their plantation capacity just as slavery was abolished imported East Indian indentured labor with concomitant implications for their contemporary social structure (Mintz, 1959; Stinchcombe, 1996). In the latter example, of course, the sources for unskilled labor are disparate and this somewhat complicates the picture, but we will not pursue an analysis of this topic here (see, for example, Williams, 1991; Miller, 1994; Smith 1996). More broadly, however, the plantation society model also helps to explain similarities in the structure of later colonial societies such as parts of Dutch Southeast Asia (Stoler, 1985), and, indeed, the racialization of "underdevelopment" in contemporary plantation societies (Beckford, 1983). However, it has proved less successful at explaining the more finely grained historical, political, and social detail in different plantation societies. Partly, this has to do with historically contingent factors such as the nature of the political relationship between metropolis and plantation colony which affected the nationalist aspirations of planter elites and the political salience of free colored populations (Stinchcombe, 1996), or the character of the counterplantation system and the ability of individuals to withdraw partly or fully from the social order of the plantation. But it also arises because models which postulate that exogenous economic or ecological factors wholly determine the social order are never fully able to account for the particular, fine-grained character of that order.

The plantation society thesis bequeaths the idea that the slave societies of the Caribbean were part societies, oriented to their metropolises and dependent upon them not only in a social and economic sense, but also militarily. Slave plantation production was based upon an inhumanly exploitative labor regimen which, particularly in societies where the free population was often heavily outnumbered by the slaves, could only be sustained by the savage disciplining of the slave's body and complete denigration of his or her personality. In Gwendolyn Midlo Hall's words, "paralyzing the hand that might strike down the master through the most naked forms of terror was the cement that held the system together" (Hall, 1996: 80). Nevertheless, it *was* a system, and the brutal logic imposed by the metropolitan instrumentality of production and the local instrumentality of social control was subject to cultural elaboration by the different groups of people it encompassed.

It is this idea of part societies bound together by pure and simple force that characterizes the plural society thesis associated especially with M. G. Smith (e.g. 1984a). Smith consistently applied this model – albeit with refinements over the years – to analyses of the Anglophone Caribbean from the end of the slavery period to the present day, arguing that the white upper class, "brown" middle class, and black working class constitute distinct corporate sections of society, practicing their own distinct cultures and entertaining their own versions of societal institutions, with the ultimate monopoly of power in the hands of the white elite, such that "the monopoly of power by one cultural section is the essential precondition for the maintenance of the total society" (Smith, 1984b: 183). In some respects, Smith's thesis resembles a simple model of social stratification which conceives a society as comprising ranked, bounded subgroups. However, it differs fundamentally from the plantation society thesis and all similarly reductionist theories in which cultural (or racial) identity is a marker for or a derivative of socioeconomic position unmediated by culture, since the essence of the model is that society comprises completely distinct blocs conjoining race, culture, and class. Class is not an exogenous factor for which race or culture are a superstructural carapace; rather, these factors each constitute a distinct and mutually derivable modality of a given corporate section and are therefore irreducibly inflected by the experience of being a member of *that* particular group. Thus, Smith's model contains none of the processual character of Marxist class theory, with its sense of internal contradiction constituting contestatory class politics within a single domain of social action. These features of Smith's model display an affinity with aspects of poststructuralist social theory which are currently influential. Both reject "metanarratives" like class theory with their emphasis on a directed historical change; both also tend to place analytical emphasis upon the plurality of social experiences whose incommensurability lends them an analytically irreducible character, even if poststructuralist theory tends to operate with a concept of power which is more pervasive and finely grained and which thereby draws attention to the micro-processes through which "subaltern" narratives are silenced or subjugated. In this respect, the models share a kind of primordialism – perhaps even a primitivism – in which particular subject positions are regarded as involving an irreducible authenticity which can be rearticulated analytically as the basis for a critique of the rationalist pretensions of social science. The plural society is not a society at all, but a collection of societies whose jostling can only be contained within a single political order by the exercise of domination (the contradictions of this position are criticized in Smith, 1996, and Bolland, 1997; see also chapter 7).

The plural society model transposes from the plantation society thesis the idea of a radical disjunction in the social order accompanying the plantation, and this in turn leads to considerable problems for the development of a postcolonial or postplantation civil society. This point was made by the Cuban historian Manuel Moreno Fraginals, who argued that the distinction between nation and plantation constituted the great political dilemma in the emergence of a Caribbean civic culture (Rivera, 1996). However, proponents of the creole society thesis – the third model – argue that such a civic culture *was* created out of the tissue of social relations forged in both the plantation and the counterplantation systems.

In the plantation and plural society models, emphasis is placed upon the alien origins of all parties to the social order of the plantation colony (with the exception of "mixed race" people of color), and the perpetuation of their alienness through the dichotomous logic of that order. Pushed to the extreme, the Caribbean region in this view becomes merely a neutral terrain upon which Europeans and Africans waged their battles. Since the odds were stacked heavily against the latter, attention then focuses on the extent to which Europeans obliterated the cultural forms of the Africans and instilled in them derivatives of European culture, or whether any African forms survived intact. In a well-known debate during the 1930s, the anthropologist Melville Herskovits argued for the persistence of African cultural traits, a position rejected by his interlocutor, E. Franklin Frazier, who propounded the now wearily familiar argument that the erasure of African culture in the American slave was the reason for many of the woes of contemporary blacks. Few scholars today would argue that Caribbean culture contains no African content but, more pertinently, the very terms of the debate have changed. As Mintz and Price (1992) have suggested, the issue is not so much whether this or that cultural trait can be traced back to Africa, but rather the way that enslaved Africans brought with them

– if they brought with them little else – prior capacities to make sense of their new world and shape it in distinctive ways, an approach which seems to have outlasted attempts during the 1980s and early 1990s to show that different regional Afro-American cultures preserved distinct "ethnic" heritages from Africa (Morgan, 1997). The essence of the creole society thesis, then, is that America was the site of a new cultural synthesis which emerged from but was not reducible to its African and European constituents.

The historical work of Edward Kamau Brathwaite has been influential in formulating this view. Focusing on Jamaica in the late eighteenth and early nineteenth centuries, Brathwaite (1971) tried to rebut the plantation or colonial society models, which suggested that the island was merely an agglomeration of plantations whose debased order was artificially maintained through external colonial force. Instead, he suggested that a distinctively Jamaican social order emerged during the period in question, in which whites, rich and poor, free coloreds and black slaves, participated in the creation of an integrative – albeit hierarchical – society grounded in local customs and a local institutional framework, even though it was consistently confounded by a persisting colonial culture. The idea can be developed in even more radical directions, as for example in Drummond's (1980) work on Guyana, in which racial categories are understood as cultural referents within a creole order rather than as distinctive groups within society. Drummond argues that putatively racial or ethnic categories such as "white," "potugee," "chinee," "coolie," "buck," and "douga" are not simply descriptors of actual groups but involve stereotypical identifications drawn from Guyanese history which people use in various social circumstances in order to create social distinctions or emphasize particular characteristics.

In these respects, creolization denotes processes of homogenization. This contrasts with its use in a good deal of contemporary theoretical writing where "creolization" marks a sense of social diversity and plurality which, it is implied, sociologists once leveled into the idea of homogeneous "societies" because of the grip of the nationalist ideologies that recourse to conceptions of the "creole" now seek to loosen (Mintz, 1995). Herein lies one source for criticism of the creole society thesis, insofar as it overstates the homogeneity of Caribbean societies that during and after slavery (and still today) remained massively polarized. At the same time, the implication that identical territorial boundaries can be drawn around identifiable and disparate social groups to make them conjoint parts of a distinctive "society" flies in the face of much contemporary sociological wisdom about the basis of social identity. The idea of a creole society emerging from indigenous processes of homogenization is, it has been argued, consonant with a contemporary Caribbean nationalism which attempts to replace the idea of colonial or class-stratification with a model of societal integration. This putative ethnogenesis is affected, for example, in the Jamaican national motto "out of many, one people." Yet, as we saw in the previous chapter, the idea of a common indigenous culture may entertain a more ambiguous character as an ideology of middle-class political rule in the postcolonial context which effaces class divisions. So, for example, Rastafari in Jamaica – originally a vehicle for a societally transcendent black separatism among working-class men – is incorporated into the nationalist fold as an expression of Jamaica's African roots and an exemplar of Afro-Jamaican cultural ingenuity, which it is possible to package commercially through the "ethnic culture" industry via reggae sunsplash festivals and the like, simultaneously undermining the radical political vision which underlies it. Diane Austin-Broos (1994) has developed this point into a broader critique of the creole society thesis, arguing that although it aims to recover the agency of Jamaicans – and particularly black working-class Jamaicans – in creating a distinctive sociocultural order which is not some mere derivative of colonial domination, it results in the rather conservative postulate that Jamaica's color–class hierarchy is a historically invariant property of all social classes. Austin-Broos shows the utility of carefully distinguishing the different models of the social order held by groups variously placed within its hierarchy. This is taken further by Bolland in his more general critique of the creole society model, when he argues "creolization . . . is not a homogenizing process, but rather a process of *contention* between people who are members of social formations and carriers of cultures" (Bolland, 1997: 25).

Bolland thus preserves a sense of distinct and opposed European and African groups within "creolized" Caribbean societies. But there is perhaps a danger here that the excessive dualism of approaches to cultural process in sociological theory (society as *either* homogeneous *or* heterogeneous, as grounded in *either* consensus *or* conflict) demands false distinctions of us. As Raymond Smith has put it in relation to the Anglophone Caribbean,

> Britons and Africans together created a creole society. The Britons no more preserved their customs than did the Africans; between them, and out of their hatreds, exploitations, copulations, mutual dependencies, and sometimes even love, they created a new social order, an order that has been accorded any social value with only the most grudging reluctance. (Smith, 1996: 85)

The critical point which emerges from the creole society thesis, then, is the idea of creolization as a process of cultural homogenization (rather than a state of cultural homogeneity) in which social conflicts find expression via cultural models rearticulated from the heterogeneous cultural resources of colonial society, models which are themselves partially constitutive of these conflicts. Moreover, there need be no incompatibility between creolization and the idea of conflict, ambivalence, or transformation between levels of power and meaning, as Brathwaite (1977) himself demonstrates in his brilliant analysis of Samuel Sharpe's 1831 slave revolt. In this sense, one can accept Bolland's criticism of creolization conceived as mere blending, without endorsing the opposite swing of the pendulum to the view that Caribbean society comprises only a set of inherent oppositions. The idea that a particular culture or society has been forged from diverse elements need not imply that the resulting social order admits to no conflict. As Talal Asad has argued in a different context,

> To demonstrate that elements making up a given cultural unit have diverse origins . . . is no proof that a unity does not exist. . . . To argue that "a culture" must be seen as a process does not exclude the possibility that it is a unified process. A unified culture is not necessarily one without contradictions; rather relations of contradiction between (cultural) elements themselves presuppose an embracing unity, however temporary. (Asad, 1990: 472)

Asad's final point, that the idea of conflict implies a societal order which provides its arena, is important and requires further elucidation. Theorists of American culture have produced many engaging if contrived metaphors of heating and combination to try to capture the sense in which American creole has emerged from its Old World antecedents, of which the "melting pot" of the United States is but the most famous. It is tempting to counterpose the melting pot metaphor, and its idea of a homogeneous new alloy strengthened by admixture, with the idea of a soup in which the "primordial" ingredients are brought together but remain identifiably unassimilated in the final product, which is something like Bolland's position. However, as Brackette Williams has argued, we are forced to recant this because "we have found in huge, long-simmering pots of vichyssoise not identifiable lumps of potato and leek, but, suddenly, chunks of meat and skins of apples which were not present when the lid of a 'common political system' was capped" (Williams, 1991: 10). Although thereby validating the creole society model as a theory of cultural creativity, Williams draws our attention to a common assumption of all three models, namely that particular, limited elements are poured into a sealed vessel which contains and bounds them, a container which sociologists have conventionally invoked as "society."

In attempting to avoid the shortcomings of this assumption, recent writers have opted for the alternative view that the domain of local social processes is forged through the flow of material from a global ecumene encompassing people, artefacts, ideas, and knowledge. For example, questioning whether the assumption of cultural distinction and wholeness common to the various approaches examined above constitutes a useful basis from which to analyze Caribbean societies, Karen Fog Olwig (1995) seeks to show how, after emancipation, the former slaves on the island of Nevis constructed a particular cultural orientation to their newfound circumstances through drawing upon three cultural traditions: the ostentatious lifestyle of the patriarchal plantation family which was often articulated around older European festive traditions such as Christmas mumming; the frugality of Methodist missionaries and their attempts to foster the emergence of the respectable "Christian black"; and Afro-creole traditions of kinship and land tenure worked out in proto-peasant, counterplantation adaptations to slavery.

In refusing to identify cultural forms as the property of particular socially constituted groups, this approach avoids the assumption that social identifications in the Caribbean can be decomposed into sets of unitary wholes (Olwig, 1995: 102–3). Moreover, the idea of "cultural flows" means that we do not need to read anything derivative or merely "oppositional" in local cultural forms such as the appropriation of the missionaries' "Christian black" model. This and other available models become ways of creating group distinctions at the local level. However, while Olwig is surely correct to argue that the emphasis upon unitary, bounded wholes in anthropology's analytic models stems from the hidden assumptions of European nationalist ideology which are imported into the theoretical discourse of the discipline, it is also the case that, in view of Europe's extreme colonial dominance of the Caribbean, historically these assumptions provided much of the raw material for creating postcolonial political communities in the region. In this respect, Olwig's argument – though not her empirical analysis of Nevis – courts the danger of suggesting that social identities are formed through a kind of global pick-and-mix, thereby effacing the very specific cultural and political processes through which particular flows are, as it were, "transmitted" and "received." Thus, in shifting the analytical focus from local "society" to global "flow," important questions about how such flows are articulated within local domains of hierarchy are too easily neglected. Let us consider such questions by examining the emergence of several different visions of Caribbean political community which I group under the labels "Euro-creole" and "Afro-creole."

Euro-creole

The political discourse of the eighteenth century brought the idea of "liberty," with all of its contradictions, to center stage. The American and

French revolutions involved attempts to free the political apparatus of the state respectively from colonial power and aristocratic rule. More generally, the "bourgeois" political climate of which these revolutions formed a part was characterized by other ideas of freedom, notably the rhetoric of "free" wage labor associated with an incipient industrial capitalism and the liberatory agenda of abolitionist movements directed towards the emancipation of American slaves. These developments posed a series of challenges to white creole elites in the Caribbean. Many were drawn to the discourse of anti-colonial sovereignty articulated in the American Revolution against the exactions of the distant metropolis, but they then had to confront the realities of constructing a postcolonial order. Far more than in the USA, this posed problems in societies where the mass of the population were slaves who possessed no affinity with the elite anti-colonial agenda.

It is interesting to compare the kind of creole historiography that emerges in these circumstances. In the USA, the eighteenth-century secessionist intellectual discourse that had railed against the high-handedness of the British colonial regime was to be re-evaluated in the middle of the nineteenth century by historians confronting the secession of the Confederate slave states, but by the end of the nineteenth century it was possible for Frederick Jackson Turner (1894) to produce a confident nationalist history based upon a secure independence, famously invoking the American frontier as a utopian Lamarckian trope, where the mingling of different populations was to produce a new and lustier breed of person. Turner was in some respects quite positive about the role that the American Indians played in this process, but he could afford to be; by the time he was writing the Indians had been all but annihilated, and could then be safely restored to a symbolic place within a fully Europeanized national firmament (see Pagden, 1987, for some Spanish-American analogies). A parallel situation could hardly be said to obtain in the slave societies of the eighteenth-century Caribbean. There, historians like Edward Long of Jamaica could only articulate their brand of white creole nationalism by insisting on rigid internal boundaries between the races, a point which emerges in the following passage where Long bemoans the upbringing of white creole women:

> Another misfortune is, the constant intercourse from their birth with Negroe domestics, whose drawling dissonant gibberish they insensibly adopt, and with it no small tincture of their awkward carriage and vulgar manners; all which they do not easily get rid of, even after an English education, unless sent away extremely young. (1774: II, 278)

This represents the very opposite of the blending demanded in Turner's frontier hypothesis. Indeed, Long felt that there were "extremely potent reasons for believing, that the White and the Negroe are two distinct species," an idea he felt able "to account for those diversities of feature, skin, and intellect, observable among mankind; which cannot be accounted for in any other way, without running into a thousand absurdities" (ibid.: 336). Long's polygenism has sometimes been taken to be a precursor of the biologization of race in nineteenth-century writers such as Gobineau, the "father of racism" (though it was hardly as unprecedented as has sometimes been supposed). However, it is perhaps better read alongside his fulminations against the sources of white creole degeneracy as an attempt to delimit and police the "freedom" he advocated for creole whites. For his part, Gobineau can be read in quite the opposite terms as an attempt to update models for aristocratic rule in the context of the populist, proto-fascist "Caesarism" of Louis Bonaparte's regime in France, which sought alliances with the populace and not with the aristocracy. Mocking comparisons in Europe (not least those of Marx's *Eighteenth Brumaire*) between Louis Bonaparte and the repressive regime of the illiterate black general Faustin Soulouque in Haiti underscore this emerging discourse, which conjoined race and class, albeit with both aristocratic and liberal-bourgeois inflections.

The same theme had been played out earlier in Saint-Domingue itself. The colonial writer Moreau de Saint-Méry (1796) had enthused over the voluptuous spectacle of mixed race dancing, but such examples of creolization appeared distinctly dystopian in relation to emerging European bourgeois values as well as the status concerns of the *petits blancs*. Towards the end of the eighteenth century, colonial legislators attempted to rebuff the growing confidence and prosperity of the *affranchis* through repressive legislation, which included sumptuary laws against wearing fine clothing and the Indian headscarves favored by colored women. Yet its effectiveness was compromised by the fact that this characteristic apparel of the *mulâtresse* had come to objectify the exotic sexual allure stereotypically associated with her, such that white women began to effect the same dress and comportment (Dayan, 1995: 180). Once again, this blending of genres or creolization was the bane of elites who saw in it a challenge to the categorical distinctions which vouchsafed their own authority. In Cuba, too, the white creole elite of the late nineteenth century adjusted to the incipient fact of a postcolonial civic culture by attempting to preserve aristocratic privileges no longer guaranteed by the colonial politico-economic order through fine attention to routines of "proper" comportment, and thus by "somatising manners," to use Rivera's (1996) phrase. Here we confront a somewhat ironic reversal of the nineteenth-century biostate described by Foucault (1981) and Stoler (1995). Whereas this biostate represented a "progressive" bourgeois triumph over the conservatism of a landed aristocracy, which nevertheless took over the preceding racial discourse to code social distinctions ever more finely as its nationalism expanded to include a widening citizenry, in Cuba the same tactic became the tool of a "reactionary" landed aristocracy attempting to preserve its privilege within the postcolonial order.

In Saint-Domingue at least, these white creole sensibilities became an irrelevance after 1804. So too did the kind of future envisaged for Jamaica by Long after emancipation and the tightening of metropolitan control during the nineteenth century, although the contest between freed Afro-Jamaicans, a racist plantocracy, and the metropolis – excellently described by Holt (1992) – animated a good deal of the racial politics of the island during that century. In Cuba, the egalitarian hopes of the anti-colonial nationalists quickly succumbed to the grip of a white oligarchy under the aegis of the USA, an oligarchy which crushed independent Afro-Cuban political organization in 1912 (Helg, 1995). Later on, this oligarchy was to be ousted by Castro's socialist revolution. In this sense, taking these three countries as broadly representative of different postplantation directions in Caribbean history, it might be said that the moment of Euro-creole nationalism in the Caribbean has passed. This is not, however, the case for Afro-creole culture, the topic of the next section.

Afro-creole

Caribbean slaves enjoyed few real possibilities for full and collective escape from the plantation order. In these circumstances, counterplantation strategies were more mediated, as with the proto-peasant adaptations undertaken in slave provision grounds or with appropriations of the colonizer's Christian religion. The St Lucian poet Derek Walcott captures these points thus:

> The subject African . . . understood too quickly the Christian rituals of a whipped, tortured and murdered redeemer, though he may have recoiled at dividing and eating his flesh for in primal cultures gods defeat each other like warriors and for warriors there is no conversion in defeat. There are many such warriors in the history of the archipelago, but the true history is of the tribe's conversion. (Walcott, 1974: 11)

Walcott's manifesto for creolization splendidly displaces the racist trope of African cannibalism onto the religion of the Europeans who ate the flesh of Christ. As I argued in chapter 2, racism and nationalism has been the bitter aftertaste of this meal. But here I want to discuss the ways in which the conversion of Walcott's "tribe" has also involved the transformation of racist and nationalist ideologies, by examining some aspects of Afro-creole religion in Jamaica and Haiti.

We have already encountered the important role played by Nonconformist missionaries in helping to establish the terms of the Jamaican postemancipation order. The missionaries' free village movement was instrumental in facilitating access to land for the freed slaves and the free villages have remained bastions of their distinctive interpretations of missionary Baptism to the present day (Besson, 1998). In 1860–1 – some five years before a popular insurrection over land tenure at Morant Bay led by the black Baptist preacher Paul Bogle so terrified the local plantocracy that it willingly surrendered its political control of the island to the metropolis – Jamaica's Great Revival, which followed the revivals in US and British Nonconformist Protestantism during the 1850s, gave added impetus to the emerging Afro-creole religious synthesis. This Revival Zion religion created a pantheon from Christian sources, in which the distant figure of the supreme God was complemented by a panoply of other spirits, from Christ down through angels, apostles, and prophets to spirits of the dead, fallen angels and, ultimately, Satan, all of whom could be propitiated in different ways and with different consequences (Chevannes, 1998a). In this respect, it represents one among several Caribbean religious forms – Haitian vodou is another obvious example – which reconstituted aspects of West African religious cosmology within a new colonial, Christian framing. Another West African import in Jamaica was the Trickster figure of Anancy. In Ashanti cosmology Anancy represents a mocking, "liminal" figure who subverts normal worldly categories like sky and earth, male and female, and so on. In Jamaican versions, he loses this cosmic role and emerges as a cunning underdog who turns the adverse circumstances of everyday life to his advantage. Parallels between Anancy and one modality of slave existence are not hard to discern, but his mocking spirit was also turned against the Puritan seriousness of the missionaries' "Christian black" model and perhaps invested the "outside" realm of postemancipation working-class Jamaican life more generally. No wonder, then, that one clergyman criticized Jamaicans for a "levity" which, he believed, vitiated their chance of full spiritual redemption (Austin-Broos, 1997).

This point underlines a more general subaltern tendency in the Caribbean for an irreverent fascination with colonial ceremony (Abrahams, 1970; Price, 1985). Another example is the Nevis "tea meeting" which originated in church fundraising events but was to assume a very different performative shape. In the tea meeting, a king, queen, and court are appointed, extravagant costumes are donned, convoluted speeches are performed before a heckling audience, tea and cakes are consumed, and the whole process is compered by "chairmen" who try to outdo all others in the hyperbolic virtuosity of their speech. Caribbean history is replete with examples of this kind of performance which colonial commentators often took as evidence of the slaves' buffoonery and childish imitation of European festivities, without perhaps appreciating how much the joke was at the expense of their own pomposity. Indeed, whether or not one concurs with Aime Césaire's view that fascism was merely colonialism meted out by Europeans upon themselves, to set the humor of the tea meeting against the preening seriousness of fascist national ceremonial makes one wonder who had the last laugh.

It is not possible for us to trace the complex genealogy of Zion Revival and other Afro-creole appropriations of Christianity through to the religious life of contemporary Jamaica (see Austin-Broos, 1997; Chevannes, 1998b), but let us briefly examine two strands of this religious life which are strongly marked by the legacy of Zion Revival, namely Rastafari and Pentecostalism, and which reveal some of its tensions.

The immediate social origins of the Rastafari movement lie in the experience of Jamaican men mainly with a rural "peasant" background, whose increasing impoverishment in the early part of the twentieth century led them into migratory unskilled labor in urban Jamaica and in the circum-Caribbean region. They experienced therein the full force of colonial racism, which led to a reappraisal of the "white" God in Afro-Jamaican forms of Christianity and to a new cosmology of a specifically black transcendence. This has been elaborated over time. Drawing upon a longer tradition of Ethiopianism in Jamaica, Rastafari divinizes Haile Selassie – emperor of Ethiopia from 1930 to 1974 – as part of its logic of this-worldly black transcendence. Among other things, this logic involves a constant substitution of subjectivity for all forms of objectification and differentiation, condensed in the pervasive Rasta trope of "I" and well captured in Bunny Wailer's Rastafarian song quoted at the start of chapter 1. In Rastafari, "I and I" stands not only for "we" but also for the sense of oneness that it asserts above all hierarchies and divisions. The Rastafarian seeks this oneness through meditations which level self–other distinctions and through which God comes to "indwell" in the self. Rastafari also refashions the colonial legacy of derision in Jamaica for Africa and its supposed primitivism along with aspects of working-class life and the ideology of "outsiderhood", sacralizing the use of marijuana and the wearing of uncombed and uncut "dreadlock" hair, and valorizing the verbal virtuosity of the "man of words." It places emphasis on "natural" food and the austere lifestyle of the artisan or self-sufficient cultivator, which in the view of some scholars betokens its peasant roots (Lewis, 1994). Concomitantly, it articulates a thorough contempt for the (white) capitalist world order and its manifestations in the neocolonial hierarchy of Jamaican society which – in keeping with a religious cosmology steeped in Old Testament tradition and an identification with the suffering of the Israelites – is described as "Babylon." As Littlewood (1998) has pointed out, many features of the Rastafari movement resemble the more radical edge of Puritanism: a critique of worldly hierarchy, an emphasis on untrammelled associational living, an identification with the Old Testament and its discourse of a "chosen" people, and – a point Littlewood does not emphasize – a stern moral self-scrutiny. While these elements may manifest themselves through direct "diffusion" via Jamaican traditions of Puritanism, as Littlewood cautiously suggests, it may also be fruitful to see them as "independent inventions," reversals whose logic is immanent in Christian cosmology and the socioeconomic hierarchy of colonial society.

Rastafari is also notoriously associated with the derogation of women, and despite a growing feminist critique of patriarchy within Rastafari (Rowe, 1998; Tafari-Ama, 1998), the movement continues to appeal principally to men. Traditionally, although the Rastawoman is celebrated as an "African queen," her access to redemption is through the controlling hand of her "Kingman." One sociological accounting for Rastafarian patriarchy is provided by Diane Austin-Broos (1987; 1997), who argues that the movement positions itself in relation to what she regards as Jamaica's national myth of origin, which transposes the biblical story of Eve's transgression in the Garden of Eden onto the racial treachery of the black slave woman's sexual union with white men. From this, of course, derives the dual marriage system which marginalizes the black working-class men who are the main constituency of Rastafari. Austin-Broos argues, therefore, that Rastafarian patriarchy represents an attempt to reconstitute black working-class men within the norms of the dual marriage system by exerting control over women.

Homiak (1998) purveys a quite different argument, placing emphasis upon renunciative celibacy rather than sexual freedom as the cause of Rastafarian circumspection with regard to women. But even if he is correct – and, of course, there may be room for both arguments within the totality of Rastafari – there remains here an association of transcendence with a masculine freedom which supervenes over the female, and whose axis is provided in the origin myth described by Austin-Broos.

Let us now briefly consider Pentecostalism, whose principal appeal in Jamaica is to working-class women rather than men. In certain respects, Pentecostalism appears the antithesis of Rastafari. Politically conservative, energized by US proselytization, and emphasizing the purity and decency of the Pentecostal female "saint," the distinction perhaps evinces Wilson's (1973) contrast between (Pentecostal) female "respectability" and (Rastafarian) male "reputation." But similarities could also be emphasized. Aspects of Afro-Christian Revival Zion have merged with Pentecostalism (Chevannes, 1998a), while Pentecostal devotional forms such as glossolalia ("speaking in tongues") represent a method of this-worldly transcendence which parallels Rastafarian cosmology. At the same time, the ideology of the "saint" deployed by the predominantly male Pentecostal clergy articulates another version of the origin myth in emphasizing the dangers of the "impure" female. On the other hand, as Austin-Broos has argued,

> Pentecostal women . . . deploy the experience of their own bodies to reposition themselves significantly within the biblical patriarchal order. By remaining part of the larger society, they also command certain powers as their period of childbearing passes and they emerge as self-sufficient household heads. They thereby offer a challenge to the cultural logic that positions them at the intersection of the origin myth and the myth of the Fall. (Austin-Broos, 1997: 241)

Thus, in the context of a social and a global order which provides constant challenges to the dignity of black working-class women – challenges often compounded in relations with their male counterparts – Pentecostalism provides one source of reprieve.

A good deal of writing on Jamaican religious and folk traditions – and perhaps of Afro-American culture more generally – displays a concern to evaluate them in terms of their oppositional or anti-colonial capacities, and the supporters of Rastafari in particular frequently proclaim its transcendence of Jamaica's mentality of colonial dependence and inferiority in contrast to Afro-Christianity, Anancyism, and so on (Chevannes, 1998c; McFarlane, 1998). Yet while there is little reason to doubt that Rastafari has had a beneficial effect upon a reevaluation of the African and the Afro-creole in Jamaica, one might register several objections to arguments of this kind. For one thing, it would be quite possible to argue that the "Puritan" seriousness of Rastafari and its patriarchal discourse is more redolent of the missionaries' colonial "Christian black" model than the mocking "levity" of Anancyism, and no more radical than the subversion of female subjection worked by Pentecostal women. More broadly, perhaps one should refrain from determining on behalf of working-class Jamaicans which strategy constitutes their best or most authentic avenue of resistance from the Olympian (or maybe Babylonian) heights of sociological theory. Instead, what I hope to have suggested, albeit from those same heights, is that Afro-Christianity, Anancyism, Rastafari, and Pentecostalism are part of an ongoing and developing argument within Jamaican Afro-creole traditions.

Afro-creole culture in Haiti has involved similar arguments, but ones articulated with its very different political history. Let us now turn to the example of a Haitian Afro-creole religion, vodou, and link it to the broader theme of this chapter by showing how vodou structures some wider postulates concerning the themes of race and forms of state power.

We will begin with a brief description of vodou. Haiti possesses many different spirit cults which vary from the specific family spirits objectified in the local landscape described in the previous chapter, to regional cults and thence to a pantheon of nationally recognized spirit figures. "Vodou" is often used rather indiscriminately as a generic term for all of these variants; here we will focus upon aspects of this broader "national" pantheon. At this level, the structure of vodou resembles in some respects the pantheon of Jamaican Zion Revival, with a remote supreme God complemented by a panoply of spirits or *lwa* who intercede more immediately in daily life, through to a variety of ghosts and evil spirits. And, as with Zion Revival, vodou is a creole synthesis despite its strong African referents: the *lwa*, though of West African provenance, are also associated with the Catholic pantheon of saints and organized into distinct families whose cosmogony maps the geopolitical coordinates of colonialism. Thus, the aspect of the African *Rada* spirits is typically homely and comforting, while the creole *Petwa* spirits reveal a more vengeful and dangerous aspect; particular *lwa* may have different *Rada* and *Petwa* forms with corresponding personae (Dayan, 1995; Brown, 1997). Like most Afro-creole religions, *vodou* lacks an organized institutional structure but ceremonies are often performed by local priests and priestesses (*houngans* and *mambos*). As with aspects of Jamaican Afro-creole religion, vodou practice typically involves an intense subjectification in the form of possession by the *lwa*, and it emphasizes a collective and performative rather than an individual and contemplative form of religious transcendence (Lowenthal, 1978).

The relationship between vodou and Haitian politics is complex. In the colonial period, it appeared to be a repository of slave resistance if we take at face value planter anxiety over "vaudoux dancing" and stories of the vodou ceremony held by the slave leader Boukman at Bois-Caïman which, legend has it, marked the start of the Haitian Revolution. In the complex postrevolutionary politics of the nineteenth century, vodou was successively repressed, courted, or ignored by Haitian leaders but, among the educated minority, it was typically scorned as an embarrassing throwback to the country's roots in primitive Africa. The occupation of the country by the USA from 1915 to 1934 marked something of a turning point. Opposition to the occupation among elements of the elite manifested itself in the construction or "imagination" of a new and homogeneous national community in which the Afro-creole folkways of the peasantry were elevated as markers of Haitian authenticity. Concomitantly, this *mouvement indigéniste* involved a positive reevaluation of vodou, as in Price-Mars' influential book *Ainsi Parle L'Oncle* (1928). At the same time, the occupation and its development program helped consolidate the emergence of a black middle class, while simultaneously buttressing the political dominance of *clair* elites. In the aftermath of the occupation, the new black elite was able to articulate the older political program of *noirisme* with renewed assurance against *clair* dominance, precipitating a successful assault upon political control in 1946 which was to culminate eleven years later in the election of François Duvalier on a *noirist* platform. This was quickly abandoned in all but name for the single-minded pursuit of power (Trouillot, 1990), a pursuit which included an assiduous courting of vodou cults and their *houngans* (together with the repression or murder of the recalcitrant) in order to create local bases of power. Indeed, many *houngans* became associated with the *makouts*, Duvalier's notorious militia.

In an incisively cynical paper, Rémy Bastien (1966) has argued that the political uses of vodou have corresponded with its scholarly representation among both locals and outsiders. Tales of cannibalism and evil rituals purveyed by foreign writers in the nineteenth century suited the racist international ostracism of the lonely "black republic," but gave way to the positive evaluations of the *mouvement indigéniste* and foreign ethnographers searching for a new ethic of postcolonial nationalism, only to succumb once more under the excesses of Duvalier to gothic images of obscene rituals in the National Palace. But it is nevertheless possible to suggest that vodou continued to provide a structure for rural life. Although he is unable to take seriously what he calls the "clown-like shenanigans" of vodou practice, Gerald Murray (1980) has shown convincingly how economic exchanges associated with vodou ritual function to safeguard peasant land tenures, long the measure of successful Afro-creole adaptation. In keeping with his "cultural materialism," Murray describes some of the elements of vodou – dancing, drumming, possession, sacrifice – as behavioral norms whose origins are merely contingent to its contemporary role in mediating land tenure. This distancing of historical form from contemporary function allows him to represent vodou as a slightly deluded mechanism for economic adjustment which might otherwise be conceived more rationally. Sidney Mintz provides an alternative way of thinking, in which the sociological imperative to render the bizarre as intelligible and ordinary unfurls not through an analytic privileging of an "ordinary" latent function, but through the ordinariness of vodou to the participants themselves. Here, historical integrity is preserved as a central feature of the meaning of vodou:

Vaudou, like any other complex of belief and practice, is a vital, living body of ideas and behaviors, carried in time by its practitioners, and responsive to the changing character of social life. This must have been true from its very beginning as a transatlantic system of faith, when African slaves from a score of different societies first attempted to implant their symbolic pasts in the hearts and minds of their children. . . . Beneath the apparent absence of any unified social or ideological superstructure, there is a body of basic beliefs and practices that typify *vaudou* throughout Haiti . . . [which provides] a core of belief – one might almost say a series of philosophical postulates about reality. (Mintz, 1972: 12–13)

The reality of Caribbean colonial slavery included the hyperdevelopment of features which occupied the central space of the Enlightenment's progressive, civil order, turning the classification and disciplining of the secularized body into the most extreme and degrading forms of colonial violence. Some of the grotesque in vodou – the transience and abandon of possession, the violence of its symbolism – doubtless operates as a kind of ontology which domesticates the extremes of this colonial context. Thus, as Joan Dayan (1995) engagingly hints in the prologue to her book on Haiti, scholarly attempts to characterize vodou in ways which are sensitive to the meanings it holds for its participants court the danger of pandering to the sensationalist exoticism from which Haiti has too often suffered in the accounts of outsiders, through the legacy of scholarly traditions which are incapable of recognizing such "perversions" of rationalism as anything other than qualities which are absolutely distinct from their own epistemology. The point is significant insofar as it helps to establish a more sophisticated way of reading the characteristically dualistic structures of much Caribbean cultural representation. Such a structure is easy to discern in the case of the broader cosmology of vodou, with its distinctions between the *Rada* and *Petwa* families of *lwa*, and with the ambivalent characteristics imputed to *lwa*like "Mistress Ezili." In her *Rada* forms she often manifests herself in the guise of the beautiful, pampered, coquettish stereotype of the *mulâtresse* concubine, yet in hideous or vengeful *Petwa* forms such as Ezili-je-wouj and Ezili-kokobe, seems to reveal the rage and misery of a woman denied any role but this adjunct to colonial hierarchy. Similarly, the *lwa* *Ogou* is both an indomitable fighter for his people, and the agent of a fearsome rage against them. European/African, white/black, free/slave, plantation/peasant, respectability/reputation, *leta/mounn andewó*, marriage/outside union – each seems to make the disjunction of the colonial order a matter of fundamental cultural import reproduced in the structure of contemporary relations. This does not, however, warrant the assumption that each term of the duality represents a singular sociopolitical order which opposes itself to the other. Karen McCarthy Brown (1997) makes this point especially well in her analysis of Ogou's place in vodou cosmology. For Brown, the *Rada* and *Petwa* pantheons concretize these dualities of inside/outside, family/stranger, oppressed/oppressor in Haitian thought. In her words, "the [Petwa] *lwa* represent an effort to expropriate the power of slaveholding and its contemporary transmutations – oppression, prejudice, economic discrimination – and to use that power against itself" (ibid.: 68). These *lwa* are effective for individualistic, self-interested ends such as the pursuit of monetary gain, but wield an uncontrollable and potentially malevolent force which the devotee invokes at his or her peril. Ogou and the *Gède lwa*, by contrast, mediate the contradiction between the individualism, alienation, and oppression of the world at large symbolized by the *Petwa lwa* and the undifferentiated, "inside" world of family through their respective strategies of struggle and Tricksterish humor. The point is not that individualistic self-interest is an alien incursion into the life of Haitian working people which is symbolically represented through recourse to the colonial symbolism of outsiderhood and evil, an argument which has been advanced for cultural identities between money and the devil for black peasantries elsewhere in Latin America (Taussig, 1980). Rather, it represents one pole in a *single* cultural system within which people are created as subjects in a capitalist "world system," yet are necessarily attuned to their status as objects in its neocolonial order and, even more so, to the absolute objectification which that order worked upon their ancestors. In the same historicizing manner through which colonial thought proceeds, this system renders the extant order intelligible through "homely materials" which in Saint-Domingue and Haiti were European as well as African. However, following the earlier discussion, arguments for the singularity of the cultural system are not intended to imply a harmonious political culture. This would certainly be an inappropriate reading of the way that vodou has figured in Haitian postcolonial history, which might better be regarded as a wary play of forces, of appropriations and negations (Dayan, 1995).

In 1986, amid the collapse of Jean-Claude Duvalier's dictatorship, *raras* bands celebrating the Petwa *lwas* in Haiti's annual Mardi Gras roamed the streets of Port-au-Prince killing prominent *makouts* and Duvalierists. Thus, the cult that François Duvalier had so assiduously courted was now providing a model for violent struggle against the repressive regime of his son (Desmangles, 1992). The extent to which vodou acts as a progressive or a reactionary force has been a living issue in Haitian politics but, I would argue, it behoves the sociologist neither to romanticize the cult as a source of uncorrupted popular resistance, nor to derogate it as a clownish throwback to battles long past. A more modest and more achievable goal is to explicate the different layers of meaning which it encodes. These layers of meaning are likely to evince a more complex reading of the political order than those permissible in official discourses which function in inherently homogenizing ways. Thus, the Dessalines portrayed in nineteenth-century Haitian historiography – always oriented as it was to the political present – emerged either as the national founding father, for the *noiriste* faction, or as the crude and brutal tyrant of the *mulâtre* faction (Nicholls, 1996). The later reevaluation by Price-Mars and other *indigéniste* intellectuals of popular traditions in the context of the US occupation made a more nuanced picture of Haitian life available to political discourse, but its longer term legacy was in a sense to strengthen the rather specific class politics of *noirisme* rather than to establish a broader national politics. More generally, though it is possible to appropriate Dessalines as an icon of anti-colonial black liberation, the Dessalines of vodou, identified with Ogou, is more complex and less comforting (Dayan, 1995: 28). Vengeful and intemperate, but implacably opposed to the oppression of his people, the versions of Dessalines – and of Ogou more generally – which emerge in the structure of vodou defy homogenizing analysis which holds that progressive political action must entail *this* and not *that*. A similar ambivalence has attended the responses of Haitian vodouists to their colonial or neocolonial conditions, which are met either with Ogou's wrathful sword or a sardonic *Gède* laugh, often almost simultaneously (Brown, 1997: 85).

We have touched several times upon the gendered aspects of vodou cosmology, notably in the form of the *lwa* Ezili. In addition to her representation of colonial dualism, Ezili condenses a rich array of symbols concerning purity, fecundity, sexuality, and abandonment. She is associated with the Catholic Virgin but – rather like the female "Christian black" of the Anglophone Caribbean – her virginity connotes purity rather than sexual innocence. In these respects, even though she is constituted through conventionally idealized and objectified categories of the "pure" and "impure" woman, she seems to hold out the promise of their transcendence. In the words of Maya Deren,

> Voudoun has given woman, in the figure of [Ezili], exclusive title to that which distinguishes humans from all other forms: their capacity to conceive beyond reality, to desire beyond adequacy, to create beyond need. (Deren, 1953: 138)

Nonetheless, the gender imagery is predicated on an inherent dualism which is constantly susceptible to a collapse into the separation of woman idolized or violated. Ezili is but one of a set of actual and mythical women in the cultural repertoire of contemporary Haiti whose sexual acts symbolize the generation of the nation itself. This identification of females and female reproductive capacities with the peopling of the land is a common trope of nationalist ideology, since it enables blank territory to be constituted into a domain of specific social homogeneity. However, in Haiti and in the Americas more generally the generation of an indigenous nation connotes not homogeneity but mixture, as in Turner's frontier or the emergence of a creole class of coloreds. Haitian myths of national origin display an ambivalence which works against the lineaments of Christian models where the sacrality of the nation is established through symbolic inversions like the birth of an omnipotent redeemer to a virgin girl, and his death at the hands of a rabble. In one common myth of national origin, the nation is born not through immaculate conception but through the rape of a black woman, Sister Rose (Dayan, 1995), while – as we have seen – the identification of the liberator Dessalines with the *lwa* Ogou hedges his redemptive qualities with ambivalence. The legend of Sister Rose is told by Timoléon Brutus in a biography of Dessalines, whereby Haiti begins "with a woman brutally fertilized by a slave in heat or a drunken White, a criminal escaped from Cayenne or a degenerate from feudal nobility" (cited in Dayan, 1995: 49).

Brutus's version expresses the ambivalence of an explicitly creole nationalism. The aggressor could have been any of these various racial stereotypes. It does not matter which because "the origin of everyone is common." That such sentiments should be expressed in a book published in 1946 – the same year that the *noiriste* "revolution" ousted the *mulâtrist* regime of President Lescot – is, however, no coincidence. Indeed, another modality of struggles over the nation in the Caribbean has been the way that anticolonial black consciousness has worked against creole nationalism, in particular by recuperating the homogeneous imagery of European nationalism through idolized images of the black woman, and defining itself against the outrage of colonialism in relation to her violation by white men.

This identification of women with property – violable objectifications of a collective claim to land – reveals nationalism in its patriarchal aspect. Whether in Brutus's version of Haiti as a woman violated by a medley of men, or in the anti-colonial slant of *noiriste* versions, it is men making claims to other men through women, who are thereby reduced to a set of categorical identifications (see hooks, 1992, and also Das, 1996, for a parallel argument in relation to Indian nationalism). Joan Dayan draws upon literary examples to show how women have contested the nationalist homology of woman and nation and its trope of the raped woman, citing the Haitian novelist Marie Vieux Chauvet's trilogy *Amour, Colère et Folie*, which invokes the specters of Ezili and Sister Rose and updates them in the story of the light-skinned virgin Rose, who is martyred through agreeing to "excruciating daily sex" with a black Duvalierist thug in a contract to protect the family's property, but muses upon her own participation in it, "Docile, too docile for a virgin. Am I virgin? Accomplice? Am I not getting used to him, looking to him for my pleasure?" (Dayan, 1995: 123). Chauvet uses the unsettling image of a woman enjoying her own rape to disturb not only its status as a ritual of male domination but also the use of ideas concerning women's purity as markers for collective "national" boundaries.

This example of Haitian violence represents a fitting epilogue to my argument. The creolization of race in the Caribbean has certainly not vitiated violent political conflicts, conflicts in which race or color have – as here – often been an idiom. Nor is it possible to generate any pan-Caribbean account of political ideologies from this aspect of regional history alone. Nevertheless, we can trace a creole ambivalence here which involves an *appropriation* of racial ideology, an explicit reckoning of its historical character, particularly in forms of Afro-creole culture contesting subordination in class society. However, unlike Paul Gilroy's (1993b) concept of the "Black Atlantic" culture – which strikes me as a somewhat idealized normative articulation of a postnational political vision – there is no reason to suppose that creole political discourse is immune from forms of closure and exclusion which entrench ethnonationalist conceptions of the postcolonial order.

Caudillismo

In the preceding sections we discussed the question of creating a national political community in race-divided plantation and postplantation societies. However, the same question presented itself rather differently in parts of the Americas which were not tied so ineluctably to the colonial plantation system. This situation applied to much of postcolonial Latin America and the Latin Caribbean in the nineteenth century, where local elites inherited an essentially colonial economic order characterized mainly by less intensive economic activities such as ranching and manorial agriculture worked by Indian, black, and "mixed race" laborers under various degrees of coercion. Facing "national" populations of subject Indian and black laborers, their problem was how to create new independent states on the basis of a shattered colonial order in militarized, regionally fragmented, and class divided societies characterized by very localized ties of political loyalty – hardly fertile ground for national ethnogenesis. Indeed, with the idea of national government lacking any enduring legitimacy, the stage was open for political bosses with highly localized support – based upon a personalist style of leadership, which combined patronage of allies with uncompromising violence against enemies – for ephemeral occupation of the political center. Yet no sooner had such a figure promised to stabilize the political order than a *coup d'état* would burst from some regional center to depose him.

This is the essence of *caudillismo*, which has been defined more formally in terms of the repeated emergence of armed patron–client sets formed around personalist ties; the lack of institutionalized political succession; the use of violence in political competition; and the chronic failure of incumbent rulers to guarantee their political tenure (Wolf and Hansen, 1967). Wolf and Hansen understand *caudillismo* as the outcome of unsuccessful political centralization in the particular context of the postcolonial manorial economy and the tension in these circumstances between a propertied white creole elite and propertyless *mestizo* or *pardo* opportunists, which was such that the locus of political authority pulsated between central and local forces until *caudillismo* gave way in the late nineteenth century to more centralized "*caudillo* dictatorships" like that of Porfirio Díaz in Mexico (a Caribbean parallel might be Ulises Heureaux of the Dominican Republic) in circumstances of capitalist penetration. However, even in the countries which were least centralized and integrated into the capitalist world economy at the zenith of *caudillismo* during the first half of the nineteenth century, notably Haiti, Venezuela, and the Dominican Republic, studies have revealed the class character of the socioracial order (Trouillot, 1990; Wright, 1990; Betances, 1995). This, I would argue, indicates not so much that race is fundamentally a modality of class, as a materialist argument would have it, but mainly that even in circumstances where the colonial order had broken down the political imaginary remained determined by the available colonial models of ranking hierarchy. In a similar vein, Stinchcombe (1996) has argued more generally that *caudillismo* represented the attempt to connect local politico-economic orders to what he calls the "world-system forces" which provided the resources and the impetus for state formation. In his words,

> By defining the *caudillo* complex by what it could do and how it could do it, we more easily understand where it solved problems people had. When did people's problems have the solution on a more macroscopic level than their resources and ties of loyalty normally reached? (Stinchcombe, 1996: 291)

Stinchcombe emphasizes the problem of creating a viable postcolonial political order with the resources to hand. He evokes the aura or "detached shell" of the colonial state as a kind of historical residue through which that order had to be imagined, but this state was now no longer invested either with sufficient military–administrative capacities to sustain it, or sufficient popular legitimacy for its smooth articulation with a sense of postcolonial national community. Indeed, often enough *caudillismo* did not attempt to create such a community. The political model of *caudillismo* was patronage (and murder), with the personalist domination of local bosses expanding beyond the ambit of its regional power base to fill the shell of the colonial state, only to collapse once again. Thus, anti-colonial nationalists had to draw upon quite different resources in order to create models of national citizenship. Nevertheless, I want to argue that *caudillismo* was structured within the same kind of closed diametric model associated with the "world system forces" described by Stinchcombe, a point we will now pursue briefly in relation to Stinchcombe's application of *caudillismo* to Haiti.

Caudillismo, Stinchcombe says, solved people's problems, but which people's problems did it solve? The model is addressed to the problem of building a postcolonial political community integrated within the "world system," but this is precisely what had been rejected by the mass of the Haitian population. Creating a usable political ideology out of the colonial order was a formidable problem for nationalist intellectuals, which they tackled by drawing in particular upon the ideals of *liberté* in French revolutionary republicanism while blaming the evils of Saint-Domingue upon the colonists rather than the metropole (Hoffmann, 1984). But there were not many nationalist intellectuals in Haiti. From the inception of the slave revolt in 1791, freedom to the Haitian masses had generally been couched less in terms of abstract political models and more in terms of secure access to land and its product. The Haitian peasantry displayed a resolute proclivity for land acquisition and cultivation for local consumption. Thus, the political problem in Haiti was really the converse of the one posed by Stinchcombe: how could the macroscopic level of the state ensure its own viability and solvency by encapsulating the microscopic level of the peasantry?

The result was a class struggle overlain by competing models of political order and inflected by prior color identities. Within a decade or two of independence, a *de facto* agrarian order had emerged which was characterized predominantly by small-scale cultivation, and which subsequent efforts at centralization were incapable of altering. This led to a peculiar class structure, with an educated *clair* commercial elite concentrated in the few coastal towns, and an aspirant black elite of rural landholders whose wealth and standing largely derived from military service but who, through the reconstitution of a peasant labor process, had little command over resources to cultivate their land. For this reason, Trouillot (1990: 76) describes the landlord class as a "continuously disintegrating" one. Landlords attempted to shore up their fortunes by recourse to state patronage, and – not least because of their color legitimacy – the more successful ones became rulers. Yet, as Trouillot points out, they were often "nothing but rulers," because they were bypassed by foreign merchants working through the commercial elite who extracted surplus from the peasantry. The peasantry was internally stratified, and members of the richer stratum developed local power bases through leasing land, acting as merchant intermediaries, and providing the civil infrastructure for the state in the countryside. The *cacos* peasant rebels who toppled successive nineteenth-century governments came from this class, but these were *caudillos* who rarely assumed control of the state, instead furnishing support in the context of the state's weakness and lack of popular legitimacy to the hidden interests of broader "world system" forces.

In these respects, "world system forces" invested the political world of *caudillismo* not just at the point where it attempted to stabilize local political orders in relation to a broader capitalist economic and political system; the class or status-ordered models of the social world entertained in those forces thoroughly invested the civil societies within which *caudillos* operated, even if they were unable to dominate those civil societies in the manner of the nation-state. *Caudillismo* cannot therefore be regarded as a center–periphery model of political authority at odds with the model of ranking hierarchy we have derived elsewhere as a fundamental feature of Euro-American political ideology. Hoetink has commented that

> The prestige of a *caudillo* derived . . . from his capacity to weld personal relationships, on the basis of actual and promised transactions of goods, privileges and loyalties, into a durable and multi-layered network of patronage, of which the leader was both the centre and the apex. (Hoetink, 1986: 289)

And, indeed, it is precisely this apical character – the intendedness towards exclusive claims over political authority, and the class order that emerges in such circumstances – which, even though frustrated for structural reasons, differentiates *caudillismo* from center–periphery models of political power of the kind we encountered earlier in relation to the Indian "galactic polity." Parallels certainly exist insofar as structural factors impeding political centralization created opportunities for local political brokers to emerge both in India and Latin America, but the wider sociopolitical environment within which these brokers operated was very different in the two cases. On the other hand, some of these differences – though not, I shall argue, all of them – began to break down with India's increasing incorporation into the global capitalist world system from the eighteenth century onwards, a process associated with British colonization and then a decolonization which has brought similar problems of national ethnogenesis to the subcontinent. It is to this issue that we now turn.

Caste, Communalism, and the Nation in Contemporary India

Although many aspects of the caste order which we have described in previous chapters are germane to contemporary life in much of India, particularly in rural areas, they figure within a sociopolitical landscape which differs radically from earlier formations, most obviously since the postcolonial state now affects an exclusive sovereign claim over a territorial domain of a kind which previously characterized European rather than Indian polities. In this respect, it might be argued that caste ideology with its complex interactional order, Brahmanic political models, and so on, is breaking down, or has already done so. This is one of the questions which will be examined in the present section. On the one hand, aspects of the contemporary political scene seem to refigure caste identifications, such as the emergence of caste groups as political associations in the domain of electoral politics, or the challenge to both established electoral politics and the caste order through Dalit (untouchable) and "backward caste" political activism. Other aspects seem less obviously related to caste identification, such as the emergence in rural areas of semi-autonomist forms of political activism among the wealthier stratum of small "peasant" cultivators (the so-called "new farmers movements"), regional autonomist movements which in some cases, like the Punjab or Kashmir, are inflected by religious identifications, and the recent emergence of "communal" violence mainly directed at Muslims and associated with the rise of an authoritarian nationalism which, ostensibly at least, seems to dissolve caste identification through a metanarrative of Hindu revivalism. We shall be particularly concerned with the latter in order to probe the utility of models which hold that communalism represents, like fascism or forms of racist nationalism, a pathology of modernity which, in the Indian case, has swept aside "traditional" caste identifications. First, however, it is necessary to sketch some aspects of modern Indian history in order to provide a context for understanding these phenomena.

We will begin the story in the mid-eighteenth century, when declining Mughal suzerainty began to give way to regional powers and ultimately to British colonial domination. The Mughals were a Turkic Muslim dynasty from Central Asia whose power in the Indian subcontinent was first established under Babur (1483–1530) and then consolidated under his successors, most notably his grandson Akbar (1542–1605). The key politico-economic institution in the Mughal polity was the allocation of alienable grants to local agrarian product. The grant-holders or *zamindars* (a term later used by the British synonymously with "landlord") – of whom the *jagirdars* or holders of land as recompense for government service were especially important – constituted an Islamicized elite of both local and Central Asian origins. Mughal policy was directed at securing the allegiance of this elite through patrimonial means – mainly by a constant perambulation of the court through its domains, bringing both the promise of patronage and the threat of force to the potentially recalcitrant – rather than at developing any broader "nationalist" ideology which engaged the mass of the indigenous population (Bayly, 1983; Blake, 1997). In traditional scholarship it has been argued that the Mughal polity fell into crisis in the eighteenth century because of high revenue demands upon local cultivators from *jagir* holders, provoking economic stagnation and increasingly organized corporate regional resistance from "brotherhoods" of cultivators, such as the Sikhs, Jats, and Marathas, against whom the Mughals had developed no countervailing claim to political legitimacy. Recent scholarship suggests that this picture must be revised by recognizing a regional dynamism which circumvented the obligation to direct political allegiances and economic resources to the center. This established more streamlined regional polities, including retrenched Mughal states, for which the Mughal polity had paved the way and which were the arena for an economic dynamism under the aegis of commercially minded *zamindars*, Vaishnavite merchants associated with temple endowment, and itinerant Shaivite ascetics who used their pilgrimage routes to establish mercantile networks (Bayly, 1983; Alam, 1993; van der Veer, 1994).

Despite this more positive picture, it is nevertheless true that political tenure during the eighteenth century *was* less secure than hitherto. *Zamindars*, merchant castes, peasant brotherhoods, and erstwhile military associates of the Mughals such as Dost Muhammad Khan – who began life as a foot soldier, became a Mughal revenue farmer, and thence carved out his own petty kingdom – were all in the business of trying to extend political claims against other pretenders. That the British were later to distort this into a theory of political "chaos" justifying colonial intervention does not alter the fact of a complex and competitive eighteenth-century political environment. Here, it is tempting to apply the American model of *caudillismo* in Stinchcombe's sense of a political order where local "big men" attempted to fill the detached shell of the earlier, larger polity. There is a further similarity inasmuch as this detached shell retained its aura of legitimacy. So, for example, corporate "brotherhoods" such as the Marathas did not, in their struggle with the Mughal state, offer a countervailing egalitarian or "indigenous" political ideology; on the contrary, when the opportunity came to entrench their own political rule, they did so by a hierarchalization after the fashion of the Mughal polity, and even submitted nominally to Mughal suzerainty (Bayly, 1983; Bose and Jalal, 1998). But this was always subject to contestation. Indeed, the difference between the American and Indian cases lies in the central ideological difference I have posited throughout this book, namely that where political authority in Euro-American contexts always seemed to culminate in a single, apical point (even if it was one that was hard to reconstruct in the postcolonial period, especially in a country like Haiti), corresponding conceptions in

India entertained more plural notions of rule. Chief among the serviceable models in the cultural repertoire which were relevant to eighteenth-century circumstances was the *kshatriya* ideology which, as Gordon (1978) points out, neatly mapped the secular, martial legitimacy of ancient Indian warrior-kings onto pretenders like Dost Muhammad Khan.

Earlier, we mentioned the peregrinations of the Mughal court as part of its strategy of power, and recourse to the *kshatriya* model brings to mind another kind of movement in the form of the Vedic horse sacrifice and the martial wanderings of the warrior-king. The ascetic merchants previously mentioned as major economic and political players in the eighteenth century, but probably established long before that, provide yet another example. Thus, in contrast to the religious and political models of European Christendom, one can speak more generally of the constitutive role of procession in Indian conceptions of authority. Indeed, wandering ascetics of Shaivite and Vaishnavite monastic orders were instrumental in extending and regularizing their respective versions of Hinduism over the vast area of the Indian subcontinent, often by reconstituting the sites of local religious cults within the broader sacred geography of a higher deity. Van der Veer (1994) points out that the hierarchical logic of Hindu cosmology is especially amenable to this. Local deities can be incorporated as manifestations or avatars of higher deities like Vishnu and Shiva, who can themselves be encompassed by higher ideals of unity. The argument nevertheless implicitly invokes a cultural metacontext in the form of a prior orientation to the general logic of encompassing hierarchy, even if the incorporation of local religious practices was not always smooth (Thapar, 1992; Schnepel, 1995). The ascetics referred to here were not usually mendicant, "outside-the-world" renouncers, but were connected with powerful and wealthy monastic orders. The leaders of these orders represent yet another "big man" model of localized authority. Here, the status accruing to asceticism is convertible into political and economic capital, albeit of a finely balanced kind, since too assiduous a pursuit of these worldly goals undermines the logic of ascetic renunciation which potentiates them (Mines and Gourishankar, 1990).

Thus, eighteenth-century India was characterized by a variety of intersecting claims to political authority, and itinerancy was an important modality through which it was possible to articulate some of these claims. But in order to link these points to the later history of nationalism we need to consider the effects of British colonialism. Unlike the American situation, the early European presence in India represented a precarious toehold in the South Asian trading world, established under the sufferance of the Mughals. This was long the situation of the English East India Company which, though founded in 1600, did not begin to flex its imperialist muscles until the latter part of the eighteenth century in the aftermath of the Anglo-French Seven Years War (1756–63). This marked a decisive shift in approach which led, in less than a hundred years, to the consolidation of virtually the whole subcontinent under direct or indirect Company rule, and then under British Crown rule after 1858 (Lawson, 1993). The reasons for the Company's shift in an imperialist direction are somewhat obscure. Perhaps more to the point are the reasons for its success. Whereas traditional imperial histories attribute this to the military prowess of Company employees like Robert Clive, the general superiority of European technology and the "divisiveness" of Indian caste society, more recent historiography suggests that this "divisiveness" is better reformulated in terms of the plural loci of Indian political authority, and that British colonial ambitions were in any case largely realized through the exploitation of indigenous political schisms and through alliances with local "modernizing" economic elites in pursuance of what seemed to be mutual interests (Bayly, 1983; Washbrook, 1988; Peabody, 1991b). Thus, in the words of David Washbrook (1988: 76), "colonialism was the logical outcome of South Asia's own history of capitalist development." Unsurprisingly, so blunt a reversal of the narrative of colonial violence has not gone unchallenged. For example, Partha Chatterjee (1993) and Gyan Prakash (1990; 1992) offer sophisticated critiques of Washbrook's somewhat inflexible Marxist historiography, although – in keeping with the later Subalternist historiographic school to which they subscribe – they tend to lapse, particularly Chatterjee, into a rather mystical discourse of anti-colonial primitivism which recuperates a singular Indian tradition of resistance to the colonial transformation of Indian society. However, these authors do not confront the empirical point Washbrook raises about the confluence of certain British and Indian economic interests, nor do they pay much attention to Washbrook's (1982; 1988) own account of colonial transformation which in fact says quite a lot about the character of the structural transformation wrought by British colonialism in India. Let us briefly summarize his main points.

First, the economic cornerstone of British rule was built upon a concretization of the (often Muslim or Islamicized) *zamindars* as local property-holding landlords. It also involved a "peasantization" of Indian society, partly because of deindustrialization and the constitution of a rural proletariat as the commercial imperatives of Indian economic elites were subordinated to Britain's own, and partly since the removal of various precolonial forms of political authority meant that access to the land became the only really secure economic base. Second, at the intellectual level, British scholars produced a vast corpus of knowledge about India which was fundamentally geared to – though was not, I would argue, entirely reducible to – the imperatives of colonial rule (cf. Cohn, 1987; Trautmann, 1997). In particular, they constructed the image of a once great but now decadent and corrupted Aryan people, whose civilization they reified through the production of putatively authoritative versions of ancient texts. At the same time, they viewed the fine distinctions of status and custom they encountered in India through the lens of their own nationalist sense of racial homogeneity, seeing in them evidence of many different "peoples." In eliminating threats to their political dominance and attempting to rule "indirectly" through indigenous elites they excised royal authority and elevated the status of *brahmans* through drawing upon them as a colonial bureaucracy and reifying Brahmanic codes as "native law." Later on, the enormous bureaucratic enterprise of census collection further reified categories like "untouchable," "Hindu," and "Muslim" and, through census counting, constituted particular categories as "minorities" or "majorities" at local, regional, and national level (Cohn, 1987: 224–54). Together with the British inability or unwillingness to consider political representation in forms other than these "communal" identities (e.g. programs for "depressed castes" rather than "the poor"), all this had a profoundly concretizing effect upon caste principles, though it did not, I would submit, actually *create* caste, as some scholars have argued (Inden, 1990). Thus, it is now widely argued that much of what was once thought to be representative of traditional India – and in particular the caste system – emerged in the course of Muslim and particularly British rule though, as I have tried to suggest throughout this book, part of what was understood by recourse to the idea of a "traditional caste system" did in fact conform to a cultural metacontext of the *longue dureé*.

The nineteenth century saw the emergence of a more regulative, liberal-bourgeois style of British colonial intervention in India and elsewhere. The character of this general transformation is revealed nowhere better than in the thought of William Wilberforce (1759–1833). A tireless campaigner against the Atlantic slave trade, Wilberforce opposed trade union organization at home in Britain and looked with horror at the coercion of labor in the Indian countryside and, most of all, at Hindu religious practices. He described Hinduism as "the grossest, the darkest, and most depraving system of idolatrous superstition that almost ever existed upon earth" and came to regard the Christian conversion of Hindus as a cause even more pressing than the abolition of the slave trade (Furneaux, 1974: 322). Such sentiments were elaborated, albeit from a utilitarian rather than an evangelical position, in James Mill's scathing *History of India* (1817), which was part of the successful ideological struggle in Britain against the more positive and romantic view of India held by the earlier imperialists. This transformation was to have significant effects upon the course of colonial policy, including land reform and the despatch of Christian missions to the subcontinent.

We cannot dwell here upon the full impact of this embourgeoisement of colonialism, but I wish to focus on some aspects of it which were to have longer term consequences. First, it is noteworthy that the missionaries of the nineteenth century had extremely limited success in their goal of mass conversion. Perhaps unsurprisingly, their greatest impact was among untouchables who had least to gain from the extant status order, though mere Christian conversion scarcely altered their position within it. In fact, somewhat in contrast to contemporaneous Nonconformist missionary activity in the Caribbean, the missionaries in India were often more interested in saving souls than in redressing status inequalities, and to the extent that they leant effective help to untouchables in resisting aspects of their degradation it was usually in relation to practices which most offended Christian sensibilities, such as subordinate participation in temple rituals or high caste sanctions against women from some untouchable castes covering their breasts (Mosse, 1994). More generally, low caste leaders of the later pre-Independence period like B. R. Ambedkar and E. V. Ramaswamy Naicker ("E.V.R.") arguably enjoyed their greatest successes on issues like forcing entry to temples from which untouchables were debarred, campaigns which fit more readily into a model of Sanskritization rather than a radical egalitarian critique of untouchability. When these leaders later articulated such critiques their success was generally more modest.

Missionaries also participated in the Orientalist construction of an Indian "racial" history. For example, Dirks (1996) has shown how the mid-nineteenth century writings on South India of the missionary Robert Caldwell elaborated the thesis of an "Aryan" conquest of "Dravidian" South India which was implicitly motivated by an attempt to constitute and engage a non-*brahman* Dravidian people more receptive to Christianity in the face of Brahmanic opposition to missionary proselytization. This thesis was later appropriated in the discourse of South Indian untouchable political mobilization – which renders untouchables as "Adi-Dravida," the "original Dravidians" – and more generally in anti-Brahmanic Tamil nationalist movements which coalesced after independence into the Dravida Munnetra Kazhagam (DMK) party. The DMK, together with the rival AIADMK formed after a 1960s schism, has dominated regional politics. The populist rule of the AIADMK "film star" politicians Marutha Gopala Ramachandran and Jayalalitha has been seen by some commentators as a derogation of the DMK's original anti-Brahmanic radicalism, not least because Jayalalitha – herself a *brahman* – courted various Brahmanic interests. In this respect, as Dirks argues, the discourse of caste – now in the form of "communalized" and "racialized" distinctions, particularly between *brahmans* and non-

brahmans – continues to invest contemporary South Indian political discourse. Indeed, it could be suggested more generally that the twentieth century has witnessed a concretization of caste in the arena of politics throughout India via forms of patronage and machine voting so that, in ethnosociological terms, caste as "code for conduct" has given way to a discourse of "natural" communities which are supported by political caste associations (Barnett, 1977; P. Brass, 1994; Mitra, 1994).

This South Indian appropriation of Orientalism has not, however, been the only response to Christianity in the subcontinent. Christian ideas and the impact of British colonialism more generally inflected various strands of reformism in nineteenth-century India, particularly among the "westernized" elite. The best-known examples are that of Rammohun Roy (1772–1833) and the "Renaissance" in the British colonial heartlands of Bengal which spawned the Bengali Brahmo Samaj, and the later Arya Samaj founded by Dayananda Sarasvati in 1875, which was to have a major impact among Hindus in the Punjab against the background of perceived Christian, Muslim, and Sikh encroachment. While there are many differences between the various manifestations of Hindu reformism, they generally borrowed from Orientalist discourse the view of an Indian degeneration from earlier glories and imbued it with a proto-nationalist emphasis on the need for a revival to slough off the "weakness" which had permitted British colonialism. Usually, this involved a critique of ritualism and the starkest manifestations of caste hierarchy, together with an attempt to construct a canonical scripture from ancient Sanskrit texts as the basis for a nationalist historiography. Another appropriation of Orientalism which emerged in the discourse of Hindu reformism was opposition to the supposed passivity of the other-worldly Hindu resigned to the decadence of the *kaliyuga* in the cyclical order of things. In the words of the early nationalist writer Bankimchandra Chattopadhyay,

> Europeans are devotees of power. That is the key to their advancement. We are negligent towards power: that is the key to our downfall. Europeans pursue a goal which they must reach in this world: they are victorious on earth. We pursue a goal which lies in the world beyond, which is why we have failed to win on earth. (Cited in Chatterjee, 1986: 57)

Thus, the reformists counterposed the logic of ranking hierarchy which approached redemption through reconstituting the divine into the mundane world by human agency, to what they perceived to be an anachronistic Indian other-worldliness. In this respect, their thought contributed to a wider trend within nineteenth-century colonial society which van der Veer has described as the "laicization of institutionalized religion," in which a "lay Hindu and Muslim public had come to occupy a sphere that was previously the domain of sacred specialists" (van der Veer, 1996: 260). Whatever other factors may account for communal conflict, this constitution of a generalized public sphere with specific conceptions of the public good – not dissimilar to the modern publics which began to emerge in Europe from the late medieval period – would seem to be a precondition for it (Habermas, 1989; Bhatt, 1997). The British also contributed to this trend by repressing much of the political ambit of sacred specialists, and by sponsoring the development of communications technology such as railways and print media which helped constitute a broader public sphere. It was in this context that secular nationalists were able to articulate an increasingly persuasive politics of anti-colonial emancipation. Its major voice was the Indian National Congress, formed in 1885, which was instrumental in taking India to independence in 1947. However, the main architect of independence within Congress was, of course, Mohandas K. Gandhi (1869–1948), who certainly cannot be regarded simply as a secular nationalist. This is not the place for an extensive analysis of Gandhi's complex thought, but an abiding feature of it which makes it especially interesting from the broader perspective of this book is the way that Gandhi attempted to reconstitute a basically Hindu conception of complete transcendence within the confines of a "modern," territorial sense of nationhood (Duara, 1995). Part of his success as a politician lay in his ability to articulate religious (or "cultural") symbolism to nationalist (or "political") ends, albeit that this rationalist distinction between religion and politics found no place in his own thought. But whether, from that same rationalist perspective, Gandhi should be regarded as a secularizer of the religious or a sacralizer of the political is perhaps less to the point than the fact that he assumed the mantle of sacrality as a Hindu ascetic or "saint" without, however, participating in the usual modes of religious legitimation, thereby helping to constitute a lay sphere of religious and political discourse (van der Veer, 1994). At the same time, he drew upon the legacy of Orientalism and reformism in constructing a political vision of autarkic village communities undergirded by a scriptural and anti-caste Hinduism.

We might make two more observations which further confound attempts to locate Gandhi within the duality of modernity and tradition. First, his anti-casteism – and particularly his attitude to untouchables – can be seen as both "modernist" and "traditional." It was "modernist" in the sense that it represented an attempt to create the homogeneous national society supposedly necessary for a successful anti-colonial struggle and a viable postcolonial state (particularly since questions as to whether or not untouchables were actually Hindus had significant political implications in the context of separate Hindu and Muslim electorates). It was "traditional" in that it represented a critique or reversal of encompassing hierarchy (where those who were "untouchable" become "Harijans" or "children of god") from a *bhakti* standpoint which, like the *bhakti* movement more generally, remained within the overall compass of Brahmanism. In either case, the vision was not radically egalitarian and indeed was criticized contemporaneously for its paternalism, not least by low caste leaders like Ambedkar and E.V.R. who, however, were unable themselves to build an entirely successful contestatory politics. Second, part of Gandhi's success lay in his embodiment of a certain "traditional" political type which he was uniquely able to manipulate for his "modern" purposes. This, according to Marriott (1976), was the ascetic, celibate "*vaishya*" guise of the minimal transactor, which was counterposed to the optimal "brahman" guise of the other major nationalist figure, Jawaharlal Nehru. To this we might add a new political type in the pessimal "*shudra*" guise of E.V.R., whom Dirks describes as a kind of "Rabelaisian Tamil alter ego for Gandhi," reviling the latter "by proclaiming his massive and carnivorous diet, his prowess in matters sexual, his interest in the things money could buy" (Dirks, 1996: 281). And a converse "traditional" model for untouchable political action was embodied in Ambedkar's conversion to Buddhism, with its emphasis on a renunciative egalitarianism (Khare, 1984). Thus, we encounter once again political agency which casts itself within the very mold that it seeks to break. The same perhaps could be said of more localized untouchable organizations, such as the Ad Dharm movement of the Punjab, which were built around the discourse of an aboriginal "chosen" people defeated and enslaved by Aryan invaders, politico-religious devotion to low caste "saints," opposition to manifestations of caste hierarchy, ascetic mores, rejection of elite forms of untouchable "upliftment" as, for example, represented by the Arya Samaj, and an approbation of the "wild" or "disorderly" lifestyle of the untouchables (Juergensmeyer, 1982). In these respects, and despite the many obvious differences, parallels with Afro-creole forms of politico-religious consciousness in the Caribbean such as Rastafari can perhaps be discerned.

The element most obviously missing from Marriott's list of traditional political types is the *kshatriya*. This model was appropriated within strands of anti-colonial nationalist thought in opposition to Gandhian pacifism but, as we shall see, many other aspects of the political discourse of the so-called "Hindu right" with which it was associated are far from traditional. Eclipsed for some time after Indian independence, not least because of its association with Gandhi's assassination, the Hindu right has recently enjoyed a major resurgence in the Indian political scene. So too has the "communal" violence usually associated with it. The destruction by Hindu activists in 1992 of the Babri Masjid, a mosque in the Hindu holy city of Ayodhya, which led to murderous rioting across the country between Hindus and Muslims, is but the best-known example of widespread urban violence and realignments of urban space in contemporary India along such communal lines (Bhatt, 1997; Deshpande, 1998).

These events have occasioned a profound debate in India about the political direction of the country, but also scholarly debates about the nature of communalism. Prominent within both debates has been a concern with locating contemporary communalism within its proper historical context. There is some evidence to suggest that violence of a not dissimilar character occurred in the precolonial period when militant Shaivite and, latterly, Vaishnavite ascetics combined their mercantile and religious itinerance with sectarian violence, and when the turbulent eighteenth-century political scene undermined local arrangements like the relationship between Muslim *zamindars* and non-Muslim cultivators (Bayly, 1985b; van der Veer, 1994; Pinch, 1996). However, it is widely recognized that British colonial rule was in important respects constitutive of contemporary conflicts through the processes mentioned earlier: economic policies which favored Muslim *zamindars*, Orientalist scholarship which counterposed an "Aryan" tradition to later Muslim conquest, the objectification of Muslim and Hindu populations in the census, the constitution of a unitary public sphere, the orientation of the colonial state to "communal" representation, and the communalization of its decolonization policy, which ultimately led via the establishment of separate Hindu and Muslim electoral representation to Partition, where in 1948 the subcontinent was divided into mainly Muslim Pakistan and mainly Hindu India amid widespread violence.

Communal violence in these novel circumstances probably first found expression in the "Cow Protection Movement" which emerged in the late nineteenth century, and which was directed at preventing the butchering of the sacred "Mother Cow" by Muslims and the British. As van der Veer (1994) has shown, there is a significant gender imagery in thus identifying the femaleness of a high cosmological principle with the threatened body of the territorial nation, to which we shall return. Later on, various Hindu organizations were formed within and without the broader umbrella of the nationalist movement. These included the Hindu Mahasabha, one of whose activists, Vinayak Savarkar, wrote the influential *Hindutva: Who is a Hindu?* (1923). Among other things, Savarkar identified Hinduism territorially with "Sindhu" – the "land between the Indus and the seas" – and thereby established a logic of religious nationalism which demanded the reconversion of those "natives" who, in the course of history, had converted to Islam. Like M. S. Golwalkar – an early leader of the Rashtriya Swayamsevak Sangh (RSS), which was formed in 1925 as a cadre Hindu nationalist organization outside the broader nationalist movement – Savarkar also drew upon the race literature of nineteenth- and early twentieth-century European scholarship, and looked to European fascism and Nazism as models for an Indian ethnonationalism couched in a discourse of Hindu "blood" transcending caste and other social divisions (Jaffrelot, 1995; Bhatt, 1997). More recently, other organizations have been formed under the umbrella of the RSS, most notably the Vishva Hindu Parishad (VHP) – a more explicitly religious organization – and the Bharatiya Janata Party (BJP), formed in 1984 out of the Jan Sangh party, which during the 1990s has been a main political party in local and national governments.

The RSS, VHP, and BJP, together with authoritarian regional parties like the Shiv Sena of Bombay, are generally regarded as the key institutional nexus of the contemporary Hindu right and its ideology of Hindutva ("Hinduness") which, in the view of many commentators, has been the driving force behind communal violence. Its recent rise to prominence has been linked with the decline of the Congress Party and the secular and weakly socialist corporate politics it had pursued, particularly under the leadership of Nehru. Congress patronage was for some time able more or less to contain a great diversity of political interests: the Hindu right; untouchable and "backward caste" movements; regional ethnonationalisms; secular liberal, socialist, and communist movements; and a middle peasantry which had emerged in the wake of post-independence *zamindar* abolition, and whose own recent mobilization in rural politics has been considered by some commentators as a social movement motivated by an anti-statist environmentalism, and by others as a new, authoritarian form of dominant casteism imbued with a *volkische* ideology drawn from European fascism or nineteenth-century nationalism (T. Brass, 1994). At any rate, increasingly from the 1970s, Congress no longer secured the loyalty of these groups, despite its attempt to court with the agenda of the Hindu right, leading to a much more turbulent political scene and its exit from government three times from 1977 to the present. Under the Janata Party government (1977–80) the Mandal Commission was appointed to consider caste reservations (or "affirmative action") for public sector employment, recommending that they be extended from untouchables to the so called "other backward castes." In 1990 V. P. Singh, prime minister of the Janata Dal government, announced the implementation of the report, provoking fierce public debate, but electoral difficulties for any party which openly rejected Mandal. The subsequent Congress government introduced somewhat watered-down measures.

Let us now look very briefly at some of the major political mobilizations by the Hindu right during this turbulent recent period. Most prominently, this has taken the form of three processions through the Hindu nationalist heartlands of North India under the aegis of the VHP. The first, in 1983, was the very tellingly titled "Sacrifice for Unanimity" campaign, in which pots of water from the holy River Ganges were carried to towns and villages along the procession route, the pots being refilled with water from local sacred sites to create a nationwide reservoir (Davis, 1996: 40). Next, focusing attention upon the putative history of temple desecration by Islamic invaders, the VHP established a campaign in which people throughout the country were asked to make a brick which would be collected and used to reconstruct desecrated temples. Both cases seem to epitomize Benedict Anderson's (1991) view of nationalism as a process of "imagining" a political community, in which the consciousness of political and cultural connections to others who one does not personally know creates an affective sense of family or community within a wider political sphere and, certainly in this case, does so explicitly by excluding other locals from that sphere. Finally, in 1990 the VHP established the *Ramjanmabhumi* ("birthplace of Rama") campaign – which the BJP joined – in the form of a procession of King Rama's chariot to the Babri Masjid mosque in Ayodhya, the supposed birthplace of the god-king Rama upon which it was alleged the Mughal Babur had built the mosque after destroying a Rama temple on the site. This was but the most spectacular example of more widespread challenges to the religious architecture of Islam in India under the aegis of the Hindu right, which Deshpande (1998) aptly describes as a "hegemonic spatial strategy" its protagonists cannot lose; either their Muslim adversaries will humiliatingly concede defeat or they will face up to the threat and thereby confirm their recalcitrance to the nationalist project.

How can communalism and the rise of the Hindu right in India be explained? Very broadly, we might suggest three different kinds of explanation involving distinct periodizations of the phenomenon. First, there are explanations which emphasize continuities in Indian history between contemporary manifestations of communalism and precolonial contexts. One such argument is that of the Hindu right itself, which holds that the opposed religious identities of Islam and Hinduism are an intrinsic or primordial feature of Indian history that has risen again after the false dawn of Congress secularism. It is hard to find much warrant for this view in historical or sociological scholarship but, as we have seen, it is nevertheless possible to argue that there *was* a relevant precolonial history of Hindu–Muslim conflict which has not simply been elaborated as such after the fact (Bayly, 1985b; van der Veer, 1994).

Second, it has been argued that communalism is a consequence, and to some extent an invention, of British colonial intervention in India which exacerbated or invented civic divisions to secure its hegemony and, as an expedient exercise in colonial governmentality, leveled different kinds of civic violence into the catchall category of the "communal riot" (e.g. Pandey,

1990). This is quite a compelling view in the light of our foregoing analysis of the colonial regime, but the argument cannot explain its changing fortunes during the postcolonial period very well. Moreover, it seems to occupy the somewhat problematic nativist modality of Subalternist historiography, which proffers a critique of the homogenizing discourses of colonial governance by recuperating indigenous agency as always inherently fragmentary rather than systemic.

The third kind of explanation is that communalism has resulted from India's contemporary condition of modernity, although there are several quite different versions of this argument. First, there is the view – particularly associated with Partha Chatterjee (1986) – that communalism is an artefact of the anti-colonial nationalist struggle, a "derivative discourse" of European nationalism which imported its violent aporias into India. However, like the "colonial discourse" argument, this does not explain the recent vicissitudes of communalism well, and – now in the "synthetic" or essentialist modality of the Subalternist project – its implicit distinction between an "authentic" popular anti-colonialism and the Eurocentric discourse of the Indian nationalist intelligentsia could be accused of its own kind of Orientalist move.

A second view, perhaps most associated with traditional leftist positions, is that Hindutva represents a hegemonic ideology which preserves elite interests by dissolving counter-claims such as regional autonomism or untouchable and "backward caste" activism into a generalizing discourse of putative Hindu unity (e.g. Thapar, 1992; Upadhyaya, 1992; Basu, 1996; Vanaik, 1997; Bose and Jalal, 1998). One advantage of such arguments is that they do explain the timing of recent events rather well, as for example in the 1990 withdrawal of the BJP from V. P. Singh's coalition government in the context of its implementation of the Mandal recommendations. In this respect, BJP support for the VHP's *Ramjanmabhumi* campaign can be seen as politically contingent. Basu (1996) and Vanaik (1997) both argue that at root the BJP is a conservative high caste movement which mobilizes opportunistically under various banners including Hindutva, profiting from a general antipathy to the state as represented by Congress among various constituencies and thereby directing political violence of several kinds in determinate directions. As Basu points out, where the BJP was able to rally political support without recourse to communalism, it did so. Possibly, these arguments understate the degree of connection between the BJP and Hindutva organizations, but they do go a long way to account for the specific timing and character of recent political events. The limitation of this kind of explanation is that – like most arguments which derive ultimately from Marxist theories of ideology – it cannot explain the appeal of Hindutva and thus its relative success except in terms of politico-economic class interest. Even if it is true that support for the Hindu right comes disproportionately, but not exclusively, from high castes – though this is less the case for movements like Shiv Sena – this is to neglect the symbolic power of the nationalist imaginary that it envehicles.

Finally, there is the view that there is little or nothing specifically Indian about communalism. Rather, it can be understood as a constitutional pathology of contemporary global modernity which, like Nazism or Serbian nationalism, is of a piece with contemporary racisms elsewhere (Chakrabarty, 1995; Fox, 1996). Against the tendency of this view to invoke modernity as a monolithic essence, Chetan Bhatt (1997) offers a more nuanced account of Hindutva as one of several authoritarian religious movements which constitutes a postcolonial or "Third World" response to global modernity by holding out the promise of living a proper, worthwhile, moral life against the threats both of "enemies within" like Muslims and other minorities and of the West's hegemonic modernity, even as it is imbued with Western modernity's most fundamental precepts of progress, secular transcendence, private morality, and so on. However, Bhatt understresses the specificity of Hindutva by emphasizing its congruence with European Nazism, fascism, and biological racisms. Although many clear parallels exist, there are also important differences. As Jaffrelot (1995) has commented, the thought of the Hindutva theorists has been able to assimilate the "Lamarckian" racism of much nineteenth-century European scholarship, which emphasized the heritability of acquired characteristics, but not that of German nationalism which, in the hands of the Nazis, represented the most extreme development of those European conceptions of nature and natural difference examined in earlier chapters. Indeed, the Hindutva rhetoric of "purity," its emphasis upon the reconversion of Muslims to bring them back into the Hindu fold, and its associated theme of an encompassing universalism, represent a "traditional Indian xenology" (Jaffrelot, 1995) with an "unmistakable brahminical accent" (Hansen, 1996a), considerably removed from the eugenic discourse of Nazism.

This is not to suggest that Hindutva ideology represents a simple continuity with a prior cultural order. Very clearly, it has been addressed to novel colonial and postcolonial situations which have provided its context and much of its substance. But the implication running through several of the positions examined above that it is a thoroughly modernist, alien transformation of a pristine – and implicitly static – traditional order cannot be sustained. The distinction between a precolonial order erased by British colonial intervention which ushered in modernity and its aporias can be replaced with the idea discussed in chapter 2 of the continous elicitation of cultural representations through which conceptions of the political order are made, re-made, and sometimes actualized across the colonizer–colonized or precolonial–postcolonial distinctions, although, with this caveat, there is no denying the plausibility of the various arguments outlined above which jointly go a considerable way to explaining the provenance of communal violence in contemporary India. Nevertheless, it is worth pointing to the way that the passions of communalism respond to the associative logic of cultural symbols drawn from a historical repertoire, and here we might remark more closely upon the particular symbolics of the *Ramjanmabhumi* campaign. Evidence for the desecration of Hindu temples by Muslim conquerors is much stronger for sites other than Ayodhya, but Ayodhya served the VHP's purposes better because it is the heart of the Rama cult. In chapter 3 we encountered Sheldon Pollock's (1993) argument that the story of Rama as told in the *Ramayana* involves an idea of territorial sovereignty absent in other Indian epic traditions, while simultaneously demonizing the enemies of the just king. Thus, it provides a much better model for contemporary nationalism than the transcendence offered by deities like Shiva or Krishna. There is in addition a significant gender imagery at play here: while Krishna is strongly associated with love in the form of both "cognatic" mother's love and his "conjugal" love as the consort of cowherdesses, and Shiva is associated with a nonhuman asceticism, the *Ramayana* casts Rama in the role of the autonomous husband whose political agency is a function of his detachment from and control over his loyal wife, Sita, enabling him to connect with higher (female) principles of devotion. In the contemporary context – and in keeping with the *kshatriya* ideology appropriated by the Hindu right against the "effeminacy" of Gandhian thought – this has been associated syllogistically with masculine agency in resisting threats to both the national "motherland" and the actual women it contains, thus representing an indigenous twist to the familiar nationalist imagery of passive women whose protection or rape is constitutive of the nation's wellbeing, although in India aspects of the nationalist movement both appropriate and repress a more active female role in relation to the fearsome Durga–Kali goddess complex (Bhatt, 1997; cf. Hansen, 1996b: 141). Finally, the destruction of the *Babri Masjid* occurred during the *kumbh* festival, long associated with martial religious pilgrimage. Thus, the *Ramjanmabhumi* campaign invoked a veritable bricolage of useful symbols from Hindu traditions: the politically constituting procession; the just sovereign king ranged against evil enemies; the committed warrior; the female-protecting, self-directed man.

Here we come to an interesting aspect of the debate about the politics of communalism. Many commentators have criticized the Hindu right for its selective, if not fraudulent use of ancient Indian tradition in support of its very contemporary agenda. In one sense, the argument carries considerable force. Despite the continuities noted above, the recourse of the Hindu right to its particular version of the past cannot be understood outside the context of an authoritarian social movement engaged with a specific contemporary condition of modernity. But this would be a strange argument to level against it from the perspective of contemporary sociological theory, with its grounding in the critiques of essentialism and Orientalism which consistently posit the dynamic and transformative capacity of human agency to create new social and political forms from past social formations. This points to an evasiveness in certain versions of contemporary social theory which reject "metanarratives" like socialist class politics and yet only lend their approval to social or political movements which can be regarded as "progressive" through the conventions of these same metanarratives. As Bhatt (1997) has argued, perhaps this stems from the indebtedness of social theory to a political tradition which elaborates a critique of the state from the perspective of civil liberty rather than theorizing the repressive character of civil society, a tradition which is readily intelligible as a countercurrent to the Western core symbol examined in chapter 2.

The implications of this point can be illustrated in relation to the intervention in the Ayodhya issue of Indian academic historians who marshaled considerable evidence against the veracity of the notion that Babur had destroyed a temple dedicated to Rama at his birthplace, concluding that the notion is "a matter of faith, not of historical evidence" (in van der Veer, 1994: 159). The VHP response to this kind of argument was predictable:

> We expect others to respect the Hindu faith that Lord Rama was born at the spot where the Ayodhya structure stood. Matters of faith are beyond the jurisdiction of Courts, acceptance by historians, or approval of government agencies. (Cited in Pollock, 1993: 289–92)

Thus, the academic demotion of "faith" beneath "evidence" is simply reversed in the logic of religious discourse. Achin Vanaik has argued that the problem here is that this Hindu "faith" conceals the bad faith of vested interests. With reference to the intervention of the historians he continues:

> The point is not that such a "rationalist exposure" could by itself (in the absence of mass political counter-mobilization against the forces of Hindutva) check the construction of bad faith, or even play a major role in this. But that this effort was a morally, intellectually and politically important one necessitated by the very deliberate and systematic construction of bad faith on such a wide scale. (Vanaik, 1997: 120)

Without disagreeing with any of this, the direction in which Vanaik's argument leads can readily be seen: another vested interest which supposes the "good faith" of a rational secularism and implicitly demands the allegiance of academic social scientists who might otherwise treat the debate between rational secularism – based, as we have seen, upon its own invisible nationalist assumptions – and religious nationalism as the subject matter for critical investigation in its own right (so long as whichever party to the debate holds the reins of political power permits them to continue working within the rationalist framework of social science.)

We shall return to this argument in the final chapter, which picks up two threads of the discussion from the present one; namely, can there be progressive political resistance to the inegalitarian implications of societies predicated upon natural hierarchy, and what is or should be the relationship between sociological analysis and political activism in this regard? What I hope to have shown in this chapter is that aspects of contemporary life in the Caribbean and India draw upon transformations of antecedent cultural representations concerning race and caste hierarchy (just as these representations in turn transformed earlier ones). In particular, we have seen some of the ways in which colonial racial discourse has been "creolized," a process which in certain respects involves an entrenchment of race as an idiom of contemporary social life at the same time as it calls into question projects of racist and nationalist inferiorization. And we have seen how caste has in turn become "racialized" under conditions of colonial and postcolonial modernity in India, a racialization which figures within very different contemporary political projects among elites and non-elites in the subcontinent, but has not erased its grounding in prior political realities.

7 | Hierarchy and Politics

Hierarchy and a Sociology of Politics

The corollary of a consistent hierarchical orientation to redemption in Euro-American thought – which I have argued in previous chapters provides the context both for colonial ideologies like racism and for their political and intellectual critique – is a constant tendency to split into dualities the messy fields of cultural process within which such ideologies are formed. Thus, colonial societies have long been the arena for a historiography of either apologia or critique, their critique a story of either oppression or struggle, just as much anti-racist activism has elaborated the clarion call of Malcolm X: "either you're part of the solution, or you're part of the problem." This certainly does capture a critical aspect of the dynamics of racism and colonialism but, as I hope to have shown in this book, it does not exhaust what can be said about them. In the contemporary social sciences, these questions figure within a broader theoretical debate between foundational and post-foundational approaches to the normative basis of human action, each of which – through their respective universalisms and particularisms – threatens to deconstruct natural hierarchies as analytical objects. We will conclude with some comments on this point and its implications in the light of the theoretical and empirical focus we have taken throughout the book.

Foundational political narratives have generally sought to invest certain political strategies, and not others, with the status of genuine resistance or transformation. In relation to recent writings on colonial culture in the two regions upon which we have principally focused in this book, we might in this respect contrast the foundational historiography of India in the Subaltern Studies school, which has tended to valorize the struggles of rural working people over those of the anti-colonial nationalist elite (Guha, 1982; Chatterjee, 1993), with Richard Burton's (1997) foundational narrative of cultural forms among Caribbean working peoples, who he finds trapped within a colonial heritage which vitiates the possibility of any true resistance. Thus, insofar as forms of Afro-creole culture such as the post-emancipation cult of female domesticity or the religious imagery of Rastafari and vodou draw upon European-derived ideologies and often thereby articulate a sense of racial identity, Burton rejects them as diversions from "true" resistance, whose model is the bourgeois desire for instrumental manipulation and escape from history. In his words, "Power manipulated is power accepted, however reluctantly, and even consolidated by the manipulator's success" (ibid.: 60). The major theoretical defect of this line of argument in Burton's otherwise impressively detailed and sensitive analysis is the idea that some historically prior order – or some revolutionary teleology – is available wholesale as an authentic resource for contemporary struggles. It is this that leads him to make quite inappropriate distinctions between slave revolts as *resistance* where they originated predominantly among African-origin slaves and as mere *opposition* where they originated in creole activism, based upon a distinction of de Certeau's (1980) which, quite to the contrary of Burton's reading, I interpret as an approbation of contingent political struggles and a rejection of some pure alternate order. In more contemporary vein, Burton suggests that the routine humiliations inflicted over recent years by Caribbean cricket teams upon the English team is a Pyrrhic victory for Caribbean people, because it is only won

> at the price of confirming the grip of the colonial legacy over them, blurring the truly significant fact of their history: not that they regularly beat Massa at his own game and regularly make him *look foolish*, but that they are playing his game in the first place. (Ibid.: 185)

We could register several objections to this argument. First, it might be said that the mastery of "Massa's" game on "Massa's" precise terms is the very opposite of the supposed sycophancy in the "Quashie" personality (cf. Craton, 1996: 127). To thus construct a model of "true" resistance which appears closed to all possible empirical examples in the Caribbean would seem to involve an *a priori* commitment to the cultural inferiority of the region as a whole. And, indeed, we might ask by what act of "racial" appropriation does the game of cricket introduced by "massa" to his slaves become the singular property of contemporary Britons? After all, it was an aristocratic Indian – K. S. Ranjitsinhji – who invented that staple of modern batsmanship, the leg glance, which English contemporaries decried as unfair, a performative innovation we would now regard as being a part of "cricket." Here, we have an example – albeit perhaps a rather trivial one – of the attempt to regulate between "central" and "peripheral" actions or meanings, which was criticized in chapter 2 by drawing upon Vološinov's theory of language. We might also consider the example through Gramsci's (1971) model of "transformism." The threat of "resistance" in Afro-creole culture is defused by incorporating it into the domain of a national or a colonial culture; the participation of Afro-creole subalterns in that culture is then derided as evidence of their inauthenticity, but their contribution to its forms through this participation goes unrecognized (cf. Williams, 1991). My argument, in contrast, is that examples of Afro-creole culture like vodou, Rastafari or perhaps even cricket represent normative attempts to objectify the experience of oppressed peoples in ways which are not obviously inferior to the normative attempt of foundational critiques like Marxism to objectify it as the economic experience of a "class-for-itself." Yet, at the same time, simply to accord these cultural forms their autonomy leaves us in much the same discursive space. So, although I have tried neither to dismiss nor romanticize forms of Afro-creole culture, I have nevertheless construed them within the theoretical discourse of sociology, which by permitting me the luxury of doing one or the other subordinates them to an exterior principle. Perhaps they can thus be regarded as examples of what Foucault (1980) called "subjugated knowledges," those local, popular modes of representation and knowing which official, "scientific" knowledge disqualifies as trivial or mistaken. But in construing them as such sociologically, the "insurrection" they threaten is reappropriated to a unitary discourse. As Foucault admonishes:

> Is it not perhaps the case that these fragments . . . are no sooner brought to light . . . than they run the risk of re-codification, re-colonization? In fact, those unitary discourses, which first disqualified and then ignored them when they made their appearance, are, it seems, quite ready now to annex them, to take them back within the fold of their own discourse and to invest them with everything this implies in terms of their effects of knowledge and power. And if we want to protect these only lately liberated fragments are we not in danger of ourselves constructing . . . that unitary discourse? (Ibid.: 86)

This, then, is the problem with a foundationalist counter-argument to Burton which would merely approbate the autonomy or the political vivacity of Afro-creole culture. Indeed, such counter-arguments permit some rather extraordinary juxtapositions, as for example where the career of a Caribbean cricketer is considered an example of subaltern resistance on a par with Toussaint Louverture's (Beckles, 1998), while Toussaint himself together with his fellow revolutionaries are frequently criticized for failing to achieve a revolutionary redemption of the Haitian people. My own view is that scholarly analysis and political activism need to move beyond the search for some redemptive rupture with all forms of hierarchy, at least without a more reflexive appreciation of the way that such ruptures are grounded in the forms they contest. Instead, I suggest that conceptions like racial identity are better thematized within the framework of a specific culture-historical consciousness rather than simply effaced. To explain what I mean by this requires a brief digression into non-foundational accounts of human action which can be broached through further reference to Foucault's work on the epistemology of the social sciences.

In his earlier writings, Foucault (e.g. 1970; 1972) propounded an "archaeology of knowledge" which could describe discrete and more or less integrated orders of knowledge or claims about truth placed determinately in time or place, such as the differing worldviews of Renaissance and modern Europe. However, the excavation of such "epistemes" presupposes a specific ground or standpoint from which the particularity of their claims over truth can be seen as such. This implies some meta-epistemic interpretive position. Foucault attempted to dissolve this in later work (e.g. Foucault, 1977; 1981) through his "genealogy of discourse," which claimed to track the diffuse workings of power without supposing origins or epistemic ruptures (see also chapter 2). He thereby attempted to break definitively with an epistemology of the social sciences which involved some transcendental, foundational, or metaphysical commitment to an unencompassable axis or center, whether it was couched in terms of a divine power, human agency, material constraint, or whatever. This has been extremely influential upon attempts within poststructuralist and postcolonial theory to "de-center" "Western" forms of reason which, as in Orientalism, are regarded as powerfully constitutive of the putative reality of the "non-West." But its difficulty is that this de-centring seems merely to be a displacement which necessarily invokes its own grounds and which, as Chetan Bhatt has nicely put it, "in disrupting a specifically Western foundationalism . . . form[s] a kind of political imaginary, postmodern theory's own utopia, its unintelligible horizon" (Bhatt, 1997: 5). Indeed, insofar as this project can be described as a kind of hyper-empiricist philosophy of history in which nothing exists beyond the self-compass of historical agents, so that the historian aims for a "pure state" in which "all 'isms' should be evacuated" (Habermas, 1987: 275), its very self-effacement is perhaps a clue to the problems involved in the genealogical method, particularly where it is proffered as a political critique. The extent to which Foucault's later position is compatible with any normative opposition to the disciplinary power which he has analyzed has been the focus of considerable debate. I am inclined to side with those who argue that his position vacillates between presupposing the kind of transcendent, normative, liberal framework he claimed to reject and a thorough empiricism with quietist political implications (Fraser, 1981; Habermas, 1987; Taylor, 1989; cf. Spivak, 1996). In the empiricist mode, Foucault deliberately eschewed the "cultural plane of peace" which we have reconstructed from the writings of Hobbes and Mauss, substituting it for a concern with power and domination (Pasquino, 1993), a procedure to which we could perhaps object along the lines of Habermas's criticism of Foucault's "uncircumspect leveling of culture and politics to immediate substrates of the application of violence" (Habermas, 1987: 290).

Habermas, by contrast, has consistently argued that a truly critical theory must be able to ground or justify its own claims to oppose extant social orders, a point he has pursued in his more recent work by attempting to reconstruct universal criteria for social relationships undistorted by the exercise of domination (e.g. Habermas, 1979). His approach has been widely criticized because it involves a finalist claim, however mounted, about normative values, precisely the kind of meta-epistemic position which Foucault tried to avoid. This problem has been described by George Trey as "the authoritative rhetoric of universality," constituting "the power move that lends dominion to consensus" (Trey, 1992: 422). Trey contrasts Habermas's ethical universalism with the philosophy of Emmanuel Levinas, whose position – more uncompromisingly anti-foundational even than a writer like Foucault – represents a philosophy of "the Other" *par excellence*. For Levinas, there is no question of critical engagement with the Other, of debate or evaluation, only an obligation to the Other in its full alterity, regardless of what it demands. The ethical extremity of this position has some force in a global context where rationalist opposition to cultural relativism – articulated not uncommonly through recourse to the most potent examples of "traditional" domination (like female circumcision) as metonyms for the "backwardness" of entire regions, religions, or cultures – often represents a barely concealed liberal triumphalism which both reifies and sanitizes an image of "the West." Indeed, although it is true that strong cultural relativism is willing to entertain various practices that would scarcely be tolerated in secular, liberal cultures it is worth suggesting that totalizing attempts to measure the value of one culture against another represent an essentially colonial problematic which is never politically innocent in the contemporary world, where those same secular, liberal societies possess a global monopoly on the means of violence. Nevertheless, Trey argues convincingly that Levinas's argument involves a power strategy of its own:

> In order to maintain the ineffable status of the other, the possibility of a mediated subjectivity . . . has to be excluded. It is this gesture . . . that is necessary if the powerless authority of the ineffable other is to be preserved. (Trey, 1992: 422)

Thus, Levinas – along with other strongly anti-foundational theorists – purveys a kind of primitivism which, in failing to find a place for the vulgarities, excesses, and contradictions of the Other, recuperates it as the moral consciousness of the self. In doing so, much anti-foundational and anti-modernist or postmodernist philosophy remains trapped in a modernist logic of redemption.

One of the problems in the debate between foundationalism and anti-foundationalism is the extremity of the choice that its protagonists often seem to offer: one must either cling to the belief in a single foundational metanarrative, or suppose that there are only so many narratives which provide no metanarrative grounds for interpreting them. Trey's reference to "mediated subjectivities" holds out the promise of defining such middle ground. So too does the philosophy of Paul Ricoeur, who speaks of an "imperfect mediation" which "can preserve the impetus Hegel gave to the process of totalization, without giving in to the temptation of a completed totality" (Ricoeur, 1984–8: III, 102–3). In this book I have traced some of the ways that race and caste hierarchies have developed historically by constructing two different cultural planes of "imperfect mediation" through which they have respectively been elicited, pointing to some of the more or less violent aporias they have involved. Within this foundation, my approach has been that of a descriptive or empirical sociologist, but it seems to me that the foundation also involves an inherent normative position, not in terms of what the right kind of politics are but in terms of what the right way to construct the political process is. This position emerges from the contention that different and apparently antithetical orientations to race or caste ideologies, such as ethnonationalism and anti-racism, or Brahmanism and untouchable assertion, do not figure in an asocial domain, a "war of all against all," but are each grounded within singular discursive fields of cultural contestation which, in the postcolonial world, increasingly are the same field. This approximates to what I have called the cultural metacontext and what Philip Kain (1992) refers to as "umbrella agreements," those deeper shared commitments to a normative social project which people hold that transcend the many different and competing ways they might construe it. Such commitments involve a logic of negation or extension, as with the separation of persons from things which provided a context both for slavery and its elimination. Where their basis becomes more or less explicit, this logic is readily interpretable as a political program, as with the American Declaration of Independence which, though it only held the equality of "men" to be self-evident, provided a model both for the equality of women and for the possibility that slaves could become men and women. This logic is not teleological. It does not inevitably progress in some positive direction, but it does imply specific developmental possibilities which, often in combination with other fields or agreements, seems at particular times and places to impose overwhelming choices. One such choice at the present time concerns the discourse of sovereignty, whether the ever-proliferating misery of racial and ethnonationalist violence it envehicles can be overcome and with what, with all that this implies for race and caste hierarchies. Foucault (almost) identified himself with this struggle:

> If one wants to look for a non-disciplinary form of power, or rather, to struggle against disciplines and disciplinary power, it is not towards the ancient right of sovereignty that one should turn, but towards the possibility of a new form of right, one which must indeed be anti-disciplinarian, but at the same time liberated from the principle of sovereignty. (Foucault, 1980: 108)

Kain (1992) detects a similar argument in Marx's *Critique of the Gotha Programme* (1875), representing a shift from the concept of "people's sovereignty" which he had articulated in his earlier writings. Power is now conceived as a negative power, preventing the exercise of domination. Developing a practical conception of such power is seen by many people today as an urgent political and intellectual task. Often it enjoins a return to discussions of the politics of community, which provides historical precedents sobering to various degrees – Rastafari or Puritan self-governing communities, nationalist xenophobia, caste society, communism, fascism, and so on – and poses questions to a new politics of community about how relations of power within and between communities along various dimensions, including the residual identifications of race or caste, together with gender, sexuality, and religion, could be managed in the absence of sovereignty. In India – where debates over foundationalism are probably of much more immediate political significance than in Europe or the Americas – the problematic conjunction of caste, community, and nation-state has produced some of the most sophisticated thinking to date from social scientists on the idea of community (e.g. Das, 1996; Bharucha, 1998). So too has the question of race in Euro-American contexts (Gilroy, 1993b; Appiah, 1996). Indeed, I would generalize to the global level Bharucha's argument that

> The tantalising task for any cultural critic in India today is to figure out the increasingly indeterminate relationships between the local, the regional and the national. These shifts demand an infinitely more complex cultural vigilance than a mere demonization of the nation-state cast within the overdetermined, Foucauldian categories of discipline, regimentation, surveillance and the policing of borders, by which citizens are constructed. (Bharucha, 1998: 177)

There are many different and plausible arguments within this new cultural politics. Paul Gilroy (1993b) has argued for a politics of memory which narrates the history of slavery and racism not just within what he calls the Black Atlantic diaspora but as an intrinsic part of a general consciousness of modernity. Derek Walcott, on the other hand, has argued for a sense of historical forgetting which, in contrast to Gilroy's black British grounding, is perhaps more consonant with an explicitly creolized Caribbean identity:

> I accept this archipelago of the Americas. I say to the ancestor who sold me, and to the ancestor who bought me I have no father, I want no such father, although I can understand you, black ghost, white ghost, when you both whisper "history," for if I attempt to forgive you both I am falling into your idea of history which justifies and explains and expiates, and it is not mine to forgive, my memory cannot summon any filial love, since your features are anonymous and erased and I have no wish and no power to pardon. . . . To you . . . I give the strange and bitter and yet ennobling thanks for the monumental groaning and soldering of two great worlds, like the halves of a fruit seamed by its own bitter juice, that exiled from your own Edens you have placed me in the wonder of another, and that was my inheritance and your gift. (Walcott, 1974: 27)

In the aftermath of Ayodhya, Indian intellectuals have also spoken of an "ethics of forgetting." Sheldon Pollock (1993) has argued that this attempt to lighten the burden of the past is illusory, and that the principled intellectual stance is to deconstruct the way that history is engaged politically, thereby helping to neutralize its force. To my mind, this is an optimistic view not only because the narrative of deconstruction is never likely to make much sense outside academic contexts, but also because the very grounds upon which it is predicated, namely a secular liberalism, are precisely the ones that are open to contest, as Pollock's own analysis admirably demonstrates.

The post-foundational turn in contemporary social theory seems to have marked an inability to produce a "new theory of right," in Foucault's phrase, which is anything other than agonistic. To expose the power strategies and hidden exclusions involved in the various attempts to define forms of liberal universalism associated with writers like Jürgen Habermas, Charles Taylor, and Richard Rorty is not unprincipled, but it too often results in what Rorty calls the "knowingness" which substitutes "knowing theorization for awe, and resentment over the failures of the past for visions of a better future" (Rorty, 1998: 127). This is a compelling observation, but whereas Rorty's objections are directed mainly at poststructuralist cultural criticism, the charge of "knowingness" could be turned against his own complacent confidence in the essential benevolence of US-style liberal democracy, or against writers like Fox (1996), whose critique of the "quest for re-enchantment" in communal and communitarian movements is grounded on a foundational belief in individual liberty, positions which involve their own quite problematic enchantment of freedom, prosperity, or happiness. I would argue on the contrary for the need to embrace the urge for a re-enchantment or resacralization in these movements, an endorsement of symbolic density, while rejecting their characteristic tendency to invoke singular logics of redemption which carry with them a potentially genocidal exclusionary capacity. Exactly how to do so is, of course, another matter entirely, but a good starting point might be to move beyond political claims based on unilateral subjectivities. This would obviously apply to racist and ethnonationalist movements themselves, but also to the valorization of the male working class within orthodox Marxism and to elements of postcolonial theory such as the injunction Landry and Maclean (1996: 4) derive from Spivak's work of "unlearning one's privilege by considering it as one's loss," a terminology which dubiously recuperates the moral superiority of the subaltern. Spivak herself has aptly criticized what she calls "the banality of leftist intellectuals' lists of self-knowing, politically canny subalterns," whereby in "representing them, the intellectuals represent themselves as transparent" (Spivak, 1994: 70). However, one of the least impressive aspects of her own writing and that of others, like Edward Said, who have influenced postcolonial theory, is the way that they deploy their own self-representation as visible, political, diasporic intellectuals as a rhetorical strategy to vouchsafe the authority of their intellectual discourse, one that is no less complicit in the silencing or refiguration of subaltern forms of consciousness (Ahmad, 1992; Bhatt, 1997; Friedman, 1997).

Despite the emptiness of the injunction to "unlearn privilege," it does at least have the merit of an implicit advocacy for the reconstruction of social identifications like racial subjectivities within contemporary public political discourse, rather than their deconstruction which has too often been the goal of liberal critique and has now been taken even further in much poststructuralist theory. It is, I would argue, important to thematize such subjectivities rather than to elide them, not only because of the hidden strategies of power which inevitably accompany claims to a normative universalism, but also because of the injuries caused by racism, colonialism, and nationalism which afflict their perpetrators as well as their victims (Nandy, 1983). Nancy Fraser (1992) provides a more fully developed conception of a political process along these lines, based upon multiple and contestatory, if sometimes overlapping, sites of mobilization around collective interests which she terms "subaltern counterpublics." In this, she builds upon the concept of the "public sphere" developed by Habermas (1989) at an early stage in his intellectual career, in which the idea of a foundational normativity was understood in relation to the contingent, empirical emergence of a collective arena for rational political debate in the course of West European history, rather than as a transcendent quality immanent in human interaction, as in his later theory of communicative rationality. But a limitation of Fraser's conception is not only that it neglects to engage with the possibility that the genesis of a counterpublic is determined in a wider transformative context, it also implicitly requires a unitary and transcendent metaspace of the kind Habermas constructs as a specific historical contingency (Postone, 1992). This ahistoricality, which also applies to Spivak's validation of "strategic essentialism" in pursuance of political goals, transcendentalizes the agency invested in extant collectivities at the expense of appreciating the grounds upon which they are constructed. In chapter 2 I attempted to incorporate these grounds into the theoretical basis for my own historical account of natural hierarchies by developing a theory of specific and contingently historical cultural metacontexts. But there may be a more universal sense in which the pain caused by the conflicts engendered through these metacontexts demands expiation. This, perhaps, is captured by Paul Ricoeur when he says that,

> We tell stories because in the last analysis human lives need and merit being narrated. This remark takes on its full force when we refer to the necessity to save the history of the defeated and the lost. The whole history of suffering cries out for vengeance and calls for narrative. (Ricoeur, 1984–8: I, 75)

Yet if, as I am inclined to believe, the history of suffering narrated by Rastafari probably does need to be told today, whereas the history of suffering narrated by Hindutva probably does not, then we need to appraise very carefully just who can validate their political claims by recourse to history, and how, in ways that go far beyond standard sociological discussions of "oppression" and "identity." In an earlier work, Ricoeur provided some useful markers for doing so in arguing:

> When one has penetrated to the depths of singularity, one feels that it is harmonious with every other in a way that cannot be put into words. I am convinced that a progressive Islamic or Hindu world in which the old ways of thinking would inspire a new history, would have with our European culture and civilization that specific affinity that all creative men share. I think that skepticism ends here. For the European, in particular, the problem is not to share in a sort of vague belief which would be acceptable to everyone; . . . we have to go back to our Greek, Hebrew, and Christian origins so as to be worthy participants in the great debate of cultures. In order to confront a self other than one's own self, one must first have a self. . . . Human truth lies only in this process in which civilizations confront each other with what is most living and creative in them. Man's history will progressively become a

vast explanation in which each civilization will work out its perception of the world by confronting all others. But this process has hardly begun. It is probably the task of generations to come. No one can say what will become of our civilization when it has really met different civilizations by means other than the shock of conquest and domination. But we have to admit that this encounter has not yet taken place at the level of an authentic dialogue. That is why we are in a kind of lull or interregnum in which we can no longer practice the dogmatism of a single truth and in which we are not yet capable of conquering the skepticism into which we have stepped. (Ricoeur, 1965: 283–4)

The enduring force of this insight is not undermined by recognizing that defining what constitutes "our civilization" is likely to be more complicated and contingent than Ricoeur appears to think. Indeed, although it would be possible to play with the view that Hindutva evinces continuities with the traditions of Indic civilization, whereas Rastafari is derivative of a European Christian tradition considerably removed from its African affectations, the legitimacy of Rastafari's historical narrative over and above Hindutva's seems to me to inhere in an authenticity of the kind described by Ricoeur which is established at some deep level in the way that contemporary social life authorizes historical perception. Nevertheless, the vast acceleration under contemporary technological conditions of modernity in the degree to which cultural representations can be communicated across the geopolitical obstacles which once helped territorialize the metacontexts of civilizational thought is likely to disrupt any final civilizational accounting of the kind invoked by Ricoeur. It is possible to be more (Appadurai, 1994) or less (Lévi-Strauss, 1985) sanguine about the consequences of this but, as I hope to have shown through the discussion of Caribbean creolization and Hindu nationalism in chapter 6, there is no reason to suppose that the idea of the fragment or the mixture as against the totality or the singularity will finally abolish the aporias of natural hierarchy. In this respect, while we can anticipate the continued relevance of immanent critique as both an academic project and a motor of social process, any teleological commitment to its finality or transcendence must be rejected along with the commitment to a vanguardist political role for academic discourses concerning natural hierarchy.

Hierarchy and a Politics of Sociology

Let us, then, finally consider the implications of the foregoing discussion for the role of sociology in the cultural politics which are attempting to transform natural hierarchies. To put it at its bluntest, my argument is that sociology has no role to play in these politics at all, and scholars cannot warrant their arguments through claims to being "profoundly political," as Landry and Maclean (1996) warrant Spivak. As should be obvious from earlier chapters, this is not because I think that sociology has some transcendent status above politics, but precisely for the opposite reason. Nor am I arguing that sociologists should refrain from involvement with political struggles. Only that such involvement cannot be the first justification for a sociology of natural hierarchies *qua* sociology as the theorization of social ontologies. One reason for this is the syllogism that because the content of sociological theory is intrinsically "political," sociologists therefore have a responsibility to be politically engaged. The problem with this argument – which perhaps one hears in the ephemeral discourse of the discipline such as conference discussions more than in its textual products – is that it recuperates the capacity of the discipline to make authoritative interventions into political debates in the very movement by which it claims to deconstruct sociological authority. I would argue by contrast that sociologists are no better placed than anyone else to proffer political solutions and that sociology in any case is not directed to this goal. Pierre Bourdieu has argued:

> If social science is not to be merely a way of pursuing politics by other means, social scientists must take as their object the intention of assigning others to classes and of thereby telling them what they are and what they have to be . . . they must analyze, in order to repudiate it, the ambition of the creative world vision, that sort of *intuitus_originarius* that would make things exist in conformity with its vision. (Bourdieu, 1991: 243)

Yet, as I argued in relation to Sheldon Pollock's position, the products of this kind of analysis are not likely to be rendered in formats which readily enable this repudiation to make much sense to anyone except other social scientists.

Another factor complicating the attempt of sociology to offer itself *qua* sociology in political struggles over natural hierarchies is that if the institutional distinction between academic and political arenas is willingly blurred then the potentialities of disciplinary judgment are lost. Dirks (1996) describes how his influential book on South Indian history (*The Hollow Crown*) was interpreted in some circles within India as a defence of Brahmanic privilege. Similarly, I would argue that Inden's (1990) critique of Orientalist assumptions in the sociology of India could easily be read as a manifesto for Hindutva. Within the institutional order of academic social science it would be easy and fair for both Dirks and Inden to refute these interpretations of their books. But it would not be possible to do so in a context where this institutional distinction was not recognized, and sociological analysis was always proffered as political prescription.

The preceding point rests upon the assumption that sharp distinctions can be made between institutional orders like the academic university and the world of politics, distinctions which are themselves "natural" or apolitical. A major aspect of Foucault's work was to argue that such assumptions are illusory, concealing the historical labor that goes into constituting the politically "neutral" spaces which claim the ability to pronounce authoritatively on different features of the social universe. If we take this argument seriously, it is possible to appreciate the sense in which the contemporary university with its emphasis on free speech and disinterested enquiry constitutes one of the sacred spaces of modernity whose sacrality inheres in its very irrelevance to worldly political discourse. This is surely part of the reason why the various traditions of anti-racism within social science have, to the bemusement of some of its practitioners, had so little effect upon banishing racial ideologies (another reason is the nature of cultural process, as argued in this book). Naturally, it is possible for social scientists to use their academic base in order to wage political struggles and build political alliances. However, rather like ascetic renouncers in India who cultivate worldly political goals, too assiduous a pursuit of the latter necessarily undermines the standing gained in the former which potentiates it. Of course, like most forms of sacrality, the academy is not quite as disinterested or other-worldly as its ideal representation would have us believe. There is much to be said for using academic circuits to further the interests of the oppressed and the disadvantaged, just as they are routinely used to further the interests of the powerful, though – as Weber has taught us and Dirks, discussed above, reiterates – the political world does not confront us with simple choices between good and evil, and it is all too easy for one's work to have quite unfortunate and unintended consequences. Nevertheless, I would argue that the call to be more "political" has to be made intelligible within the discourse of those frameworks if it is to be anything except another authoritarianism, particularly since it cannot be assumed that the subaltern political discourses which might contest those frameworks are not systematized through the same metacontext (cf. Habermas, 1992a; 1992b). Thus, while not necessarily disagreeing with Rorty's (1998) view that universities should act as centers of social protest, I would argue that intellectual enquiry is not reducible to this function, and his argument that the academic left should put a moratorium on theory does not seem a convincing manifesto for academic and political invigoration.

If sociology or anthropology and their grounding within the privileged "neutrality" of the university are assailed for their quietism by leftist and liberatory movements, and for their rationalist bias from right-wing and fundamentalist movements, there is nothing to be gained by conceding the argument and trying to justify their practice on the grounds of political instrumentality. I would argue that sociology, and these political discourses too, are derivative of deeper historical processes which sociology has attempted to make explicit in various ways. Perhaps a certain humility or resignation is required to suggest that sociological theory can only construct the cultural and political spheres which provide their ground; it cannot of itself solve the political problems which emerge from these spheres. Even if its practice has been guided by, and depends upon, a secular humanism which can be articulated against the invidious politics of hierarchy, sociology cannot find its own justification in this fact.

References

Abrahams, R. 1970. Patterns of performance in the British West Indies. In Whitten, N. and Szwed, J. (eds.) *Afro-American Anthropology: Contemporary Perspectives.* New York: Free Press.

Abrahams, R. 1983. *The Man of Words in the West Indies.* Baltimore: Johns Hopkins University Press.

Ahmad, A. 1992. *In Theory: Classes, Nations, Literatures.* London: Verso.

Alam, M. 1993. *The Crisis of Empire in Mughal North India, Awadh and the Punjab, 1707–1748.* Delhi: Oxford University Press.

Alexander, J. 1977. The culture of race in middle-class Kingston, Jamaica. *American Ethnologist* 4: 413–35.

Alexander, J. 1984. Love, race, slavery and sexuality in Jamaican images of the family. In Smith, R. T. (ed.) *Kinship, Ideology and Practice in Latin America.* Chapel Hill: University of North Carolina Press.

Allen, T. 1994. *The Invention of the White Race. Volume One: Racial Oppression and Social Control.* London: Verso.

Allen, T. 1997. *The Invention of the White Race, Volume Two: The Origins of Racial Oppression in Anglo-America.* London: Verso.

Anderson, B. 1991. *Imagined Communities: Reflections on the Origins and Spread of Nationalism.* London: Verso.

Anderson, P. 1974. *Passages from Antiquity to Feudalism.* London: Verso.

Appadurai, A. 1981. *Worship and Conflict Under Colonial Rule: A South Indian Case.* Cambridge: Cambridge University Press.

Appadurai, A. 1986. Is homo hierarchicus? *American Ethnologist* 13: 745–61.

Appadurai, A. 1994. Disjuncture and difference in the global cultural economy. In Williams, P. and Chrisman, L. (eds.) *Colonial Discourse and Postcolonial Theory.* Hemel Hempstead: Harvester Wheatsheaf.

Appadurai, A. and Breckenridge, C. 1976. The South Indian temple: authority, honour and redistribution. *Contributions to Indian Sociology* 10: 187–211.

Appiah, A. 1996. Race, culture, identity: misunderstood connections. In Appiah, A. and Gutman, A. (eds.) *Color Conscious: The Political Morality of Race.* Princeton, NJ: Princeton University Press.

Arendt, H. 1967. *The Origins of Totalitarianism.* London: George Allen and Unwin.

Asad, T. 1987. Are there histories of peoples without Europe? *Comparative Studies in Society and History* 29: 594–607.

Asad, T. 1990. Multiculturalism and British identity in the wake of the Rushdie affair. *Politics and Society* 18: 455–80.

Austin, D. 1979. History and symbols in ideology. *Man* n.s. 14: 297–314.

Austin, D. 1983. Culture and ideology in the English-speaking Caribbean: A view from Jamaica. *American Ethnologist* 102: 223–40.

Austin-Broos, D. 1987. Pentecostals and Rastafarians: Cultural, political, and gender relations of two religious movements. *Social and Economic Studies* 36: 1–39.

Austin-Broos, D. 1992. Redefining the moral order: Interpretations of Christianity in post-emancipation Jamaica. In McGlynn, F. and Drescher, S. (eds.) *The Meaning of Freedom: Economics, Politics and Culture after Slavery*. Pittsburgh: University of Pittsburgh Press.

Austin-Broos, D. 1994. Race/class: Jamaica's discourse of heritable identity. *New West Indian Guide* 68: 213–33.

Austin-Broos, D. 1997. *Jamaica Genesis: Religion and the Politics of Moral Order*. Chicago: University of Chicago Press.

Baechler, J. 1988. The origins of modernity: Caste and feudality (India, Europe and Japan). In Baechler, J., Hall, J., and Mann, M. (eds.) *Europe and the Rise of Capitalism*. Oxford: Blackwell Publishers.

Baechler, J., Hall, J., and Mann, M. 1988. *Europe and the Rise of Capitalism*. Oxford: Blackwell Publishers.

Bakhtin, M. 1984. *Rabelais and His World*. Bloomington: Indiana University Press.

Barnett, S. 1976. Coconuts and gold: Relational identity in a south Indian caste. *Contributions to Indian Sociology* 10: 133–56.

Barnett, S. 1977. Identity choice and caste ideology in contemporary South India. In Dolgin, J., Kemmitzer, D., and Schneider, D. (eds.) *Symbolic Anthropology: A Reader in the Study of Symbols and Meanings*. New York: Columbia University Press.

Barth, F. 1969. Introduction. In Barth, F. (ed.) *Ethnic Groups and Boundaries*. London: George Allen and Unwin.

Bastien, R. 1966. Vodoun and politics in Haiti. In Courlander, H. and Bastien, R., *Religion and Politics in Haiti*. New York: Institute for Cross-Cultural Research.

Basu, A. 1996. Mass movement or elite conspiracy? The puzzle of Hindu nationalism. In Ludden, D. (ed.) *Contesting the Nation: Religion, Community and the Politics of Democracy in India*. Philadelphia: University of Pennsylvania Press.

Battaglia, O. de 1962. The nobility in the European Middle Ages. *Comparative Studies in Society and History* 5: 60–75.

Baudrillard, J. 1975. *The Mirror of Production*. St Louis: Telos Press.

Bayly, C. 1983. *Rulers, Townsmen and Bazaars: North Indian Society in the Age of British Expansion*. Cambridge: Cambridge University Press.

Bayly, C. 1985a. State and economy in India over seven hundred years. *Economic History Review* 38: 583–96.

Bayly, C. 1985b. The pre-history of communalism? Religious conflict in India, 1700–1850. *Modern Asian Studies* 19: 177–204.

Bayly, C. 1989. *Imperial Meridian: The British Empire and the World, 1780–1830*. London: Longman.

Bayly, S. 1986. Islam in southern India: "Purist" or "syncretic"? In Bayly, C. and

Kolff, D. (eds.) *Two Colonial Empires: Comparative Essays on the History of India and Indonesia in the 19th Century*. Leiden: Martinus Nijhoff.

Beckford, G. 1983. *Persistent Poverty: Underdevelopment in Plantation Economies of the Third World*. London: Zed Books.

Beckles, H. 1998. *A Spirit of Dominance: Cricket and Nationalism in the West Indies*. Kingston: Canoe Press.

Benítez-Rojo, A. 1996. *The Repeating Island: The Caribbean and the Postmoderns' Perspective*. Durham, NC: Duke University Press.

Bennett, L. 1969. *Before the Mayflower: A History of Black America*. Chicago: Johnson Publishing.

Benson, R. 1982. The Gelasian doctrine: Uses and transformations. In Makdisi, G., Sourdel, D., and Sourdel-Thomine, J. (eds.) *La Notion d'autorité au moyen age Islam, Byzance, Occident*. Paris: Presses Universitaires de France.

Bentley, G. 1991. Response to Yelvington. *Comparative Studies in Society and History* 33: 169–75.

Berger, P. 1967. *The Sacred Canopy: Elements of a Sociological Theory of Religion*. New York: Anchor.

Bernal, M. 1987. *Black Athena: The Afroasiatic Roots of Classical Civilization*. London: Free Association Books.

Berreman, G. 1979. *Caste and Other Inequities: Essays on Inequality*. Meerut: Folklore Institute.

Besson, J. 1979. Symbolic aspects of land tenure and transmission of land rights among Caribbean peasantries. In Cross, M. and Marks, A. (eds.) *Peasants, Plantations and Rural Communities in the Caribbean*. Guildford and Leiden: Department of Sociology, University of Surrey and Department of Caribbean Studies, University of Leiden.

Besson, J. 1988. Agrarian relations and perceptions of land in a Jamaican peasant village. In Brierly, J. and Rubenstein, H. (eds.) *Small Farming and Peasant Resources in the Caribbean*. Winnipeg: University of Manitoba Press.

Besson, J. 1992. Freedom and community: The British West Indies. In McGlynn, F. and Drescher, S. (eds.) *The Meaning of Freedom: Economics, Politics and Culture after Slavery*. Pittsburgh: University of Pittsburgh Press.

Besson, J. 1998. Religion as resistance in Jamaican peasant life: The Baptist Church, Revival worldview and Rastafari movement. In Chevannes, B. (ed.) *Rastafari and Other African–Caribbean Worldviews*. Basingstoke: Macmillan.

Betances, E. 1995. *State and Society in the Dominican Republic*. Boulder, Col.: Westview Press.

Béteille, A. 1967. Race and descent as social categories in India. *Daedalus*, spring: 444–63.

Béteille, A. 1990. Race, caste and gender. *Man* 25: 489–504.

Bharucha, R. 1998. The shifting sites of secularism: Cultural politics and activism in India today. *Economic and Political Weekly* 33: 167–80.

Bhatt, C. 1997. *Liberation and Purity: Race, New Religious Movements and the Ethics of Postmodernity*. London: UCL Press.

Blackburn, R. 1988. *The Overthrow of Colonial Slavery 1776–1848*. London: Verso.

Blackburn, R. 1997. *The Making of New World Slavery: From the Baroque to the*

Modern, 1492–1800. London: Verso.

Blake, S. 1997. The patrimonial–bureaucratic empire of the Mughals. In Kulke, H. (ed.) *The State in India 1000–1700*. Delhi: Oxford University Press.

Bolland, O. 1997. *Creolization and Creole Societies: A Cultural Nationalist View of Caribbean Social History*. Belize City: Angelus Press.

Bose, S. and Jalal, A. 1998. *Modern South Asia: History, Culture, Political Economy*. London: Routledge.

Bourdieu, P. 1977. *Outline of a Theory of Practice*. Cambridge: Cambridge University Press.

Bourdieu, P. 1984. *Distinction: A Social Critique of the Judgement of Taste*. Cambridge, Mass.: Harvard University Press.

Bourdieu, P. 1991. *Language and Symbolic Power*. Cambridge: Polity Press.

Boxer, C. 1965. *The Dutch Seaborne Empire, 1600–1800*. Harmondsworth: Penguin Books.

Brass, P. 1994. *The Politics of India since Independence*. Cambridge: Cambridge University Press.

Brass, T. 1994. Introduction: The New Farmers Movements in India. *Journal of Peasant Studies* 21: 3–26.

Brathwaite, E. 1971. *The Development of Creole Society in Jamaica, 1770–1820*. Oxford: Clarendon Press.

Brathwaite, E. 1977. Caliban, Ariel, and Unprospero in the conflict of creolization: A study of the slave revolt in Jamaica in 1831–32. *Annals of the New York Academy of Sciences* 292: 41–62.

Braudel, F. 1972–4. *The Mediterranean and the Mediterranean World in the Age of Phillip II*. New York: Harper and Row.

Brodber, E. 1987. Black consciousness and popular music in Jamaica in the 1960s and 1970s. *New West Indian Guide* 61: 145–60.

Brown, K. 1997. Systematic remembering, systematic forgetting: Ogou in Haiti. In Barnes, S. (ed.) *Africa's Ogun: Old World and New*. Bloomington: Indiana University Press.

Burghart, R. 1996. *The Conditions of Listening*. Delhi: Oxford University Press.

Burke, P. 1978. *Popular Culture in Early Modern Europe*. London: Temple Smith.

Burton, R. 1997. *Afro-Creole: Power, Opposition and Play in the Caribbean*. Ithaca, NY: Cornell University Press.

Busby, C. 1997. Of marriage and marriageability: Gender and Dravidian kinship. *Journal of the Royal Anthropological Institute* 3: 21–42.

Calhoun, C. 1995. *Critical Social Theory*. Oxford: Blackwell Publishers.

Cameron, E. 1991. *The European Reformation*. Oxford: Clarendon Press.

Canning, J. 1996. *A History of Medieval Political Thought, 300–1450*. London: Routledge.

Canny, N. and Pagden, A. 1987. *Colonial Identity in the Atlantic World, 1500–1800*. Princeton, NJ: Princeton University Press.

Carnegie, C. 1987. Is family land an institution? In Carnegie, C. (ed.) *Afro-Caribbean Villages in Historical Perspective*. Kingston: African–Caribbean Institute of Jamaica.

Carter, A. 1973. A comparative analysis of systems of kinship and marriage in South

Asia. *Proceedings of the Royal Anthropological Institute* 1972: 29–54.

Caspary, G. 1979. *Politics and Exegesis: Origen and the Two Swords*. Berkeley: University of California Press.

Certeau, M. de 1980. On the oppositional practices of everyday life. *Social Text* 3: 3–43.

Chakrabarty, D. 1995. Modernity and ethnicity in India: A history for the present. *Economic and Political Weekly* 30: 3373–80.

Chatterjee, P. 1986. *Nationalist Thought and the Postcolonial World: A Derivative Discourse*. London: Zed Books.

Chatterjee, P. 1993. *The Nation and its Fragments: Colonial and Postcolonial Histories*. Princeton, NJ: Princeton University Press.

Chattopadhyaya, B. 1994. *The Making of Early Medieval India*. Delhi: Oxford University Press.

Chevannes, B. 1998a. Introducing the native religions of Jamaica. In Chevannes, B. (ed.) *Rastafari and Other African–Caribbean Worldviews*. Basingstoke: Macmillan.

Chevannes, B. 1998b. *Rastafari and Other African–Caribbean Worldviews*. Basingstoke: Macmillan.

Chevannes, B. 1998c. Rastafari and the exorcism of the ideology of racism and classism in Jamaica. In Murrell, N., Spencer, W., and McFarlane, A. (eds.) *Chanting Down Babylon: The Rastafari Reader*. Philadelphia: Temple University Press.

Clark, S. 1990. *Paul Ricoeur*. London: Routledge.

Clarke, E. 1966. *My Mother Who Fathered Me: A Study of the Family in Three Selected Communities in Jamaica*. London: George Allen and Unwin.

Cohen, W. 1980. *The French Encounter with Africans: White Response to Blacks, 1530–1880*. Bloomington: Indiana University Press.

Cohn, B. 1987. *An Anthropologist Among the Historians and Other Essays*. Oxford: Oxford University Press.

Cohn, N. 1957. *The Pursuit of the Millennium*. London: Paladin.

Colella, P. 1982. Mercantilism and Hobbes' Leviathan. *Journal of Thought* 17: 89–99.

Comaroff, J. 1987. Of totemism and ethnicity: Consciousness, practice and the signs of inequality. *Ethnos* 52: 301–23.

Cox, O. 1948. *Caste, Class and Race*. New York: Monthly Review Press.

Cox, O. 1987. *Race, Class and the World System: The Sociology of Oliver C. Cox*. New York: Monthly Review Press.

Craton, M. 1996. A recipe for the perfect calalu: Island and regional identity in the British West Indies. In Beckles, H. (ed.) *Inside Slavery: Process and Legacy in the Caribbean Experience*. Kingston: Canoe Press.

Curtin, P. 1990. *The Rise and Fall of the Plantation Complex: Essays in Atlantic History*. Cambridge: Cambridge University Press.

Curtis, L. 1968. *Anglo-Saxons and Celts: A Study of Anti-Irish Prejudice in Victorian England*. Bridgeport, Conn.: University of Bridgeport Press.

Daniel, E. 1984. *Fluid Signs: Being a Person the Tamil Way*. Berkeley: University of California Press.

Das, V. 1996. *Critical Events: An Anthropological Perspective on Contemporary In-*

dia. Delhi: Oxford University Press.

Davies, W. 1996. On servile status in the early Middle Ages. In Bush, M. (ed.) *Serfdom and Slavery: Studies in Legal Bondage.* Harlow: Longman.

Davis, D. 1966. *The Problem of Slavery in Western Culture.* Ithaca, NY: Cornell University Press.

Davis, R. 1996. The iconography of Rama's chariot. In Ludden, D. (ed.) *Contesting the Nation: Religion, Community and the Politics of Democracy in India.* Philadelphia: University of Pennsylvania Press.

Dayan, J. 1995. *Haiti, History and the Gods.* Berkeley: University of California Press.

Degler, C. 1959. Slavery and the genesis of American race prejudice. *Comparative Studies in Society and History* 2: 49–66.

Degler, C. 1971. *Neither Black Nor White: Slavery and Race Relations in Brazil and the United States.* New York: Macmillan.

Deliège, R. 1991. Replication and consensus: Untouchability, caste and ideology in India. *Man* 25: 155–73.

Denich, B. 1994. Dismembering Yugoslavia: Nationalist ideologies and the symbolic revival of genocide. *American Ethnologist* 21: 367–90.

Deren, M. 1953. *Divine Horsemen: The Living Gods of Haiti.* London: Thames and Hudson.

Deshpande, S. 1998. Hegemonic spatial strategies: The nation-space and Hindu communalism in twentieth-century India. *Public Culture* 10: 249–83.

Desmangles, L. 1992. *The Faces of the Gods: Vodou and Roman Catholicism in Haiti.* Chapel Hill: University of North Carolina Press.

Diaz-Royo, A. 1979. Dignidad and Respeto: Two core themes in the traditional Puerto Rican family culture. In Cross, M. and Marks, A. (eds.) *Peasants, Plantations and Rural Communities in the Caribbean.* Guildford and Leiden: Department of Sociology, University of Surrey and Department of Caribbean Studies, University of Leiden.

Dirks, N. 1989. The invention of caste: Civil society in colonial India. *Social Analysis* 25: 42–52.

Dirks, N. 1993. *The Hollow Crown: The Ethnohistory of an Indian Kingdom.* Ann Arbor: University of Michigan Press.

Dirks, N. 1996. Recasting Tamil society: The politics of caste and race in contemporary Southern India. In Fuller, C. (ed.) *Caste Today.* Oxford: Oxford University Press.

Dominguez, V. 1977. Social classification in creole Louisiana. *American Ethnologist* 4: 589–602.

Drescher, S. 1990. The ending of the slave trade and the evolution of European scientific racism. *Social Science History* 14: 415–49.

Dreyfus, H. and Rabinow, P. 1993. Can there be a science of existential structure and social meaning? In Calhoun, C., LiPuma, E., and Postone, M. (eds.) *Bourdieu: Critical Perspectives.* Cambridge: Polity Press.

Drummond, L. 1980. The cultural continuum: A theory of intersystems. *Man* 15: 352–74.

Duara, P. 1995. *Rescuing History From the Nation: Questioning Narratives of Mod-*

ern China. Chicago: University of Chicago Press.

Duby, G. 1968. The diffusion of cultural patterns in feudal society. *Past and Present* 41: 3–10.

Duby, G. 1974. *The Early Growth of the European Economy: Warriors and Peasants from the Seventh to the Twelfth Century*. Ithaca, NY: Cornell University Press.

Dumont, L. 1964. A note on locality in relation to descent. *Contributions to Indian Sociology* 7: 71–6.

Dumont, L. 1965. The functional equivalents of the individual in caste society. *Contributions to Indian Sociology* 8: 85–99.

Dumont, L. 1970. Religion, politics and society in the individualistic universe. *Proceedings of the Royal Anthropological Institute*: 31–41.

Dumont, L. 1977. *From Mandeville to Marx: The Genesis and Triumph of Economic Ideology*. Chicago: University of Chicago Press.

Dumont, L. 1980. *Homo Hierarchicus: The Caste System and its Implications*. Revd. edn. Chicago: University of Chicago Press.

Dumont, L. 1983. *Affinity as a Value: Marriage Alliance in South India, with Comparative Essays on Australia*. Chicago: University of Chicago Press.

Dumont, L. 1986. *Essays on Individualism: Modern Ideology in Anthropological Perspective*. Chicago: University of Chicago Press.

Dunn, R. 1972. *Sugar and Slaves: The Rise of the Planter Class in the English West Indies, 1624–1713*. New York: Norton.

Duplessis, R. 1997. *Transitions to Capitalism in Early Modern Europe*. Cambridge: Cambridge University Press.

Durkheim, E. (1965). *The Elementary Forms of Religious Life*. New York: Free Press.

Eisenstadt, S. 1997. Historical experience, cultural traditions, state formation and political dynamics in India and Europe. In Doornbos, M. and Kaviraj, S. (eds.) *Dynamics of State Formation: India and Europe Compared*. New Delhi: Sage.

Ekeh, P. 1990. Social anthropology and two uses of tribalism in Africa. *Comparative Studies in Society and History*: 660–700.

Elliott, J. 1963. *Imperial Spain, 1469–1716*. Harmondsworth: Penguin Books.

Elliott, J. 1984. The Spanish conquest and settlement of America. In Bethell, L. (ed.) *The Cambridge History of Latin America, Volume I: Colonial Latin America*. Cambridge: Cambridge University Press.

Eltis, D. 1993. Europeans and the rise and fall of African slavery in the Americas: An interpretation. *American Historical Review* 98: 1399–1423.

Embree, A. 1977. Frontiers into boundaries: From the traditional to the modern state. In Fox, R. (ed.) *Realm and Region in Traditional India*. New Delhi: Vikas Publishing House.

Embree, A. 1985. Indian civilization and regional cultures: The two realities. In Wallace, P. (ed.) *Region and Nation in India*. New Delhi: Oxford University Press.

Ertman, T. 1997. *Birth of the Leviathan: Building States and Regimes in Medieval and Early Modern Europe*. Cambridge: Cambridge University Press.

Evans, W. 1980. From the land of Canaan to the land of Guinea: The strange odyssey of the "Sons of Ham". *American Historical Review* 85: 15–43.

Evans-Pritchard, E. 1940. *The Nuer: A Description of the Modes of Livelihood and Political Institutions of a Nilotic People.* Oxford: Oxford University Press.

Evans-Pritchard, E. 1948 (1962). *Social Anthropology and Other Essays.* New York: Free Press.

Fabian, J. 1983. *Time and the Other: How Anthropology Makes its Object.* New York: Columbia University Press.

Feeley-Harnik, G. 1985. Issues in divine kingship. *Annual Review of Anthropology* 14: 272–313.

Fields, B. 1990. Slavery, race and ideology in the United States of America. *New Left Review* 181: 95–118.

Flandrin, J.-L. 1979. *Families in Former Times: Kinship, Household and Sexuality.* Cambridge: Cambridge University Press.

Foucault, M. 1970. *The Order of Things.* New York: Vintage.

Foucault, M. 1972. *The Archaeology of Knowledge and the Discourse on Language.* New York: Pantheon Books.

Foucault, M. 1977. Nietzsche, genealogy, history. In Bouchard, D. (ed.) *Language, Counter-Memory, Practice.* Ithaca, NY: Cornell University Press.

Foucault, M. 1980. *Power/Knowledge: Selected Interviews and Other Writings 1972–77.* Brighton: Harvester.

Foucault, M. 1981. *The History of Sexuality: An Introduction.* Harmondsworth: Penguin Books.

Fox, R. 1970. Urban settlements and Rajput "clans" in Northern India. In Fox, R. (ed.) *Urban India: Society, Space and Image.* Durham, NC: Duke University Press.

Fox, R. 1996. Communalism and modernity. In Ludden, D. (ed.) *Contesting the Nation: Religion, Community and the Politics of Democracy in India.* Philadelphia: University of Pennsylvania Press.

Fraser, N. 1981. Foucault on modern power: Empirical insights and normative confusions. *Praxis International* 1: 272–87.

Fraser, N. 1992. Rethinking the public sphere: A contribution to the critique of actually existing democracy. In Calhoun, C. (ed.) *Habermas and the Public Sphere.* Cambridge, Mass.: MIT Press.

Frazer, J. 1922. *The Golden Bough: A Study in Magic and Religion.* Basingstoke: Macmillan.

Friedman, J. 1997. Global crises, the struggle for cultural identity and intellectual porkbarrelling: Cosmopolitans versus locals, ethnics and nationals in an era of de-hegemonization. In Werbner, P. and Modood, T. (eds.) *Debating Cultural Hybridity: Multi-Cultural Identities and the Politics of Anti-Racism.* London: Zed Books.

Fuller, C. 1977. British India or traditional India? An anthropological problem. *Ethnos* 3–4: 95–121.

Fuller, C. 1989. Misconceiving the grain heap: A critique of the concept of the Indian jajmani system. In Parry, J. and Bloch, M. (eds.) *Money and the Morality of Exchange.* Cambridge: Cambridge University Press.

Fuller, C. 1992. *The Camphor Flame: Popular Hinduism and Society in India.* Princeton, NJ: Princeton University Press.

Furneaux, R. 1974. *William Wilberforce*. London: Hamish Hamilton.

Garrigus, J. 1996. Colour, class and identity on the eve of the Haitian revolution: Saint-Domingue's free coloured elite as *colors américains*. In Landers, J. (ed.) *Against the Odds: Free Blacks in the Slave Societies of the Americas*. London: Frank Cass.

Geertz, C. 1983. Centers, kings and charisma: Reflections on the symbolics of power. In Geertz, C., *Local Knowledge: Further Essays in Interpretive Anthropology*. New York: Basic Books.

Gellner, E. 1983. *Nations and Nationalism*. Oxford: Blackwell Publishers.

Gersh, S. 1978. *From Iamblichus to Eriugena: An Investigation of the Prehistory and Evolution of the Pseudo-Dionysian Tradition*. Leiden: E. J. Brill.

Gilroy, P. 1993a. *Small Acts: Thoughts on the Politics of Black Cultures*. London: Serpent's Tail.

Gilroy, P. 1993b. *The Black Atlantic: Modernity and Double Consciousness*. London: Verso.

Gilroy, P. 1998. Race ends here. *Ethnic and Racial Studies* 21: 838–47.

Gonda, J. 1969. *Ancient Indian Kingship from the Religious Point of View*. Leiden: E. J. Brill.

Goody, J. 1983. *The Development of the Family and Marriage in Europe*. Cambridge: Cambridge University Press.

Gordon, S. 1978. Legitimacy and loyalty in some successor states of the eighteenth century. In Richards, J. (ed.) *Kingship and Authority in South Asia*. Madison: University of Wisconsin–Madison.

Gramsci, A. 1971. *Selections from the Prison Notebooks*. London: Lawrence and Wishart.

Greenblatt, S. 1991. *Marvelous Possessions: The Wonder of the New World*. Oxford: Clarendon Press.

Greene, J. 1986. *Peripheries and Center: Constitutional Development in the Extended Polities of the British Empire and the United States, 1607–1788*. New York: W. W. Norton.

Guenée, B. 1985. *States and Rulers in Later Medieval Europe*. Oxford: Blackwell Publishers.

Guha, R. 1982. On some aspects of the historiography of colonial India. In Guha, R. (ed.) *Subaltern Studies I: Writings on South Asian History and Society*. Delhi: Oxford University Press.

Habermas, J. 1971. *Knowledge and Human Interests*. Boston: Beacon Press.

Habermas, J. 1979. *Communication and the Evolution of Society*. Cambridge: Polity Press.

Habermas, J. 1987. *The Philosophical Discourse of Modernity*. Cambridge: Polity Press.

Habermas, J. 1989. *The Structural Transformation of the Public Sphere: An Inquiry into a Category of Bourgeois Society*. Cambridge, Mass.: MIT Press.

Habermas, J. 1992a. *Postmetaphysical Thinking*. Cambridge: Polity Press.

Habermas, J. 1992b. Concluding remarks. In Calhoun, C. (ed.) *Habermas and the Public Sphere*. Cambridge, Mass.: MIT Press.

Habib, I. 1992. *Medieval India 1: Researches into the History of India 1200–1750*.

Delhi: Oxford University Press.

Hall, G. 1996. *Social Control in Slave Plantation Societies: A Comparison of St. Domingue and Cuba.* Baton Rouge: Louisiana State University Press.

Hall, J. 1985. *Powers and Liberties: The Causes and Consequences of the Rise of the West.* Harmondsworth: Penguin Books.

Hall, J. 1988. States and societies: The miracle in comparative perspective. In Baechler, J., Hall, J., and Mann, M. (eds.) *Europe and the Rise of Capitalism.* Oxford: Blackwell Publishers.

Handlin, O. and Handlin, M. 1950. Origins of the Southern labor system. *William and Mary Quarterly* 3d ser. 7: 199–222.

Hanke, L. 1959. *Aristotle and the American Indians.* London: Hollis and Carter.

Hannaford, I. 1996. *Race: The History of an Idea in the West.* Baltimore: Johns Hopkins University Press.

Hansen, T. 1996a. Globalisation and nationalist imaginations. *Economic and Political Weekly* 31: 603–16.

Hansen, T. 1996b. Recuperating masculinity: Hindu nationalism, violence and the exorcism of the Muslim 'Other'. *Critique of Anthropology* 16: 137–72.

Hastings, A. 1997. *The Construction of Nationhood: Ethnicity, Religion and Nationalism.* Cambridge: Cambridge University Press.

Hazeltine, H. 1968. Roman and Canon law in the Middle Ages. In Tanner, J., Prévite-Orton, C., and Brooke, Z. (eds.) *The Cambridge Medieval History Volume 5.* Cambridge: Cambridge University Press.

Heesterman, J. 1985. *The Inner Conflict of Tradition: Essays in Indian Ritual, Kingship and Society.* Chicago: University of Chicago Press.

Heesterman, J. 1989. King and warrior. *History and Anthropology* 4: 97–122..

Heesterman, J. 1997. Traditional empire and modern state. In Doornbos, M. and Kaviraj, S. (eds.) *Dynamics of State Formation: India and Europe Compared.* New Delhi: Sage.

Heitzman, J. 1997. State formation in South India, 850–1280. In Kulke, H. (ed.) *The State in India 1000–1700.* Delhi: Oxford University Press.

Helg, A. 1995. *Our Rightful Share: The Afro-Cuban Struggle for Equality, 1886–1912.* Chapel Hill: University of North Carolina Press.

Hess, L. 1983. *The Bijak of Kabir.* Delhi: Motilal Banarsidass.

Hesse, K. 1996. No reciprocation? Wife-givers and wife-takers and the bartan of the samskara among the Khatris of Mandi, Himachal Pradesh. *Contributions to Indian Sociology* n.s. 30: 109–40.

Hobbes, T. 1968. *Leviathan.* Harmondsworth: Penguin Books.

Hobsbawm, E. 1983. Introduction: Inventing traditions. In Hobsbawm, E. and Ranger, T. (eds.) *The Invention of Tradition.* Cambridge: Cambridge University Press.

Hocart, A. M. 1936 (1970). *Kings and Councillors: An Essay in the Comparative Anatomy of Human Society.* Chicago: University of Chicago Press.

Hoetink, H. 1973. *Slavery and Race Relations in the Americas: An Inquiry into their Nature and Nexus.* New York: Harper and Row.

Hoetink, H. 1986. The Dominican Republic c.1870–1930. In Bethell, L. (ed.) *The Cambridge History of Latin America, Volume V: c. 1870 to 1930.* Cambridge:

Cambridge University Press.

Hoffmann, L.-F. 1984. Francophilia and cultural nationalism in Haiti. In Foster, C. and Valdman, A. (eds.) *Haiti – Today and Tomorrow: An Interdisciplinary Study*. New York: University Press of America.

Hollis, P. 1980. Anti-slavery and British working-class radicalism in the years of reform. In Bolt, C. and Drescher, S. (eds.) *Anti-Slavery, Religion and Reform: Essays in Memory of Roger Anstey*. Folkestone: Dawson.

Holt, T. 1992. *The Problem of Freedom: Race, Labor and Politics in Jamaica and Britain, 1832–1938*. Baltimore: Johns Hopkins University Press.

Holy, L. 1996. *Anthropological Perspectives on Kinship*. London: Pluto Press.

Homiak, J. 1998. Dub history: Soundings on Rastafari livity and language. In Chevannes, B. (ed.) *Rastafari and Other African–Caribbean Worldviews*. Basingstoke: Macmillan.

hooks, b. 1992. *Yearning: Race, Gender and Cultural Politics*. London: Turnaround.

Horn, J. 1994. *Adapting to a New World: English Society in the Seventeenth Century Chesapeake*. Chapel Hill: University of North Carolina Press.

Hulme, P. 1990. The spontaneous hand of nature: Savagery, colonialism and the Enlightenment. In Hulme, P. and Jordanova, L. (eds.) *The Enlightenment and its Shadows*. London: Routledge.

Inden, R. 1976. *Marriage and Rank in Bengali Culture*. Berkeley: University of California Press.

Inden, R. 1986. Tradition against itself. *American Ethnologist* 13: 762–75.

Inden, R. 1990. *Imagining India*. Oxford: Blackwell Publishers.

Inden, R. 1995. Embodying God: From imperial progresses to national progress in India. *Economy and Society* 24: 245–78.

Inden, R. and Nicholas, R. 1977. *Kinship in Bengali Culture*. Chicago: Chicago University Press.

Jacobs, W. 1969. British-colonial attitudes and policies toward the Indian in the American colonies. In Peckham, H. and Gibson, C. (eds.) *Attitudes of Colonial Powers toward the American Indian*. Salt Lake City: University of Utah Press.

Jaffrelot, C. 1995. The ideas of the Hindu race in the writings of Hindu nationalist ideologues in the 1920s and 1930s: A concept between two cultures. In Robb, P. (ed.) *The Concept of Race in South Asia*. Delhi: Oxford University Press.

Jamous, R. 1992. The brother–married sister relationship and marriage ceremonies as sacrificial rites: A case study from northern India. In Coppet, D. de (ed.) *Understanding Rituals*. London: Routledge.

Jha, D. 1987. *Feudal Social Formation in Early India*. Delhi: Chanakya Publications.

Johnson, L. 1995. Imagining communities: Medieval and modern. In Forde, S., Johnson, L., and Murray, A. (eds.) *Concepts of National Identity in the Middle Ages*. Leeds: Leeds Texts and Monographs.

Jordan, W. 1968. *White Over Black: American Attitudes Towards the Negro, 1550–1812*. Chapel Hill: University of North Carolina Press.

Juergensmeyer, M. 1982. *Religion as Social Vision: The Movement against Untouchability in Twentieth Century Punjab*. Berkeley: University of California

Press.

Kain, P. 1992. Marx and pluralism. *Praxis International* 11: 465–86.

Kantorowicz, E. 1957. *The King's Two Bodies: A Study in Medieval Political Theology*. Princeton, NJ: Princeton University Press.

Kapferer, B. 1988. *Legends of People, Myths of State: Violence, Intolerance and Political Culture in Sri Lanka and Australia*. Washington, DC: Smithsonian Institution Press.

Khan, M. 1994. *Kashmir's Transition to Islam: The Role of Muslim Rishis (Fifteenth to Eighteenth Centuries)*. Delhi: Manohar.

Khare, R. 1984. *The Untouchable as Himself: Ideology, Identity and Pragmatism among the Lucknow Chamars*. Cambridge: Cambridge University Press.

Klein, H. 1999. *The Atlantic Slave Trade*. Cambridge: Cambridge University Press.

Kulke, H. 1997. *The State in India 1000–1700*. Delhi: Oxford University Press.

Kumar, D. 1985. Private property in Asia: The case of medieval South India. *Comparative Studies in Society and History* 27: 340–66.

Kuper, A. 1988. *The Invention of Primitive Society: Transformations of an Illusion*. London: Routledge.

Landry, D. and Maclean, G. 1996. Introduction: Reading Spivak. In Landry, D. and Maclean, G. (eds.) *The Spivak Reader*. London: Routledge.

Lawson, P. 1993. *The East India Company: A History*. Harlow: Longman.

Lazarus-Black, M. 1994. *Legitimate Acts and Illegal Encounters: Law and Society in Antigua and Barbuda*. Washington, DC: Smithsonian Institution Press.

Lerche, J. 1993. Dominant castes, rajas, Brahmins and inter-caste exchange relations in coastal Orissa: Behind the facade of the "jajmani" system. *Contributions to Indian Sociology* n.s. 27: 237–66.

Lévi-Strauss, C. 1963. *Structural Anthropology*. Harmondsworth: Penguin Books.

Lévi-Strauss, C. 1966. *The Savage Mind*. London: George Weidenfeld & Nicolson.

Lévi-Strauss, C. 1969. *The Elementary Structures of Kinship*. London: Eyre and Spottiswoode.

Lévi-Strauss, C. 1970. *The Raw and the Cooked*. London: Jonathan Cape.

Lévi-Strauss, C. 1985. *The View From Afar*. Chicago: University of Chicago Press.

Lewandowski, S. 1985. Merchants and kingship: An interpretation of Indian urban history. *Journal of Urban History* 11: 151–79.

Lewis, B. 1971. *Race and Color in Islam*. New York: Harper and Row.

Lewis, G. 1983. *Main Currents in Caribbean Thought*. Baltimore: Johns Hopkins University Press.

Lewis, L. 1995. Spanish ideology and the practice of inequality in the New World. In Bowser, B. (ed.) *Racism and Anti-racism in World Perspective*. London: Sage.

Lewis, W. 1994. The social drama of the Rastafari. *Dialectical Anthropology* 19: 283–94.

Littlewood, R. 1998. History, memory and appropriation: Some problems in the analysis of origins. In Chevannes, B. (ed.) *Rastafari and Other African–Caribbean Worldviews*. Basingstoke: Macmillan.

Llobera, J. 1994. *The God of Modernity: The Development of Nationalism in Western Europe*. Oxford: Berg.

Long, E. 1774 (1970). *The History of Jamaica*. 2 vols. London: Frank Cass.

Lowenthal, I. 1978. Ritual performance and religious experience: A service for the gods in southern Haiti. *Journal of Anthropological Research* 34: 392–414.

Lowenthal, I. 1984. Labour, sexuality and the conjugal contract in rural Haiti. In Foster, C. and Valdman, A. (eds.) *Haiti – Today and Tomorrow: An Interdisciplinary Study.* New York: University Press of America.

Lynch, J. 1992. *The Medieval Church: A Brief History.* Harlow: Longman.

Lyotard, J.-F. 1984. *The Postmodern Condition: A Report on Knowledge.* Manchester: Manchester University Press.

McCall, J. 1995. Rethinking ancestors in Africa. *Africa* 65: 256–70.

McFarlane, A. 1998. The epistemological significance of "I–an–I" as a response to Quashie and Anancyism in Jamaican culture. In Murrell, N., Spencer, W., and McFarlane, A. (eds.) *Chanting Down Babylon: The Rastafari Reader.* Philadelphia: Temple University Press.

MacKay, A. 1977. *Spain in the Middle Ages: From Frontier to Empire, 1009–1500.* Basingstoke: Macmillan.

McKee, J. 1993. *Sociology and the Race Problem: The Failure of a Perspective.* Urbana: University of Illinois Press.

Malamoud, C. 1981. On the rhetoric and semantics of *Purusartha. Contributions to Indian Sociology* 15: 33–54.

Malamoud, C. 1992. Brothers and sisters in Brahmanic India. In de Coppet, D. (ed.) *Understanding Rituals.* London: Routledge.

Malik, K. 1996. *The Meaning of Race: Race, History and Culture in Western Society.* Basingstoke: Macmillan.

Mann, M. 1986. *The Sources of Social Power: A History of Power from the Beginning to A.D. 1760.* Cambridge: Cambridge University Press.

Mann, M. 1988. European development: Approaching a historical explanation. In Baechler, J., Hall, J., and Mann, M. (eds.) *Europe and the Rise of Capitalism.* Oxford: Blackwell Publishers.

Marriott, M. 1968. Caste ranking and food transactions: A matrix analysis. In Cohn, B. and Singer, M. (eds.) *Structure and Change in Indian Society.* Chicago: Aldine.

Marriott, M. 1976. Hindu transactions: Diversity without dualism. In Kapferer, B. (ed.) *Transaction and Meaning: Directions in the Anthropology of Exchange and Symbolic Behavior.* Philadelphia: Institute for the Study of Human Issues.

Marriott, M. 1989. Constructing an Indian ethnosociology. *Contributions to Indian Sociology* n.s. 23: 1–39.

Martinez-Alier, V. 1989. *Marriage, Class and Color in Nineteenth-Century Cuba: A Study of Racial Attitudes and Sexual Values in a Slave Society.* Ann Arbor: University of Michigan Press.

Marx, K. and Engels, F. 1975–96. *Collected Works.* 47 vols. London: Lawrence and Wishart.

Mauss, M. 1922 (1979). *The Gift: The Form and Function of Exchange in Archaic Societies.* London: Routledge.

Mauss, M. 1979. *Sociology and Psychology.* London: Routledge and Kegan Paul.

Mendelsohn, O. 1993. The transformation of authority in rural India. *Modern Asian Studies* 27: 805–42.

Mendelsohn, O. and Vicziany, M. 1998. *The Untouchables: Subordination, Poverty and the State in Modern India*. Cambridge: Cambridge University Press.

Miles, R. 1982. *Racism and Migrant Labour*. London: Routledge and Kegan Paul.

Miles, R. 1987. *Capitalism and Unfree Labour: Anomaly or Necessity?* London: Tavistock.

Miles, R. 1989. *Racism*. London: Routledge.

Miles, R. 1993. *Racism After Race Relations*. London: Routledge.

Miller, D. 1986. Exchange and alienation in the jajmani system. *Journal of Anthropological Research* 42: 534–56.

Miller, D. 1994. *Modernity, An Ethnographic Approach: Dualism and Mass Consumption in Trinidad*. Oxford: Berg.

Milner, M. 1994. *Status and Sacredness: A General Theory of Status Relations and an Analysis of Indian Culture*. New York: Oxford University Press.

Mines, M. and Gourishankar, V. 1990. Leadership and individuality in South Asia: The case of the South Indian big man. *Journal of Asian Studies* 49: 761–86.

Mintz, S. 1959. Labor and sugar in Puerto Rico and Jamaica. *Comparative Studies in Society and History* 7: 273–83.

Mintz, S. 1972. Introduction. In Métraux, A., *Voodoo in Haiti*. London: André Deutsch.

Mintz, S. 1974. *Caribbean Transformations*. Baltimore: Johns Hopkins University Press.

Mintz, S. 1977. The so-called world system: Local initiative and local response. *Dialectical Anthropology* 2: 253–70.

Mintz, S. 1978. Was the plantation slave a proletarian? *Review* 2: 81–98.

Mintz, S. 1985. *Sweetness and Power: The Place of Sugar in Modern History*. Harmondsworth: Penguin Books.

Mintz, S. 1995. Enduring substances, trying theories: The Caribbean region as *oikumene*. *Journal of the Royal Anthropological Institute* n.s. 2: 289–311.

Mintz, S. 1996. Ethnic difference, plantation sameness. In Oostindie, G. (ed.) *Ethnicity in the Caribbean*. Basingstoke: Macmillan.

Mintz, S. and Price, R. 1992. *The Birth of African–American Culture: An Anthropological Perspective*. Boston: Beacon Press.

Mitra, S. 1994. Caste, democracy and the politics of community formation in India. In Searle-Chatterjee, M. and Sharma, U. (eds.) *Contextualising Caste: Post-Dumontian Approaches*. Oxford: Blackwell Publishers.

Moffatt, M. 1979. *An Untouchable Community in South India: Structure and Consensus*. Princeton, NJ: Princeton University Press.

Moore, R. 1990. *The Formation of a Persecuting Society: Power and Deviance in Western Europe, 950–1250*. Oxford: Blackwell Publishers.

Moreau de St.Méry, M. 1796 (1976). *Dance*. New York: Dance Horizons.

Morgan, E. 1975. *American Slavery, American Freedom: The Ordeal of Colonial Virginia*. New York: W. W. Norton.

Morgan, P. 1997. The cultural implications of the Atlantic slave trade: African regional origins, American destinations and New World developments. In Eltis, D. and Richardson, D. (eds.) *Routes to Slavery: Direction, Ethnicity and Mortality in the Atlantic Slave Trade*. London: Frank Cass.

Mörner, M. 1967. *Race Mixture in the History of Latin America*. Boston: Little

Brown.

Mosse, D. 1994. Idioms of subordination and styles of protest among Christian and Hindu Harijan castes in Tamil-Nadu. *Contributions to Indian Sociology* 28: 67–106.

Mosse, G. 1979. *Towards the Final Solution: A History of European Racism*. London: J. M. Dent.

Mosse, G. 1995. Racism and nationalism. *Nations and Nationalism* 1: 163–73.

Mukhia, H. 1997. Was there feudalism in Indian history? In Kulke, H. (ed.) *The State in India 1000–1700*. Delhi: Oxford University Press.

Munn, N. 1971. The transformation of subjects into objects in Walbiri and Pitjantjatjara myths. In Berndt, R. (ed.) *Australian Aboriginal Anthropology*. Nedlands: University of Western Australia Press.

Murray, G. 1980. Population pressure, land tenure and voodoo: The economics of Haitian peasant ritual. In Ross, E. (ed.) *Beyond the Myths of Culture: Essays in Cultural Materialism*. New York: Academic Press.

Myrdal, G. 1944 (1964). *An American Dilemma: Volume 1*. New York: McGraw Hill.

Nandy, A. 1983. *The Intimate Enemy: Loss and Recovery of Self under Colonialism*. Delhi: Oxford University Press.

Nicholls, D. 1996. *From Dessalines to Duvalier: Race, Color and National Independence in Haiti*. New Brunswick: Rutgers University Press.

Nozick, R. 1974. *Anarchy, State and Utopia*. New York: Basic Books.

Olwig, K. 1995. Cultural complexity after freedom: Nevis and beyond. In Olwig, K. (ed.) *Small Islands, Large Questions: Society, Culture and Resistance in the Post-Emancipation Caribbean*. London: Frank Cass.

Östör, Á., Fruzzetti, L., and Barnett, S. 1992. *Concepts of Person: Kinship, Caste and Marriage in India*. Oxford: Oxford University Press.

Pagden, A. 1987. Identity formation in Spanish America. In Canny, N. and Pagden, A. (eds.) *Colonial Identity in the Atlantic World, 1500–1800*. Princeton, NJ: Princeton University Press.

Pagden, A. 1990. *Spanish Imperialism and the Political Imagination*. New Haven, Conn.: Yale University Press.

Pagden, A. 1993. *European Encounters with the New World*. New Haven, Conn.: Yale University Press.

Pagden, A. 1995. *Lords of All the World: Ideologies of Empire in Spain, Britain and France c. 1500–c. 1800*. New Haven, Conn.: Yale University Press.

Pagden, A. and Canny, N. 1987. Afterword: From identity to independence. In Canny, N. and Pagden, A. (eds.) *Colonial Identity in the Atlantic World, 1500–1800*. Princeton, NJ: Princeton University Press.

Palat, R. A. 1986. Popular revolts and the state in medieval South India. *Bijdragen Tot de Taal – Land – en Volkenkunde* 142: 128–44.

Pandey, G. 1990. *The Construction of Communalism in Colonial North India*. Delhi: Oxford University Press.

Parekh, B. 1995. Liberalism and colonialism: A critique of Locke and Mill. In Pieterse, J. N. and Parekh, B. (eds.) *The Decolonization of Imagination: Culture, Knowledge and Power*. London: Zed Books.

Parry, J. 1979. *Caste and Kinship in Kangra*. London: Routledge and Kegan Paul.

Parry, J. 1980. Ghosts, greed and sin: The occupational identity of Benares funeral priests. *Man* n.s. 15: 88–111.

Parry, J. 1986. The Gift, the Indian Gift and the Indian 'Gift'. *Man* n.s. 21: 453–73.

Parry, J. 1989. On the moral perils of exchange. In Parry, J. and Bloch, M. (eds.) *Money and the Morality of Exchange*. Cambridge: Cambridge University Press.

Pasquino, P. 1993. Political theory of war and peace: Foucault and the history of modern political theory. *Economy and Society* 22: 77–88.

Patterson, O. 1977. The structural origins of slavery: A critique of the Nieboer–Domar hypothesis from a comparative perspective. *Annals of the New York Academy of Sciences* 292: 12–40.

Patterson, O. 1982. *Slavery and Social Death*. Cambridge, Mass.: Harvard University Press.

Peabody, N. 1991a. In whose turban does the lord reside? The objectification of charisma and the fetishism of objects in the Hindu kingdom of Kota. *Comparative Studies in Society and History* 33: 726–54.

Peabody, N. 1991b. *Kota mahajagat*, or the great universe of Kota: Sovereignty and territory in 18th century Rajasthan. *Contributions to Indian Sociology* 25: 29–56.

Peirce, C. 1932. *Collected Papers*. 6 vols. Cambridge, Mass.: Harvard University Press.

Phillips, W. 1985. *Slavery from Roman Times to the Early Transatlantic Trade*. Manchester: Manchester University Press.

Pinch, W. 1996. Soldier monks and militant sadhus. In Ludden, D. (ed.) *Contesting the Nation: Religion, Community and the Politics of Democracy in India*. Philadelphia: University of Pennsylvania Press.

Poliakov, L. 1971. *The Aryan Myth: A History of Racist and Nationalist Ideas in Europe*. New York: New York Library.

Poliakov, L. 1974. *The History of Anti-Semitism: Volume I – From Roman Times to the Court Jews*. London: Routledge & Kegan Paul.

Pollock, S. 1984. The divine king in the Indian epic. *Journal of the American Orientalist Society* 104: 505–28.

Pollock, S. 1993. Ramayana and political imagination in India. *Journal of Asian Studies* 52: 261–97.

Pollock, S. 1998. The cosmopolitan vernacular. *Journal of Asian Studies* 57: 6–37.

Postone, M. 1992. Political theory and historical analysis. In Calhoun, C. (ed.) *Habermas and the Public Sphere*. Cambridge, Mass.: MIT Press.

Prakash, G. 1990. Writing post-Orientalist histories of the Third World: Perspectives from Indian historiography. *Comparative Studies in Society and History* 32: 383–408.

Prakash, G. 1992. Can the "subaltern" ride? A reply to O'Hanlon and Washbrook. *Comparative Studies in Society and History* 34: 168–84.

Price, R. 1985. An absence of ruins? Seeking Caribbean historical consciousness. *Caribbean Review* 14: 24–45.

Quigley, D. 1993. *The Interpretation of Caste*. Oxford: Clarendon Press.

Raheja, G. 1988. *The Poison in the Gift: Ritual, Prestation and the Dominant Caste in a North Indian Village.* Chicago: University of Chicago Press.

Raheja, G. 1989. Centrality, mutuality and hierarchy: Shifting aspects of inter-caste relationships in North India. *Contributions to Indian Sociology* 23: 79–101.

Ricoeur, P. 1965. *History and Truth.* Evanston, Ill.: Northwestern University Press.

Ricoeur, P. 1984–8. *Time and Narrative.* 3 vols. Chicago: University of Chicago Press.

Rigby, P. 1996. *African Images: Racism and the End of Anthropology.* Oxford: Berg.

Rivera, A. 1996. The somatology of manners: Class, race and gender in the history of dance etiquette in the Hispanic Caribbean. In Oostindie, G. (ed.) *Ethnicity in the Caribbean.* Basingstoke: Macmillan.

Rorty, R. 1998. *Achieving Our Country: Leftist Thought in Twentieth Century America.* Cambridge, Mass.: Harvard University Press.

Rowe, M. 1998. Gender and family relations in Rastafarī: A personal perspective. In Murrell, N., Spencer, W., and McFarlane, A. (eds.) *Chanting Down Babylon: The Rastafari Reader.* Philadelphia: Temple University Press.

Rudner, D. 1994. *Caste and Capitalism in Colonial India.* Berkeley: University of California Press.

Rudolph, L. and Rudolph, S. 1985. The subcontinental empire and regional kingdom in Indian state formation. In Wallace, P. (ed.) *Region and Nation in India.* New Delhi: Oxford University Press.

Ryan, M. 1981. Assimilating new worlds in the sixteenth and seventeenth centuries. *Comparative Studies in Society and History:* 519–38.

Sahlins, M. 1974. *Stone Age Economics.* London: Tavistock.

Sahlins, M. 1976. *Culture and Practical Reason.* Chicago: University of Chicago Press.

Sahlins, M. 1985. *Islands of History.* London: Tavistock.

Said, E. 1978. *Orientalism.* New York: Vintage Books.

Sanders, R. 1978. *Lost Tribes and Promised Lands: The Origins of American Racism.* Boston: Little, Brown.

Saussure, F. de 1983. *Course in General Linguistics.* London: Duckworth.

Scammell, G. 1989. *The First Imperial Age: European Overseas Expansion c.1400–1715.* London: Routledge.

Schneider, D. 1968. *American Kinship: A Cultural Account.* Chicago: University of Chicago Press.

Schneider, D. 1977. Kinship, nationality and religion in American culture: Toward a definition of kinship. In Dolgin, J., Kemmitzer, D., and Schneider, D. (eds.) *Symbolic Anthropology: A Reader in the Study of Symbols and Meanings.* New York: Columbia University Press.

Schnepel, B. 1995. Durga and the king: Ethnohistorical aspects of politico-ritual life in a South Orissan jungle kingdom. *Journal of the Royal Anthropological Institute* 1: 145–66.

Schwartz, S. 1997. Spaniards, pardos, and the missing mestizos: Identities and racial categories in the early Hispanic Caribbean. *New West Indian Guide* 71: 5–19.

Seneviratne, H. 1987. Kingship and polity in Buddhism and Hinduism. *Contributions to Indian Sociology* n.s. 21: 147–55.

Shulman, D. 1980. *Tamil Temple Myths: Sacrifice and Divine Marriage in the South Indian Saiva Tradition*. Princeton, NJ: Princeton University Press.

Shulman, D. 1984. The enemy within: Idealism and dissent in South Indian Hinduism. In Eisenstadt, S., Kahane, R., and Shulman, D. (eds.) *Orthodoxy, Heterodoxy and Dissent in India*. Berlin: Mouton.

Shulman, D. 1985. *The King and the Clown in South Indian Myth and Poetry*. Princeton, NJ: Princeton University Press.

Simmel, G. 1968. *The Conflict in Modern Culture and Other Essays*. New York: New York Teachers College Press.

Sinha, S. 1965. Tribe–caste and tribe–peasant continua in Central India. *Man in India* 45: 57–83.

Sinha, S. 1997. State formation and Rajput myth in tribal Central India. In Kulke, H. (ed.) *The State in India 1000–1700*. Delhi: Oxford University Press.

Skaria, A. 1997. Shades of wildness: Tribe, caste and gender in Western India. *Journal of Asian Studies* 56: 726–45.

Skinner, Q. 1978. *The Foundations of Modern Political Thought – Volume Two: The Age of Reformation*. Cambridge: Cambridge University Press.

Smith, A. 1991. *National Identity*. Harmondsworth: Penguin Books.

Smith, M. 1984a. *Culture, Race and Class in the Commonwealth Caribbean*. Mona: University of West Indies Press.

Smith, M. 1984b. Comment on Austin's "Culture and ideology in the English-speaking Caribbean." *American Ethnologist* 11: 183–5.

Smith, R. 1978. The family and the modern world system: Some observations from the Caribbean. *Journal of Family History* 3: 337–60.

Smith, R. 1996. *The Matrifocal Family: Power, Pluralism and Politics*. London: Routledge.

Sperber, D. 1996. *Explaining Culture: A Naturalistic Approach*. Oxford: Blackwell Publishers.

Spivak, G. 1994. Can the subaltern speak? In Williams, P. and Chrisman, L. (eds.) *Colonial Discourse and Postcolonial Theory*. Hemel Hempstead: Harvester Wheatsheaf.

Spivak, G. 1996. Scattered speculations on the question of value. In Landry, D. and Maclean, G. (eds.) *The Spivak Reader*. London: Routledge.

Spruyt, H. 1994. *The Sovereign State and its Competitors: An Analysis of Systems Change*. Princeton, NJ: Princeton University Press.

Srinivas, M. 1956. Sanskritization and westernization. *Far Eastern Quarterly* XIV: 481–96.

Srinivas, M. 1987. *The Dominant Caste and Other Essays*. Oxford: Oxford University Press.

Stein, B. 1980. *Peasant State and Society in Medieval South India*. Delhi: Oxford University Press.

Stein, B. 1997. The segmentary state: Interim reflections. In Kulke, H. (ed.) *The State in India 1000–1700*. Delhi: Oxford University Press.

Stern, H. 1977. Power in traditional India: Territory, caste and kinship in Rajasthan.

In Fox, R. (ed.) *Realm and Region in Traditional India*. New Delhi: Vikas Publishing House.

Stinchcombe, A. 1995. *Sugar Island Slavery in the Age of Enlightenment*. Princeton, NJ: Princeton University Press.

Stocking, G. 1968. *Race, Culture and Evolution: Essays in the History of Anthropology*. Chicago: University of Chicago Press.

Stoler, A. 1985. *Capitalism and Confrontation in Sumatra's Plantation Belt, 1870–1979*. New Haven, Conn.: Yale University Press.

Stoler, A. 1995. *Race and the Education of Desire: Foucault's History of Sexuality and the Colonial Order of Things*. Durham, NC: Duke University Press.

Stone, L. 1990. *The Family, Sex and Marriage in England 1500–1800*. Harmondsworth: Penguin Books.

Strathern, M. 1985. Kinship and economy: Constitutive orders of a provisional kind. *American Ethnologist* 12: 191–209.

Strathern, M. 1988. *The Gender of the Gift: Problems with Women and Problems with Society in Melanesia*. Berkeley: University of California Press.

Strathern, M. 1992. *After Nature: English Kinship in the Late Twentieth Century*. Cambridge: Cambridge University Press.

Strayer, J. 1970. *On the Medieval Origins of the Modern State*. Princeton, NJ: Princeton University Press.

Subbarayalu, Y. 1982. The Cola state. *Studies in History* 4: 265–306.

Subrahmanyam, S. 1994. *Money and the Market in India 1100–1700*. Delhi: Oxford University Press.

Tafari-Ama, I. 1998. Rastawoman as rebel: Case studies in Jamaica. In Murrell, N., Spencer, W., and McFarlane, A. (eds.) *Chanting Down Babylon: The Rastafari Reader*. Philadelphia: Temple University Press.

Tambiah, S. 1985. *Culture, Thought and Social Action*. Cambridge, Mass.: Harvard University Press.

Taussig, M. 1980. *The Devil and Commodity Fetishism in South America*. Chapel Hill: University of North Carolina Press.

Taylor, C. 1989. *Sources of the Self: The Making of the Modern Identity*. Cambridge: Cambridge University Press.

Tcherkezoff, S. 1993. The illusion of dualism in Samoa. In del Valle, T. (ed.) *Gendered Anthropology*. London: Routledge.

Temperley, H. 1996. New World slavery, Old World slavery. In Bush, M. (ed.) *Serfdom and Slavery: Studies in Legal Bondage*. Harlow: Longman.

Thapar, R. 1989. Epic and History: Tradition, dissent and politics in India. *Past and Present* 125: 3–26.

Thapar, R. 1992. *Interpreting Early India*. Delhi: Oxford University Press.

Thapar, R. 1996. *Time as a Metaphor of History: Early India*. Delhi: Oxford University Press.

Thibault, P. 1997. *Re-reading Saussure: The Dynamics of Signs in Social Life*. London: Routledge.

Thomas, K. 1984. *Man and the Natural World: Changing Attitudes in England 1500–1800*. Harmondsworth: Penguin Books.

Tilly, C. 1990. *Coercion, Capital and European States, AD 990–1992*. Oxford:

Blackwell Publishers.

Trautmann, T. 1981. *Dravidian Kinship*. New Delhi: Oxford University Press.

Trautmann, T. 1997. *Aryans and British India*. Berkeley: University of California Press.

Trawick, M. 1990. *Notes on Love in a Tamil Family*. Berkeley: University of California Press.

Trey, G. 1992. Communicative ethics in the face of alterity: Habermas, Levinas and the problem of post-conventional universalism. *Praxis International* 11: 412–27.

Trouillot, M.-R. 1982. Motion in the system: Coffee, color and slavery in eighteenth-century Saint Domingue. *Review* 5: 331–88.

Trouillot, M.-R. 1990. *Haiti, State Against Nation: The Origins and Legacy of Duvalierism*. New York: Monthly Review Press.

Tuck, R. 1993. *Philosophy and Government, 1572–1651*. Cambridge: Cambridge University Press.

Tully, J. 1993. *An Approach to Political Philosophy: Locke in Contexts*. Cambridge: Cambridge University Press.

Turner, F. 1894 (1966). *The Significance of the Frontier in American History*. Ann Arbor, Mich.: University Microfilms.

Turner, S. 1994. *The Social Theory of Practices: Tradition, Tacit Knowledge and Presuppositions*. Cambridge: Polity Press.

Turner, V. 1974. *Dramas, Fields and Metaphors: Symbolic Action in Human Societies*. Ithaca, NY: Cornell University Press.

Uberoi, P. 1993. *Family, Kinship and Marriage in India*. Delhi: Oxford University Press.

Unnithan, M. 1994. Girasias and the politics of difference in Rajasthan: 'Caste', kinship and gender in a marginalised society. In Searle-Chatterjee, M. and Sharma, U. (eds.) *Contextualising Caste*. Oxford: Blackwell Publishers.

Upadhyaya, P. 1992. The politics of Indian secularism. *Modern Asian Studies* 26: 815–53.

van den Boogaart, E. 1982. Colour prejudice and the yardstick of civility: The initial Dutch confrontation with Black Africans, 1590–1635. In Ross, R. (ed.) *Racism and Colonialism: Essays on Ideology and Social Structure*. The Hague: Martinus Nijhoff.

van der Veer, P. 1994. *Religious Nationalism: Hindus and Muslims in India*. Berkeley: University of California Press.

van der Veer, P. 1996. Writing violence. In Ludden, D. (ed.) *Contesting the Nation: Religion, Community and the Politics of Democracy in India*. Philadelphia: University of Pennsylvania Press.

Vanaik, A. 1997. *The Furies of Indian Communalism: Religion, Modernity and Secularization*. London: Verso.

Vaughan, A. 1995. *Roots of American Racism*. Oxford: Oxford University Press.

Vološinov, V. 1929 (1986). *Marxism and the Philosophy of Language*. Cambridge, Mass.: Harvard University Press.

Wagner, R. 1977. Analogic kinship: A Daribi example. *American Ethnologist* 4: 623–42.

Wagner, R. 1986. *Symbols That Stand For Themselves.* Chicago: University of Chicago Press.

Walcott, D. 1974. The muse of history: An essay. In Coombs, O. (ed.) *Is Massa Day Dead?* New York: Anchor Books.

Wallerstein, I. 1974. *The Modern World-System: Capitalist Agriculture and the Origins of the European World-Economy in the Sixteenth Century.* New York: Academic Press.

Walvin, J. 1973. *Black and White: The Negro and English Society, 1555–1945.* London: Allen and Unwin.

Washbrook, D. 1982. Ethnicity and racialism in colonial Indian society. In Ross, R. (ed.) *Racism and Colonialism: Essays on Ideology and Social Structure.* The Hague: Martinus Nijhoff.

Washbrook, D. 1988. Progress and problems: South Asian economic and social history c. 1720–1860. *Modern Asian Studies* 22: 57–96.

Weber, M. 1930. *The Protestant Ethic and the Spirit of Capitalism.* London: Routledge.

Weber, M. 1946. *From Max Weber.* New York: Oxford University Press.

Westfall, R. 1970. *Science and Religion in Seventeenth-Century England.* London: Archon Books.

White, H. 1973. *Metahistory: The Historical Imagination in Nineteenth-Century Europe.* Baltimore: Johns Hopkins University Press.

Wieviorka, M. 1995. *The Arena of Racism.* London: Sage.

Williams, B. 1991. *Stains On My Name, War In My Veins: Guyana and the Politics of Cultural Struggle.* Durham, NC: Duke University Press.

Williams, B. 1995. Classification systems revisited: Kinship, caste, race and nationality as the flow of blood and the spread of rights. In Yanagisako, S. and Delaney, C. (eds.) *Naturalizing Power: Essays in Feminist Cultural Analysis.* London: Routledge.

Williams, E. 1944. *Capitalism and Slavery.* Chapel Hill: University of North Carolina Press.

Wilson, P. 1969. Reputation and respectability: A suggestion for Caribbean ethnography. *Man* 4: 70–84.

Wilson, P. 1973. *Crab Antics: The Social Anthropology of English Speaking Negro Societies of the Caribbean.* New Haven, Conn.: Yale University Press.

Wink, A. 1990. *Al-Hind: The Making of the Indo-Islamic World.* Leiden: E. J. Brill.

Wittgenstein, L. 1953. *Philosophical Investigations.* Oxford: Blackwell Publishers.

Wolf, E. 1982. *Europe and the People Without History.* Berkeley: University of California Press.

Wolf, E. and Hansen, E. 1967. *Caudillo* politics: A structural analysis. *Comparative Studies in Society and History* 9: 168–79.

Wood, P. 1995. "If toads could speak": How the myth of race took hold and flourished in the minds of Europe's Renaissance colonizers. In Bowser, B. (ed.) *Racism and Anti-racism in World Perspective.* London: Sage.

Wright, W. 1990. *Café Con Leche: Race, Class and National Image in Venezuela.* Austin: University of Texas Press.

Yalman, N. 1963. On the purity of women in the castes of Ceylon and Malabar.

Journal of the Royal Anthropological Institute 93: 25–58.

Ziegler, N. P. 1978. Some notes on Rajput loyalties during the Mughal period. In Richards, J. F. (ed.) *Kingship and Authority in South Asia*. Madison: University of Wisconsin–Madison.

Zuckerman, M. 1987. Identity in British America: Unease in Eden. In Canny, N. and Pagden, A. (eds.) *Colonial Identity in the Atlantic World, 1500–1800*. Princeton, NJ: Princeton University Press.

Index